Fortress Rabaul

Fortress Rabaul

The Battle for
the Southwest Pacific

January 1942–April 1943

Bruce Gamble

ZENITH PRESS

First published in 2010 by Zenith Press, an imprint of MBI Publishing Company, 400 First Avenue North, Suite 300, Minneapolis, MN 55401 USA

Zenith Press titles are also available at discounts in bulk quantity for industrial or sales-promotional use. For details write to Special Sales Manager at MBI Publishing Company, 400 First Avenue North, Suite 300, Minneapolis, MN 55401 USA.

To find out more about our books, join us online at www.zenithpress.com.

Library of Congress Cataloging-in-Publication Data
Gamble, Bruce.
  Fortress Rabaul : the battle for the Southwest Pacific, January 1942-April 1943 / Bruce Gamble.
    p. cm.
  Includes bibliographical references and index.
  ISBN 978-0-7603-2350-2 (hbk. w/jkt)
  1. World War, 1939-1945--Campaigns--Papua New Guinea--Rabaul. 2. World War, 1939-1945--Aerial operations, Japanese. 3. World War, 1939-1945--Aerial operations, American. 4. Rabaul (Papua New Guinea)--History, Military--20th century. 5. Air pilots, Military--United States--Biography. 6. Medal of Honor--Biography. I. Title.
  D767.99.N444G36 2010
  940.54'26585--dc22
                                2009042353
On the cover: A U.S. Army 5th Air Force raid on the Japanese-held air and naval base at Rabaul, New Britain. *AP Photo*
Maps by: Bruce Gamble
Design Manager: Brenda C. Canales
Layout by: Diana Boger
Cover designed by: Simon Larkin

Printed in the United States of America

To my aunt and uncle:

Margaret Gamble Steinbinder (1918–2009)
Physical therapist, Walter Reed Army Hospital

John J. Steinbinder (1918–2002)
Captain, USAAF, forty-three combat missions
in the Southwest Pacific

Contents

Preface

FOR WELL OVER FORTY YEARS I've been proud of the fact that my uncle, John J. Steinbinder, served as a B-17 navigator in the Southwest Pacific. Sadly, I learned little about his combat experiences during my youth, and by the time I became seriously interested in researching and writing about the war, he had been diagnosed with Alzheimer's.

The disease inevitably claimed Uncle Johnny, but there was a silver lining. Not long before his passing, I took temporary possession of a large footlocker that contained his military papers and memorabilia. Among them was a diary filled with details of Johnny's overseas tour in 1942, and I was fascinated to discover that he was a member of the first American squadron to attack Rabaul. By the completion of his ten-month tour, Johnny had logged at least nineteen combat missions over Japan's mightiest stronghold.

My personal interest in Rabaul, aside from the stories Uncle Johnny shared, began while writing *The Black Sheep*. The way the veteran pilots spoke of Rabaul, even sixty years after the war, made me realize that it was no mere target. In early 2001, I had the pleasure of conducting a lengthy interview with Capt. William F. Krantz, USN, whose carrier-based bomber was forced down at sea after attacking Rabaul in 1943. Krantz and his two crewmen spent ten harrowing days in a raft before washing up on New Britain, where Rabaul is located. Although the island was in Japanese hands, the three airmen were aided by natives who guided them to an Australian coastwatcher. Three months later, the Americans were rescued by a PT boat.

Krantz in turn put me in touch with the coastwatcher, Peter Figgis, who had been a member of the Australian army garrison at Rabaul when the war began. After sharing his own remarkable story, Figgis referred me to other veterans of the unit, known as Lark Force. The ripple effect continued, and soon I was hooked on the early history of Rabaul and the tragic fate of the garrison. The end result was *Darkest Hour: The True Story of Lark Force at Rabaul—Australia's Worst Military Disaster of World War II*, published by Zenith Press in 2006.

While working on that project, I realized that no one had yet published a comprehensive account of the air war over Rabaul. This is really remarkable, since Rabaul was the focus of Allied air attacks from January 1942 until the end of the war, making it the longest battle of World War II. A virtually impregnable fortress, Rabaul grew in notoriety until it became an icon of the Pacific war. Always dangerous, the stronghold rivaled the most infamous targets in Europe—places like Ploesti, Schweinfurt, and Berlin. No less than six Medals of Honor were awarded to American airmen for actions over Rabaul, five of them posthumously, underscoring the intensity of the air battles.

Soon after *Darkest Hour* was released, I set out to write a detailed narrative about Rabaul and the war's longest air campaign. I firmly believe that extraordinary events are best told by the people who experienced them, so from the outset of this project my goal was to include material from numerous participants to help explain events from both the Japanese and Allied perspectives. In doing this, however, it became apparent that a comprehensive account of the *entire* forty-four-month-long air war would simply be too large for publication as a single volume. A manageable approach for the topic was easy to establish, for there were two distinct phases in the Pacific War. The first, which lasted about seventeen months, began with the massive Southern Offensive as Japan captured numerous territories. Among them was Rabaul, which the Japanese quickly developed into a major military complex that dominated the region. *Fortress Rabaul* focuses on that opening phase of the conflict, when Rabaul served as a springboard for several new offensives. It begins with a brief history of New Britain and a synopsis of the Lark Force story, and then focuses on the air war over Rabaul from January 1942 to April 1943. At that time, having suffered irreplaceable losses in the battles for Guadalcanal and New Guinea, Admiral Isoroku Yamamoto shifted his headquarters to Rabaul to oversee a major new aerial offensive. Barely two weeks later, he was shot down during an audacious and perfectly timed fighter mission. His death heralded the beginning of the end for Japan, which increasingly dug in and fought a defensive war.

It is my hope to describe the second phase of the war in a future volume, for there are obviously still many great tales of heroism and sacrifice to narrate.

A FEW CONVENTIONS warrant mention here. First, the twenty-four-hour military clock is used. During the war the Japanese followed Tokyo time (Japan Standard Time), which at Rabaul was two hours ahead of the local time used by the Allies. In the interest of consistency, the necessary adjustments have been made to the times referenced in Japanese sources. For the same purpose, the identification of Japanese individuals adheres to the Western custom of given name first followed by the surname. Japanese aircraft are identified by a combination of official terminology and model/year designations for the first twenty chapters. Although somewhat awkward, the method is true to the system employed by Allied intelligence during the first several months of the war. Eventually a series of simple code names was developed, and these are used throughout the last six chapters of the book. Lastly, distances are given in statute miles unless otherwise noted, as the vast majority of readers will relate more easily to "highway" miles than nautical miles.

Acknowledgments

I WOULD LIKE TO THANK Richard Kane, editorial director of Zenith Press, for his great patience and support. I am equally grateful for the many improvements suggested by Scott Pearson, associate editor at Zenith, who is just as patient as Richard.

I must also extend my gratitude to the professional staffs at three repositories in the United States: the National Archives and Records Administration in College Park, Maryland; the Air Force Historical Research Agency at Maxwell Air Force Base outside Montgomery, Alabama; and the MacArthur Memorial in Norfolk, Virginia. Equally important research facilities Down Under include the Australian War Memorial and the Australian National Archives, both in Canberra.

Like any author, I relied heavily on the assistance of numerous friends and colleagues to complete this project. Without their help, I don't believe the story could have been told. In Australia, the many who gave cheerfully of their time and wisdom include Mark Brennan, Peter Cundall, Peter Dunn, Michael Elliott, James Ford, Tim Gambrill, Lex McAulay, Hank Nelson, Peter Stone, David Vincent, David Wilson, and Brian Wimborne. The following veterans of World War II also participated Down Under, either directly or with helpful recommendations: Catalina pilot Sir Richard Kingsland, Benn Selby (brother of antiaircraft battery commander Lt. David Selby), Chap. John May, Hudson pilot John Murphy, and intelligence officer Des Martin.

The list of people who supported this project in North America is much longer. Some are noted authors, others are dedicated historians who work behind the scenes, and still others are relatives of those who served in the Southwest Pacific. I'm equally grateful to them all and pleased to count many of them among my friends. They are William Davis, Rick Dunn, Richard Frank, Jon Guttman, Eric Hammel, Bill Hess, Larry Hickey, Randy Jacobson, Herb Kadowaki, Curtis Keel, Jim Landsdale, Josephine Lerew, John Lundstrom, Roger Mansell, Allyn Nevitt, Shuko Nilson, Andrew Obluski, Janice Olson, Frank Olynyk, Edward Rogers, Henry Sakaida, Jim Sawruk, Michael Smith, Osamu Tagaya, Justin Taylan, Barrett Tillman, Anthony Tully, Douglas Walker, Ron Werneth, and James Zobel.

Last, but never least, the following USAAF veterans gave generously of their time, documents, and photo collections in support of this book. I am proud to have had the opportunity to work with these members of the "greatest generation" who unflinchingly served their country. Perry Dahl, pilot, 475th Fighter Group; Jim Dieffenderfer, pilot, 43rd Bomb Group; Joe Forrester, pilot, 475th Fighter Group; Jim Harcrow, pilot, 43rd Bomb Group; Frank Hohmann, crewmember, 19th Bomb Group; Cyril Klimesh, crewmember, 22nd Bomb Group; John Loisel, pilot, 475th Fighter Group; Carthon Phillips, crewmember, 19th Bomb Group; John Watkins, pilot, 22nd Bomb Group; and Roger Vargas, navigator, 43rd Bomb Group. If I've overlooked anyone, I pray that I'm forgiven.

Maps

Rank Abbreviations

1st Lt.—First Lieutenant
Adm.—Admiral
Air Cdre.—Air Commodore
AVM—Air Vice Marshal
Brig. Gen.—Brigadier General
Capt.—Captain
Chap.—Chaplain
Cmdr.—Commander
Col.—Colonel
Cpl.—Corporal
CPO—Chief Petty Officer
Ens.—Ensign
Flt. Lt.—Flight Lieutenant
Flt. Sgt.—Flight Sergeant
Flg. Off.—Flying Officer
FPO—Flight Petty Officer
Gen.—General
LAC—Leading Aircraftman
Lt.—Lieutenant

Lt. Cmdr.—Lieutenant
   Commander
Lt. Col.—Lieutenant Colonel
Lt. j.g.—Lieutenant Junior Grade
Maj.—Major
Maj. Gen.—Major General
Master Sgt.—Master Sergeant
Midn.—Midshipman
PO—Petty Officer
Pfc.—Private First Class
Plt. Off.—Pilot Officer
Pvt.—Private
Rear Adm.—Rear Admiral
Sgt.—Sergeant
Sgt. Maj.—Sergeant Major
Sqn. Ldr.—Squadron Leader
Vice Adm.—Vice Admiral
Wing Cmdr.—Wing Commander
WO—Warrant Officer

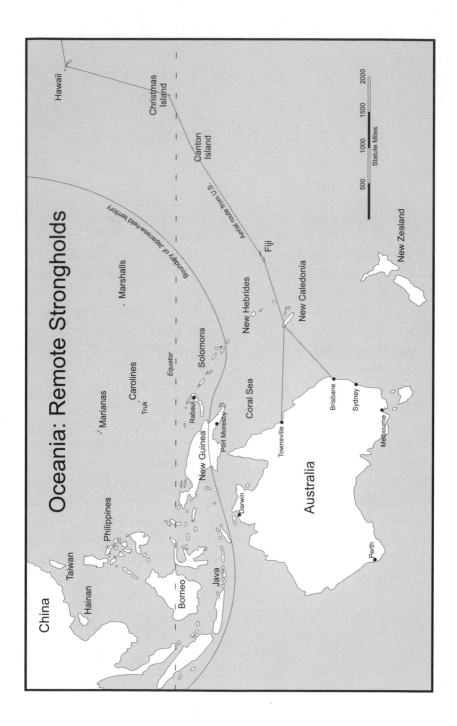

Oceania: Remote Strongholds

China

Taiwan

Hainan

Philippines

Marianas

Carolines

Truk

Marshalls

Equator

Boundary of Japanese-held territory

Borneo

Java

New Guinea

Rabaul

Port Moresby

Solomons

Darwin

Coral Sea

Townsville

Australia

Brisbane

Sydney

Melbourne

Perth

New Hebrides

New Caledonia

Fiji

Aerial route from U.S.

Canton Island

Christmas Island

Hawaii

New Zealand

Statute Miles

500   1000   1500   2000

Prologue

Melbourne, Victoria,
2350 Hours, Friday, January 23, 1942

A T TEN MINUTES to midnight, the lights still burned brightly
at Victoria Barracks, the stately combined headquarters of the
Australian armed forces. On a normal evening, the military staffs were
shooed out promptly at 1700 (5 p.m.) so that the cleaning crews could get
in, but on this balmy night, many of the Commonwealth's top leaders were
gathered in the Central War Room. They had a crisis on their hands.

For the past thirty hours, no one had heard from the small garrison at
Rabaul, the former capital of the Mandated Territory of New Guinea, 2,300
miles to the north in the Bismarck Archipelago. The garrison, code-named
Lark Force, consisted of a lightly armed infantry battalion, a battery of small
antitank guns, and a field ambulance detachment, the latter staffed by two
doctors, twenty orderlies, and six nurses. Heavy weapons were limited to a
pair of coastal defense guns, manned by a detachment of Royal Australian
Artillery, and two aging antiaircraft guns—one with a cracked breach—
manned by young militiamen. With a grand total of about 1,400 troops,
Lark Force was tasked with defending two airdromes, a large harbor, and
more than fifteen miles of New Britain's rugged coastline.

The prolonged silence from Rabaul was ominous, but the men at
Victoria Barracks had a fairly clear idea of what had transpired. In early
January, planes of the Imperial Japanese Navy based at Truk had initiated
a series of bombing attacks against Rabaul, receiving little opposition

1

despite the presence of a Royal Australian Air Force squadron. Then on January 20, a raid by more than one hundred Japanese carrier planes practically wiped out the squadron and badly damaged the fortifications at Rabaul. Two days later, another attack by carrier planes destroyed what remained of the fixed defenses.

At noon on January 22, an enemy invasion fleet was sighted on the northern horizon. Hours later, all communications with Rabaul abruptly ceased. It was all too apparent that New Britain had been invaded.

The outcome should have been no surprise, for the fate of Lark Force had been decided long before the Japanese arrived. On December 12, 1941, only a few days after the surprise attack on Pearl Harbor, the government decided not to risk any ships to deliver additional men or material to Rabaul. There would be no evacuation, no resupply. In a secret cable to diplomats in Washington D.C., the chief of naval staff attempted to rationalize the cabinet's decision, writing, "Under the circumstances . . . it is considered better to maintain Rabaul only as an advance air operational base, its present small garrison being regarded as hostages to fortune."

Incredible as it seems, the Rabaul garrison was given up as lost more than a month before the invasion occurred.

The government's one concession was to evacuate the noncombatants. Over a period of eight days beginning just before Christmas, approximately eight hundred women and children were taken from the Mandated Territory by commercial ships and aircraft. The civilian men—more than two hundred at Rabaul alone—were left behind to face an uncertain future. They included Harold Page, the acting administrator of the territory, whose older brother was a former prime minister and one of Australia's most prominent citizens. Despite his connections, Page could do nothing to help himself or the others left behind. As the weeks went by and the threat of invasion loomed, he sent urgent messages requesting instructions for the evacuation of the men, but the bureaucrats in Canberra had ignored his pleas for help.

Now it was too late. The last ship capable of providing safe passage from New Britain had been set ablaze by Japanese dive-bombers on January 20.

DOWN IN THE DIM basement corridors of Victoria Barracks, newspaper correspondents waited anxiously for an official statement about the situation at Rabaul. As midnight approached, some were concerned about the deadline for the morning editions, but additional minutes dragged by while staff officers argued over the wording of a press release. Finally a brief communiqué was issued. It stated simply that all radio traffic from Rabaul had ceased at 1600 hours on January 22, and a Japanese invasion force had landed before dawn the next morning. The remnants of Lark Force, driven from their fortifications, were believed to be putting up "resistance in the hills."

Over the next few days, the Australian government carefully controlled the information provided to the general population, much of it presented by Francis M. "Frank" Forde, the deputy prime minister as well as minister of the army. On the evening of Friday, January 23, he preempted the military communiqué by several hours in stating that the "only known landing" had occurred at Kieta, on the big island of Bougainville in the northern Solomon Islands. Acknowledging the presence of a Japanese fleet near Rabaul, he told the press, "Australia was facing the most serious threat in its history."

To ensure that his statements were taken seriously, Forde continued to emphasize the magnitude of the situation.

> The Premier of Japan (General Tojo) had declared that Japan would show no mercy if we continued to resist, but resist we will to the utmost of our capacity. If the enemy lands at Rabaul two events of tremendous gravity will occur. These were that territory under the control of an Australian Government will be assailed for the first time, and that Australian militia will be in action for the first time. We cannot delude ourselves about the fact that Australians will have to fight as they never fought before for our very existence.

The next afternoon, Forde stated that the Japanese had presumably landed at Rabaul, based on the loss of communication with the garrison. But in the wake of the initial report, nothing more was learned. After several days of silence, some newspapers resorted to speculation. "Military experts believe that the Rabaul garrison should be able to hold out until sufficient aid arrives," invented the Sydney *Sun* on January 28.

But it was pure propaganda. Nobody in Australia, least of all the press, knew what was happening at Rabaul.

CHAPTER 1

Volcanoes, God,
and Coconuts

A FEW WEEKS AFTER the Pacific war began, newspaper correspondent George H. Johnston posed a rhetorical question about Rabaul: "Why are the Japs striking at this little tropical outpost less than five degrees below the equator?"

The short answer is that Rabaul boasts one of the finest harbors in the Pacific. Its numerous deepwater anchorages are ringed by rugged mountains, with a relatively narrow passage in the southeast quadrant that opens to the sea. The main basin, measuring approximately seven-and-a-half miles long by five miles wide, is surrounded with volcanoes that stand shoulder to shoulder like sentinels. They are magnificent reminders of the extreme geological violence that formed the landscape and its anchorage.

Located at the northeastern tip of crescent-shaped New Britain, largest of the more than two hundred islands that make up the Bismarck Archipelago, the town of Rabaul sits atop a seismic time bomb. This is largely because Rabaul lies within a huge circular fault line—a geological phenomenon known as a ring fracture—which defines a fragile, loose-fitting lid over a subterranean chamber of magma. The ground is highly unstable. Rabaul is shaken routinely by earthquakes—a hundred per

4

month is not unusual—and during "crisis periods" of heightened seismic activity, they sometimes come in swarms. During the mid-1980s, for example, Rabaul was rocked by tens of thousands of quakes, with one extraordinary spike of nearly fourteen thousand measurable tremors in a single month—an average of well over four hundred quakes per day.

For all the excitement they cause, the earthquakes that rattle New Britain are not particularly damaging. The inherent danger lies in the potential of the ring fracture to violently erupt. More than thirty such events have occurred in just the past five hundred thousand years, some lasting for days or even weeks as enormous amounts of magma burst from the ring fracture. In several cases, so much material was ejected from the magma chamber that the loose-fitting lid above it collapsed like a soufflé. With each subsequent eruption the depression grew larger, and is known today as the Rabaul *caldera*. TheSpanish word for caldron, it is an appropriate description indeed.

One of the most devastating volcanic events occurred a mere 1,400 years ago. In the estimation of Dr. C. Daniel Miller, a volcanologist with the U.S. Geological Survey, "a very violent eruption" ejected approximately ten cubic kilometers of magma and debris from the subterranean chamber. The amount of destructive force necessary to blast so much material from the earth is almost inconceivable. "It would be like hundreds of H-bombs going off—one every thirty seconds for ten hours," says Miller. "That's the kind of energy we're talking about."

The subsequent collapse of the empty magma chamber must have been spectacular, but there was no one alive to see it. Virtually every human being within thirty miles of ground zero had been killed, including those on nearby islands. One can only imagine the stupendous sight as twenty square miles of terrain suddenly dropped six hundred feet or more. That event was followed by flooding of biblical proportions as the ocean poured through a breach in the southeastern quadrant of the depression. Once the dust settled and the waters calmed, the result was a large basin of seawater surrounded by a bizarre moonscape of pumice and ash.

Thanks to the tropical climate with its copious amounts of annual rainfall, the volcanic soil was covered by fast-growing kunai grasses and other vegetation in a relatively short time. Native islanders eventually returned to the area, building new villages and resuming the familiar patterns of their ancestors. They tended gardens, defended their villages, and practiced the timeworn rituals passed down from generation to generation. For the next thousand years, the giant caldera remained silent, and eventually the great eruption was forgotten.

THE FIRST KNOWN European to sail completely around the crescent-shaped island, English explorer William Dampier, arrived in 1700. He named the island New Britain and charted its coastline, but for many years thereafter, explorers avoided the island because of justifiable fears of malaria and cannibals. Seafarers may have anchored in the caldera on rare occasions, but their shore parties did not stray far from the beach. For the next 150 years, the island remained shrouded in obscurity.

By the mid-nineteenth century, much of the fear associated with headhunters and malaria had been overcome by the inexorable spread of Christianity. After bringing the gospel to Polynesia, white missionaries headed for Melanesia, the "black islands," with noble ideas of turning the savages into children of God. In 1872, Capt. Cortland Simpson of the Royal Navy sailed HMS *Blanche* into the caldera and claimed its "discovery." He named the inner harbor for himself and the outer bay for his ship, thus adding Simpson Harbor and Blanche Bay to the nautical charts. Contrary to Simpson's claim of discovery, the caldera had been mapped a full century earlier by another English explorer, Philip Carteret, who had named the volcanic mountains surrounding the basin. The largest was the North Daughter, soaring 1,600 feet above Simpson Harbor; the South Daughter anchored the southeastern tip of the volcanic peninsula; and the Mother stood between them, her twin peaks resembling breasts.

After Simpson's visit, dozens of traders and missionaries began to settle New Britain, and its population steadily increased throughout the late 1800s. Competition between Catholic and Protestant mission-aries sometimes confused the natives, but the practices of headhunting and cannibalism gradually waned. Interestingly, the Christians failed to change the islanders' beliefs in the supernatural. Thanks to the earth-quakes (*gurias* in the native Tolai language) that shook New Britain almost daily, the islanders were convinced that malevolent spirits called *kaia* inhabited the volcanoes. Some of the big mountains were long extinct, but there was still plenty of volcanic activity. In 1791, English explorer John Hunter observed a vent near the South Daughter erupting a large column of steam; and sixty years later another eruption occurred along an odorous gully known as Sulphur Creek, which empties into Simpson Harbor.

There was nothing supernatural about the eruptions, of course. Hot magma still occupied the subterranean chamber, which alternately swelled and contracted over the centuries. One odd-looking result, the Davapia Rocks, protruded like obelisks from the middle of Simpson Harbor. Locals called them "the Beehives." A mile to the east stood another geological phenomenon, Matupit Island, which had risen from the caldera like a blister until it reached more than thirty feet above sea level. Nearby squatted an ugly, menacing volcano named Tavurvur, which Hunter had witnessed erupting in 1791. Yet another volcano, Rabalanakaia, was nestled in the shadow of the Mother, which in turn was flanked by the North Daughter and South Daughter, and at least three unnamed vents lined the banks of the aptly named Sulphur Creek. With so many different vents and fumaroles present, the finger of land around Simpson Harbor and Blanche Bay became known as Crater Peninsula.

COMPARED WITH THE influence of Christianity and even the awesome power of volcanoes, nothing changed New Britain like the humble coconut. In the mid-nineteenth century, coconut oil gained popularity as a key ingredient in candles and soap. German companies perfected methods of cutting up coconuts and processing the meat, which was then packed in burlap bags and shipped to the Fatherland, where factory presses extracted the oil. Thus was born the copra industry. Plantations sprang up all across the Pacific, and the volume of shipping traffic exploded. New Britain was no exception. The industry expanded rapidly throughout the archipelago, claimed by Germany as a protectorate in 1884 and named after the first chancellor, Otto Von Bismarck. A year later, Germany annexed a large portion of eastern New Guinea (the Netherlands claimed the western half, calling it Dutch New Guinea, while Great Britain claimed the southeastern portion, including much of the Papuan Peninsula). The privately held New Guinea Company received a charter to administer the territory, but rampant malaria forced the company to move its headquarters to New Britain.

The administration settled at Kokopo (pronounced *Cocka-pō*), a community on the shore of St. George's Channel. The choice was influenced by the town's proximity to Vunapope (*Vuna-pōpay*), the regional center for the Order of the Sacred Heart, a Roman Catholic organization. Easily the largest mission on New Britain, Vunapope occupied a handsome, sprawling campus overlooking the sea. As a location for the territorial headquarters, however, Kokopo proved to be undesirable, mainly because its harbor was inadequate for large ships.

In the early 1890s, the German government took over the administration of the protectorate and sent Dr. Albert Hahl to serve as its first governor. Eager to move the headquarters into the protected waters of Simpson Harbor, Hahl acquired the swampy land at the north end of the anchorage in the name of the government. The area had been deemed unsuitable for development, but with efficient German engineering the mangrove swamps were drained and cleared, a wharf was constructed in 1904, and the first buildings were erected the following year. Tram lines were laid to move goods from warehouses to wharves on narrow-gauge carts, and the Germans even cut a tunnel through the side of the caldera to reach a village on New Britain's north shore.

By 1910 the territorial government was established in the new town, named Rabaul, meaning "place of mangroves." It featured wide boulevards and hundreds of shade trees, a bustling commercial district, and attractive bungalows along the pleasant side streets. Hahl resided in Government House, an impressive mansion on Namanula Hill. Nearby was a modern hospital, raised on piers so that air could circulate underneath, and surrounded by deep verandas that took advantage of the hilltop's pleasant sea breezes.

Rabaul and its superb anchorage soon gained favor as a shipping port. Entrepreneurs arrived from Europe and Asia, bringing more sophistication to the tropical town. A few years after this idyllic start, however, World War I interrupted progress. The British Admiralty, concerned that Germany would send commerce raiders into the Pacific, appealed to Australia for help in capturing key ports and other installations in German New Guinea. The Royal Australian Navy responded by sending an expeditionary force, which arrived at Rabaul on September 11, 1914. Troops went ashore that afternoon to search for wireless stations, and one platoon met stiff resistance en route to Bita Paka, where the Germans had erected a giant steel radio mast. Five Australians were killed in action—the Commonwealth's first casualties of World War I—but the transmitter was successfully captured. The

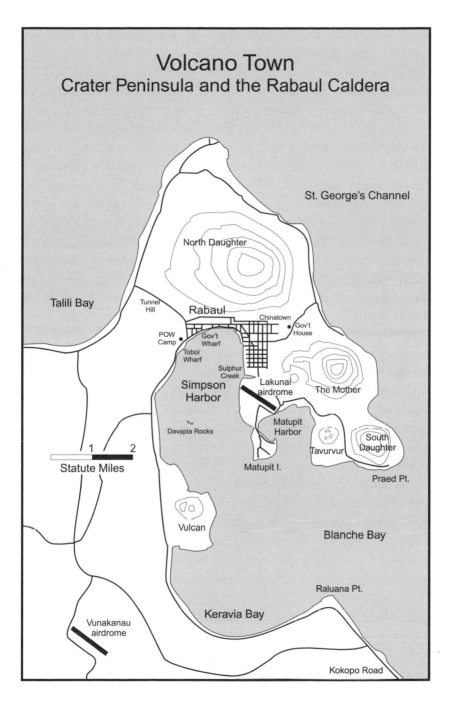

Volcano Town
Crater Peninsula and the Rabaul Caldera

St. George's Channel

North Daughter

Talili Bay

Tunnel Hill

Rabaul

Chinatown

Gov't House

POW Camp

Gov't Wharf

Toboi Wharf

Sulphur Creek

Lakunai airdrome

The Mother

Simpson Harbor

Davapia Rocks

Matupit Harbor

Tavurvur

South Daughter

1   2

Statute Miles

Matupit I.

Praed Pt.

Vulcan

Blanche Bay

Raluana Pt.

Vunakanau airdrome

Keravia Bay

Kokopo Road

Aussies occupied Rabaul without a fight the next day, and four days later Germany surrendered the entire territory.

For the duration of the war and two years thereafter, the Australian Army maintained martial law over the captured region. The League of Nations granted portions of the former German territory to the Commonwealth in 1921, at which time the acquisition was renamed the Mandated Territory of New Guinea. Scattered among its hundreds of inhabited islands were innumerable native villages, coconut plantations, and mission stations with an eclectic mix of residents. The biggest islands featured coastal towns with bustling waterfronts, such as Kavieng at the northern tip of New Ireland.

By the mid-1930s, Rabaul was well established as the largest and most cosmopolitan town in the territory. Its citizens shopped at department stores operated by some of Australia's biggest trading conglomerates, including Burns, Philp & Company and W. R. Carpenter & Company. Rabaul boasted a movie theater, a library, a book club, social clubs, pharmacists, a printing office, taxi stands, pool halls, gas stations, and an ice-making and cold storage plant. Among the sporting venues were a large concrete swimming pool, a cricket field, a baseball diamond, and even a golf course. There were also two airdromes: Lakunai, about two miles southeast of Rabaul along the shore of Simpson Harbor, and Vunakanau, eleven miles south of Rabaul, used by the RAAF as a forward operating base. Near the outlet of Sulphur Creek in Simpson Harbor, a seaplane terminal and ramps were built for Queensland and Northern Territory Aerial Services (QANTAS), the oldest airline in the English-speaking world. Thus, George Johnston's description of Rabaul as a "little tropical outpost" was misleading. By the start of World War II, Rabaul was a bustling town with well over three hundred permanent buildings and a population of approximately one thousand Caucasians, three thousand Asians, and six thousand Melanesian islanders.

In many ways Rabaul was a pleasant tropical town, but its habitability was severely tested one Saturday afternoon in the spring of 1937, when a harmless-looking islet near the western shore of Simpson Harbor suddenly erupted. Compared with the cataclysmic event that had occurred some 1,400 years earlier, this eruption was small, disgorging perhaps half a cubic kilometer of *ejecta*. But even a small eruption near a populated area can be both terrifying and devastating. In this case, a dark column of smoke and debris exploded from the vent. Flashes of lightning darted almost constantly from the volcanic cloud, and thunder added its din to the roar of the eruption. Muddy seawater, sucked into the cloud by convection, fell to the ground in torrents of dirty rain. The biggest disaster occurred when the outer portions of the eruption column collapsed, producing a *pyroclastic* avalanche that wiped out two Tolai villages and incinerated five hundred natives.

As the eruption gained strength, heavy ash began to fall downwind. The citizens of Rabaul, having dropped whatever they were doing to watch the spectacle, suddenly realized they were in the path of the fallout. Only two roads led north out of the caldera, both of which became jammed with thousands of refugees. Daylight turned to night as the thick, gray clouds overtook them, and the booming of thunder made it seem as though doomsday had arrived.

Sunrise the next morning revealed an amazing sight. The small islet in Simpson Harbor had been transformed overnight into a conical mountain more than seven hundred feet high. A wisp of steam drifted from its cone, but the eruption was over. Later that afternoon, the squat volcano named Tavurvur erupted with its own blast of steam and heavy smoke. The flaming debris was frightening to behold, but the eruption soon subsided. Rabaul was abandoned for two weeks, its once-lovely streets in ruins. Trees had snapped under the weight of several inches of wet ash, cars lay buried as though by a gray blizzard, and ships were aground, scattered at odd angles on the beaches. The task of cleaning up was a long and frustrating affair.

In the wake of the devastating eruption, the Australian government decided to move the capital of the mandated territory elsewhere. But the only viable alternatives were on the malaria-ridden coast of New Guinea, and two years of bickering ensued. Eventually the town of Lae, known as the site where Amelia Earhart and Fred Noonan began the last leg of their ill-fated attempt to cross the Pacific, was selected as the future capital. Before an official move could begin, however, Adolf Hitler launched his blitzkrieg on Western Europe. With that, Rabaul was all but forgotten as the Australian government turned its attention to the war on the other side of the globe.

CHAPTER 2

24 Squadron

IF THE UNITED STATES WAS said to be "a sleeping giant" at the onset of World War II, Australia was nearly comatose.* The Commonwealth was still in dire economic straits in 1941, thanks to a painfully slow recovery from the worldwide economic depression of the previous decade. Australia was neither wealthy nor powerful, and a large percentage of its economy and military strength went to support British interests. Tens of thousands of its soldiers were sent to North Africa to fight the Germans, such that by the end of 1941 almost three whole divisions had been committed. As a result, Australia lacked adequate manpower to defend her own backyard. Her weakness was sharply criticized in official postwar assessments, which lamented the Commonwealth's tiny navy, lack of weapons and supplies, and an air defense that was hardly more than "a paper plan."

Almost twenty years earlier, the Royal Geographical Society had warned against the dangers of one country gaining control over the Pacific. After visiting several island groups of Australia's mandated territory in 1921, the Honorable J. P. Thomson had written: "On each of these groups

---

*The famous quote, "I fear all we have done is to awaken a sleeping giant . . . " is widely attributed to Adm. Isoroku Yamamoto, commander in chief of the Combined Fleet. The line was popularized in two major films, *Tora! Tora! Tora!* and *Pearl Harbor*, but Yamamoto probably did not utter the words.

enumerated a naval base could be established and its position rendered secure against attack by suitable fortifications and the natural advantages afforded by the coral-reef structures. Once this was done a hostile power would be in a position practically to dominate the whole of the Pacific Ocean. With submarines and a fleet of destroyers, it would be a simple matter to isolate Australia and New Zealand."

Thomson's assessment was remarkably prophetic, but the Allies failed to pay attention. Canberra seemed more interested in the gold fields of New Guinea until World War II began, when the military importance of the mandated territory was finally addressed.

The first noteworthy effort to link the islands with a communications network was achieved by Lt. Cmdr. Eric N. Feldt of the Royal Australian Navy, who set out in the fall of 1939 to enlist as many men as possible in a coastwatching organization. Traveling from island to island between New Guinea and the New Hebrides, Feldt enrolled dozens of plantation owners, traders, government officials, and other civilians into a loosely organized group. His achievement was brilliant: in the coming years the scattered coastwatchers provided useful intelligence and performed extraordinary feats, many at the cost of their lives.

Aside from a small volunteer militia company formed in 1939 at Rabaul, there was almost no military presence on New Britain until late 1940, when the War Cabinet approved a motion to encourage Dutch warships to visit Simpson Harbor. As an incentive, the politicians voted to install a pair of 6-inch coastal artillery guns at the entrance to the harbor, though actual delivery would not take place for months. At about the same time, the RAAF established an advance operational base (AOB) for flying boats near the outlet of Sulphur Creek. Thereafter, fortification of the islands gained momentum. The War Cabinet announced in early 1941 that it was deploying the 23rd Brigade to defend what it called the "Malay Barrier," a grandiose name for three small island bases hundreds of miles apart.

The three garrisons, culled from the 8th Division, 2nd Australian Imperial Force, were inexplicably named for small birds. Sparrow Force, consisting mainly of the 2/40th Infantry Battalion, fortified the island of Timor; Gull Force, with the 2/21st Infantry Battalion as its nucleus, was deployed two hundred miles farther north to Ambon; and Lark Force, built around the 2/22nd Infantry Battalion, went to Rabaul.

Lark Force arrived at Rabaul in contingents between April and September of 1941. Initially the soldiers set up camp near Simpson Harbor, but in early June the squat volcano named Tavurvur erupted again, and for months thereafter it spewed clouds of noxious vapor. Everyone grew weary of the stench of sulfur and the corrosive effects of the falling ash, which rotted tent fabric and uniforms and pitted exposed metal surfaces. To escape the fallout, Lark Force built a more permanent encampment of wood-framed buildings along Malaguna Road on the west side of Rabaul. The camp afforded a direct view of the nearby harbor—on the other side of which the volcano continued to erupt, sometimes with spectacular fireworks, for months to come.

PRIOR TO THE ARRIVAL of Lark Force, aerial defenses on New Britain were nonexistent. That changed in mid-August 1941 when the liner *Neptuna* delivered a pair of World War I–vintage antiaircraft guns to Rabaul. Crewed by a militia unit of two officers and fifty-two men, the guns had no predictor, no height finder, and only a primitive ring-sight for aiming. Even worse, the breach of the Number 2 gun was cracked, so neither weapon was fired during practice. Instead, the crews trained by pretending to shoot down the weekly mail plane when it approached and departed every Saturday. This resulted in merciless teasing from the regular AIF personnel, but the militiamen redeemed themselves by winning several bouts in a hard-fought boxing tournament.

Aside from the two old antiaircraft guns, there were no improvements in the aerial defenses until December, when an undermanned RAAF composite squadron was transferred to Rabaul from Townsville, Queensland. Led by Wing Cmdr. John M. Lerew, 24 Squadron brought ten CA-1 Wirraways and four Lockheed Hudsons for air defense and reconnaissance. The problem was that neither type of aircraft had been designed for combat.

On the eve of the Pacific war, the RAAF had but 180 frontline aircraft in operation. The service openly admitted that its planes were "not very formidable, the best being Hudsons, Catalinas, and Empire flying boats." The blunt appraisal, which appeared in the official postwar history, was most notable for the fact that none of the aircraft named were fighters. In mid-1941, the RAAF simply didn't have any.

The closest thing to a fighter in the inventory was the Wirraway, which derived its name from an old aboriginal word meaning "challenger." Built under license by the Commonwealth Aircraft Corporation, it was a copy of the renowned North American AT-6 two-seat trainer (the Harvard in Commonwealth service) with a few add-ons: three light machine guns, a more powerful radial engine, and a three-bladed propeller. Despite the improvements, the aircraft was woefully underpowered, with a maximum speed of only 220 miles per hour and an agonizingly slow rate of climb.

The RAAF had known for years that the Wirraway had no business serving as a fighter. During a visit from London in 1937, the inspector general of the Royal Air Force had cautioned that the Wirraway "could only be regarded as an advanced training aircraft." But four years later, the RAAF still had nothing better to replace it with.

The American-built Hudson was another example of compromise in the RAAF. After starting life as a civilian airliner—the twin-engine Lockheed Electra made famous by the likes of Amelia Earhart—the military export version evolved when the Royal Air Force requested a navigational trainer. The Hudson was not designed for heavy combat duty, but the RAAF employed it in every manner conceivable, from maritime patrol to bombing to long-range reconnaissance. It was reasonably fast at 250 miles per hour, carried a crew of five, and was armed with seven .303-caliber machine guns for defense. However, it proved vulnerable to enemy fighter attack, especially from the rear, and could carry only 1,000 pounds of bombs. Even then its range was severely limited; therefore, the Hudsons in 24 Squadron typically carried half the rated load: two bombs, each weighing 250 pounds.

On December 7, the day prior to the attack on Pearl Harbor in time zones west of the International Date Line, Flt. Lt. John F. Murphy led the first three Hudsons to Rabaul. Landing at Vunakanau airdrome, the crews were dismayed to find no permanent facilities. There was only a dirt runway hacked out of the kunai grass, a "hangar" made from a piece of corrugated roofing supported by four poles, and a few thatch-roofed huts for accommodation. Murphy's biggest concern was the lack of dispersal sites. With no revetments available, the Hudsons were parked like sitting ducks alongside the runway.

The fourth Lockheed arrived on December 8 after undergoing an engine change. By then, word of the Japanese attacks had reached the squadron. As officer-in-charge of the four Hudsons, Murphy began sending out armed patrols and made his first operational flight on December 9. He attempted to intercept a high-flying aircraft, strongly suspected to be a Japanese reconnaissance plane, but was not successful.

Six days later, Flt. Lt. Kenneth J. Erwin hit pay dirt during a photographic mission over Kapingamarangi Atoll, about four hundred miles northeast of Rabaul. The site of a refueling station for Japanese seaplanes, it was the only enemy installation within range of the Hudsons. Making two passes over the atoll that morning, Erwin counted nineteen barges, a variety of shore facilities, and a merchant ship. The latter fired at him with its small-caliber guns.

Erwin returned to Vunakanau and reported his findings, whereupon Murphy ordered a bombing mission. Two additional Hudsons were available, so Erwin guided Murphy and a third crew back to the target area. Finding the merchantman about twenty miles north of Kapingamarangi, the three Hudsons made individual attack runs. "I was the first to drop a bomb," Murphy wrote later, "and therefore believe I was the first pilot in the Southwest Pacific Area to attack the enemy." It is a point worth emphasizing: just a week after the attack on Pearl Harbor, a flight of three RAAF Hudsons from Rabaul made an impromptu attack against a Japanese merchant ship. For the record, Australia attacked first, not the other way around.

But dropping a bomb is only half of the equation. Actually hitting a moving target, especially a zigzagging ship, is difficult. The pilots of 24 Squadron had never practiced it in training, and to make matters worse, they had to attack the ship from high altitude to avoid damaging their own aircraft. "At that time we only had instantaneous fuses," recalled Murphy, "and so had to attack at altitude with bomb sights that were anything but accurate."

Making two bomb runs apiece, the Hudsons caused no apparent damage. Had they attacked in formation, releasing their bombs in a salvo, they might have gotten lucky. As it was, the merchantman had a relatively easy time dodging the six small bombs dropped individually.

Deeply frustrated by the mission's outcome, Murphy and the others expected some negative reaction from RAAF headquarters, but no one was prepared for the hostile wave of criticism that ensued. Wing Commander Lerew, arriving at Rabaul with a flight of Wirraways the day after the mission, caught the worst of it. As soon as he climbed down from his aircraft, he was handed a decoded message. "It was addressed to me from the Chief of Air Staff, Sir Charles Burnett," Lerew remembered. "He expressed clearly his disappointment with the poor effort that had been put up by the squadron in missing the ship and stated that unless better results were achieved, the entire squadron would be replaced immediately."

Lerew was flabbergasted by the threat from the top man in the RAAF. Burnett, born in Minnesota and raised in England, had spent twenty-two years in the Royal Air Force prior to his appointment in Australia. His criticism seemed to stem from a monumental ego, as though he might force 24 Squadron to improve by sheer will. He had the option of replacing Lerew and bringing him back to Australia in disgrace, but he took no action. Thus, his message accomplished little except to antagonize the squadron.

Lerew was also reprimanded by Wing Cmdr. William H. "Bull" Garing, the senior air staff officer at Townsville, regional headquarters for the North East Area. Using phrases like "wasted effort," "utter failure," and "extreme disappointment," Garing battered the squadron's performance in a letter that concluded with: "The Empire expects much from a few." Perhaps Garing intended the words to be inspirational, like those of Winston Churchill after the Battle of Britain, but to Lerew the phrase sounded like a load of drivel. Military historian Lex McAulay gives Garing some allowance for his demeanor, describing him as "a fireball" whose short temper and abrasiveness were not uncommon for the time. Garing had earned a Distinguished Flying Cross during the early months of the war in Europe, and he expected everyone in the RAAF to perform as well as he had against the Luftwaffe.

Fortunately for 24 Squadron, Lerew could tolerate Garing's abuse. Proud of his Huguenot ancestry, Lerew was stubborn, resilient, resourceful, and occasionally devilish—characteristics that would help him face the numerous challenges that lay ahead.

Kapingamarangi Atoll was targeted a few more times during the last two weeks of 1941, but something seemed to go wrong with every mission. The worst culprit proved to be the bombs, which too often failed to explode. Still disgruntled, Lerew's superiors ordered him to write a detailed situation report explaining the squadron's failures. He complied but his response contained a measure of the "impish irreverence" he had become famous for. Lerew itemized the numerous handicaps his squadron faced every day: minimal aircrews, lack of maintenance personnel, lack of proper repair facilities, no utility vehicles, poor communication links, miles of rough roads, and finally, "Disappointment in the lack of assistance rendered by the Almighty."

To be absolutely certain his superiors understood the level of his frustration, Lerew closed the report with a deliberate jab at Garing: "The Empire expects much, repeat much, of a few."

While the Hudson crews struggled to improve their results, the Wirraway flyers had even worse luck. Lerew divided the fighters into two groups, retaining B Flight at Vunakanau and sending A Flight to Lakunai airdrome under the guidance of his second-in-command, Flt. Lt. Wilfred D. "Bill" Brookes. The move was made on the afternoon of December 18, some hours after another encounter with enemy aircraft. Two unidentified reconnaissance aircraft appeared, and four Wirraways attempted to intercept them, but as Brookes later lamented, they were unable to catch the snoopers "owing to lack of speed." It was a sorry situation when so-called fighters were not fast enough overtake reconnaissance planes.

Lakunai was in need of numerous physical improvements, but Brookes's detachment consisted of only ten airmen and six ground personnel—not nearly enough men for the necessary construction project. Brookes acquired forty Tolai laborers from the local administration, but even with the extra manpower the RAAF men had to roll up their sleeves and work. Together with the natives they built their own living quarters, constructed dispersal areas among the coconut trees of the adjacent plantation, and lined the taxiways with planks to keep the planes from sinking into the soft volcanic soil. Unaccustomed to heavy physical work in such extreme humidity, the airmen cursed the "lower 'drome." Their frustrations mounted as torrential rains periodically washed out the roads and disrupted the single telephone line that linked Lakunai with Vunakanau.

The day after Christmas, a pair of Japanese Type 97 flying boats reconnoitered Rabaul. Again the Wirraways failed to intercept them, so the mechanics stripped the little planes of every unnecessary pound in an effort to increase their performance. The results proved negligible. The Wirraways were simply too underpowered to catch even the largest, heaviest seaplanes in the Imperial Navy.

On New Year's Day, 1942, the squadron finally enjoyed some success. Ordnance personnel armed four Hudsons with bombs fused for eleven-second delays, allowing the crews to attack "Kap" Atoll at a low altitude without blowing their own tails off. Of the eight bombs dropped, five were direct hits on shore facilities. One was scored by John Murphy, whose copilot, Flg. Off. Alfred S. Hermes, climbed from his seat to observe the results of their attack on a large building. Unfortunately, the delayed-action fuses worked too well. When Murphy released his first bomb, Hermes chimed, "It's in the front door," followed a few heartbeats later by, "It's out the back door." Murphy laughed it off, happy with the knowledge that he could at least hit a target.

GEORGE JOHNSTON'S rhetorical question about Rabaul would have interested the Japanese. For more than three decades, going back as far as the rule of Emperor Meiji, they had been quietly preparing for war against the West—specifically the United States. Having defeated Russia's fleet in 1905, the Imperial Navy developed a "fundamental strategy" of one day drawing the U.S. Pacific Fleet into an ambush. Steven Bullard, historian and translator of Japanese military documents for the Australian War Memorial, explained the development of the policy: "The waters near the Japanese mainland were initially chosen as the site of this decisive battle. However, advances in military technology and the changing strategic situation resulted in a re-evaluation in 1936 that moved the site to the seas west of the Marianas (with a reconnaissance line in the Marshall Islands). By 1940, the seas to the east of the Marianas and to the north of the Marshall Islands were the planned location."

Because of that shift in location, the Imperial Navy developed a forward base for the Combined Fleet at Truk Atoll in the Caroline Islands. Formerly a possession of Germany, the Carolines (along with the Marshalls and Marianas) were occupied by Japan during World War I. The right to govern them was later granted by the League of Nations, but Japan withdrew from the League in 1933, thus freeing herself from treaty restrictions that forbade the fortification of mandated territories. The Imperial Navy began to construct several bases among the islands, and by 1940 Truk had become a formidable bastion, nicknamed the "Gibraltar of the Pacific" by the press. Despite the moniker, the Japanese were concerned about the base's vulnerability to air attack. The perceived threat was Rabaul, slightly less than seven hundred miles to the south. Never mind that its two airdromes were primitive grass strips without permanent facilities;

never mind that the RAAF did not possess any long-range bombers. The new American B-17 Flying Fortresses *could* reach Truk from Rabaul, and that was enough to cause worry.

During the tumultuous summer of 1941, the increasingly militant Japanese began to actively formulate a plan for war. Imperial General Headquarters laid the groundwork for a massive operation called the Southern Offensive, a multi-pronged invasion designed to swiftly overwhelm territories held by Great Britain, the United States, and the Netherlands East Indies. The main component, the Southern Army, would invade the Philippines, Malaya, and other important territories, while a smaller organization called the *Nankai Shitai* (South Seas Force) captured Guam and the Bismarck Archipelago.

During a briefing on the Southern Offensive presented to Emperor Hirohito on November 3, the occupation of Rabaul was identified as one of the primary goals—a testament to its vital importance in Tokyo's strategy. Three days later, Imperial General Headquarters issued orders to the army and navy to mobilize their forces for war.

As an independent unit under the direct command of Imperial General Headquarters, the South Seas Force was created to establish a strong defensive perimeter of island bases around the territories seized by the Southern Army. Combined with existing fortifications, Japan would control the Pacific from the Kurile Islands southward to the Gilberts in the Central Pacific, then westward through the Solomons and Bismarcks to New Guinea, and finally around Java and Sumatra to Burma—a chain of strongholds more than twelve thousand miles in length. As the linchpin of what the Japanese called the Southeast Area, Rabaul would be developed into an impregnable military complex, a hub from which to launch additional campaigns and further extend Japan's grip on the southern hemisphere.

In other words, the Japanese planned to transform Rabaul, with its huge anchorage and excellent topographical features, into the mightiest fortress in the Pacific.

THERE WAS GOOD REASON for a direct chain of command from Tokyo to the South Seas Force. The Imperial Army and Navy were parochial, neither one willing to be subordinate to the other, particularly at the start of what promised to be a glorious offensive. But with Imperial General

Headquarters in charge of operations, the typical rivalries were avoided. As insurance, the services were bluntly ordered to work together. The South Seas Force, for example, received Great Army Instruction No. 992 on November 8, 1941, which emphasized, in part: "The army and navy will cooperate."

There wasn't an officer alive in either service who would dare to question the directive's legitimacy. *Every* direct order in the Japanese military system, whether written or verbal, was regarded as though Emperor Hirohito himself had issued it. As a result, the army and navy components of the South Seas Force not only cooperated but conducted a near-flawless operation against Guam.

When the Southern Offensive commenced on December 8, Tokyo time, several troop transports and a sizeable convoy of Fourth Fleet warships were already en route to Guam, an American possession in the Mariana Islands. Land-based naval aircraft from Saipan softened up the island's defenses for two days, and when the invasion troops stormed ashore on December 10, the garrison of 153 U.S. Marines and the local militia surrendered within minutes.

After securing Guam, the South Seas Force spent the rest of December preparing for the invasion of the Bismarcks. On January 3, 1942, Maj. Gen. Tomitaro Horii and his battalion commanders flew more than 630 miles to Truk for a planning session with their navy counterparts. Boarding the cruiser *Kashima* in Truk lagoon, they met with Vice Adm. Shigeyoshi Inoue, commander of the Fourth Fleet, and hammered out the various details of "R" Operation, as the coming invasion was called. The meeting concluded with the signing of a cooperation agreement between Horii and Inoue, ostensibly to satisfy the dictates of Tokyo, after which Horii and his staff flew back to Guam.

The following day, the Imperial Navy's 24th Air Flotilla received orders to begin attacking Rabaul from its base at Truk. Having already conducted several high-altitude reconnaissance flights over the area, the aircrews were undoubtedly anxious to initiate combat. None, however, could have foreseen that the air war over Rabaul would continue unabated for almost four years. The longest battle of World War II was about to begin.

CHAPTER 3

Gladiators

THE WAR CAME TO RABAUL on a pleasant Sunday morning, the fourth day of 1942. Dawn broke rapidly, as it always does in the equatorial latitudes, giving the antiaircraft gunners atop the North Daughter a breathtaking sunrise. Accustomed to such splendor after weeks of sitting at their posts, they might have assumed that yet another monotonous day awaited them. If so, they were in for a surprise.

At approximately 1000 hours, plantation manager Cornelius L. Page sent an urgent radio message from the tiny island of Tabar, ninety miles north of New Britain. Recruited two years earlier into the network of coastwatchers, he had observed a flight of Japanese bombers as they passed over his coconut plantation on a direct course for Rabaul.

The formation consisted of sixteen Navy Type 96 land attack aircraft of the Chitose Air Group, currently attached to the 24th Air Flotilla at Truk. Known to the Allies as Mitsubishi G3Ms, the twin-engine aircraft were fast and well armed. They also possessed an extraordinary combat radius that allowed them to reach Rabaul easily from their airfield seven hundred miles away. The Imperial Navy's unique category of land-based attack aircraft, *rikujo kogeki-ki* (commonly abbreviated as *rikko*), emphasized the use of aerial torpedoes against ships, but the aircraft could also carry bombs, and on this mission the Mitsubishis were armed with 60-kilogram fragmentation bombs.

The air-raid sirens began to wail in Rabaul shortly after 1100. High atop the North Daughter, the young antiaircraft gunners fidgeted with excitement as they strained to catch a first glimpse of the enemy. Suddenly the planes appeared—sixteen bombers coming straight toward the gunners in perfect V formation. The Aussies were enthralled by the size and splendor of the enemy formation, and many thought the planes looked beautiful in the sunlight.

One keyed-up teenager, having never experienced the guns in action, asked, "Can we really fire this time?"

"Too right we can," answered Lt. David M. Selby, the battery's commanding officer. He gave the order to fire, and the old guns belched flame a split second apart, causing the gunners to flinch reflexively. They held their collective breath until the shells detonated at thirteen thousand feet, far below the enemy planes. Recovering from their surprise at the initial blast of heat and noise, the gunners set the fuses for the maximum range of fifteen thosand feet and quickly settled into the familiar routine they had practiced for months, getting off round after round from the two vintage weapons. But still the shells failed to reach the enemy planes. The only noteworthy outcome was the successful performance of the cracked breach; otherwise the Japanese bombers continued toward Lakunai airdrome with nary a scratch.

At the airdrome, Flight Lieutenant Brookes and Sqn. Ldr. Archibald R. Tindal scrambled aloft in two Wirraways just as the bombs began falling. They should have been airborne much sooner, but for unknown reasons the fighters did not take off in time to intercept the formation. Not that the delay made much difference: the Japanese bombers were at least ten miles per hour faster than the Wirraways. Two other Wirraway crews tried to scramble from Lakunai but were forced to abort, their vision obscured by thick clouds of volcanic dust churned up by the exploding enemy bombs.

Without interference from the Wirraways or the antiaircraft battery, the Japanese should have smashed the airdrome. Surprisingly, however, only three bombs out of forty actually hit the target. Twenty struck the water, and the other seventeen landed within the Rapindik native housing complex and infirmary adjacent to the airdrome. Shrapnel from the small fragmentation bombs caused horrific casualties in the confined area, killing a dozen islanders outright and severely injuring thirty others.

Shortly before dusk, eleven Navy Type 97 flying boats (Kawanishi H6Ks) of the Yokohama Air Group attacked Vunakanau airdrome. With their long parasol wings and slender fuselages curving upward toward twin vertical stabilizers, the four-engine seaplanes resembled giant dragonflies as they droned overhead. An estimated forty bombs were dropped, all of which missed Vunakanau by a wide margin due to the rapidly waning daylight. Twilight fell so quickly, in fact, that the antiaircraft gunners did not even fire at the formation.

The first raids on Rabaul made headlines in Japanese newspapers. One article, citing a report from Melbourne, stated that the "radio station" had been an objective of the attacks. But the bombers were clearly targeting the airdromes, and the powerful civilian radio facility operated by Amalgamated Wireless of Australasia was untouched.

The next raid occurred on the afternoon of January 6, when nine huge Kawanishi flying boats returned to hit Vunakanau again. This time, with no early warning from "Con" Page, the attack caused serious damage: a direction-finding station smashed, a Wirraway destroyed, a Hudson damaged by a near miss, and the runway pocked with craters. The Japanese reported "intense" antiaircraft fire, which caused minor damage to one Kawanishi. Four Wirraways took off to intercept the flying boats, but due to their pitiful climb rate only one managed to get close enough to open fire. Flight Lieutenant Bruce H. Anderson chased the formation beyond New Ireland and expended all of his ammunition at a retreating bomber from maximum range. Although he failed to register any hits, he was credited with being the first Allied fighter pilot to engage the enemy in the Southwest Pacific. The achievement counted for very little, however, and Bill Brookes noted sourly that "the enemy took advantage of cloud cover and their superior height to get away."

The following morning, another *rikko* formation attacked Vunakanau. Page radioed the alarm at 1030, having counted eighteen Type 96 bombers overhead. Wirraways took off immediately, but the Japanese bombers dropped their ordnance on the airdrome without opposition because the Australian planes were too underpowered to catch them.

On this occasion the bombardiers' aim was accurate. Two parked planes—the Wirraway assigned to Bruce Anderson and a Hudson loaded with bombs—caught fire. Anderson and another pilot attempted to save the Wirraway, but John Lerew noticed the danger posed by the burning

Hudson and shouted a warning. The squadron doctor drove up in his sedan just as the bomber's fuel tank erupted, and all four men dived under the vehicle. Seconds later the Hudson's bombs exploded, peppering the car with debris. After struggling from beneath the car, Lerew marveled at the shallow space he and the others had squeezed into when the need was urgent.

THE JAPANESE CEASED raiding for several days, sending only a few reconnaissance flights over Rabaul instead of bombers. During the same period, a specially prepared Hudson of 6 Squadron flew a photoreconnaissance mission from Kavieng to Truk lagoon on January 9. The crew returned from the daring flight, the longest undertaken by the RAAF to date, with evidence that a large enemy fleet was gathering in the lagoon.

The 24th Air Flotilla resumed its bombing campaign on the morning of January 16, when another formation of *rikko* destroyed stockpiles of fuel, bombs, and flares at Vunakanau. Two Wirraways tried to intercept the Mitsubishis but never got closer than a thousand yards—nowhere near effective gunnery range. "Owing to the superior speed of the enemy," noted Brookes, "they had no trouble escaping."

Six hours after the first attack, a handful of flying boats dropped strings of fragmentation bombs on Lakunai, narrowly missing the ordnance dumps. Bombs exploded all around Lerew and several other men sheltering in slit trenches, but no one on the ground was hurt. From the systematic nature of the attacks, it was obvious to everyone in Rabaul that the Japanese were preparing to invade. Harold Page, the senior territorial official, pleaded with the government in Canberra to evacuate the remaining civilians. The Norwegian freighter *Herstein*, docked at Rabaul since early January after unloading a cargo of aviation fuel and bombs, had plenty of space available, but the officials in Canberra were adamant: the vessel was to take on a load of copra. Stunned that the government was more concerned about a few tons of coconut meat than two hundred civilians, Page continued to appeal for evacuation. Finally he received a terse message: "No one is to take the place of the copra on the *Herstein*."

FLUSH WITH VICTORY after the easy conquest of Guam, Major General Horii and the troops of the South Seas Force were already en route by the time Page got his answer. R Operation commenced on January 14 when the invasion fleet, escorted by a powerful screening force of three light cruisers, nine destroyers, and two large minelayers, departed Guam and headed south toward New Britain.

Three days later, according to plan, a much more powerful fleet of warships sailed from Truk lagoon. Commanded by Vice Adm. Chuichi Nagumo, the aircraft carriers of the First Air Fleet had just replenished in Japan after their triumphant return from Pearl Harbor. The fleet was reduced from six aircraft carriers to four for R Operation, but these were four of the best. From the 1st Carrier Division came the big flattops *Akagi* and *Kaga*, with a combined complement of fifty-four Type 0 carrier-borne fighters (Mitsubishi A6M2s), forty-five Type 99 carrier-borne bombers (Aichi D3A1s), and fifty-four Type 97 carrier-borne attack planes (Nakajima B5N2s). *Zuikaku* and *Shokaku* of the 5th Carrier Division brought an additional thirty A6M2s, fifty-four D3A1s, and fifty-four B5N2s. To protect this floating arsenal, Nagumo had battleships *Hiei* and *Kirishima* for fleet support, which in turn were shielded by the heavy cruisers *Tone* and *Chikuma*, the light cruiser *Abukuma*, and nine destroyers. Additionally, two squadrons of submarines were deployed from Truk to secure the sea lanes around the Bismarcks.

Nagumo planned to rendezvous with the South Seas Force on January 20 at the equator. Horii's invasion fleet crossed the line at 0500, whereupon the South Seas Force held a ceremony to commemorate their achievement as the first army force to cross the equator in Japan's 2,600-year history. Nagumo's fleet joined them at mid-morning, and soon thereafter the carriers began launching a massive strike against Rabaul. The attack force consisted of eighteen horizontal bombers and nine fighters from *Akagi*, twenty-seven horizontal bombers and nine fighters from *Kaga*, and nineteen dive-bombers each from *Shokaku* and *Zuikaku*.

The strike leader, thirty-nine-year-old Cmdr. Mitsuo Fuchida, was trained as an airborne observer rather than a pilot. A 1924 graduate of the Imperial Japanese Naval Academy at Etajima, he was renowned for his brilliant tactical ideas and leadership of the attack on Pearl Harbor. Eminently qualified to lead the first carrier strike against Rabaul, he coordinated the assorted air groups by radio from the cockpit of a B5N2.

Fuchida's trademark method was to attack the target from multiple directions simultaneously. For the strike on Rabaul, he separated the attackers into three groups—the smallest numbering about twenty planes, the largest more than fifty. The groups headed outbound from the carriers in three different directions; then, on Fuchida's cue, they converged on the target from the east, west, and north.

AT 1214 ON JANUARY 20, Cornelius Page reported twenty aircraft passing over his plantation. Half an hour later, the antiaircraft gunners at Rabaul watched slack-jawed as Zeros roared overhead in flights of three.

The militiamen's reaction was not uncommon. All across the Pacific, the Allies were stunned by their first encounters with the celebrated fighter known to the Japanese as *Rei Shiki Sento Ki* (Type 0 carrier-borne fighter), commonly abbreviated as *Rei-sen*. No other aircraft better represented the dominance of Japanese air power at the beginning of World War II. Designed in the late 1930s and accepted by the Imperial Navy in 1940, the Zero was a marvel of economical engineering. The A6M2 Model 21 weighed only a little more than 5,300 pounds fully loaded (about the same as a modern-day SUV), yet its 950-horsepower radial engine gave the diminutive fighter tremendous speed, an astonishing rate of climb, and superior aerobatic capability. The Zero's armament—a pair of rifle-caliber machine guns in the nose and two 20mm automatic cannons in the wings—was fairly effective, and the Imperial Navy pilots were thoroughly trained. Their favorite tactic was to single out an enemy aircraft and overwhelm it with superior numbers.

When the *Rei-sens* appeared over Rabaul at 1248 that afternoon, two Wirraways were already airborne on routine patrols. Three others scrambled from Vunakanau, and three more attempted to take off from Lakunai, but the Aussie crews were at a terrible disadvantage. Displaying what David Selby later called "desperate gallantry," they rose skyward like so many gladiators to face the Japanese.

Only two of the Wirraways at Lakunai actually got airborne. The engine on Bruce Anderson's plane faltered, and he crashed-landed on the runway, injuring both himself and Plt. Off. Colin A. Butterworth in the legs. Thus a total of five Wirraways took off to join the two already on patrol.

Seven underpowered fighters—nothing more than glorified trainers—would face 109 of the Imperial Navy's best.

The *Rei-sen* pilots did not wait for the Aussies to get organized. "There could be only one conclusion to this fantastically uneven combat," wrote Selby after witnessing the action from his perch atop the North Daughter.

"There was a puff of white smoke from the cannon of a Zero, a red flash as the shell found its mark on one of our planes, and before the boom of the explosion floated down to us a Wirraway was screeching earthward, angry red flames and black smoke pouring from it."

The first to die were Flg. Off. John C. Lowe and his observer, Sgt. Albert C. Ashford. Both were twenty-six years old when their Wirraway spiraled into the waters off Praed Point.

In the other patrolling Wirraway, the two crewmen were a study in contrasts. The rear seat observer, Plt. Off. Albert George Claire, was eight years older than the pilot, Sgt. George Albert Herring, and outranked him by several pay grades. But Herring, who had turned twenty-one only the day before, was a capable pilot. When a swarm of Zeros fired on the Wirraway, hitting both men in the legs and mangling the plane's tail, the aircraft went out of control. At the last possible moment, Herring regained control of the spinning fighter and bellied in at Lakunai. Both men were pulled to safety moments before Zeros swooped down and strafed the crumpled Wirraway, destroying what was left of it.

Several miles to the south, Sgt. Charles F. Bromley and his observer, Sgt. Richard Walsh, took off from Vunakanau and were still clawing for altitude when six Zeros attacked them over Blanche Bay. The two Aussies never stood a chance. Bromley, only nineteen, was killed instantly by a bullet to the head. Walsh evidently tried to jump just before the Wirraway hit the shallows near Praed Point, but his chute did not fully deploy.

Of the two Wirraways that took off successfully from Lakunai, one was flown by Sgt. William O. K. Hewitt, who had dashed to a parked plane and gotten it started while Flg. Off. John "Jack" Tyrrell manned the rear gun. After getting airborne and working his way up to nine thousand feet, Hewitt spotted a formation of enemy planes attacking the wharves at Rabaul. He turned toward them, but before he could get into a firing position, he saw a Zero heading him off from above. Pulling up in a hard, climbing turn, Hewitt tried to meet the Japanese fighter head-on, but his anemic Wirraway could not sustain the climb and stalled.

For a few seconds the Aussie fighter hung almost motionless in the air. Hewitt was completely vulnerable, and the Japanese pilot immediately took advantage. Pieces of Hewitt's unarmored plane flew off as bullets and cannon shells ripped through the little Wirraway. One 20mm shell exploded in the cockpit, severing hydraulic lines and wounding Hewitt in the left knee.

The Wirraway pitched over, nosing down so abruptly that the negative g-forces lifted Jack Tyrrell completely out of his seat. Flailing as he fell, he grabbed for the D-ring of his parachute and discovered to his horror that it was gone. Moments later, the parachute obliged him by opening. Tyrell drifted serenely over the plateau south of the caldera and landed unharmed in the branches of a tree. Later, while walking cross-country toward Vunakanau, he came across a group of Lark Force soldiers hunting for "a supposed Japanese parachutist."

Hewitt, meanwhile, his knee full of shrapnel and his face covered with hydraulic fluid, steered the damaged Wirraway toward the sanctuary of a cloud. He remained hidden until conditions were clear and then crash-landed at Vunakanau without further difficulty. He would live to fight another day, but the Wirraway was beyond repair.

In another Wirraway, Sgt. Ronald C. G. Little and his gunner, Sgt. Donald R. Sheppard, endured a similar experience. More than a dozen Zeros attacked them, damaging the tail of their aircraft, but Little managed to duck into a cloud. Each time he tried to poke out of it, however, he was forced to hide again by the swarming Zeros. Eventually he made a dash for Vunakanau and landed safely with no injuries to either crewman.

Twenty-year-old Sgt. Robert A. Blackman took off from Vunakanau and was last seen "in combat with several Zeros." But nothing more was heard thereafter from either Blackman or his gunner, Sgt. Stanley E. Woodcroft. Eventually their official status was changed from missing to dead.

Only one Australian pilot, Sgt. Malcolm G. Milne, landed with an undamaged Wirraway. After taking off from Lakunai with Sgt. Raymond S. Harber in the back seat, Milne headed straight into a cloud. According to the official RAAF history, he played "a grim game of 'tag' with a greatly superior force of Zeros," but they failed to draw him into combat. Eventually the Japanese withdrew to concentrate on stationary targets, and Milne returned to Lakunai without a scratch.

The fight was over in seven minutes. Selby later observed, "There was something sickening in that sudden merciless extermination, something inspiring in the cold-blooded heroism of those Wirraway pilots, diving splendidly to what each man must have realized meant certain death.

Every incident of that horrible fight had been visible to us, but we were powerless to help."

The casualties suffered by 24 Squadron were heavy, if not as absolute as Selby implied. Of the eight Wirraways that participated, one crashed during takeoff, three were shot down in combat, two crash-landed with irreparable damage, one landed with moderate damage, and one came back without engaging in combat. The final toll among the airmen was six dead and five wounded. There is no evidence that any of the attacking Zeros were damaged, making for a completely lopsided massacre.

That the defenders took off against such an overwhelming force should be considered one of the great sacrifices of the Pacific war—but not a single medal was awarded by the RAAF. Responding in 1946 to an official inquiry about this grievous oversight, the defense ministry stated that no citations could be issued because no enemy planes had been shot down. By that twisted logic, no man who ever jumped on a grenade to save his buddies would deserve a medal either, because his self-sacrifice caused no harm to the enemy.

AFTER ANNIHILATING the Wirraways, the Japanese concentrated on stationary targets. At Vunakanau, where the 2/22nd Battalion had a few Lewis machine guns for antiaircraft defense, the soldiers had a difficult time compensating for the speed of the enemy planes. This was their first experience with single-engine carrier planes. During previous attacks they had watched as formations of medium bombers and giant seaplanes passed high overhead; but the Aichi dive-bombers and nimble Zeros seemed phenomenally fast as they bombed and strafed from all directions. Among the dozens of bombs that landed on the airdrome, many were duds. Some penetrated up to fifteen feet into the soft earth, and the troops later spent hours digging them out. Miraculously, no one was hurt during the delicate process.

HIGH ATOP THE SLOPES of the North Daughter, Lieutenant Selby's two antiaircraft guns swiveled around to face a large formation of Type 97 bombers. The old guns put up a steady barrage, but the Japanese came on resolutely, heading toward the eastern shore of Simpson Harbor on a course that would bring them close to the battery.

Stacked in three *chutais* of nine aircraft each, the formation was led initially by Lt. Cmdr. Takashi Hashiguchi, *hikotaicho* (air group commander) of *Kaga*'s carrier attack unit. But he, like Fuchida, was primarily an observer. Shortly before commencing the bomb run, he signaled the crew of the number-two plane to take the lead. Petty Officer 1st Class Tatsuya Sugihara, specially trained at horizontal bombing, moved to the front of the *chutai*. He was teamed with the unit's top bombardier, PO Katsuo Yamamoto, whose bomb release would cue the other pilots to drop their ordnance. Some carried six 60-kilogram "daisy cutters," while others toted an 800-kilogram (1,764-pound) bomb.

One of the latter was carried by Ens. Takeshi Maeda, flying the number-three position in the lead element. When the first two planes switched positions, he removed the safety device from his release mechanism. Moments later, while he prepared for the bomb run, the barrage from the Australian guns rocked the *chutai* on all sides. "Our aircraft shook a lot from all this antiaircraft fire," he recalled. "I paid attention to the leading Type 97 and released our bomb, which caused our aircraft to rise up. Suddenly, Sugihara's aircraft was hit by antiaircraft fire and dropped out of our formation. Then it became engulfed in flames and slammed into the mid-slope of Mt. Hanasaki, a volcano on Rabaul. I believe this was a direct hit, and everything happened in just a matter of seconds. If it had not been on the 'bomb run,' the *taicho*'s Type 97 and our aircraft would have been in danger." *

Only six weeks earlier, Sugihara and his crew had participated in the glorious attack on Pearl Harbor. Now it was their distinction to become the first Japanese airmen to die at Rabaul.

SOME OF THE DAY'S MOST impressive attacks were made by the Type 99 dive-bombers from *Shokaku* and *Zuikaku*. Selby and his gunners had a stadium view as three of the big fixed-gear bombers swooped down on the Norwegian freighter *Herstein*, still loading copra at the Burns, Philp & Company wharf. Three bombs hit the merchant ship squarely, igniting the cargo of oily copra. In the superstructure, a defiant sailor fought back with a mounted machine gun until the rising flames forced him to evacuate his post. The mooring lines burned through, and *Herstein* began to drift slowly across the harbor, her hull glowing cherry red.

---

*Mt. Hanasaki was the Japanese name for the Mother, largest of the extinct volcanoes adjacent to Rabaul.

Another group of Type 99s concentrated on an even bigger ship, *Westralia*, a former passenger liner that served as a floating coal bunker. An easy target, the stationary hulk was blasted by bombs and sank out of sight.

Carrier planes also attacked Lakunai, dropping bombs and machine-gunning the adjacent coconut groves to destroy the dispersal areas hidden among the trees. The coastal defense battery at Praed Point likewise received attention, after which the Japanese tried without success to knock out the antiaircraft guns. Because they were situated on a razorback ridge, nothing but a pinpoint hit would destroy them. As it was, several bombs tumbled harmlessly into a ravine before exploding.

Ending the attack at approximately 1330, the Japanese performed a deliberate aerial pageant over Rabaul to flaunt their power. They had reason to celebrate: out of 109 participating aircraft, only the Type 97 flown by Sugihara had been shot down.

But not all of the others got away cleanly. Describing the mission as "frightful," Ens. Haruo Yoshino stated that five additional Type 97s were damaged by the heavy barrage from the Australian antiaircraft guns. His own plane was hit in the engine, which caused a disconcerting vibration. The long overwater flight back to the aircraft carrier was particularly nerve-wracking. "I was scared that the engine might stop at any moment because of the vibration," Yoshino later said. "A bunch of electrical wires in the engine were hit. Around that area fragments from antiaircraft shells were scattered inside. So, I thought that there was something in that area that didn't explode yet; I desperately wanted to go back."

Yoshino succeeded in making an emergency landing aboard *Kaga*, but the crew of another Type 97 was forced to ditch alongside the carrier. The Australian gunners had also damaged a Type 99 dive-bomber. The pilot attempted an emergency landing aboard *Shokaku* but crashed on the flight deck, killing both himself and the rear gunner. Selby and his young militiamen thought they had downed just one attacker, but their accurate gunnery cost the Japanese a total of three aircraft.

Commander Fuchida felt "like a hunter sent to stalk a mouse with an elephant gun." Frustrated with the outcome of the mission, especially the wasteful use of precious fuel and ordnance on a virtually defenseless target, he went straight to Nagumo after landing back aboard *Akagi* and told him it was "ridiculous to use all these aircraft in such an operation."

§

IN THE MIDST of the attack, John Lerew had sent an urgent message to Area Headquarters at Townsville: "Waves of enemy fighters shot down Wirraways. Waves of bombers attacking aerodromes. Over one hundred aircraft seen so far. [Strafing] on Praed Point." After the attack, he fired off an amplifying message. "Sending A16-38 [the lone remaining Hudson] to Moresby with casualties. Two Wirraways useless defense. Will you now please send some fighters?"

But the staff at Townsville could only reply: "Regret inability to supply fighters. If we had them you would get them."

Faced with the stark realization that no reinforcements were coming, Lerew consolidated the remains of 24 Squadron at Vunakanau. Anything of value that could be brought from Lakunai was placed on trucks, after which the airdrome was rigged for demolition. That afternoon, the personnel gathered at Vunakanau to find a whole new rash of problems caused by the Japanese attacks, including a shortage of drinking water and inadequate facilities for feeding and housing everyone.

COLUMNS OF BLACK SMOKE rose quietly above Rabaul, fed by the burning wharves and copra sheds and the drifting *Herstein*. Casualties on the ground had been surprisingly light, but eleven sailors from *Herstein* were dead, and several others had suffered burns. The injured Norwegians were taken to the civilian hospital on Namanula Hill, the only facility at Rabaul with an operating room. They were joined by Bruce Anderson, Colin Butterworth, Albert Claire, George Herring, and Bill Hewitt, all from 24 Squadron, who had suffered an assortment of broken bones and bullet wounds.

The hectic activity at the hospital came to a hushed standstill when a utility truck arrived carrying the bodies of Charles Bromley and Dick Walsh. Alice Bowman, a civilian nurse, later recalled: "The battered bodies were almost unrecognizable as the young men we had laughed and joked with a few days ago. One who looked no older than a schoolboy had been shot through the head. The other lay like a discarded puppet; his shattered, broken body had come down in the sea and his partially opened parachute covered him now like a sodden shroud."

Arrangements were made to bury the two airmen in the local cemetery, but as there was no time for embalming the bodies, they had to be interred quickly before decomposition set in. The squadron could not provide a chaplain or enough personnel for a proper military funeral, so the Protestant chaplain from Lark Force agreed to conduct a quick memorial service. Early the next morning, Chap. John L. May read the burial rites for Bromley and Walsh as they were laid to rest in the Rabaul Cemetery.

Immediately afterward, the padre accompanied John Lerew and Flg. Off. Geoffrey R. Lempriere, the squadron intelligence officer, to Lerew's office. "The three of us were much moved by various aspects of our situation," recalled May. "Not only did we grieve for the loss of the men who had been killed, we were saddened and frustrated by the failure of the Australian authorities to understand what was happening at Rabaul."

Everyone was exasperated, particularly with the government's mindless inefficiency. The 17th Antitank Battery had been supplied with only twenty rounds per gun, all solid shot, useless for anything but target practice. No other ammunition had arrived from Australia, but in December the garrison had received plenty of turkeys for Christmas Dinner. "It would not be too much," May continued, "to say that we felt bitter."

After venting their frustration, the three men hatched an idea that evolved into one of the most famous messages in RAAF lore. May, who had graduated from the University of Tasmania with a degree in liberal arts, was well versed in Latin and knew of a centuries-old legend that bore similarities to their present situation. "At about that point in the talk between the three of us," he recalled, "there was some reference to the gladiators in the Roman arena, and the recollection of the salute which the Roman historian Suetonius, in his *Life of Claudius*, says was given by the gladiators. Translated, it reads, 'Hail, Emperor, those who are about to die salute you.' It seemed appropriate to alter these words to, 'We who are about to die salute you.'"

The Latin translation required only three words, "*Morituri vos salutamus*," which May provided to Lempriere for encoding and transmittal. The defiant message, all the more clever because of its simplicity, originated from Rabaul at 0845 hours on January 21. Historically the message has been attributed to Lerew, but credit for suggesting the phrase *and* providing the Latin belong properly to Chaplain May.

About three hours later, a reply came back from the forward area headquarters at Port Moresby: Lerew was to proceed there and assume command of a new squadron being cobbled together from the remnants of 24 Squadron and other units. Bill Brookes would then take over the "Rabaul detachment," having received a spot promotion to acting squadron leader. Lerew had not been demoted or sanctioned, but as one RAAF historian later put it, the brass in Melbourne plainly wanted "the chief gladiator . . . removed from the arena."

Lerew had his own ideas. If he complied with the order, he would have to fly the lone remaining Hudson, which could be put to better use transporting the wounded men. If not evacuated, they would be at the mercy of the Japanese when the invasion finally came. Thus, it was an easy decision on his part: he ignored the order.

CHAPTER 4

Desperate Hours

FROM MELBOURNE TO Townsville, from Port Moresby to Rabaul, Australia's military leaders were anxious to learn the whereabouts of the Japanese fleet. With 24 Squadron all but wiped out, the task of locating the ships went to a small detachment of 20 Squadron operating from a forward base in the Solomons. At dawn on January 21, a twin-engine Catalina flying boat piloted by Flt. Lt. Robert H. Thompson lifted off from the calm waters near Buka Island, just off the northern tip of Bougainville. The long reconnaissance flight, expected to last twelve hours or more, would not be altogether uncomfortable for the eight-man crew. Suspended beneath the Catalina's parasol wing was a spacious V-shaped hull with enough cabin space for several bunks and even a small galley. Thompson and his crew relaxed as the "Cat-boat" paralleled the coast of New Ireland, but they kept a close watch on the ocean below.

The copilot, Flt. Lt. Paul M. Metzler, was at the controls approximately six hours after takeoff when he spotted what looked like "a number of gray logs" on the surface. Thompson, sitting to Metzler's left, counted four cruisers and reported them by radio to Port Moresby. But before he could transmit additional details, bursts of antiaircraft fire exploded nearby. Steering the Catalina into a nearby cloud, Metzler caught "a hazy glimpse" of Zeros taking off from the deck of an aircraft carrier.

36

Unaware of the threat, headquarters at Port Moresby ordered the Catalina to maintain surveillance. Taking over the controls, Thompson poked in and out of the clouds at eleven thousand feet to give the crew an occasional look at the ships below, but the game of hide-and-seek lasted only a few minutes before the enemy fighters reached their altitude.

Led by WO Yoshio Kodama of the *Zuikaku* fighter unit, a three-plane *shotai* of Zeros attacked the Catalina from astern. Thompson hauled back on the controls, pulling the big plane around in sweeping turns while Metzler tried to direct the gunners over the intercom, but the Japanese fighters were much too agile. Their gunfire shredded the lumbering seaplane.

In the ventral tunnel at the rear of the Catalina's fuselage, LAC Kenneth G. Parkyns endured a terrifying experience as he tried to fight back with a Lewis machine gun. Zeros bored in again and again, firing directly at his position. Parkyns was hit several times, but amazingly the wounds proved to be mostly superficial.

The three Japanese pilots expended more than one hundred cannon shells and 1,400 bullets at the Catalina, concentrating much of their gunfire in the flying boat's midsection. Leading Aircraftman James L. Cox was killed while manning a machine gun in one of the side blisters, and four other crewmembers were wounded in the main cabin. Suddenly, the situation turned even more nightmarish as the fuel in the perforated wing tanks ignited. Streams of flaming gasoline poured from the tanks down into the cabin, creating an inferno that temporarily engulfed Sgt. Leo T. Clarke and Cpl. John Perrett.

Up in the cockpit, Thompson rolled the big aircraft into a tight, spiraling dive while Metzler worked the throttles to keep the aircraft under control. Flames from the punctured fuel tanks also spread across the upper wing surfaces, eating away the fabric covering the ailerons, which made controlled flight nearly impossible.

The Catalina appeared to be in its death plunge, but as Metzler later explained, there was still time for a miracle:

The Japs were not firing at us, but we were going down fast enough for an imminent crash. Then everything happened at once. Thompson heaved back with both hands on the heavy column. At the same time I pushed both throttles right open, the nose came up and we were level. Next instant the Catalina touched the water faster than any Catalina had ever done before. The first skip must have been a good two hundred yards and with each succeeding skip the boat charged through the water with a noise like thunder. We abandoned ship before it could explode, with the boat still doing a good rate of knots; in fact it careered around us several times burning and crackling like a bushfire. All the Very [flares] of various colors exploded like fireworks, one after another. Finally it came to rest and burnt right out in the middle with the nose and the tail tilting up, and then disappeared with a terrific hiss of salt water on hot metal.

The body of airman Cox went down with the plane, but everyone else managed to jump from the burning seaplane. However, Clarke and Perret soon died from their horrible burns, leaving five survivors in the water with no raft. Among them, only Thompson had escaped without some sort of wound. Metzler, a strong swimmer, thought he could see the mountains of New Hanover in the distance and got the men started in that direction.

Two hours later they had barely made any progress when someone shouted, "Christ Almighty, here comes a bloody cruiser!" The Japanese heavy cruiser *Aoba* slid alongside the swimmers, who started performing the Australian crawl to show they had plenty of stamina. "Keep swimming," advised Thompson. "Don't turn or look around, and for the love of God, don't wave at the bastards."

But the Aussies had only two choices: drown in the Bismarck Sea or be taken prisoner. Wisely they chose the latter. *Aoba*'s crew saved them from certain death, and the ship's medical officer treated their wounds. Transported to Japan, all five Australians survived the duration of the war in various POW camps.

WITH THE NEAR-ANNIHILATION of 24 Squadron over Rabaul on January 20, Vice Admiral Nagumo had come close to fulfilling his main objective, the destruction of enemy air power in the region. But there were still a few airdromes to neutralize on New Ireland and New Guinea. Even as Bob Thompson and his crewmen winged toward their fateful encounter, Nagumo launched the necessary strikes.

Soon after dawn on January 21, fifty-two aircraft from *Akagi* and *Kaga* bombed Kavieng. Reports of the early morning attack were received by

Fortress Signals, the communications unit at Rabaul, which also picked up the grim news that Thompson's crew had found the Japanese fleet off New Ireland. Throughout the day, as additional messages arrived from Port Moresby with updates about the Japanese fleet, the picture gradually developed in all its frightening clarity. An enemy invasion force consisting of four cruisers, at least two carriers, five to seven troop transports, and numerous other ships was converging on Rabaul.

Colonel John J. Scanlan, the commander of Lark Force, realized that the enemy would be within gunnery range of Rabaul by nightfall. A decorated veteran of World War I, he gathered his staff for a hasty conference. Scanlan's first order was to evacuate the encampment on Malaguna Road, which was completely exposed to naval bombardment. It was a wise decision, but in the next breath Scanlan issued a puzzling instruction: the troops were not to be told about the approaching enemy fleet. Instead, they were instructed to prepare for a battalion exercise lasting two or three days. As a result, the Aussie soldiers loaded their haversacks with only a minimum of supplies.

AMAZINGLY, AS IF unaware that 24 Squadron had been nearly wiped out, Townsville ordered Lerew to go on the offensive. A message received at 1630 on January 21 instructed him to use "all available aircraft to . . . attack the enemy shipping concentration southwest of Kavieng." Lerew was exasperated. He had already informed his superiors that he had only two airworthy planes. What was he supposed to accomplish by sending one Hudson and a Wirraway against a fleet of forty enemy ships?

Despite his frustration, Lerew understood intrinsically that he could not disobey the order. His duty, as Lord Tennyson had expressed so eloquently in his 1854 poem, "The Charge of the Light Brigade," was "not to reason why . . . but to do or die."

Bill Brookes volunteered to pilot the Wirraway, but when he and an ordnance man inspected it that afternoon, they found that the wing-mounted bomb racks had been removed to configure the plane as a fighter. That left the Hudson, which had been hidden in a stand of trees at Vunakanau. Dozens of native laborers muscled it out into the open and hauled it to the runway, where Sqn. Ldr. Jack Sharp climbed aboard with his copilot and two gunners. Just before dusk, the four men courageously took off to find the approaching fleet. Fortunately for them, darkness fell rapidly after the sun dipped below the horizon, and an approaching weather system made visibility even worse. Forced to abandon the search, Sharp returned safely to Vunakanau.

With the Hudson back in one piece, Lerew signaled his intention to evacuate the wounded airmen using the bomber as an ambulance. The reply, from Air Cdre. Francis M. Bladin at Townsville, was blunt: "Rabaul not yet fallen. Assist Army in keeping airdrome open. Maintain communications as long as possible."

Lerew ignored Bladen as well. Heading to the hospital on Namanula Hill, he picked up the men who had been wounded on the 20th. The doctor advised that they were unfit to travel, but Lerew insisted on their release. Leaving them to the Japanese was not an option. Thus, wearing casts and fresh dressings, still dopey from the effects of morphine, they were driven to Vunakanau airdrome in the middle of the night.

A light rain fell as the wounded were loaded aboard the Hudson. At 0300 on January 22, with Jack Sharp back at the controls, the Lockheed accelerated down the soggy runway and lurched into the air, one propeller over-revving loudly due to a problem with its constant-speed control. Other mechanical troubles plagued the journey, but the last Allied plane out of Rabaul stayed in the air long enough to reach Port Moresby. After refueling, Sharp continued to Australia with his cargo of wounded airmen. Thanks to his determination and Lerew's stubbornness, they would heal—and return to fight again.

WHATEVER SATISFACTION Lerew may have felt as he watched the Hudson depart lasted only a couple of hours. Just before dawn, forty-five carrier planes from *Akagi* and *Kaga* returned to finish the job of destroying the fixed defenses at Rabaul. Dive-bombers pounded the coastal gun battery at Praed Point, and this time succeeded in dislodging the upper gun from its emplacement. The heavy weapon tumbled down the steep slope onto the lower gun, killing or wounding more than twenty artillerymen. Other carrier planes attacked the two airdromes, and several dive-bombers tried, again without success, to knock out the antiaircraft battery.

The Aussie gunners apparently scored hits on at least two of *Kaga*'s Type 99 dive-bombers, which later made forced landings in the water alongside the carrier. If their loss was indeed the result of damage from antiaircraft fire, then Selby's young militiamen accounted for a total of five enemy carrier planes—a tremendous accomplishment considering the gunners' lack of experience and unsophisticated weaponry.

Soon after the raid ended, lookouts on Watom Island observed the enemy fleet only twenty miles north of their position. By midday, the ships could be seen from Rabaul itself, leaving no doubt whatsoever that an invasion was imminent.

AT HIS NEW headquarters on high ground near Vunakanau, Colonel Scanlan decided he was no longer bound by his original orders regarding the defense of Rabaul. With the coastal guns in ruins and 24 Squadron out of action, Lark Force's essential purpose had all but evaporated.

Determined to leave nothing useful to the enemy, Scanlan issued orders to demolish the two airdromes and the antiaircraft guns. The rigged explosions added to the chaos that gripped Rabaul that afternoon, but the biggest blast was yet to come. At 1600 hours, a stockpile of approximately two thousand bombs, offloaded from the freighter *Herstein* a week earlier, was destroyed by Lark Force engineers. Lacking the time to do the job methodically, they set off the entire dump in what was later described as a "rather botched demolition." The explosion was disastrous, leveling houses and buildings within a quarter-mile radius and causing extensive damage as far away as half a mile. Electrical service was knocked out all over town, and the delicate glass vacuum tubes in the radio transmitters were smashed. In the blink of an eye, communication with the outside world was cut off. Even worse, several local natives had been caught in the open. Their corpses, torn open grotesquely by the massive concussion, lay in the middle of the street.

LATE THAT AFTERNOON, Lerew paid a visit to Scanlan's new head- quarters to make a determination about his squadron. Almost all of his remaining men were either mechanics or support personnel, he told Scanlan. None had received any infantry training, and only a few had fired a rifle during basic training. Should they stay and fight with the infantry?

The weather was beginning to deteriorate, matching Scanlan's mood. Sharing a last drink with Lerew, he decided after a brief deliberation that the RAAF personnel would be more of a hindrance than an asset and gave Lerew his consent to withdraw. Shortly thereafter, the remnants of 24 Squadron started toward the south coast of New Britain in an assortment of trucks and staff cars.

§

WORKING STEADILY throughout the afternoon to treat the wounded men brought in from the wrecked coastal guns, the medical personnel on Namanula Hill were nearly oblivious to the crisis developing outside the hospital. But when the explosion of the bomb dump cut electrical power, they decided to move the sick and wounded to a safer location. Nearly eighty patients were transported in a caravan of ambulances, utility trucks, and other vehicles to Vunapope, where Bishop Isidoro Leone Scharmach, the vicar apostolic of Rabaul, made the mission's "native boys' hospital" available. It was well after midnight by the time the vehicles rounded the caldera and arrived at the clinic, normally used by male islanders. After settling the patients, the six army nurses attached to the 2/10 Field Ambulance trudged up the hill to a women's dormitory for a few hours' sleep. But there would be no rest for the two doctors, Maj. Edward C. Palmer and Capt. Sandy E. J. Robertson, who elected to return to Rabaul. They were battlefield surgeons and intended to perform their duty with the troops. It was not an easy decision. Sooner or later, everyone left behind at Vunapope would be captured by the Japanese.

Before leaving, Palmer approached Chaplain May and said, "You'll stay, will you, Padre?"

It was not a question. Both men understood that the doctor was politely telling May to assume responsibly for the patients, nurses, and orderlies from the 2/10 Field Ambulance, not to mention the civilians from the administration hospital and local missions. The chaplain, responding with a simple "Yes," knew that he would be one of the first officers captured.

WHILE 24 SQUADRON put some distance between themselves and Rabaul, a radio operator raced ahead to hunt for a working radio. Finding one at Tol plantation on Wide Bay, Sgt. Frederick G. Higgs encrypted a short message to Port Moresby: "Send flying-boats. [The men] will identify themselves with torch."

By this time, dozens of other evacuees, including civilians and even a few army personnel, had joined the exodus from Rabaul. When the last segment of navigable roadway ended at the Warangoi River, the rabble numbered 150 men.

Due to the heavy rainfall, the river was now a raging torrent. Two native canoes were available for crossing the river, but the process took hours. Afterward, the men continued on foot through the dripping jungle, fording another river before they finally reached a large, stylish plantation called Put Put in the middle of the night. Allowing only a brief rest, Lerew split the group into two parties. He put Bill Brookes in charge of the civilians and married RAAF personnel, numbering about fifty men, and commandeered two boats to take them the rest of the way to Tol plantation.

Brookes was appalled by the behavior he witnessed that night among certain civilians. "Numerous cases occurred where [men] were deliberately dumped and left behind," he reported, "in order that a particular person could make his escape either a little more certain or faster."

Among those left behind was Harold Page, the former territorial administrator. No longer a young man, he decided to walk back to Rabaul with three other officials. Reaching the convoy of trucks abandoned at the Warangoi River on January 25, they made camp and waited for the Japanese to pick them up.

Lerew and his party, meanwhile, continued their journey from Put Put on foot, covering another fifteen miles to Adler Bay. Stopping at another plantation to rest at midday on January 23, they were driven under cover a few times when enemy scout planes flew over. That afternoon, the drone of aircraft engines sent the men scurrying under the trees again. But then some of the men, probably mechanics, recognized the distinctive note of Bristol Pegasus engines. An Empire flying boat was somewhere nearby.

As it turned out, two of the gigantic, four-engine seaplanes, formerly used by Qantas for luxury international passenger service, were searching for Lerew and his men. The radio message sent by Sergeant Higgs had been received at Port Moresby the previous day, and 20 Squadron sent the Empires on a rescue mission. The crews had elected to stop for the night at Samarai on the tip of the Papuan Peninsula, then took off again on the morning of January 23 and searched along the coast of New Britain. Eventually they made contact with Lerew's party at Sum Sum plantation.

Ninety-eight men were ferried out to the two seaplanes, which were so overloaded they could not break contact with the water on their first two attempts. Only after dumping fuel were they able to stagger aloft. The planes landed at Samarai, where the evacuees received clean clothing and spent the night in a company store. The following day, one of the Empires returned to New Britain and picked up Brookes's party at Wide Bay.

Considering the shoestring nature of the mission, the rescue of 24 Squadron was almost miraculous. Unfortunately, as word of the successful airlifts trickled back to the men of Lark Force by "jungle telegraph," scores of soldiers struggled across the rugged mountains to Wide Bay in the mistaken belief that the RAAF would send more flying boats.

Cruelly, disastrously, the rumors proved false.

CHAPTER 5

The Fall of Rabaul

CONTRARY TO THE WISHFUL, speculative stories published in Australian newspapers, Lark Force suffered a humiliating defeat. During the moonless night of January 22, Japanese troopships carrying approximately five thousand soldiers of the South Seas Force and hundreds of naval infantrymen moved stealthily to their embarkation points in Blanche Bay. Amphibious operations commenced shortly after midnight, and by 0230 the landings were underway at three different beachheads around the caldera. Lark Force fought back at two locations, but the enemy forces easily overwhelmed the Australian defenses. Resistance weakened rapidly as the Japanese poured troops ashore, taking full advantage of their military supremacy on the ground and in the air.

Planes from *Akagi* and *Kaga* roamed the skies with almost no opposition, streaking down to strafe and dive-bomb targets identified by reconnaissance floatplanes. Only one pilot, a member of *Kaga*'s fighter air group, was lost during the entire day of operations. Before taking off that morning, FPO 2nd Class Isao Hiraishi had offered his parachute to Lt. Yoshio Shiga, his section leader. A descendant of the old samurai class and the son of a rear admiral, Shiga felt compelled to turn it down.

They wouldn't need parachutes, he told Hiraishi, as there were no enemy fighters to oppose them.

But the twenty-seven-year-old lieutenant later regretted his optimism:

> As I predicted we saw no enemy fighters over Rabaul, and ground targets also were scarce. I went low for a single strafing run and Hiraishi-san followed me down. After pulling out I saw him speeding towards [my aircraft] to join formation. I was alarmed to see fire shooting out of his exhaust stacks. Hiraichi-san pointed to his mouth, which was a gesture for not having enough fuel and that he couldn't return to the carrier. He then banked sharply, and I saw that his Zero fighter was shot in the belly by ground fire. Sadly, Hiraishi-san went into a split-S and crashed into the sea. I still blame myself for his loss because I told him not to wear a parachute.

Despite the death of Hiraishi, the air attacks proved effective at breaking down the Australians' flimsy communications system. Within hours Colonel Scanlan lost control over his scattered rifle companies, which began to fall back in disarray.

SEVERAL WEEKS PRIOR to the invasion, Scanlan had chastened subordinates for suggesting that food and supplies should be cached in the jungle, berating their attitude as "defeatist." He reinforced his point on New Year's Day with two unyielding proclamations, distributed to all hands: "EVERY MAN WILL FIGHT TO THE LAST," and "THERE SHALL BE NO WITHDRAWAL."

But on January 23, as his defenses fell apart around him, Scanlan reversed his position. During his last radio contact with Lt. Col. Howard H. Carr, commanding officer of the 2/22nd Battalion, Scanlan stated that the situation appeared hopeless. It had become, he said, a matter of "every man for himself." The unimaginative Carr, interpreting Scanlan's words as a directive, ordered the phrase transmitted to the scattered companies. He even sent out runners to make certain the message was delivered.

Scanlan then did the unthinkable. Accompanied by several members of his staff and a native houseboy, he walked off the battlefield while the fighting was still in progress. A short while later, all resistance by Lark

Force collapsed. What had begun as an organized withdrawal degenerated into a pell-mell dash for the sanctuary of the jungle.

Among the hundreds of Australians who "went bush," almost none were prepared for long-term survival in the wilds of New Britain. Much of the blame lies with Scanlan's bizarre decision to deliberately mislead his men into believing they were deploying on an exercise of two or three days' duration. His earlier refusal to allow caches of food to be hidden in the jungle also came back to haunt him, because there were several trailheads and other strategic locations where supply dumps might have been placed. A veteran of trench warfare, Scanlan had no background in jungle fighting. As a direct result of his intractability, hundreds of men entered the jungle with little more than the lightweight khaki uniforms they wore.

A FEW OF THE firefights, though brief, had been intense. At various sites, mostly on the plateau south of the caldera, fifty-seven Australians lay dead, and dozens more were wounded. The Japanese captured most of those who could still walk, but men immobilized by their wounds were generally finished off.

At least five Lark Force officers were murdered by General Horii's soldiers. On January 26, Lt. Lennox D. Henry, an infantry officer, and Capt. Herbert N. Silverman, a medical officer with the Royal Australian Artillery, were captured with a small party of evaders following a skirmish northwest of Rabaul. The Japanese beheaded Henry on the spot and took Silverman to Rabaul, only to execute him four days later after refusing to recognize his status as a doctor. Captain Richard E. Travers, who led a rifle company in the 2/22nd Battalion, voluntarily surrendered with approximately one hundred of his men on January 27 and was immediately murdered. His death was apparently intended as a warning to other Australians contemplating evasion.

In the minds of the Japanese, the killings were justified. On the day of the invasion, thousands of leaflets had been air-dropped to the Australians hiding in the jungle, warning them in no uncertain terms that their situation was hopeless:

To the Officers and Soldiers of this Island!
SURRENDER AT ONCE!

And we will guarantee your life, treating you as war prisoners. Those who RESIST US WILL BE KILLED ONE AND ALL. Consider seriously, you can find neither food nor way of escape in this island and you will only die of hunger unless you surrender.

January 23rd, 1942

Japanese Commander in Chief

Horii must have anticipated quick compliance, for that was how the system worked in the Imperial Army. His decree was more than a warning: it was a direct order. But the Australians had no intention of complying. As the days passed, only a few surrendered, mainly because no one in Lark Force took the threats seriously. Their defiance proved to be a huge mistake. Horii was undoubtedly offended when Scanlan and hundreds of Aussies, including all of the senior officers, disregarded his decree.

To make matters worse, while the Japanese chased the Australians through the jungle, a sudden outbreak of malaria caused numerous deaths among Horii's men and incapacitated hundreds of others. Almost the entire 1st Battalion and a significant percentage of the 3rd Battalion fell ill, creating a near catastrophe for the medical staff of the South Seas Force. The doctors failed to diagnose the disease for days after the outbreak began, which resulted in far more casualties from malaria than from Australian bullets.

Pulling his troops back from the jungle, Horii decided to monitor the evaders rather than pursue them. Imperial Navy ships patrolled the coastal areas, reconnaissance aircraft watched the jungle trails from above, and villagers were bribed or forced to reveal the whereabouts of Aussie soldiers. By the beginning of February, Horii was satisfied that two large groups of Australians were encamped at plantations on the south coast. He was correct. Due to the rumors that had spread after the successful airlift of 24 Squadron, dozens of Aussies had headed for Wide Bay. Ultimately some two hundred men gathered near Tol plantation, most having arrived by way of the precipitous Baining Mountains.

For almost every individual, the trek to Wide Bay had been a nightmare. Hungry and dejected, they had climbed countless ridges, forded raging rivers, and pushed through suffocating jungle, only to wait in vain once they reached Tol plantation. Soon malaria set in, and by the time the men realized that the flying boats weren't coming back, many lost the will to

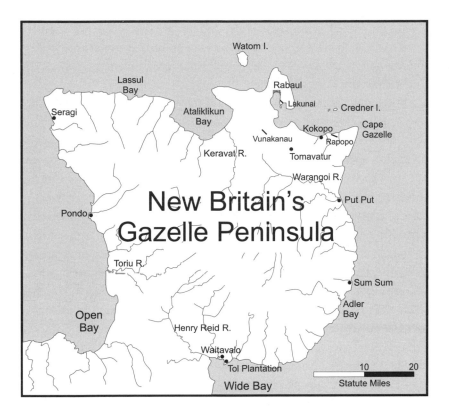

continue evading the Japanese. The notion of surrender no longer seemed so terrible. Depressed and lethargic, the Australians were content to pass the days sleeping or scrounging for food.

The other large group of evaders had gathered at Adler Bay within an abandoned plantation. Although they were significantly better off in terms of food, with ample livestock and rice, they were advised by a medical officer to surrender. It was probably Captain Robertson who bluntly explained that to continue evading would result in "almost certain death from starvation or malaria." He subsequently moved south to Tol plantation, and the men at Adler Bay placed a white flag at the water's edge where it could be seen from the sea.

Angry and frustrated with the Australians, General Horii was more than ready to take both groups prisoner. On February 2 he ordered Lt. Col. Masao Kuwada, commander of the 3rd Battalion at Kokopo, to organize a "pursuit by boats" to Wide Bay. The task was delegated to Lt. Tadaichi

Noda, who selected approximately 150 soldiers from the 8th Infantry Company for the operation. He also brought an interpreter assigned to the *Kempeitai*, the military police and counterespionage branch of the Imperial Army.

Noda and his men boarded five Daihatsu landing craft, which were towed by a coast-wise vessel to Wide Bay. Arriving just after dawn on February 3, the landing craft dropped their tow lines and approached the plantation under their own power. As they neared the beach, the Japanese opened fire with light machine guns and even a small howitzer, mostly shooting into the palm trees. Jolted awake by the sudden attack, the Aussies had virtually no time to run. Most were too tired to care, and only a handful escaped from the large plantation.

As soon as the firing stopped, Captain Robertson stepped forward with twenty-one men under a white flag. Within a few hours the Japanese rounded up all the rest—more than 180 men in all—and fed them a hot meal, the first decent food they'd had in days. Afterward, the prisoners lounged quietly under guard. Their initial treatment seemed to reinforce the idea that they were going to be better off in Japanese hands.

But the next morning, Lieutenant Noda was agitated. Only three commissioned officers had been identified among the captives, the most senior being Robertson. The others were Capt. John R. Gray, Royal Australian Engineers, and Lt. Hatsell G. Garrard, a young infantry officer. Colonel Scanlan and the senior officers of Lark Force were still at large.

Increasingly belligerent, Noda ordered the prisoners out of the building and lined them up. Garrard was singled out and led to the Tol plantation house, where Noda, assisted by the *Kempeitai* interpreter, began a brutal interrogation. There is no doubt that Noda demanded to know Scanlan's whereabouts, but if Garrard knew, he thwarted every question. Furious, Noda beat him on the head and body with a stout piece of wood. Garrard was periodically revived with water, but the punishment continued until he collapsed. The Japanese then tied him to a tree and left him to bake in the scorching sun.

The remaining prisoners were also marched to the plantation house, whereupon Noda attempted to identify the men who had surrendered on the beach the previous morning. At first, about forty claimed to have been part of the group. This caused some confusion among the Japanese, but eventually twenty men, Robertson and Gray among them, were separated from the main group of prisoners. Approximately 160 captives remained in the yard outside the plantation house. The Japanese confiscated all personal items, including identity disks, and then tied the captives' hands behind their backs, binding their thumbs tightly with twine or wire.

Setting up a two-way radio, Noda contacted battalion headquarters for further instructions. An exchange of messages ensued, ending with authorization—either from Colonel Kuwada or Horii himself—to proceed with the next step.

The prisoners were separated into groups of about twelve and roped together in single file. All of the groups, each escorted by an officer or noncom and several soldiers, were then marched away from the main house in different directions, taking roads and footpaths that led into the sprawling coconut groves. As they walked through sun-drenched rows of palm trees, the captives realized that they were going to be killed. Helpless to prevent it, the Aussies relied on the one trait that bound them together like no other army in the world: their *mateship*. Although fear and anguish tore at them, they refused to allow their emotions to show. Some, true to their heritage, even managed a quip or two. Each man tried to accept his fate with aplomb, if only to help steady the man next to him.

The Japanese were the cowards. Across the vast plantation, groups of roped-together prisoners were ordered to sit. A man was then pulled from each of the lines and led into a nearby thicket, where soldiers stabbed him in the back with their fifteen-inch-long bayonets. Taking their time, the executioners walked back to the waiting groups of prisoners, making a show of wiping the blood from their bayonets before summoning the next man in line.

The killing went slowly. For the captives at the end of each line, the dread of those prolonged minutes must have been intolerable.

After a while the Japanese grew impatient and began killing prisoners in twos and threes. Some were shot. At nearby Waitavalo plantation, one group of eleven men was gunned down in a single volley. Whether by bullet or bayonet, the Australians were murdered from behind.

But the killers proved to be as careless as they were craven. When Noda and his soldiers departed, they left at least nine Aussies alive among the piles of bodies. Several managed to stumble away, and one survivor helped two severely wounded men into the shelter of a utility shed. He then went to find help, but before he could return, a Japanese naval landing party found the two victims and torched the shed with them inside it.

Incredibly, six victims of the massacre recovered, including a medical orderly who was stabbed eleven times. Their survival guaranteed that the horrible atrocities at Tol would be exposed in full.

The Japanese had made no attempt to bury the 150 or so corpses scattered throughout the coconut groves. The only exception was Lieutenant Garrard, who was forced to dig his own grave. Soldiers bludgeoned and then bayoneted him before shoving his body in the shallow hole, leaving it only partially covered with dirt.

Sanctioned by Colonel Kuwada, tacitly if not verbally authorized by General Horii, the murders at Tol conveyed an unforgettable message. To emphasize the point, the Japanese left a personal note for Colonel Scanlan on the door of a plantation house stating that he was responsible for what had happened.

Scanlan himself had narrowly avoided being captured at Tol. When the message and the shocking truth of the massacre were revealed to him, he could stomach no more attempts at evasion. At a Roman Catholic mission a few miles beyond Wide Bay, he made up his mind to surrender. On February 10, accompanied by his batman, two other soldiers, and a major from the 2/22nd Battalion, he began the long walk back to Rabaul.

LIEUTENANT NODA and his men returned to Kokopo with Robertson, Gray, and the small party that had initially surrendered at Tol. Along the way, the Japanese also picked up the dozens of Australians waiting at Adler Bay. Most of the prisoners were delivered to a stockade at their own former army post on Malaguna Road, but Robertson and Gray were held at Kokopo. Robertson returned to the native hospital, where the nurses, upset over being abandoned on the eve of the invasion, gave him a cold reception.

Gray was destined for much worse. The *Kempeitai*, more determined than ever to capture Scanlan, set up a cordon of outposts across the lower Gazelle Peninsula to guard the main trails. Almost daily, exhausted Aussies walked out of the jungle and turned themselves in, but Scanlan remained at large for two weeks after the massacre at Tol. The *Kempeitai* were not stupid. By this time they realized that Gray, having earlier accompanied Scanlan across the Baining Mountains, probably knew more about the colonel's intentions than anyone on the island. Thus, they subjected the thirty-four-year-old engineer to their unique brand of interrogation.

On the morning of February 20, Gray was led to a palm tree about fifty yards from the bishop's residence at Vunapope. He was lashed to the tree and tortured for several hours. At one point a soldier scooped up a nest of red ants and threw them on Gray, who squirmed and twisted against the ropes as the insects bit him. The day-long interrogation was witnessed at various times by four local islanders—two villagers and two native catechists—who later provided testimony about Gray's torture.

Finally untied from the tree, Gray fell to the ground but got back on his feet in a silent show of defiance. The Japanese then led him to a remote spot where a medical doctor named Chikumi, attached to the 144th Infantry Regiment, administered "injections" and cut open Gray's chest. The captain was still alive when his heart was removed so that Chikumi could observe the results. Circumstantial evidence suggests that someone administered the *coup de grace* with a bullet. Chaplain May, on duty at the native hospital, heard the shot.

Gray died protecting the secret of Scanlan's whereabouts. But the very next day, the colonel and his party walked up to a *Kempeitai* outpost near the Warangoi River and surrendered.

CHAPTER 6

Counterattack

ALTHOUGH VIRTUALLY NO ONE in Australia knew what had happened on New Britain, the evidence was overwhelming that a Japanese force now controlled the island. Rabaul had changed hands. Overnight, it had become the most important target in the Southwest Pacific. In fact, within hours of the invasion the RAAF began planning its first counterattack.

The only Australian base within range of Rabaul was Port Moresby, located on the Gulf of Papua in what was formerly British New Guinea. The colonial township boasted two airdromes—Seven Mile, named for its distance by road from the center of town, and Kila Kila, a small airstrip near the coast southeast of town—plus an excellent harbor with an RAAF seaplane facility.

The latter was especially important. Rabaul lay five hundred miles northeast of Port Moresby, and only one type of plane in the RAAF inventory was capable of delivering a load of bombs that far: the American-built Consolidated PBY Catalina. Powered by a pair of Pratt & Whitney radial engines, the ungainly flying boat could carry up to four thousand pounds of bombs on external wing racks and stay airborne for more than twenty hours. But the Cat-boat was also plodding and awkward. With a full combat load of fuel, bombs, machine gun ammunition, and eight crewmen aboard, the Catalina tipped the scales at more than seventeen tons, cruised at less than one hundred miles per hour, and had a maximum ceiling of only eighteen thousand feet.

The distance to Rabaul was not the greatest obstacle. That distinction belongs to a unique combination of the complex tropical weather systems and mountainous islands that define the Southwest Pacific. Few places on the planet are as challenging to human existence as New Guinea, the world's second largest island. The Australian territory, primarily the Papuan Peninsula, is dominated by a range of jumbled, precipitous mountains that form the peninsula's elongated spine.

Words can scarcely do justice to the Owen Stanley Mountains, which soar dramatically to more than thirteen thousand feet within a few dozen miles of Port Moresby. The lower slopes are heavily forested, with huge exotic hardwoods protruding from a jungle canopy so dense that daylight barely penetrates to the ground. The upper slopes are often invisible, shrouded by clouds of mist or drenching squalls that ride the updrafts and downdrafts like ghostly apparitions.

Beyond the mountains, aviators flying to Rabaul faced a long journey over the Solomon Sea, where the weather was frequently treacherous. The warm waters, seasonal wind patterns, and a host of other meteorological factors influenced a system known as an intertropical convergence zone (also called an intertropical front), a semipermanent disturbance capable of producing ultra-severe thunderstorms. The thunderheads frequently topped out at forty thousand feet or higher—well above the altitude limitations of most World War II aircraft—and planes that tried to penetrate the front could expect to encounter extremely violent turbulence and frequent lightning.

Because of the weather, the first attempt to hit Rabaul on the night of January 23 was unsuccessful. The next effort began the following afternoon when Thomas McBride Price, a twenty-seven-year-old squadron leader from Adelaide, South Australia, briefed five Catalina crews at the RAAF's forward area headquarters in Port Moresby. After receiving their assignments, the airmen were transported down to the waterfront, where they boarded "an ugly old bomb scow" that took them out to the Catalinas moored in the harbor.

Soon, puffs of whitish smoke drifted across the water as ten radial engines were started. Presently the seaplanes moved from their moorings and taxied sluggishly to the downwind end of the harbor, their broad hulls riding low in the water. One by one they turned into the wind and went to full throttle, their engines screaming at maximum power. It took several nerve-wracking minutes for the overloaded planes to gradually build up enough speed to break contact with the water. Once airborne, the Catalinas climbed slowly and banked to the southeast. Far too heavy to climb above the Owen Stanley Mountains, they were forced to take a lengthy detour around the Papuan Peninsula before turning northward toward Rabaul.

As daylight faded, the crews ate a meal prepared in the in-flight galley. Later that evening, the Catalinas reached the intertropical convergence zone parked over the Solomon Sea. Flying at an altitude of only a few thousand feet, barely making ninety miles per hour because of their heavy bomb load, the seaplanes plowed through the fattest, most turbulent portion of the front. Inside the storm, the aircraft bucked violently. "It was an amazing thing," recalled one pilot. "I just couldn't believe how the Catalina held together under the stresses of the sudden drops and lifts. You virtually lost control of the airplane. It was very rough indeed."

In addition to wrestling their planes through the turbulence, the pilots were periodically blinded by brilliant flashes of lightning. Often they were forced to turn the controls over to the copilot until their vision improved.

When the planes finally burst from the storm into clear skies, the contrast was almost startling: stars shimmered overhead, and the air felt as smooth as velvet. With the target still several hours away, some of the crewmen climbed into bunks to "snatch a nap like children in kinder-garten." They were lulled to sleep in minutes as the Catalinas droned slowly through the night.

When the seaplanes at last approached the northern tip of New Britain, the crews found Simpson Harbor obscured. A layer of scattered clouds was not unusual, but on this January night the volcano Tavurvur was active, spewing a thick cloud of vapor over the anchorage. As the Catalinas descended to six thousand feet, the "bomb-aimers" moved forward to the optical sights mounted in each bow. Down below, searchlight beams criss-crossed the night sky. Several antiaircraft batteries manned by the Maizaru 2nd Special Naval Landing Force, who specialized in the rapid deploy-ment of "high-angle" 80mm guns, opened fire on the intruders. Ships in the harbor joined in, firing blindly through the clouds.

Private 1st Class Akiyoshi Hisaeda, a member of the 55th Division field hospital, was aboard the troop transport *Venice Maru* when the Catalinas attacked. "Battle exchanged for about one hour between several enemy machines and our navy and army," he noted that night in his diary. "Our forces sustained at least one casualty."

Whatever damage Hisaeda referred to was evidently the result of sheer luck. The Australian bombardiers, unable to locate targets in the night, simply aimed their bombs at the antiaircraft fire coming up from below. Frustrated by the poor visibility, the Catalina crews reported only "probable hits" when they returned to Port Moresby.

Due to all the blind shooting, the Japanese caused more harm to themselves than did the attackers. Friendly fire from shipboard antiaircraft guns swept across the plateau south of Simpson Harbor, hitting elements of the South Seas Force. The 55th Transportation Company's bivouac area suffered damage and casualties, according to Lt. Col. Toshiharu Sakigawa, who described his men as "quite disturbed" by the incident.

Two nights later the Catalinas were back over Simpson Harbor, but this time only three aircraft participated in the raid. The third flying boat, piloted by Flt. Lt. Terence L. Duigan, arrived over the target approximately an hour behind the first two. He observed one ship "blazing fiercely" near the northwestern shore of Simpson Harbor and another burning in the middle of the anchorage. When the crews returned to Port Moresby, one reported a possible hit on an "aircraft carrier," but in reality the Catalinas had caused only minor damage.

Although neither of the first two attacks had caused much damage, the Australians believed they had done some harm to the Japanese. More importantly, all planes had returned safely, and the flyboys were hailed as heroes. "RAAF Shocks Japs," proclaimed the *Sydney Sun*, which added in bold type: "In the two raids on Rabaul, it is now believed that four Jap troopships have been rendered useless and others damaged."

The accompanying story consisted mostly of propaganda, but it served as a tonic for a nation already tired of gloomy war news. The resounding media coverage also spurred the RAAF, which continued to attack Rabaul every second night. The next raid was conducted by four Catalinas on the night of January 28, but due to poor visibility the results were unobserved. Two nights later, Squadron Leader Price led five Catalinas back to Simpson Harbor and claimed one hit on a ship. The Australians reported intense antiaircraft fire after the mission, an indication that heavy batteries manned by the South Seas Force were now in place.

The first week of raids did achieve some damage, as confirmed in a postwar report by the Imperial Navy: "Enemy aircraft frequently invaded the skies over the Rabaul anchorage, bombing and strafing, but our ships put up fierce resistance and repulsed them. Three enemy planes were shot down. Damage suffered—one dead, fifteen injured, and minor damages to two transports." A separate report submitted by the Imperial Army listed four dead and fifteen wounded among units of the South Seas Force.

But the claim by the Japanese that three Australian planes were shot down in late January was pure invention. No Catalinas were lost over Rabaul during the early raids, partly due to the ineffectiveness of the few shore-based antiaircraft guns, and also because there were no Japanese fighters to oppose the flying boats. Vice Admiral Nagumo had ordered *Akagi* and *Kaga* back to Truk as soon as Rabaul was secured, leaving only a few floatplanes for aviation support.

WITHIN HOURS of the invasion, the Imperial Navy's 4th Construction Detachment, assisted by an army construction battalion, commenced repairs to the runway at Lakunai airdrome. That same afternoon, Cmdr. Ryutaro Yamanaka of the land-based Chitose Air Group arrived at Rabaul from the Marshall Islands to inspect Lakunai and "encourage the army engineer troops on the scene." Such coordination between the two services was uncommon, but it got results. By the end of the month, the airdrome was completely repaired.

Rabaul's first land-based fighters, formerly assigned to the Tainan Air Group, were delivered by the aircraft transporter *Kasuga Maru* a few days after Yamanaka's visit. Less than a week later, on January 31, a contingent of fifteen fighters of the Chitose Air Group was transferred from the Marshalls.

The first fighters sent to Rabaul were not the highly regarded Zeros but obsolescent Mitsubishi A5M4s, known to the Japanese as Type 96 carrier fighters. With their fixed landing gear, open cockpit, and teardrop wheel covers, the planes resembled something from a Disney cartoon. They were also significantly slower than the Zero, and with only two 7.7mm machine guns in the nose, did not pack much firepower. However, the Type 96's gnatlike maneuverability was superb.

Although not designed or equipped for night combat, the new arrivals teamed up with the searchlight crews to challenge the Catalinas' nocturnal raids. The first combat occurred on the night of February 3, when two of the five Catalinas that attacked shipping in Simpson Harbor were caught in the beams of the powerful searchlights. One got out of trouble by diving through the volcanic steam billowing from Tavurvur, but the other, piloted by Flt. Lt. Godfrey E. Hemsworth, was held firmly by the searchlights.

Within moments, twenty-two-year-old FPO 1st Class Hiroyoshi Nishizawa darted in behind the Catalina and fired more than one hundred rounds into the main wing, fuselage, and empennage of the big plane. In turn, Nishizawa may have been startled when a stream of bullets and tracer rounds snaked toward him from the Catalina's midsection. Firing a pair of Lewis machine guns from the waist gun blister on the seaplane's port side, nineteen-year-old Sgt. Douglas F. Dick saw the Japanese fighter go into a spin. He claimed a kill and, when other crewmen later confirmed his report, was credited with a "probable" victory.

But Nishizawa had merely been dodging the return fire, for his Type 96 fighter was not damaged. Ironically, he believed he had fatally damaged the Catalina, which plunged toward the water. He was credited with a victory, the first of many attributed to the rail-thin, often sickly pilot who would eventually become one of the Imperial Navy's greatest aces.

Hemsworth and his crew were far from finished. Nishizawa's gunfire had hit the port propeller, disabling the engine, but Hemsworth used a few tricks of his own to escape. A former commercial pilot with many years of experience, he rolled the heavy seaplane into a steep dive while simultaneously feathering the damaged propeller. Leveling off at minimal altitude, he exited Simpson Harbor in the darkness on one engine.

Throughout the night, Hemsworth held the damaged Catalina aloft, the miles and the hours crawling by while raw fuel leaked into the bilges from bullet holes in the wing tanks. When he reached the Huon Gulf, Hemsworth made a flawless nighttime water landing off Salamaua so that the crew could make temporary repairs to the damaged propeller. At dawn Hemsworth took off using both engines, after which he feathered the bad prop for the remainder of the journey. He could not cross the Owen Stanley Mountains on one engine, so once again he flew the long way around the Papuan Peninsula, this time at an altitude of only fifty feet. Finally, more than twenty-five hours after starting the mission, Hemsworth landed the bullet-riddled Catalina in the harbor at Port Moresby.

§

LAND-BASED NAVY FIGHTERS also caused trouble for one of the first RAAF reconnaissance missions over Rabaul. On February 6, Flt. Lt. David W. I. Campbell and his crew from 32 Squadron crossed Simpson Harbor at ten thousand feet and noted a fighter taking off from Lakunai. Only four minutes later the enemy aircraft reached the Hudson's altitude and commenced a gunnery attack. The agile fighter, undoubtedly a Zero, raked the Hudson with machine gun bullets and cannon fire. One shell exploded among a stack of sea markers, polluting the cabin with a silvery cloud of metallic powder; another detonated in the cockpit, severing the little finger from Campbell's left hand and smashing his wrist. Shrapnel from the same shell also badly injured the copilot, fracturing bones in his left leg and arm and wounding his right hand. In the dorsal turret, Sgt. Geoffrey A. O'Hea returned fire but was himself wounded in the left leg. The only crewmember not injured was Sgt. Gordon Thomson, a twenty-one-year-old native of Manchester, England. Moving from position to position inside the fuselage, he administered first aid to the wounded men and helped Campbell fly the damaged plane. The latter, despite terrible pain and heavy loss of blood, remained at the controls for another three hours before landing safely at Port Moresby. Campbell was later awarded a Distinguished Flying Cross, and Thomson earned a Distinguished Flying Medal.

THE BUILDUP OF air power at Rabaul gained momentum with the arrival of the 24th Air Flotilla, commanded by Rear Adm. Eiji Goto, at the end of January. The transfer of his headquarters from Truk was timed to coincide with the deployment of the Yokohama Air Group, whose fourteen Kawanishi flying boats occupied the former RAAF seaplane facility near Sulphur Creek.

Goto went on the offensive almost immediately. On the night of February 2–3, six flying boats conducted the first attack on Port Moresby. The huge seaplanes dropped twenty-one bombs on Seven Mile airdrome, killing an Australian sergeant but otherwise causing little material damage. Two nights later, nine flying boats bombed the town itself, demolishing a house and two commercial buildings. The Australians, with no fighters and only a few antiaircraft guns, quickly realized that Port Moresby was virtually defenseless.

Meanwhile, less than a week after Goto commenced his bombing campaign, a small flotilla of vessels departed Simpson Harbor and sailed two hundred miles down the island's southern coast to Gasmata, known to the Japanese as Surumi. The village boasted a grass airstrip, used previously as a refueling stop by the RAAF, and on February 9 a unit of Special Naval Landing Forces went ashore and secured the site. Engineers of the 7th Establishment Squad immediately began making improvements to the field. Working quickly, they developed a forward base with a runway some 3,600 feet long and 100 feet wide.

The purpose for building the advance base was later explained by a naval correspondent: "Although the Surumi airfield . . . was capable of accommodating only a small number of fighters or serving as an emergency landing strip for land attack planes, it was highly important as a relay air base to the Port Moresby, Lae, and Salamaua areas." Unmentioned by the Japanese was the defensive element provided by the forward base, which enabled Imperial Navy fighters to patrol the skies over central New Britain and intercept Allied attackers well south of Rabaul.

FLYING OFFICER GEOFF LEMPRIERE, 24 Squadron's intelligence officer, was one of those individuals whose luck vacillated between fortune and misfortune. Remaining in Rabaul on January 22 in order to destroy classified documents, he missed the squadron's evacuation. Then, after joining up with a band of Lark Force soldiers attempting to escape south along the coast, he was slowed by a random injury to his leg that developed into a badly infected ulcer. The party he was traveling with "borrowed" a small boat from a Catholic mission in the hopes of sailing to New Guinea, but they blundered into the harbor at Gasmata on the night of February 9 and were captured. This, however, turned out to be advantageous for Lempriere, whose infected leg would likely have become gangrenous if left untreated. Instead, a Japanese doctor at Gasmata provided expert medical attention—and probably saved his life.

More ironies followed. While Lempriere underwent treatment on the afternoon of February 11, three RAAF Hudsons attacked the transports being unloaded in the harbor. The mission was led by John Lerew, who of course had no inkling that his former squadron mate was literally right under his nose.

As luck would have it, the first A5M4 fighters assigned to the newly acquired base arrived from Rabaul at that very moment. An hour and twenty minutes earlier, FPO 1st Class Satoshi Yoshino had led four of the open-cockpit fighters from Lakunai airdrome. As they approached Gasmata, Yoshino was alerted by radio that enemy bombers were attacking. His fighters were in a perfect position to strike.

For Lerew, descending to mast height to attack one of the transports, the timing could not have been worse. In a flash, Yoshino hit the Hudson in both engines. The right engine and wing caught fire, but Lerew continued his attack, releasing his bombs at an altitude of only twenty feet. He pulled up sharply, maintaining control of the burning plane long enough for the other three crewmembers to move toward the rear escape hatch. Just as the Hudson's right wing separated and the doomed plane nosed over, Lerew squirmed out of the cockpit side window and parachuted to the jungle below.

Yoshino, having fatally damaged Lerew's aircraft, next went after the Hudson piloted by Flg. Off. Graham I. Gibson. This plane also crashed, diving at a steep angle directly into a hillside. The Japanese claimed to have shot down the third Hudson as well, but Flt. Lt. William A. Pedrina and his crew managed to escape. The Aussie airmen fought hard and were officially credited with shooting down one fighter and probably destroying another, though only one Mitsubishi was actually hit, with total damage amounting to six bullet holes. After ensuring that the sky was clear of Australian bombers, Yoshino and the rest of his flight landed safely at Gasmata.

Lerew, meanwhile, survived his adventurous parachute descent into the dense jungles of New Britain and began searching for his crewmen. No trace of them was found, and it is believed that all three perished in the Hudson's fiery fuselage before they could jump. Moving deeper into the bush, Lerew lived off the land for several days while evading the Japanese. He finally encountered friendly natives and was led to a coastwatcher, who arranged for a sailing schooner to take him to Port Moresby. Ten days after being shot down, Lerew rejoined his squadron.

The daring attack had cost the RAAF two Hudsons and the lives of seven men, but for once the lightweight bombers gave as good as they got. Japanese records revealed that two transports, the 4,390-ton *Kinryu Maru* and 7,072-ton *Kizui Maru*, were damaged by direct hits at Gasmata on February 11. Although both vessels eventually returned to service, dozens of Japanese had been killed or wounded.

CHAPTER 7

Stronghold

CONSIDERING THE RAAF'S almost-embarrassing lack of resources, the long-range attacks against New Britain were nothing less than heroic. To the Japanese, however, the raids were nothing more than a minor harassment—too insignificant to affect the development of Rabaul. Indeed, as ship after ship offloaded troops and supplies onto the busy wharves and jetties, the town experienced a population explosion.

During the first hours of occupation, the Japanese grabbed everything they could lay their hands on, ransacking stores and gorging themselves on foodstuffs and liquor, but once the pickings were gone the South Seas Force was left to deal with severe overcrowding. Conditions grew worse as more personnel came ashore, and the combat troops were eventually outnumbered by support units. Temporary encampments helped relieve the housing shortage, but the Japanese also erected hundreds of hastily built wooden buildings.

Prior to the invasion, Rabaul consisted of about 330 structures of all types, including warehouses and commercial buildings. Over the next few months the Japanese tripled that figure, constructing more than 600 wooden structures for an aggregate of 2.8 million square feet of floor space. The army and navy revamped or constructed twenty-nine sawmills, mostly using native labor, which together generated an output of more than seven hundred thousand board feet of lumber per month.

Everywhere around Rabaul, engineers began enlarging and improving the military complex. Simpson Harbor could already handle three hundred thousand tons of shipping, but the Imperial Navy made it even better, adding anchorages in Keravia Bay and Matupit Harbor. Vice Admiral Inoue, the commander of the Fourth Fleet, officially dispersed the invasion fleet on January 29 and established the Rabaul Area Force. Subordinate commands included the 8th Special Base Force, the 6th Torpedo Squadron, the 14th Minesweeper Flotilla, floatplane units, a naval construction detachment, and the Special Naval Landing Force antiaircraft batteries.

Air power received similar attention. Lakunai airdrome, which the Japanese called *Rabingikku*, was established as the main base for Imperial Navy fighters, primarily because a low area near the midpoint of the runway was deemed unsuitable for constant use by heavy aircraft. Engineers added approximately one hundred revetments and planned to resurface the runway, but periodic flooding prevented that from becoming a reality. The field conditions remained substandard throughout much of 1942 thanks to the steady fall of ash from Tavurvur, only a mile from the end of the runway on the opposite side of Matupit Harbor.

Vunakanau airdrome was greatly expanded as the main base for Imperial Navy land attack aircraft as well as fighters. The runway, extended to a length of 5,200 feet and widened to 135 feet, was paved with a four-inch-thick layer of concrete. Protective revetments for sixty bombers and ninety fighters were added, along with numerous wooden buildings for storage, administration, and housing. New barracks space alone totaled some 70,000 square feet, providing accommodations for 2,500 personnel.

Many of the roads that crisscrossed the Gazelle Peninsula were likewise improved. Prior to Japanese occupation there were just over 100 miles of paved roads, most of which were built by German engineers before World War I. The Japanese expanded that mileage four-fold, bringing in the 31st Field Road Construction Unit and "special details" (a euphemism for POW labor) to build 395 miles of new roads. The completed network provided numerous options for moving large quantities of troops and supplies.

Defensive emplacements and weapons were also imposing, with batteries installed and manned independently by army and navy units. The first heavy batteries were placed by the Maizaru 2nd Special Naval Landing Force, which set up four 80mm Type 99 antiaircraft guns, followed soon thereafter by the 47th Field Antiaircraft Artillery Battalion, equipped with at least a dozen 75mm Type 88 guns. The latter, which somewhat resembled the fearsome German 88mm Flak, was not nearly as lethal, but the Japanese more than made up for the difference by installing almost a hundred Type 88 and Type 99 guns at Rabaul. In addition, two dozen 120mm and larger dual-purpose guns, which could be used against ships as well as aircraft, were placed in strategic locations around the harbor. And that was only the heavy stuff. Smaller-caliber antiaircraft weapons included approximately 100 Navy Type 96 25mm automatic cannons (in both twin- and triple-barrel versions), plus approximately 120 heavy machine guns and rapid-fire cannon manned by army units.

Each weapon had its own bubble of lethal coverage, and the Japanese placed the guns, to the extent possible, so that the kill zones overlapped. The Type 88s, for example, had a theoretical effective range of 9,000 meters (29,000 feet), while the lighter Type 96 cannon were deadly up to 5,500 meters (18,000 feet). In all, the caldera was surrounded by nearly *four hundred* antiaircraft guns, most of them concentrated in a C-shaped ring that started at the tip of Crater Peninsula and extended all the way around the basin to Kokopo. Any Allied aircraft attempting to attack Rabaul would first have to fly through this ring of fire and then run the gauntlet again in order to egress from the target.

Coastal defense systems at Rabaul were equally impressive. To streamline command and control, the Gazelle Peninsula was divided into areas of military responsibility. Simpson Harbor and Rabaul township were the navy's domain, while the army controlled most of the remaining area. Naval defense batteries included thirty-eight heavy rifles—all but one having a bore of 120mm or larger—protected by at least fifty concrete pillboxes housing heavy machine guns. The army added dozens of 150mm howitzers, 75mm infantry guns, mortars, and antitank guns to this formidable group of weapons. In the southern part of the peninsula, army zones were further subdivided into sectors, each defended by eight hundred to four thousand troops. Fortifications included numerous pillboxes, bunkers, and reinforced caves. Choke points were created with roadblocks and antitank ditches, and foot trails were sowed with land mines. Any beaches that might be used for an Allied amphibious landing—particularly Talili Bay, the Keravat River area, and Kokopo—were heavily mined.

The array of weaponry dedicated to ground defense was astounding. Potential invaders would first have to navigate through a maze of underwater obstacles designed to rip the bottoms out of landing craft, then fight inland past a hornet's nest of fixed defenses: almost 240 heavy cannon and howitzers, roughly the same number of antitank guns and field guns, 23 heavy mortars, and approximately 6,000 machine guns and grenade launchers.

In addition to building heavy fortifications, the Japanese improved local utilities. Engineers upgraded the availability of fresh water by drilling at least thirteen new wells. Total yield reached 290,000 gallons per day, some of it going into tank trucks and water bowsers for distribution to remote sites. As for electrical output, there had been only a single 200-kilowatt, diesel-powered generator in Rabaul, which lacked the capacity to fully electrify the township. The Japanese added twenty-three diesel power stations, upping the kilowatt output nearly five-fold, and placed numerous portable generators around the peninsula to provide additional lighting at night.

The communication infrastructure at Rabaul was likewise revamped. Little remained of the slapdash telephone system installed by Lark Force—most of the lines had been cut during the invasion—so the Japanese dug an extensive network of narrow ditches and laid miles of new cable. Radio communications were improved by placing new receiver/transmitter sets, which covered a broad range of frequencies, across northern New Britain and the surrounding islands, and the navy built an independent communications center at a road intersection known as Three Ways.

The newest advancement at Rabaul was radar, which the Japanese had been developing quietly. Two naval Type 1 (Model 1) sets were installed at Tomavatur Mission, placed so that each covered a separate 180-degree sector out to a maximum range of about ninety miles. Nine newer Type 1s (Model 2) were placed throughout the Bismarck Archipelago, including three sets on New Britain and two on New Ireland. Twenty smaller radars were removed from aircraft for use as ground equipment, but only eleven of these went into service. Nonetheless the Japanese successfully combined radar stations, observation posts, and the communications network into "a most satisfactory air warning system." In many instances, they were able to receive up to an hour's advance warning of approaching raids.

Fully aware that Rabaul would be viewed as the most important military target in the entire theater, the Japanese made careful preparations to withstand a lengthy siege. Using the newly built roads, the army and navy each dispersed millions of tons of food, fuel, ammunition, clothing, spare parts, and other essential supplies—enough for each service to conduct six months of warfare—among hundreds of caches hidden across the peninsula.

Not all of the improvements were implemented overnight, of course. Some developments required months to complete, and more than a year passed before all of the weapons and other defenses were installed. But the Japanese eventually accomplished what the Australians could not. Using trucks, horses, native laborers, and prisoners, they developed Rabaul into the most heavily fortified stronghold south of the equator. Indeed, the Imperial Army and Navy poured so many shiploads of troops, weapons, materials, and supplies into the effort that the garrison experienced a food shortage in the summer of 1942.

Tokyo's intentions were clear: with Rabaul as the center of operations, the Japanese could now expand their domination over the entire South Pacific, from the Solomon Islands to New Guinea—and possibly far beyond. Little did they realize, however, just how quickly the Americans would try to attack their burgeoning stronghold.

CHAPTER 8

Task Force 11

BARELY A WEEK after the Japanese captured Rabaul, events that would directly affect the fortress unfolded on opposite sides of the Pacific. Aboard the battleship *Nagato*, anchored in the Inland Sea at Hashirajima, Adm. Isoroku Yamamoto and the Combined Fleet Staff were concerned about the free-roaming carriers of the United States Navy. On February 1, aircraft from two independent task forces had attacked Japanese bases in the Marshall Islands and the Gilberts. The simultaneous raids caused only nominal destruction, but they provided the American public with an enormous boost in morale while deeply embarrassing the Japanese. Rear Adm. Matome Ugaki, the Combined Fleet chief of staff, later admitted: "After experiencing defensive weakness ourselves, we could no longer laugh at the enemy's confusion at the time of the surprise attack on Pearl Harbor."

Soon after the attacks, Imperial General Headquarters learned that a third American carrier force was loose, this time in the South Pacific. The Japanese went on high alert, broadcasting the news across the Southeast Area. Even the lowest ranks were informed. Akiyoshi Hisaeda, serving as a cook in the 55th Division field hospital at Rabaul, entered some of the details into his diary on February 7: "Enemy aircraft carrier with 50 aircraft advancing on New Britain."

The information obtained by the lowly private was not only timely but remarkably accurate. The stately USS *Lexington*, one of America's most beloved warships, had crossed the equator into the South Pacific a mere two days earlier. She carried sixty-eight aircraft and served as the flagship of Task Force 11, consisting of two heavy cruisers, seven destroyers, and a fleet oiler. Commanded by Vice Adm. Wilson Brown, the task force had departed Pearl Harbor on January 31 for a variety of escort and patrol duties. First on the agenda was a mid-ocean rendezvous with Task Force 8, under the command of Rear Adm. William F. "Bull" Halsey Jr., whose ships had raided the Marshalls on February 1. His force would need to be refueled, after which Brown would take Task Force 11 south toward Canton Island for convoy duties.

Two days out of Hawaii, Brown received new orders. Halsey's ships no longer needed refueling, so Brown headed straight for Canton. On February 6, a day after crossing the equator, his orders were amended once again: he was to proceed to the Fiji Islands and rendezvous with a newly formed multinational force known as the ANZAC squadron. A familiar name from World War I, ANZAC (Australian–New Zealand Army Corps) had been expanded to include American participation. The naval force included two American destroyers and the heavy cruiser *Chicago* along with two New Zealand light cruisers and some lightly armed corvettes. Rear Adm. John G. Crace, Royal Australian Navy, commanded the squadron aboard HMAS *Australia*, a heavy cruiser. The ships and other components of the ANZAC command were under the operational control of the senior American naval officer in Australia, Vice Adm. Herbert F. Leary. His task, as put forward by his superiors in Washington, was to seek a fight with the enemy. Since none of the Allied countries could challenge the Japanese on their own, the command had been formed to combine assets, but on the whole there wasn't much to unify. Aviation units consisted mostly of RAAF reconnaissance planes, augmented by a few U.S. Navy Catalinas operating out the Fiji Islands. A fighter group and a light bomber group of the U.S. Army Air Corps had recently arrived in Australia, but their planes had neither the range nor the endurance to support naval forces.

Leary's options improved when Task Force 11 became available. Together, the ANZAC squadron and the ships under Brown's command gave the Allies a potent striking force. With that in mind, Adm. Earnest J. King, commander-in-chief of the U.S. Fleet (COMINCH), ordered Brown and Leary to go on the offensive.

Eager to do something positive after the debacle at Pearl Harbor, Brown recommended a strike on Rabaul. It was a bold, high-risk proposal, the equivalent of an onsides kick on the first play from scrimmage. Rabaul lay 1,700 miles beyond Fiji, and the oiler *Neosho* did not carry enough fuel to supply all of Brown's ships *plus* those of the ANZAC squadron. Therefore, Task Force 11 would have to conduct the strike on its own. Despite the obvious risks, King, a former skipper of the *Lexington*, appreciated the audacity of Brown's plan and approved it.

Task Force 11 rendezvoused with the ANZAC squadron near Fiji on February 16, whereupon Brown consolidated his plans and obtained the latest intelligence on Rabaul. The most recent reconnaissance mission had been conducted two days earlier by a Hudson of 32 Squadron. The crew reported an "aircraft carrier" (probably an aircraft transporter), five warships, eleven merchant ships, and twelve flying boats in Simpson Harbor, plus several planes at Lakunai airdrome. Brown was concerned about the location of Admiral Nagumo's carriers, but the briefers assured him that the enemy flattops would not be a threat. This was true, for the ironic reason that the carrier force was sailing into position to launch a strike on the Australian mainland just three days hence.

Rabaul would be relatively unprotected, or so the experts thought. Hoping to maintain the element of surprise, Task Force 11 departed Fiji on the afternoon of February 16 and sailed deep into enemy waters.

UNKNOWN TO THE Allies, eighteen of the Imperial Navy's newest attack planes had recently arrived at Rabaul. Two *chutais* (nine-plane divisions) of Mitsubishi G4M1s, known to the Japanese as Type 1 land attack aircraft, landed at Vunakanau on February 14. Veterans of the Takao Air Group, with extensive combat experience in the Philippines and Netherlands East Indies campaigns, the crews had been transferred into the 4th Air Group, a brand-new composite unit created at Rabaul on February 10.

Commanded by Capt. Yoshiyotsu Moritama, a non-aviator whose duties were primarily administrative, the group was not yet at full strength. A third *chutai*, culled from the Chitose Air Group in the Marianas, had recently transitioned to Type Is, and the crews were still completing the training syllabus. Eventually the 4th Air Group would consist of twenty-seven Type 1s and an equal number of *Rei-sen* fighters, all drawn from veteran units; however, as of mid-February, only the eighteen aircraft at Rabaul were operational.

In service for less than a year, the Type 1 *rikko* was considered the Imperial Navy's premier land attack aircraft. Similar in appearance to the U.S. Army's Martin B-26 Marauder, the Mitsubishi was both larger and heavier. The B-26 had a slender fuselage that tapered at both ends, whereas the Type 1's fuselage was uniformly thick, prompting crewmen to nickname it *hamaki* (the cigar).

The roomy fuselage served its purpose. The *rikko* doctrine favored the use of aerial torpedoes against ships, a specialty demonstrated with stunning effectiveness on December 10, 1941, when waves of land-attack aircraft sank the British warships *Repulse* and *Prince of Wales*. The Type 1's internal weapon bay was designed to carry either a Type 91 aerial torpedo, which was more than seventeen feet long and weighed 1,820 pounds, or the equivalent weight in bombs.

Mitsubishi engineers achieved this load-carrying capability without sacrificing speed, armament, or range. The twin Kasai fourteen-cylinder radial engines generated over 1,500 horsepower each and gave the aircraft a top speed of almost 270 miles per hour. Well armed with four 7.7mm machine guns and a 20mm tail cannon, the Model 11 flown by the 4th Air Group boasted a range of more than 2,300 nautical miles.

But to attain such impressive performance, the engineers had spurned critical components known to be essential for survivability in combat. To save weight, no armor plate was installed for crew protection. The engineers also chose to forego self-sealing liners in the fuel tanks, which were integrated within the main wing. The only thing separating hundreds of gallons of high-octane gasoline from enemy bullets was a few millimeters of aluminum skin.

Author-historian Osamu Tagaya, a renowned expert on Japanese aviation units of World War II, described the rationale behind the Type 1's development:

> The use of conventional fuel tanks, fully internalized within the airframe, would have left room for the installation of protective measures, but would also have reduced fuel capacity below requirements. The navy, in its collective wisdom, would not accept any shortfall in range or

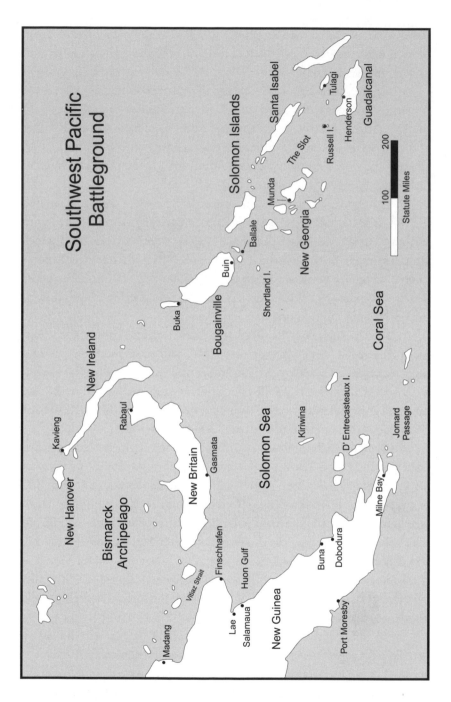

Southwest Pacific
Battleground

performance, and appeared quite willing to take the risks inherent in the design.

This was mute testimony to the extent to which a tactical doctrine favoring attack at all costs pervaded the Imperial Navy. The IJN was loath to accept the 300-kilogram weight penalty which the installation of rubber ply protection for the fuel tanks entailed. Ever focused on performance and range in pursuit of the offensive, navy airmen refused to give up that weight in bombs or fuel in exchange for a feature which many . . . considered nonessential.

The "land-attackers," as the airmen called themselves, knew their planes had an Achilles heel. Yet they possessed supreme confidence in the Type 1, which had been unstoppable during the early campaigns over China, the Philippines, and the Netherlands East Indies. History, they believed, was on their side.

FOR THE FIRST few days out of Fiji, Task Force 11 benefited from long-range forward observation provided by a squadron of B-17s. The 14th Reconnaissance Squadron, pieced together from three different units in Hawaii, had been assigned temporarily to the U.S. Navy under Vice Admiral Leary. Led by twenty-eight-year-old Maj. Richard H. Carmichael, a square-jawed West Pointer with a dazzling smile, the squadron flew lengthy patrol sectors that extended seven hundred miles from Nandi airfield in the Fijis.

Aboard *Lexington*, Vice Admiral Brown and his staff completed their strike planning. The task force would steam toward Rabaul for four days, keeping well clear of islands to avoid detection, and launch a strike on the morning of February 21. "Plentiful shipping targets were expected," wrote Capt. Frederick C. Sherman, commanding officer of the carrier. "We planned a surprise attack from north of the Solomons, with the planes approaching Rabaul over the intervening island of New Ireland and a simultaneous cruiser bombardment of the ships in the harbor."

The ambitious plans also called for Carmichael's B-17s to hit Rabaul in coordination with the navy strike. The heavy bombers were scheduled to arrive at Townsville, Australia, on February 19, then launch the following night for Rabaul. If all went well, they would arrive over the target at dawn on the twenty-first, the same time as *Lexington*'s aircraft. After refueling at Port Moresby, the Fortresses would return to Townsville, completing a mission of approximately 2,300 miles with an elapsed time of eighteen hours.

Long before anyone was in position to attack, however, the carefully laid plans began to unravel. Japanese listening posts intercepted segments of the abnormally high message traffic between admirals King, Brown, and Leary, enabling Imperial General Headquarters to issue alerts even before the task force departed from Fiji. The tension went up another notch on the afternoon of February 19, when an outpost southwest of Truk warned of enemy destroyers in the vicinity. Later it was determined to be a false alarm, but the warning prompted Rear Admiral Goto to order the Yokohama Air Group to prepare for an important mission. The flying boats would go out early the next morning with a single purpose: find the American task force.

AT DAWN ON February 20, three enormous Kawanishi H6Ks lifted majestically from the surface of Simpson Harbor and climbed eastward. The flying boats, each with a crew of ten, took slightly different headings to reach their assigned fifteen-degree sectors. For the first several hours the hunt came up empty. But just as the seaplane piloted by Lt. j.g.Noboru Sakai approached the outer turn point, a crewmember spotted the task force. At 1030 hours, Sakai radioed headquarters with the electrifying news that an enemy aircraft carrier and its screening force were 460 miles northeast of New Britain.

Sakai and his crew were undoubtedly ecstatic about their accomplishment, but they had little time to congratulate themselves. High atop the *Lexington*'s superstructure, a large, box-shaped antenna had already detected pulses of invisible energy reflected from the Japanese flying boat. The antenna was one of several integrated components that made up the carrier's first-generation CXAM search radar, which fed the electronic data to a primitive scope inside the carrier's combat information center. A trained operator called out the particulars to another man standing at an illuminated plotting board: unidentified contact, thirty-five miles, bearing one-eight-zero. Word of the "bogey" was passed by sound-powered telephones to the bridge, whereupon Captain Sherman ordered the launch of the ready CAP, or combat air patrol.

On the wooden flight deck, six gray-camouflaged Grumman F4F-3 Wildcat fighters sat with their engines idling, ready for immediate launch.

The cloth-helmeted pilots were guided by deck handlers—sailors wearing yellow jerseys—who used specialized sign language to direct the pilots into position. The deck canted slightly as the 888-foot-long *Lexington* turned into the prevailing wind, and when her course was steady a green light illuminated on the superstructure. This was the signal for the yellow-shirted Flight Deck Officer to throw a quick salute to the first pilot in line; he then leaned toward the carrier's bow, extended his right arm, and pointed forward with a flourish.

Revving his engine at full power, the first pilot released his brakes. The stubby gray fighter accelerated down the deck and was quickly airborne, its wings waggling slightly as the pilot manually cranked up the wheels. One by one the remaining Wildcats followed, forming into two-plane sections as the lead pilots checked in by radio: the 1st Division leader (Lt. Cmdr. John S. "Jimmy" Thach), second section leader (Lt. Edward H. "Butch" O'Hare), and third section leader (Lt. j.g. Onia B. "Burt" Stanley), reported their fighters up and ready.

In *Lexington*'s darkened combat information center, the fighter director officer scanned the graphics written on the plotting board and made a quick decision. Communicating with the fighters by radio, Lt. Frank F. "Red" Gill vectored Thach's section southward to investigate the bogey while holding the other four fighters in reserve over the task force.

Less than thirty minutes after the Kawanishi flying boat was detected by radar, the stage was set for *Lexington*'s first encounter with enemy aircraft.

CHAPTER 9

Medal of Honor: Edward H. "Butch" O'Hare

THIRTY-SIX-YEAR-OLD Jimmy Thach, commanding officer of Fighting Squadron 3 aboard the *Lexington*, had long been regarded as one of the navy's best pilots. Nicknamed for his likeness to an older brother who'd preceded him at the Naval Academy, Thach was the Old Man personified, with deep-set eyes, drooping cheeks, and a receding hairline. But behind the hushpuppy face was a true gunnery expert. Thach had learned to shoot as a boy in Arkansas; and later, after graduating from the Naval Academy, he accumulated more than three thousand hours in all types of aircraft, including assignments as a test pilot and flight instructor.

The morning of February 20 found Thach and Ens. Edward R. "Doc" Sellstrom Jr., his wingman, thirty-five miles southwest of the *Lexington* on the latest heading provided by the fighter director officer. Applying a combination of pilot's instinct and the information from the CXAM radar, "Red" Gill steered the two fighters to intercept an unidentified contact. It was not a simple task. The Japanese pilot was being cagey, using cumulous clouds, thick with rain, as hiding places.

But Lieutenant Sakai was merely prolonging the inevitable. The CXAM radar could "see" his enormous flying boat through the clouds, making it only a matter of time before the Wildcats were upon him.

Based on Thach's recollection, Sakai may have spotted the fighters first.

He flew into the clouds and we followed, hoping he'd come out on the same course on the other side. But he was a smart Jap. He turned inside the cloud, and when we came out, the air was vacant. We went back into the cloud, flying on instruments. There was a small opening in the cloud, and as I came into it, I looked down and not more than a thousand feet below was a huge wing with a red disc. It was my first sight of an enemy aircraft as close as that, and it nearly scared me to death.

Thus began a deadly game of Wildcat-and-mouse, except that the mouse was enormous and well armed. Knowing he could not outmaneuver the fighters, Sakai attempted to evade them by descending through the base of the cloud. But the Kawanishi was simply too massive to escape unnoticed. Bursting out of the clouds at 1,500 feet, Sakai had only one option available: he had to run.

Unlike the previous adversaries faced by the Yokohama airmen (the underpowered Wirraways of 24 Squadron), the Wildcats with their 1,200-horsepower Pratt & Whitney engines had plenty of speed. They also had the immeasurable advantage of altitude. Perched above and behind the big flying boat, Thach and Sellstrom waited until it was well out in the open before commencing their first gunnery run.

After years of practice, Thach's first firing run was flawless. The heavy slugs from his four .50-caliber machine guns punched easily through the Kawanishi's broad parasol wing, causing plumes of vaporized gasoline to spew from numerous holes in the fuel tanks. Ignited by a glowing tracer or an incendiary round, the volatile mist suddenly erupted in brilliant sheets of flame. Sakai and his men were doomed.

Thach watched as several objects tumbled from the plane, thinking at first that they were bodies. They turned out to be eight small bombs. "I could see the Japs in the forward part of the plane stand up, but they seemed to make no attempt to jump," Thach recalled. "The plane was almost completely engulfed in flames, and it hit the water with a huge explosion."

Sakai's crew perished at twelve minutes past eleven. Miles away, observing a column of black smoke on the horizon, *Lexington*'s sailors let out a cheer. Fighting Squadron 3 had scored its first victory.

THIRTY MINUTES LATER, the CXAM radar detected another bogey, this time north of the task force. Lieutenant Gill vectored Burt Stanley and his wingman, Ens. Leon M. Haynes, toward the snooper and ordered them to "buster," to which they shoved their throttles to maximum power. A short time later Haynes spied the target, another silvery Kawanishi at six thousand feet. He signaled to Stanley, who in turn radioed the ship with a tally-ho.

In his excitement, Stanley missed the master gun switch while running through the precombat checklist, and nothing happened when he squeezed the trigger. After toggling the switch, he fired three bursts into the massive wing of the Japanese plane. Haynes followed, also registering solid hits.

The flying boat, piloted by WO Kiyoshi Hayashi, began to burn. Slowly at first, then more steeply, it pitched over and fell toward the ocean, leaving a trail of greasy black smoke to mark the path of its mortal plunge. The spectacular explosion when it hit the surface at 1202 was again witnessed by *Lexington*'s crew.

Expending just a few hundred rounds of ammunition, Fighting Squadron 3 had achieved two indisputable victories. On the opposite side of the ledger, twenty Japanese airmen were dead.

IN THE CHINATOWN building that served as his headquarters, Rear Admiral Goto deliberated over the sighting report received from Sakai's patrol plane. There had been no collaborating report since the initial message, nor was any amplifying word transmitted by the other two flying boats; but Goto had already made up his mind. Sakai's information placed the American task force approximately five hours' flying time from Rabaul, well within range of the 4th Air Group's land attack aircraft. Goto was determined to destroy the approaching force but delayed the order to attack in the hopes of learning more from the patrol planes. The radio remained silent. At 1310, with nothing else to go on, Goto gave the order for the 4th Air Group to attack the American ships.

For the men at Vunakanau airdrome, the situation was less than ideal. For one thing, the land-attack component was only two-thirds complete.

The crews from the Chitose Air Group had completed their training and were en route from the Marianas with new aircraft, but they would not reach Rabaul until the following day. Thus, only eighteen aircraft were available for the mission.

Secondly, although the airmen had significant combat experience, none had ever attacked a large naval force. They would also have to fly the mission without their preferred weapon, aerial torpedoes. None had been delivered yet to Rabaul, which meant that the Type 1s would be configured as bombers with two 250-kilogram (550-pound) bombs each. Additionally, the crews were aware that they would not enjoy fighter support. Only six Zeros had been delivered to Rabaul thus far, and there were no external drop tanks for them. Without the tanks, the *Rei-sens* lacked the range to reach the American task force, engage in combat, and still make it back to Rabaul. The land-attackers would have to fend for themselves.

Despite the apparent shortcomings, the crews of the 4th Air Group had the utmost confidence in their fast, well-armed bombers. Thus far the air forces of the Imperial Navy had practically annihilated every opponent, giving the men at Vunakanau every reason to believe that the string of easy victories would be extended. Indeed, prior to boarding their aircraft, they gathered for an inspiring message from Rear Admiral Goto. "I want you to crush the enemy fleet, which is apparently a large one," he told them. "Do not fear the enemy, however powerful he may be. Do not underrate him, however small his force. Fulfill your task with coolness and composure."

The airmen then climbed aboard their twin-engine bombers, which still wore the *kumogata* (cloud pattern) camouflage scheme left over from earlier campaigns. In contrast to the green-and-brown paint, heavily weathered after three months in the tropics, the fresh white identification codes of the newly formed 4th Air Group stood out brightly on the tails of the bombers.

Lieutenant Commander Takuzo Ito, the *hikotaicho*, boarded "F-348" and sat at the rear of the bomber's spacious greenhouse cockpit. A graduate of the Etajima Naval Academy and the Kasumigaura Naval Air Training School, Ito had a wife and family at home in the quaint city of Hiroshima. All of his previous experience had been in reconnaissance floatplanes, but ten days earlier he had been assigned to the 4th Air Group as the senior air leader.

Next to Ito sat another observer, Lt. Yogoro Seto of Tokyo, the *chutaicho* (division leader) of the 1st *Chutai*. Up forward, CPO Chuzo Watanabe manned the senior pilot's seat on the right-hand side of the cockpit, while FPO 2nd Class Minoru Toyoda occupied the copilot's seat on the left—the reverse of the American system. Four additional crewmen climbed aboard, including a navigator who doubled as the bombardier/nose gunner, two radio operators, and the flight engineer. During combat, the radio operators, flight engineer, and one of the observers would man the bomber's defensive weapons: a 7.7mm machine gun in the dorsal blister, two identical guns mounted in side blisters, and a 20mm automatic cannon in the tail.

During startup, one aircraft from the 1st *Chutai* encountered mechanical problems and was scrubbed from the mission. The remaining seventeen planes taxied from their hardstands to the runway threshold, where the crews were thrilled to see hundreds of mechanics and other ground personnel lining the runway. As the first plane commenced its takeoff run at 1420, the well-wishers waved their caps over their heads and yelled "Banzai! Banzai!"*

The aviators were supremely motivated. "Off we went," recalled one, "led by a unit commander and heartily seen off by superiors and comrades. With the words, 'We won't fail you,' we headed toward mid-ocean."

But Lieutenant Commander Ito and his medium bombers encountered trouble soon after they crossed New Ireland and got over the open sea. Heavy rain squalls extended over a large percentage of the ocean, making conditions both difficult and hazardous for the large formation. Only two weeks earlier the group had lost two planes and their crews in a devastating mid-air collision, which likely influenced Ito's decision to separate the 1st and 2nd *Chutais*. The nine aircraft of the latter, commanded by Lt. Masayoshi Nakagawa, took a slightly different heading and soon disappeared from view.

UNKNOWN TO THE Japanese, Vice Admiral Brown had called off the planned strike. Rabaul was safe. The task force would soon reverse course.

Brown had no alternative but to presume that one or more of the enemy flying boats had alerted Rabaul about the task force. The Japanese would

---

* An iteration of an ancient Chinese expression for long life to the emperor, "banzai" was revived during the Meiji period as a ritualistic war cry.

be on high alert, with plenty of time to move their ships from Simpson Harbor and bolster their defenses. Without the element of surprise, *Lexington*'s airmen would face an unacceptable level of risk.

Soon after the second flying boat was shot down, Brown made the difficult decision to cancel the raid. The ever-aggressive Ted Sherman wanted to press ahead, but Brown overruled him, recommending that another attempt be made later, perhaps when a second carrier was available. As a concession, he continued to sail directly toward Rabaul in a deliberate feint. With each passing hour, Task Force 11 moved almost twenty miles closer to the enemy stronghold.

AT 1330, JIMMY THACH led his six Wildcats back to the *Lexington*, having turned the CAP over to the squadron's 2nd Division, led by Lt. Cmdr. Donald A. Lovelace. A few hours passed without incident, but the anticipation of an enemy attack gradually increased as the afternoon wore on. Therefore, with a fortuitous sense of timing, Captain Sherman ordered the launch of the next available division at 1600. Before Lt. Noel A. M. Gayler's 3rd Division had an opportunity to take off, the CXAM picked up a large contact seventy-five miles west of the carrier. Shortly thereafter the radar image vanished, only to reappear again at 1625, now fifty miles from the ship. Five minutes later a new plot showed the contact closing rapidly. An enemy attack was inbound.

Klaxon alarms sounded throughout the task force, sending sailors to their battle stations. Aboard *Lexington*, Sherman rang for flank speed—one of the carrier's best defenses. "Lady Lex" had begun life twenty years earlier as a fast battle cruiser, but her construction was nearly scrapped in 1922 due to the Limitation of Naval Armament treaty. Congress eventually came to the rescue. Authorized for completion as an aircraft carrier to circumvent the treaty limitations, *Lexington* was redesigned. Her upper works were completely transformed, but the propulsion equipment remained unchanged: sixteen oil-fired burners, four turbine generators, and eight massive electric motors generated more than two hundred thousand horsepower. Despite her great length and displacement, *Lexington* could reach a top speed of thirty-four knots—almost forty miles per hour—making her a difficult target to hit.

The carrier's shipboard weapons were no less formidable. Long-range armament consisted of a dozen 5-inch dual-purpose guns mounted on sponsons along both sides of the hull. Intermediate and close defense were handled, in turn, by 1.1-inch automatic cannon and water-cooled .50-caliber machine guns. All of the gunners were efficient, having trained almost daily against parachute flares and towed targets. Even when off duty, the crews of the 5-inch guns practiced with a mechanized loader mounted below decks.

But even more than her speed or bristling gun batteries, *Lexington* relied on her squadron of Grumman fighters for defense. Immediately after Noel Gayler's division took off, Lovelace and the 2nd Division returned to the carrier in preparation for landing. Low on fuel, they circled over *Lexington* and were thus out of position to intercept the attackers. In the meantime, Gayler's six fighters climbed toward the inbound bogey in sections of two. Heavy with fuel, they lacked the time for a division rendezvous as Gill continually fed them updated vectors.

Simultaneously, *Lexington*'s deck crewmen dealt with a unique problem. As soon as Gayler's division was airborne they had to "re-spot" the flight deck in order to recover Lovelace's fighters. This meant clearing the landing area at the aft end of the flight deck, where dozens of aircraft had been parked to make room for Gayler's Wildcats to launch. The parked planes now had to be pushed forward manually so that Lovelace's division could land.

To anyone unfamiliar with carrier operations, the whole process of deck-spotting seems complicated, but the crew was accustomed to performing these flight-deck ballets several times a day. Normally they had ample time between launch and recovery cycles, but with six Wildcats low on fuel and an attack imminent, all of the parked planes had to be moved forward in haste. However, four additional Grumman fighters and more than twenty Douglas SBD dive-bombers had just been fueled in anticipation of the next launch cycle. Filled with highly flammable aviation gas, they now represented an enormous risk. If just one enemy bomb landed among them, *Lexington* was doomed. The planes had to be launched immediately to get them out of harm's way, requiring another frenzied re-spot.

As a result, Lovelace's Wildcats were waved off and given new instructions to buster toward the incoming attackers. Some, very low on fuel, had already started coming in to land; but in response to the new orders, they raised their landing gear and headed westward at top speed.

The deck handlers, meanwhile, continued their feverish dance of pushing planes aft while keeping the four gassed-up Wildcats available at the front of the pack. Jimmy Thach and three of his pilots from the 1st Division manned them and were ready to launch again as soon as the carrier turned into the wind.

NAKAGAWA'S 2ND *Chutai* had found *Lexington* first. After all the bad weather during the flight from Rabaul, it seemed a bit ironic that the big carrier was steaming in an area of bright sunshine. The Japanese had no trouble recognizing the flattop: she was surrounded by her screen of escorts in what the Japanese called a "ring formation." Nakagawa instructed one of his radiomen (there were three qualified operators aboard his aircraft) to notify 24th Air Flotilla headquarters, and the report was sent at approximately 1630 hours.

Down below, American lookouts spotted the enemy formation ten miles from the outermost ship. The sky was so clear that Sherman later called it "a perfect day for bombing, with the oncoming planes easily visible from the bridge."

The nearest fighters were flown by Noel Gayler and his wingman, Ens. Dale W. Peterson. Due to their sluggish rate of climb, the two pilots had attained only a slight altitude advantage when they spotted the enemy planes: nine twin engine bombers in V formation at 11,500 feet, coming fast. Rolling into shallow dives, Gayler and Peterson initiated their first attack from the side of the formation at 1639.

The Japanese shot first. Streams of glowing tracer rounds reached toward the two Wildcats, but Gayler and Peterson held an important advantage. In addition to their high rate of speed, they presented only small frontal targets to the enemy gunners. Their own illuminated gun sights, meanwhile, were filled with a rapidly growing profile of the nearest bomber. Both men opened fire and scored lethal hits with their first pass. The Mitsubishi burst into flames and skidded out of the formation, revealing the ease with which the Type 1's unprotected fuel tanks could be ignited.

Moments later the rest of Gayler's division joined the fight, and in the span of two minutes another two bombers fell into the sea.

The battle intensified as the 2nd *Chutai*, now numbering just six bombers, came within range of the ships' antiaircraft guns. The screening ships opened up with their main batteries, but just at that moment, *Lexington* turned into the wind to launch the last of her vulnerable planes, forcing her gunners to hold their fire lest the muzzle blast from the 5-inchers knock a departing aircraft out of control.

High overhead, Gayler and his pilots suddenly found themselves in the midst of friendly fire as the first of the antiaircraft shells began to explode, closer to them than to the enemy bombers. Ignoring the angry black bursts, the fighters pressed their attacks against the Japanese formation. The next bomber to drop out was Nakagawa's, badly damaged by Gayler and Peterson on their second pass. Both men continued firing as they raced through the formation, and yet another Mitsubishi fell to their accurate gunnery.

Now only four bombers remained in formation. The absence of Nakagawa's lead aircraft perhaps rattled the surviving aircrews, for they flew beyond the *Lexington*, wasting critical minutes while they regrouped. Nevertheless the four aircraft wheeled around and intitiated a fresh attack run, this time from astern. Shouldering past the flak and the slicing Wildcats, they reached the bomb release point just as the *Lexington*'s last fueled-up plane climbed away from the flight deck. As if a switch had been thrown, the carrier's antiaircraft guns cut loose with a pent-up roar. Simultaneously, Sherman ordered a series of full-rudder turns to spoil the enemy's aim. The maneuvering worked. Eight large bombs tumbled from the four remaining Mitsubishis, but none landed near the speeding, twisting carrier.

Lighter now by 1,100 pounds apiece, the bombers accelerated in a bid to escape the Wildcats and antiaircraft fire. One covered only a few miles before it was shot down; the other three separated while diving to gain more speed.

Jimmy Thach and Doc Sellstrom, having just reached combat altitude after taking off from *Lexington*, immediately gave chase. They were joined by most of the pilots from the 2nd and 3rd divisions, whose blood was up. So far the Wildcats had downed six bombers in a lopsided fight, and everyone was eager to get a share of the action. This may have prompted two young pilots to approach the bombers recklessly, underestimating the Mitsubishis' lethal armament.

The first was Lt. j.g. Howard L. Johnson, whose fighter was hit by gunfire from a fleeing bomber. He boldly attempted to keep pace, but as he drifted back he was sucked directly behind the Mitsubishi. Its tail gunner slammed several 20mm rounds into the Wildcat, wounding Johnson in the legs and putting the engine out of action. After bailing out and landing safely in the water, Johnson floated for only a few minutes before one of the screening destroyers picked him up.

Not so fortunate was Ens. John W. "Jack" Wilson of the 3rd Division, whose fighter was performing sluggishly as he tried to chase down a bomber from astern. Thach saw what was about to happen and keyed his radio to shout a warning, but before he could utter a word, Wilson's canopy was smashed by a direct hit from a cannon shell. The ensign probably never knew what hit him. No parachute appeared as his fighter fell into the sea five miles from the carrier.

Thach opened fire at the offending bomber and it went down in flames, a demise that was becoming commonplace. He also aided in the destruction of another bomber, one that had probably been damaged earlier. Several other Wildcat pilots went after the last two bombers still in the air—or so everyone thought. No one noticed that Nakagawa's crewmates had miraculously regained control of their crippled bomber at very low altitude. Gradually working their way around to a new attack position, they got within two miles of *Lexington* before being detected.

Aboard the carrier, hundreds of men held their collective breath as they watched the dark-colored aircraft approach at wave-top height, knowing instinctively that the pilot intended to crash into them deliberately. Considering the size and speed of the twin-engine Mitsubishi, not to mention its load of bombs and high-octane gasoline, a holocaust would occur if the suicide attempt succeeded.

Sherman kept *Lexington* in a constant turn, presenting only her narrow stern to the attacker. When the menacing bomber got within 2,500 yards, the carrier's rapid-fire cannons and machine guns opened up with a withering blast, but the big aircraft kept coming. Finally, at three quarters of a mile, the antiaircraft fire began to take effect. Pieces flew off Nakagawa's bomber, yet it still wobbled onward, momentum carrying it to within a few dozen yards of the ship before it finally stalled and hit the water with a mighty explosion.

TWELVE MINUTES had elapsed since Noel Gayler and Dale Peterson first attacked the enemy formation. As the noise of the antiaircraft guns died away, rising plumes of smoke marked the watery graves of seven medium bombers and two fighters. Don Lovelace and his division, desperately low on fuel, circled the carrier while waiting for the deck crew to clear the landing area. Most of the remaining fighters were scattered miles away as they chased down the last two bombers. Ultimately the 2nd *Chutai* was annihilated, though one bomber got as far as eighty miles before it was finished off by a patrolling SBD dive-bomber.

In the meantime, only a single section of Wildcats remained on CAP, orbiting faithfully over the carrier. "Butch" O'Hare and his wingman, Lt. j.g. Marion W. Dufilho, were extremely unhappy with their assignment. Twice now the fighter director had held them over the ship during engagements with enemy aircraft—first when the flying boats were shot down and more recently when the medium bombers attacked—and both times O'Hare and Dufilho had missed all the action. Of course, "Red" Gill was simply doing his job by keeping a few planes in reserve. At the moment, with all of the other combat-ready Wildcats off chasing down bombers, O'Hare and Dufilho represented the only fighter defense for the entire task force.

As if on cue, the eight bombers of Lieutenant Commander Ito's 1st *Chutai* approached the warships. He had initially led them too far to the north, and by the time they found the task force, the 2nd *Chutai* had been all but destroyed. This was fortunate for Admiral Brown. Had Ito and Nakagawa arrived together and attacked with seventeen bombers simultaneously, they might have completely overwhelmed the task force's defenses. As it turned out, the fact that only two American fighters stood between his *chutai* and the enemy ships now worked in Ito's favor. "Red" Gill was so busy dealing with the first attack that he paid scant attention to the new contact, which first appeared on radar scopes at 1649. Minutes later, a lookout aboard the destroyer *Patterson* reported a visual sighting, by which time Ito's bombers were only ten miles from the outer screen. Alarmed, Gill vectored O'Hare and Dufhilo to intercept them. But while going through their combat checklists, the two pilots were dismayed to discover that Dufilho's guns did not work. Evidently the ammunition belts were stuck, a fairly common gripe with the early model Wildcat, in which negative-g maneuvers were prone to cause jams in the linked ammunition.

O'Hare, beside himself with frustration a few moments earlier, was suddenly the only Wildcat pilot capable of defending the task force. In the wings of his stubby gray fighter, the ammunition boxes held enough rounds for eighteen seconds of firing time. With that, he would have to take on the entire enemy formation alone.

At 1705, as the bombers closed on *Lexington*, Gill hollered on the radio for the other Wildcats to buster back to the task force. "The rest of us were heading his way, climbing up toward the oncoming Jap bombers," remembered Jimmy Thach, "but we all knew we could not intercept them before they reached the bomb-dropping position."

In training, O'Hare had impressed Thach with his grasp of combat theory and smooth gunnery. Now, fully aware that the enemy bombers "were coming on fast and had to be stopped," O'Hare knew that his first performance in actual combat would have to be flawless.

Down below, *Lexington* turned northward into the wind to recover Lovelace's division. This greatly simplified matters for the Japanese bombardiers, who would not have to compensate for crosswind in setting up their bomb runs. However, Ito wasted valuable time by wheeling the formation around to approach the *Lexington* from astern. This enabled O'Hare and Dufilho (who stayed with his leader despite his malfunctioning guns) to cut inside the bombers' turn.

As O'Hare closed rapidly from the right side of the enemy formation, some of the Japanese gunners opened fire, intent on killing him first. Ignoring the tracers, O'Hare took aim at the rearmost Mitsubishi and triggered a short burst with perfect deflection. The bomber piloted by FPO 2nd Class Ryosuke Kogiku careened out of formation, its starboard engine trailing smoke. O'Hare lined up his sights on the next aircraft and got the same result. Ribbons of vaporized gasoline streamed from the perforated wing of FPO 1st Class Koji Maeda's bomber, which also veered out of formation.

Pulling left to avoid the two stricken aircraft, O'Hare let his fighter's momentum carry him under the formation. He crossed to the opposite side and then climbed back into firing position behind the rearmost bomber on the left side of the formation. Aiming for the aircraft's opposite engine, he squeezed the trigger, and again his aim was true. The bomber shuddered under the impact of the heavy bullets and fell back, its right engine damaged and the left wing fuel tank punctured. O'Hare then fired a burst into the next bomber in line, which caught fire as he closed to nearly point-blank range. With just two brief firing runs, he had carved half of the bombers out of formation.

A few miles away, Thach was practically bending his throttle in an effort to join the fight. Later he marveled at his protégé's gunnery.

As we closed in I could see O'Hare making his attack runs with perfect flight form, exactly the way we had practiced. His shooting was wonderful—absolutely deadly. At one time as we closed in I could see three blazing Japanese planes falling between the formation and the water—he shot them down so quickly.

How O'Hare survived the concentrated fire of this Japanese formation I don't know. Each time he came in, the turtleback guns of the whole group were turned on him. I could see the tracer curling all around him, and it looked to us as if he would go at any second. Imagine this little gnat absolutely alone tearing into that formation.

The streams of tracer fire crisscrossing the sky so impressed Thach that he later described it as "the red rain of battle." Gunners in the Japanese formation fired hundreds of rounds at O'Hare, but incredibly only one bullet struck his Wildcat, disabling the airspeed indicator. Meanwhile, Dufilho gamely made several feints at the formation, drawing some of the heat away from O'Hare.

Although half of the 1st *Chutai* had been shot out of the formation, only the fourth of O'Hare's victims fell all the way to the sea. The first three, despite various degrees of damage, were brought under control by their well-trained pilots. No one noticed as the Mitsubishi piloted by Kogiku actually climbed back into formation. Petty Officer Maeda snuffed out his engine fire with a built-in carbon dioxide extinguisher but lagged behind the formation because of his reduced speed. The third bomber, piloted by FPO 1st Class Bin Mori, was too badly crippled to climb back into the formation, so he released his bombs over the water and withdrew, descending nearly to the ocean as he tried to escape.

When the remnants of the 1st *Chutai* neared the task force, bursts of antiaircraft fire suddenly erupted near O'Hare's Wildcat. At least two pieces of shrapnel pierced his plane, yet he continued to set up his third gunnery run. Unaware that one of the planes he had hit on his first pass was now back in formation, he was misled by the size of the attacking group. "By this time the Japs . . . were right on top of the release point. They *had* to be stopped any way at all: there were five of them still. I came in close, shot into the fifth one till he fell away, then gave the remaining four a general burst until my ammunition was exhausted."

O'Hare fired at the outermost bomber on the left side of the formation, piloted by Lt. j.g. Akira Mitani. It fell in flames, giving O'Hare a clear shot at the formation's lead aircraft. Contrary to his statement that he fired "a general burst," O'Hare targeted the port engine of Ito's bomber, and once again his aim was precise. The bullets ripped through the nacelle with such kinetic force that the fourteen-cylinder radial engine was literally torn from its mountings. The entire engine, propeller and all, tumbled crazily from the left wing, and an instant later the bomber itself spun out of control due to the sudden absence of weight and thrust.

With the lead bomber out of the way, O'Hare fired the last of his ammunition—perhaps forty rounds—into the lagging bomber flown by Petty Officer Maeda. Remarkably, despite the additional damage, the Mitsubishi stayed in the air.

BECAUSE OF O'HARE'S extraordinary shooting, only three bombers of the 1st *Chutai* were able to attack *Lexington*. Maeda, being too far out of position to bomb the carrier, aimed for the heavy cruiser *Minneapolis* off the carrier's port bow, but both of his bombs missed. At 1709, just as the last Wildcat from Lovelace's division squeaked aboard *Lexington*, the three Mitsubishis arrived at the release point and dropped their bombs. Sherman calmly ordered the rudder hard over, and all six bombs fell wide of the carrier, though one hit the water near enough to sprinkle the flight deck with shrapnel.

In all, seventeen *rikko* had charged at the carrier in two waves, yet "Lady Lex" was hit by nothing more than a few metal shards.

AT THE POINT of bomb release, two of the three attackers were still relatively unscathed. That soon changed as "Doc" Sellstrom shot one down approximately eight miles from the task force. This was probably the G4M flown by FPO 2nd Class Tokiharu Baba. The other undamaged Mitsubishi, piloted by FPO 1st Class Kosuke Ono, was subsequently hit in the starboard engine by antiaircraft fire. Several fighters gave chase, resulting in a high-speed gunfight as Ono tried to evade them at low altitude. His bomber proved unusually rugged, enduring intense attacks from both the left and the right that killed or wounded several of his crewmen. But return fire from the surviving gunners was still accurate. One bullet hit Noel Gayler's windscreen, starring the Plexiglas, and eventually the Wildcats withdrew.

Similarly, Petty Officer Mori's damaged bomber came under heavy pursuit as he tried to get away from the task force. Lieutenant Edward H. Allen of Scouting Squadron 2, having already knocked down a Mitsubishi of the 2nd *Chutai* with his Dauntless scout bomber, spotted the fleeing G4M and gave chase. Mori made no attempt to maneuver. It was a life-and-death race, with both planes going flat out. Allen's SBD was a mile or two per hour faster, and over a stretch of several minutes he gradually overtook Mori's damaged aircraft. Seeing no defensive fire from the left waist gun, Allen exploited the weak spot. He pulled almost directly beneath the bomber, as if flying in formation, and positioned the SBD so that the rear gunner could fire his flexible .30-caliber Browning machine gun straight up into the belly of the G4M at point-blank range. At least two crewmen were killed aboard Mori's aircraft, but despite the casualties and heavy damage, the *rikko* was uncharacteristically rugged and refused to fall. Lieutenant Allen, finding himself 150 miles from the carrier, had to give up the chase.

THE MOST REMARKABLE feat of flying that day—O'Hare's gunnery aside—was accomplished by the pilots in Ito's lead bomber. Somehow, after the aircraft went out of control with its port engine blown clean off, the crew not only regained control but doggedly resumed the attack. Sans engine, the *rikko* was completely unbalanced. Where its port engine should have been was a tangle of broken and twisted structural parts that produced an enormous amount of drag. The pilots countered it with full opposite rudder and maximum power on the good engine, their superb airmanship keeping the crippled bomber aloft, if only for a few minutes. Ito and his crew knew they were doomed. Despite the aerodynamic handicap, they boldly attempted a *taiatari*, literally translated as "body crashing," hoping to destroy *Lexington* with a suicide attack.

Just as with Nakagawa's attempt earlier, Ito's plane approached the carrier from astern at low level. And just as before, the rapid-fire weapons cut loose when the suicidal bomber came within range. But this time the mangled aircraft made no effort to match the ship's maneuvers. Perhaps it was all the crew could do to hold the plane straight and level; perhaps the *Lexington*'s withering gunfire killed them at the controls. Whatever the case, the bomber flew beyond the carrier and then plunged into the sea less than a mile off the port bow, leaving a slick of burning fuel that remained on the surface for several minutes.

With the skies finally clear of attackers, the Wildcats returned to *Lexington* and bounced down one by one on their narrow landing gear. Hundreds of the ship's crew converged on the flight deck, cheering wildly as the sweat-soaked pilots climbed from their cockpits. O'Hare was mobbed. Almost everyone topside in Task Force 11 had witnessed his marksmanship as he singlehandedly saved the *Lexington* from severe damage—or worse.

A FEW HOURS LATER, at approximately 1945, two battled-scarred *rikko* landed at Vunakanau. A total of four bombers from the 1st *Chutai* had escaped the immediate area of the task force, but only petty officers Kogiku and Maeda made it back to Rabaul in their damaged aircraft.

Although no other bombers returned to the airdrome, one got close. Petty Officer Mori and the survivors of his shot-up bomber struggled homeward without the benefit of maps or charts, all of which had been destroyed by a burst of antiaircraft fire. Using a navigation method known as "dead reckoning," Mori headed toward New Britain while worrying about the fuel state. The left wing tank had been punctured by Butch O'Hare's bullets, and it was obvious the remaining fuel would not last long.

Soon after night fell, the Mitsubishi ran out of gas. Mori made a wheels-up water landing in the darkness, hitting the surface with "a strong impact," and then swam clear with a few other crewmen. The wreckage sank with the bodies of the dead still inside, leaving the survivors afloat in the darkness, uncertain of their whereabouts. Seeing a distant light, they shouted wildly but got no answer. They fired a signal flare, and the light drew nearer, causing moments of apprehension. The crew agreed among themselves that if they were in enemy territory, they would commit suicide. To their great relief they heard "voices speaking in the Nippon language" and were soon rescued. Their *rikko* had come down in Simpson Harbor, only a few miles short of their destination. Considering the circumstances, it was an extraordinary feat of airmanship and navigation.

The other bomber, piloted by Petty Officer Ono, limped away from the task force with its right engine shot out, several crewmen dead, and gasoline leaking from the left wing tank. The plane was still two hundred miles from Rabaul when the left engine quit from fuel starvation, but at that very moment, "like a blessing from heaven," an island appeared. Ono had stumbled across the Nuguria Islands, a tiny atoll east of New Ireland, and he quickly ditched the bomber alongside a beach. Ono and two other crewmen survived the crash-landing and staggered ashore, where islanders offered them coconuts and food in exchange for cigarettes. After the ordeal they'd just experienced, however, the aviators were "in no mood" to eat.

The next morning they awoke to the sound of a low-flying navy plane from Rabaul. As it flew over, a parcel was tossed out. The package landed in the sea and was lost, but the castaways were relieved by the knowledge that they had been spotted. Later that day another plane flew over, dropping food along with a message indicating that a rescue party was on its way. Ono and the other two survivors spent the rest of the day cremating the bodies of the dead crew and were picked up the next day by boat.

PERHAPS TO OFFSET their catastrophic losses, the few surviving members of the 4th Air Group submitted grossly exaggerated reports. Toshio Miyake, a naval correspondent at Rabaul, spun their accounts into a major victory. Within days, newspapers across Japan announced that an enemy carrier had been blasted off "New Guinea." The accompanying story claimed that ten American planes had been shot down in a "spectacular air dual," during which "some of the Nippon planes resorted to fierce body-crashing tactics, severely damaging the aircraft carrier and causing it to burst into flames." A cruiser was also claimed as sunk, while actual Japanese losses were halved with the admission that nine planes "had failed to return."

Over the next few weeks, at least five more articles about the air battle appeared in Japanese newspapers, each filled with dramatic details glorifying the airmen who had allegedly crashed their planes into the American carrier. Ito, Mitani, Nakagawa, and Seto had all met "an honorable death" and were venerated as warrior gods. Never mind that only two crews had actually *attempted* suicide attacks, neither of which succeeded. To the Japanese, it was far more important to idolize the death of the airmen as a noble sacrifice.

The *Johokyoku* (Information Bureau), which had direct control over all news published or broadcast in Japan, made certain the people never knew the truth about the battle, which had been an absolute disaster for the 24th Air Flotilla. In the span of a few hours, Rear Admiral Goto's air groups had lost thirteen Type 1 bombers and two Type 97 flying boats in combat, and two additional bombers were forced to ditch with dead crewmen aboard. Later it was learned that the third flying boat on the morning patrol had failed to return. Although its disappearance was evidently not combat-related, the names of ten more crewmen were added to the long list of the dead. In what was by far the worst day yet for the Imperial Navy's air arm, more than 120 highly trained aviators lost their lives on February 20, including a group commander and two division leaders.

DESPITE THE FACT that the planned raid on Rabaul had been canceled, the *Lexington's* air group had plenty to celebrate as the task force withdrew to safer waters. Fourteen pilots and at least one rear gunner were officially credited with shooting down sixteen bombers and two flying boats. In exchange, Fighting Squadron 3 had lost only two Wildcats and one pilot.

Recognition for the victory came quickly. The Navy's highest medal for combat valor, the Navy Cross, was awarded to no less than seven pilots, including Thach and Gayler. Eight others received the next highest award, a Distinguished Flying Cross. The achievements were certainly important, even spectacular, but for the most part the deeds were blown out of proportion. Had the events occurred later in the war, when the guidelines for combat medals were much more rigid, most of the pilots would have received lesser awards.

And then there was Butch O'Hare, whose amazing exploits purged a family scandal. Less than three years earlier, while Butch underwent flight training at Pensacola, his father had been murdered in a gangland hit ordered by the most notorious criminal in American history, Al Capone. The assassination was not unexpected. Edgar O'Hare, known to the Chicago underworld as "Eddie," had made a fortune from the dog tracks he operated during the late 1920s and early 1930s. He was well entrenched in Capone's gang as an attorney and business partner, but he decided to cooperate with the federal government in bringing the mobster to justice. Capone was convicted of income tax evasion and served most of his sentence on "the Rock," the infamous Alcatraz Island federal penitentiary. Later, while finishing out a separate sentence at Terminal Island for a misdemeanor conviction, he ordered the hit on Eddie O'Hare. The stigma for Butch, aside from his father's association with Capone, was a persistent rumor that his appointment to Annapolis had been part of an arranged deal with the government in exchange for his father's testimony.

Wherever the truth lay, O'Hare's brilliant gunnery erased all doubts about his reputation. With just three firing passes he had knocked six bombers out of formation. At first he claimed all six as victories. He was initially supported by Thach, who reported seeing three bombers falling simultaneously, but then people began to recall that three bombers had attacked the *Lexington* while a fourth attempted to bomb the *Minneapolis*. Therefore, because everyone assumed the formation had consisted of nine planes to begin with, O'Hare was officially credited with shooting down five, making him the first American "ace-in-a-day."

Assessing the accuracy of his claims is fairly simple. The combat log of the 4th Air Group shows that the 1st *Chutai* consisted of eight bombers, not nine. O'Hare fired into six, of which only two crashed as a direct result. The other four were damaged, some severely, but Ito's bomber was finished off by *Lexington*'s antiaircraft batteries; Kojiku and Maeda landed intact at Rabaul; and Mori ditched his aircraft in Simpson Harbor. As a result, O'Hare should have earned only partial credit for the aircraft flown by Ito and Mori.

In O'Hare's defense, he had no time to confirm whether his victims fell to the sea or stayed in the air. "I figured there wasn't much to do except shoot at them," he later told correspondents. "I would go for one, let him have it, then pull out quick so that the exploding, burning plane would not fall on top of me. Then I'd go for the next one like the first."

More importantly, only three bombers attacked *Lexington*, unsuccessfully at that, because of O'Hare's aggressive attacks. Everyone was eager to proclaim him the ship's savior, and the American public desperately needed good news along with a live hero. In O'Hare, they got both. Initially he was recommended for a Navy Cross, but Admiral King upgraded the award to a Medal of Honor, and it was approved by Congress on April 16, 1942.

O'Hare, the first pilot of World War II to receive the nation's highest military award for valor, was not destined to survive the conflict. He was killed in late 1943 during night combat operations in the Central Pacific, ironically while intercepting a raid by the same type of bombers.

After the war, the city of Chicago honored him by changing the name of a local airfield from Orchard Depot to O'Hare International. In the decades since, millions of travelers have passed through the airport, one of the world's busiest, unaware of the historic links to Fortress Rabaul and the ill-fated "land attackers" of the 4th Air Group.

CHAPTER 10

Carmichael's Raid

BY THE MIDDLE OF February 1942, Japanese forces had captured vast amounts of territory. Guam, Wake, the Bismarcks, and Malaya had already fallen like so many ten-pins; and Burma, the Philippines, and the Netherlands East Indies were about to follow. Imperial General Headquarters, pleased that the Southern Offensive was "making better progress than expected," ordered Vice Admiral Inoue to capture "various important points in British New Guinea and in the Solomon Islands . . . as quickly as possible."

There was no reason to doubt that Inoue would succeed. All of his previous operations had achieved the required goals with little opposition. When the Rising Sun flag flew over New Guinea and the Solomons, the lines of supply and communication between Australia and the United States would be severed, forcing the Australians to sue for peace. With the Commonwealth out of the war, the Americans would no longer have a viable base in the theater for opposing the Southern Offensive.

Inoue's grand plan for the conquest of New Guinea was to begin with the simultaneous invasions of Lae and Salamaua, originally scheduled for March 3. However, the disastrous losses suffered by the 24th Air Flotilla on February 20 forced Inoue to delay the landings while Rear Admiral Goto rebuilt his air strength. As soon as enough aircraft and flight crews were available, Inoue intended to "inflict strong pressure on Australia by means of air power," a euphemism for pounding Port Moresby into submission.

As part of Inoue's strategy, the first attack on the Australian continent had been conducted on February 19. Once again the Japanese employed overwhelming force, sending 190 carrier planes from Nagumo's First Air Fleet, supplemented by fifty-four bombers from the Celebes, to attack the port city of Darwin. Damage was severe: eight Allied vessels sunk, thirteen others beached or damaged, and approximately two dozen aircraft destroyed, including nine USAAF P-40s shot down. The death toll exceeded 250 civilians and military personnel.

That same morning, the B-17s of Major Carmichael's 14th Reconnaissance Squadron arrived at Townsville, Queensland. At a time when Australians were sick of constant bad news, the sight of a dozen Flying Fortresses must have thrilled the local populace. Each of the four-engine bombers seemed enormous and bristled with machine guns: two .50-caliber weapons in a dorsal power turret, another pair in a remote-controlled belly turret, two more in the tail, plus individual guns at the waist positions on both sides of the fuselage. A ninth gun could be extended from a hatch above the radio compartment, and two .30-caliber guns protruded from panels in the Plexiglas nose.

Carmichael and his flight crews immediately began to prepare the bombers for action. One of the navigators, 2nd Lt. John J. Steinbinder, wrote excitedly in his diary: "Tomorrow we go on our first mission. We are to bomb Rabaul."

The original plan to attack the stronghold in coordination with Task Force 11 was still in effect, or so Carmichael thought, but the enemy raid on Darwin changed the squadron's priorities. "Mission called off due to great concentration of Japanese naval and aerial forces," noted Steinbinder. "We are to move on to Cloncurry, 450 miles in the interior of Australia, so that if the Japs bomb Townsville we shall be out of the way."

There were no Allied fighters or antiaircraft guns at Townsville to protect the B-17s, which were far too valuable to risk. So the 14th Reconnaissance Squadron moved to Cloncurry, deep into the outback, where they found little of interest except wild kangaroos, stifling heat, and hordes of flies. Recreation consisted of an open-air movie theater, and one old hotel had a small pub with enough room at the bar for perhaps ten patrons. Steinbinder described the town as "a hell hole," and who could blame him? "Flies fly into your mouth, up your nostrils, into your eyes & ears," he wrote. "Oh! They sure are hell. It's terrifically hot here: 40° Centigrade or 105 Fahrenheit."

In many ways, Steinbinder was typical of the junior officers who had joined the U.S. Army Air Corps prior to the war. Raised in a small town in middle-America, he spent his youth on a dairy farm near Oberlin, Ohio. Unlike the great majority of his peers, however, English was not Steinbinder's first language. His parents were Hungarian immigrants, and he grew up speaking their native tongue first. Diligence in high school helped him earn a scholarship to Oberlin College, where he received a degree in chemistry. After graduating in 1940, he volunteered for the U.S. Army with hopes of training as a pilot but failed to meet the service's strict vision standards. He was therefore packed off to Miami for navigator training at the Pan American Airlines facility.

A year later and ten thousand miles from home, he sat amid the flies at Cloncurry and tried to make sense of his rapidly changing world.

ON THE MORNING of February 22, the 14th Reconnaissance Squadron was ordered back to Townsville. The B-17s were to hit Rabaul on their own. Carmichael's squadron lacked ground support personnel, so the over-worked flight crews had to perform all necessary maintenance themselves. Three bombers were scrubbed from the mission for mechanical reasons, leaving nine available to fly back to Garbutt Field outside Townsville. There, the enlisted crews spent the day preparing, refueling, and arming the B-17s while the officers attended briefings.

Major Carmichael and his men were introduced to two RAAF Catalina pilots—Wing Cmdr. Julius A. "Dick" Cohen, commanding officer of 11 Squadron at Port Moresby, and Plt. Off. Norman V. Robertson, 20 Squadron—who would ride aboard two of the B-17s to assist with navigation and identification of targets.* The American airmen needed the help. Not only did they lack experience in the region, there were no navigation aids or even reliable charts available, and the first leg of the mission would be flown in total darkness over long stretches of shark-infested waters.

The RAAF's allocation of two valuable pilots demonstrated their faith in the Flying Fortress. Cohen in particular represented years of experience

---

*In 1947, then-Group Captain Cohen petitioned to change his legal name. Later knighted, he is known today as Sir Richard Kingsland.

the Australians could not afford to lose, but he remained modest about his role. "I was there for comfort," he said later. "Carmichael was a very competent pilot, and he had a competent navigator. I didn't do anything significant. It just gave them comfort to know that they had a pilot with local experience on board."

The mission profile was essentially unchanged from the original plan, which called for the crews to take off at midnight and attack Rabaul at sunrise. While waiting for the scheduled start-up time, the men endured a few restless hours. Many wrote letters to their loved ones before heading into combat for the first time. John Steinbinder penned one to his mother and another to his college sweetheart, Margaret Gamble, expressing sentiments that he wanted to share "in case anything happens."

He needn't have bothered. For his crew, led by 1st Lt. James R. DuBose Jr., the much-anticipated mission ended without the bomber moving an inch. "Our #3 engine refused to run," lamented Steinbinder in his diary. The mechanical glitch reduced the number of bombers to eight, but the squadron's troubles were just beginning. While taxiing in the darkness at Townsville, two of the remaining bombers collided and were scratched from the mission, one damaged so severely that it never flew again.

As a result of all the difficulties on the ground, only six B-17s took off from Garbutt Field that night. More trouble occurred about an hour later when the formation ran into the inter-tropic front over the Coral Sea. First Lieutenant Harry W. Spieth became temporarily lost and returned to Townsville, where he explained he could not get around the wall of cumulous clouds that towered to forty thousand feet. Nobody questioned his decision. Formation flying was challenging enough in broad daylight, but at night and in bad weather the conditions could be terrifying. Visual acuity and depth perception were diminished, and the slightest motions seemed greatly amplified.

Now down to five, the B-17s punched through the storm system in two groups. Three of the Fortresses, led by Major Carmichael, gradually fell behind the other two as they continued toward the target, costing Carmichael the distinction of being the first American to bomb Rabaul. The honors went instead to Capt. William Lewis Jr., who arrived over Simpson Harbor at 0647 with 1st Lt. Frederick C. Eaton Jr. on his wing.

Clouds and volcanic steam obscured the anchorage, so the two B-17s orbited overhead for almost half an hour before the bombardiers were able to identify targets. Lewis made a standard bomb run, dropped his four six-hundred-pounders, and turned toward Port Moresby as planned. Eaton's bombs failed to release, so he doubled back over the target for another attempt. By this time, enemy antiaircraft shells began to burst in the vicinity, and as Eaton made his second run a large-caliber shell punched clean through his B-17's right wing without exploding.

The bombers' loitering, not to mention Eaton's second run over the target, gave the Japanese ample time to scramble several fighters. Six Zeros and two Type 96s rose up from Lakunai, and while Lewis got away cleanly, Eaton was chased almost to New Guinea in a prolonged gunfight. His crew claimed two enemy fighters shot down and another "crippled," but no corresponding losses were recorded by the 4th Air Group that day. Conversely, Eaton's bomber was struck by a single cannon shell, but the crew escaped injury and the aircraft sustained only minor damage.

The bigger problem for Eaton was high fuel consumption. Calculations provided by the mission planners had been based on peacetime experience; but in actual combat the B-17s were using far more fuel than estimated. This was compounded when both Lewis and Eaton spent more than thirty minutes over the target. The second bomb run cost Eaton a lot more fuel, and after evading the fighters he discovered there wasn't enough in the tanks to make it over the Owen Stanley Mountains.

Looking for a suitable landing place northeast of the great range, Eaton spied what appeared to be a grassy plain just inland from the New Guinea coast. He made a textbook wheels-up landing, as uneventful as a crash landing could be, but the bomber decelerated quickly and then sank several feet into muck. The solid-looking field turned out to be the Agaiambo Swamp, a vast wetlands. Although Eaton and his crew climbed from the bomber unhurt, their adventure was just beginning. Five weeks later, after battling malaria and 220 miles of wretched terrain, they finally returned to Port Moresby.*

BY THE TIME Carmichael's element of three B-17s arrived over Rabaul, several minutes behind Lewis's flight, interceptors were waiting. "I don't

---

*Eaton's B-17, later nicknamed the "Swamp Ghost," is the most famous war relic in the Southwest Pacific. Private salvagers extracted it in 2006, and following years of controversies regarding ownership, the aircraft left New Guinea aboard a ship bound for the United States as this book went to press.

think the Japanese were yet ready to fight," recalled Carmichael, "so it wasn't a real severe attack."

The enemy fighters became more aggressive after the B-17s dropped their bombs. Dick Cohen, accustomed to the barebones Catalinas of the RAAF, was glad to sit on an armor-plated seat in the cockpit of Carmichael's B-17. "Some Japanese fighters came by," he remembered. "I could see the Zeros struggling to get enough height to make a pass at us. Their bullets were small, but there were quite a few holes in the B-17, and a couple of the crew were wounded."

He was right: Zeros peppered Carmichael's aircraft, causing superficial wounds to the radio operator and tail gunner, but the Flying Fortress lived up to its reputation for ruggedness. "We were a formidable platform for the Japanese to approach," Cohen added. "Our gunners were very good, the aircraft maintained good defensive formation, and I think the Japanese had a pretty rough time."

The B-17 hit hardest was flown by 1st Lt. Harry N. Brandon, who needed every bit of skill to control the bomber after his right inboard engine burst into flames and the outer engine was shut down by mistake. The forgiving B-17 stayed aloft on the two left engines while the fire was extinguished, and eventually the right outboard engine was restarted. A pilot from the 4th Air Group at Rabaul, FPO 2nd Class Motosuna Yoshida, claimed a B-17 and was credited with a victory; however, no Flying Fortresses except Eaton's were lost.

After a long return flight, four B-17s crossed the Owen Stanley Mountains and landed at Port Moresby. Cohen and Robertson returned to their RAAF squadrons, and the bombers were refueled before taking off again for Australia. Reaching Townsville on the afternoon of February 23, Carmichael's small clutch of bombers completed a mission of more than fourteen hours' duration.

For all the effort, the first American raid on Rabaul was a big disappointment. The results were officially recorded as "not observed," and Carmichael's personal assessment of the mission was equally modest. "We attacked Rabaul with whatever number of planes we had available," he said years later, "but we didn't hit anything."

Other sources support Carmichael's statement, if only by omission. Australian prisoners in the Malaguna Camp stockade were completely unaware that Simpson Harbor had been attacked by B-17s that morning, likely because of the cloud cover and the bombers' high altitude. Similarly, there was no mention of the B-17s in the diary kept by Private Hisaeda of the 55th Field Hospital, though he recorded virtually every other raid during that period. Less than twenty-four hours later, for example, he wrote of an attack by three enemy aircraft, noting that one was shot down. As usual, Hisaeda's information was accurate. Flight Lieutenant Ernest V. Beaumont and his eight-man crew, flying one of three Catalinas that raided Rabaul on February 24, failed to return from the mission.

ON FEBRUARY 26, Dick Cohen led several Catalinas back to Rabaul for another night attack. By that time he had been flying combat missions without letup for the better part of two years, including a stint with the Royal Air Force in England, and was exhausted. The tempo of operations placed enormous demands on all of the crews and their dwindling number of airworthy Catalinas, but 11 and 20 Squadrons kept pecking away at the Japanese stronghold. Unfortunately, the enemy's defenses were rapidly improving. "The Japanese were very alert," Cohen remembered. "They'd flick searchlights on us at once, and we realized that they were either very efficient or had radar."

On this night, as the flying boats approached Rabaul at seven thousand feet, the ships down in the darkened harbor looked like toys. But the bursts of antiaircraft fire shaking the Catalinas were real enough, giving the bombardiers a difficult time as they tried to align their sights. Tired and frustrated, Cohen decided that something had to give. Spotting a large Japanese ship alongside one of the wharves, he spontaneously decided to make an unorthodox attack. "We were fed up with being shot at from down below, and fed up with being attacked by fighters," he said later. "I got it into my head to attack the Toboi Wharf, which was visible on that particular night, a clear night. So I just rolled over and dived on it."

Catalinas were never intended for dive-bombing, but Cohen pushed his aircraft into a steep power dive that terrified his crew. Flight Lieutenant Robert M. Seymour, his copilot, later told Cohen it was the most frightening experience of the entire war for him. Up in the bow, the bombardier had a dizzying view as the seaplane plunged earthward. At 1,300 feet, Cohen shouted "release bombs!" over the intercom and hauled back on the control column. Twelve 250-pounders detached from their external wing racks and exploded a few seconds later, rocking the Catalina as Cohen pulled out at mast height over Simpson Harbor.

MAJOR CARMICHAEL was eager to hit Rabaul again. The 14th Reconnaissance Squadron was scheduled for its second attempt on February 28, but the mission had to be canceled when more than half the flight crews fell ill with dengue fever. The conditions at Cloncurry were ideal for the viral outbreak, which takes about a week to incubate. It waylaid dozens of men with high fevers, skin rashes, painful joints, and severe headaches. The dusty heat and swarming flies only added to the sick men's misery, which lasted several days before the infection ran its course. By the end of the first week of March, the squadron had completed only a few reconnaissance missions.

Thus far the oddball B-17 squadron, still attached to the U.S. Navy, had been completely ineffective. And for the Allies, there was more troubling news: improvements would be few and far between, and very slow in coming.

CHAPTER 11

Yanks Down Under

O N CHRISTMAS EVE 1941, almost two months before Carmichael's first raid on Rabaul, President Roosevelt met with Prime Minister Churchill and the combined service chiefs in Washington, D.C., to discuss strategy for prosecuting what had become a two-ocean war. The attendees of the conference, code-named Arcadia, examined the various priorities of the Allied forces in both the European and Pacific theaters, and concluded that Hitler was the most dangerous enemy—this despite the shock that still lingered from the launching of Japan's Southern Offensive less than three weeks earlier. Although the smoke had barely cleared over Pearl Harbor, the United States and Great Britain agreed to prosecute the war against Germany first.

Naturally, this decision did not sit well with the Allied commanders in Hawaii and Australia. Because of Arcadia, only a trickle of war materiel and personnel would be sent to the Pacific combat zone, at least until such time as the factories and training programs could catch up with the enormous demands.

To compound the problem, Allied air strength in the Southwest Pacific was being steadily whittled away. Combat losses accounted for a relatively small percentage of the total depletion, with mishaps and mechanical failures having the greatest impact on aircraft availability. The flight crews had to perform necessary repairs themselves, and it was not uncommon for them to toil eighteen hours a day under deplorable conditions. Although they often created ingenious solutions to get planes ready for missions, the repairs were stopgap measures at best. Gradually and inevitably, the rate of mechanical breakdowns increased.

Only a handful of American air units existed in Australia during the early months of 1942, and none had a full complement of maintenance or ground support personnel. Some squadrons, barely organized, were all that remained of the once-proud Far East Air Force, formerly based in the Philippines. Smashed by the Southern Offensive in the first days of the war, the survivors put up only minor resistance before withdrawing to Java. The remnants that escaped the Japanese onslaught were eventually pulled all the way across Australia to Melbourne, and the few remaining planes were in deplorable shape. The crewmembers loafed for days on end, suffering from low morale.

Another problem affecting American air operations was the complicated command structure. On January 5, 1942, Lt. Gen. George H. Brett was named commander of all U.S. forces in Australia. One of his first actions was to create seven military zones, which he called "base sections," with centers at Darwin, Townsville, Brisbane, Melbourne, Adelaide, Perth, and Sydney. The arrangement proved awkward, mainly because the RAAF had already established five different zones, each commanded by an officer who had ultimate control over all aircraft in his sector, whether American or Australian. Not surprisingly, coordination of operations between the zones and different nationalities was an administrative nightmare.

The situation in Australia was tied directly to events in the far-off Philippines, where General Douglas MacArthur had made some poor decisions. When the Southern Offensive commenced on December 8, 1941, he was so stunned that he was virtually incapacitated for the first critical hours, unavailable to his subordinates except for his chief of staff, Col. Richard K. Sutherland. MacArthur's difficulties only intensified as detachments of the Japanese Fourteenth Army landed on Luzon on December 10. Twelve days later the main invasion force went ashore near Baguio, north of Manila, and within forty-eight hours MacArthur's vaunted army folded. Tens of thousands of American and Filipino troops were forced to fight a delaying action as they retreated southward toward the Bataan Peninsula.

In the wake of the debacle at Pearl Harbor, Rear Adm. Husband Kimmel and Maj. Gen. Walter Short had been swiftly sacked, but there was not even a formal investigation into MacArthur's actions in the Philippines. To the contrary, he received a Medal of Honor, an award clearly intended to boost American morale during those grim days. MacArthur did spend several weeks under siege in a bunker at Corregidor, during which he visited the front-line troops exactly once. For that, he earned their eternal disdain and a new nickname: "Dugout Doug."

Major General Lewis H. Brereton, commander of the Far East Air Force and the man whom MacArthur blamed for its swift demise, was banished to Australia. He remained officially in charge of the air units until January 5, 1942, when General Brett took over as commander of American forces in Australia. Soon thereafter MacArthur transferred Brereton to India, thereby getting him out of the region altogether. In Australia, meanwhile, all of the Army Air Corps units were lumped into Brett's command with the exception of the 14th Reconnaissance Squadron, which remained for the time being under the control of Vice Admiral Leary.

With so many overlapping commands, it was all but impossible to keep the egos and ambitions of the top players from influencing operations. Brett, for example, cultivated a close relationship with Australia's newly elected prime minister, John Curtin. But the ousted Country Party also wooed Brett, promising him "the high command position" if they were restored to power in the next election. Brett would later deny that he pursued the offer, but he deliberately integrated his staff with numerous Australians. He also created a directorate system by which certain subordinates, including Australian officers, were authorized to issue orders in his name. Finally, he made a policy of mixing RAAF personnel among the crews of American bombers.

At Australian airdromes, American airmen were considered guests of the RAAF. They followed Aussie procedures and protocol, and although the combat missions were generally conducted with a spirit of cooperation, the Americans gradually became resentful of taking orders. Frustrations simmered. Cultural differences that at first seemed charming became exasperating. American mechanics, working side by side with their hosts to repair damaged planes and assemble new ones, were especially aggravated by the Aussies' habit of blithely stopping all work every morning and afternoon for a cup of tea and a "smoke-o."

§

THE 24TH AIR FLOTILLA resumed its bombing campaign against Port Moresby on February 24, the day after Carmichael hit Rabaul. Nine Type 1 *rikko* of the 4th Air Group, escorted by an equal number of Zeros, attacked Seven Mile airdrome from an altitude of sixteen thousand feet. Their accurate bombing destroyed a Hudson and a civilian aircraft on the ground, obliterated virtually all of the structures (along with some vitally important vehicles), and killed a member of 32 Squadron.

The Australians, lacking legitimate fighters at Port Moresby, did not attempt to intercept the attack. The only planes available were some battle-weary Hudsons and a few Wirraways. Antiaircraft defenses consisted of four 3.7-inch and six 3-inch guns, plus some Lewis machine guns manned by the militia garrison.

Wing Commander John Lerew, now in command of 32 Squadron at Seven Mile, was justifiably worried about the vulnerability of his Hudsons. Due to conditions he described as "treacherously boggy," the aircraft were parked in exposed positions along both sides of the runway. Remembering all too well what had happened at Rabaul, Lerew pushed his men hard to get dispersal areas built. He also sent sharply worded messages to Townsville requesting heavy construction equipment, but his signals went unanswered. Instead, Northeast Area Headquarters ordered him to move his planes to Horn Island, 340 miles southwest of Port Moresby in the Torres Straits. This created a logistical nightmare for Lerew, whose reconnaissance planes still had to stage through Port Moresby to conduct their patrols. As a concession, headquarters promised to provide advance notice of each mission, enabling the assigned crews to move up to Port Moresby ahead of time, but the Aussie airmen had a much bigger concern than mere logistics. Until some fighters were brought up to Port Moresby, the Japanese were guaranteed to have total air superiority over New Guinea.

As if to underscore the point, the 4th Air Group attacked again on February 28, this time with seventeen Type 1 bombers escorted by six Zeros. Concentrating on the seaplane base, the Japanese destroyed three Catalinas at their moorings and damaged another. The RAAF headquarters building received a direct hit that destroyed numerous flight records and other important documents.

The cost to the Japanese was a single Zero, piloted by FPO 1st Class Katsuaki Nagatomo. Purportedly hit by a lucky shot from an antiaircraft gun, he suffered burns but managed to parachute from his flaming Zero and drift down into Bootless Bay. Nagatomo was taken prisoner—a fate worse than death to a Japanese airman—and the disgrace of his capture was not revealed by the 4th Air Group. Instead he was listed officially as dead, but in the end it didn't matter. Sent to Australia, Nagatomo was one of more than 230 Japanese who died during a large-scale breakout attempt from a POW camp outside Cowra, New South Wales, in August 1944.

Meanwhile, the raid by the 4th Air Group left the Australians with only two Catalinas and a Hudson immediately available for duty at Port Moresby. Keeping up the pressure, the Japanese continued to attack almost daily, creating a desperate situation for the Australian garrison. Patrol missions were greatly curtailed, and the night raids by Catalinas had to be temporarily discontinued. This was exactly the result Vice Admiral Inoue had hoped for: fewer Allied reconnaissance planes meant greater freedom of movement and less risk of detection for his own units.

IN THE PHILIPPINES, key events unfolded that would soon alter the Southwest Pacific battlefront. On February 22, General MacArthur received orders to evacuate Corregidor and make his way to Australia. The directive, signed by President Roosevelt along with the U.S. Army chief of staff and the secretary of war, authorized a brief delay on Mindanao so that MacArthur could judge the feasibility of its defense; afterward he was to proceed directly to Melbourne.

An executive order from the president was essentially the only way to get MacArthur to leave the Philippines. He loathed the notion of leaving his men under a cloud of humiliation and defeat, but he had no choice: he'd been selected to assume command of all American forces in Australia, superseding George Brett. More importantly, Roosevelt and Churchill wanted him in Melbourne, the Australians wanted him in Melbourne, and the American people wanted him rescued from the Philippines. MacArthur grudgingly acquiesced but delayed his departure until the situation was stable enough, in his judgment, to avoid an adverse "psychological" affect on his men.

Because all of the airfields on Luzon were in Japanese hands, arrangements were made to transfer MacArthur, his household (wife, son, and Chinese amah), and staff members to the north coast of Mindanao in U.S. Navy PT boats. Long-range army planes would then meet the evacuees at

Del Monte Field and bring them to Australia. For that purpose, MacArthur radioed Brett on March 1 and requested three Flying Fortresses for transportation from Mindanao.

Unfortunately, the few surviving B-17s of the Far East Air Force were a sorry lot. Located in Melbourne, the 7th and 19th Bomb Groups (Heavy) had been pulled back from the combat zone after months of hardship in the Philippines and Java. Both groups suffered from low morale, and their B-17s were in dire need of overhaul. Brett therefore approached Vice Admiral Leary and requested four B-17Es, the newest in Australia, from Carmichael's 14th Reconnaissance Squadron.

Leary refused. "I'd like to help you, Brett," he said, "but it's quite impossible. We need those planes here and can't spare them for a ferry job, no matter how important it is."

Leary had good reason to hoard his assets. The Imperial Navy roamed the seas with impunity and just days earlier had soundly defeated a joint American-British-Dutch-Australian (ABDA) naval force in the Java Sea. But Leary was being less than honest when he said the B-17s could not be spared. In fact they were underutilized, thanks to the outbreak of dengue fever at Cloncurry. Whatever his real motives were, Leary remained uncooperative. Brett therefore ordered the war-weary units down in Melbourne to conduct a "special mission to the north."

On March 11, the same day that MacArthur and his party left Corregidor aboard four PT boats, a flight of four B-17s with minimal crews proceeded from Melbourne to Daly Waters, a remote airfield deep in the Northern Territory. After refueling, the bombers flew to Batchelor Field south of Darwin, where the airmen learned for the first time about their special task: they were to deliver much-needed supplies to Mindanao, then pick up General MacArthur and his party and bring them back to Australia. Extra fuel tanks were installed in the bomb bays for the three-thousand-mile round trip, scheduled to begin the next day at noon. If all went according to plan, the B-17s would arrive at Del Monte Field well after dark to minimize the possibility of interception by enemy fighters.

But the mission began badly on March 12 and went downhill from there. In the words of Capt. Henry C. Godwin, all four of the B-17s "were really in terrible shape." He did not exaggerate. One bomber failed to get off the ground due to engine trouble, another turned back for the same reason after just fifty miles, and the remaining two were plagued with additional problems as they chugged up to Del Monte. The Fortress flown by 1st Lt. Harl Pease Jr. had a partial hydraulic failure that affected several systems, including the engine superchargers and wheel brakes. Forced to fly the entire route at low level, Pease reached Del Monte at 2300 hours and landed successfully but had to bring his bomber to a stop by ground-looping it at the end of the runway.

Godwin, flying the other B-17, didn't even make it that far. While attempting to transfer fuel from the auxilliary tank into the wing tanks, the flight engineer inadvertently dumped hundreds of gallons overboard. Godwin and the copilot, distracted by the dangerously low fuel situation, neglected to update the altimeter as they descended to land at Del Monte in the darkness. The instrument gave false information, and still indicated 1,200 feet when they struck the surface of Iligan Bay a mile short of the runway. The Fortress bounced high and then plunged into the water, killing two of the crew in the rear of the plane. The five surviving crewmen, one with a badly injured back, reached shore after a harrowing four-hour swim.

At this point, MacArthur and his party were still en route to Mindanao. The seventy-seven-foot Elco PT boats, normally capable of sustaining forty miles per hour, were in rough shape after three months of combat operations. The engines had gone more than a thousand hours beyond their recommended overhaul, carburetors and spark plugs were fouled, and the boats could attain barely half their rated speed. Their double-planked mahogany hulls, reinforced with plywood, creaked and groaned as the boats pounded against unusually heavy swells. Most of the passengers were acutely seasick, including MacArthur and his son, four-year-old Arthur IV, their agony prolonged by the boats' slow progress. Ideally the 560-mile journey should have taken about twenty hours, but the exodus dragged on for thirty-five.

By the time MacArthur finally reached Mindanao on the morning of March 13, Lieutenant Pease and his B-17 were gone. Brigadier General William F. Sharp, the senior army officer on the island, had considered the bomber too unsafe for the likes of MacArthur and sent Pease back to Australia. The trip was not entirely wasted—Pease departed on March 12 carrying sixteen airmen who had been stranded in the Philippines—but when MacArthur learned that only one rickety B-17 had flown to Del Monte and then left without him, he went ballistic. (Later, stories began to circulate that the youthful-looking Pease was still on the island when MacArthur arrived. Allegedly, the general took one look at the B-17 and refused to board such a "dangerously decrepit" aircraft. Other versions have MacArthur exclaiming, "My God, he's only a boy," upon seeing Pease for the first time. Neither story actually happened. Pease, considered one of the best pilots in the 19th Bomb Group, was long gone by the time MacArthur reached Mindanao; nevertheless several biographers and historians have erroneously placed the two men together.)

MacArthur *did* lose his temper. Outraged over the inept effort to pick him up, he sent blistering messages to Brett in Australia and Gen. George C. Marshall, the U.S. Army chief of staff in Washington, D.C., demanding the "three best planes in the United States or Hawaii."

One immediate result was that Vice Admiral Leary lost operational control of the B-17s brought over by Major Carmichael. Redesignated the 40th Reconnaissance Squadron, the unit was transferred into the 19th Bomb Group, which was being reformed at Townsville, on March 14. Two days later, four B-17Es from the newly redesignated squadron flew to Batchelor Field and picked up more supplies. From there, two bombers continued north to Mindanao for another rescue attempt. Piloted by Lt. Frank P. Bostrom and Capt. Bill Lewis, the two aircraft collected MacArthur's party at Del Monte and returned to Batchelor Field by mid-morning on March 17. Richard Carmichael also got involved, flying MacArthur and his family farther south to Alice Springs. Most of the passengers were violently airsick, but somehow MacArthur's wife Jean was singled out for refusing to fly any farther. As a result, MacArthur decided to complete the trip by rail. He would come to regret it. Only one train was available, pulled by a relic of a steam locomotive, and the journey to Melbourne across the blazing hot outback lasted three miserable days.

MacArthur's arrival in Australia was accompanied by immediate changes in the command structure. First, the Australian War Cabinet approved a nomination from Prime Minister Curtin naming MacArthur "Supreme Commander of Allied Forces" in the region. Canberra agreed to include all Australian combat forces in the new command, called the Southwest Pacific Area (SWPA). Subsequently, per Australia's endorsement, the Joint Chiefs of Staff in Washington agreed to give MacArthur command of the designated area, simultaneously naming Adm. Chester W. Nimitz "Supreme Commander of the Pacific Ocean Area" (POA). Nimitz's area of responsibility, much larger in terms of square miles, consisted almost entirely of water except for a few strategic island groups. In contrast, the Southwest Pacific Area included Australia, New Guinea, Borneo, and the Philippines—roughly 90 percent of the Pacific's aggregate landmass.

MacArthur accepted his new appointment on March 18 while still aboard the train. It was the reprieve of a lifetime. Instead of being sanctioned for the disaster in the Philippines, he had been handed the resources that would allow him to eventually drive the enemy out of his beloved islands. Eager to get started, he made a vainglorious pledge to a gathering of reporters: "I came through and I shall return."

He had no idea his promise would take three years to fulfill.

A WEEK BEFORE MacArthur's rescue from Australia, the aviation component of the American army was officially renamed the United States Army Air Forces. At first glance, the strength of the air units in Australia seemed impressive: forty B-17 Flying Fortresses, seven LB-30 Liberators (the export version of the B-24 heavy bomber), twenty-seven A-24 Dauntless dive-bombers, and more than five hundred fighters of various types. But the numbers were deceptive. Of the heavy bombers, perhaps a dozen or so B-17s in the newly reconstituted 19th Bomb Group were operational. The rest were long overdue for major repairs or overhaul. The A-24 light bombers, the army's version of the highly successful Douglas SBD employed by the U.S. Navy, would prove inadequate as land-based bombers due to limitations in speed, range, and armament.

The fighter situation was hardly any better. Some 337 Curtiss P-40E Warhawks, 90 Bell P-39 Airacobras, and more than 100 Bell P-400s (the export model of the P-39) had reached Australia. However, 125 fighters had already been shot down or destroyed on the ground, another 175 were awaiting assembly or repairs, and 75 of the P-40s had been diverted to the RAAF. Consequently, only 92 P-40s, 33 P-39s, and 52 P-400s were in commission. More importantly, the American fighters were inferior to the Zeros that currently ruled the skies over the Southwest Pacific. All three models were powered by a liquid-cooled Allison inline engine, which performed well at low altitudes but turned anemic above sixteen thousand feet.

The worst reputation belonged to the P-400. Hundreds had been shipped to the Royal Air Force through the Lend-Lease program, but the

British accepted only 80 planes. The Soviet Union gladly received most of what remained, but somehow 179 fighters ended up back in American hands. They were sent to the Southwest Pacific, where Army pilots joked that P-400 stood for "a P-40 with a Zero on its tail."

And there was more bad news. MacArthur was shocked to learn that of the 25,000 American troops in Australia, most were assigned to air units. On February 25, the transports *Ancon* and *Hugh L. Scott* had docked at Brisbane with the ground echelons of the 3rd Bombardment Group (Light) and 22nd Bombardment Group (Medium) respectively. Two weeks later, the old liner *Maui* arrived at Brisbane and offloaded another 2,500 army personnel, all of whom belonged either to an air base company, a communications outfit, ordnance companies, or the 8th Pursuit Group. MacArthur had almost no infantry, no tanks, and no navy. Advised of the stark realities during his train ride to Melbourne, he is said to have exclaimed, "God have mercy on us!"

WHILE MACARTHUR'S FORCES in Australia were significantly weaker than the numbers indicated, the enemy's control of the region was growing stronger by the day. During the first week of March, Vice Admiral Inoue initiated the simultaneous invasions of Lae and Salamaua, code-named "SR" Operation. POWs from Lark Force were among the dockside laborers who helped load the transport ships gathered in Simpson Harbor. On March 3, elements of Major General Horii's South Seas Force boarded *Yokohama Maru* and *China Maru* while the Maizaru 2nd Special Naval Landing Force went aboard *Kongo Maru*, *Tenyo Maru*, and *Kokai Maru*. The Invasion Force, commanded by Rear Admiral Sadamichi Kajioka, included eleven warships protected in turn by another six cruisers of the Distant Screening Unit, which sortied from Truk.

The Invasion Force departed Rabaul on March 5 and was detected two days later by an RAAF Hudson. By that time, however, the convoy was already within fifty-five miles of the New Guinea coast, leaving the Allies powerless to stop it. At dawn on March 8, Kajioka's warships began shelling both Lae and Salamaua. No one ashore was hurt, and military damage was limited, but the local detachments of the New Guinea Volunteer Rifles melted into the jungle without putting up a fight. Unopposed, the Japanese landing forces quickly established antiaircraft and ground defenses and set up a local administration. Engineers repaired the airstrips, which had been badly damaged by Nagumo's carrier planes in January, and within thirty-six hours Lae was ready to receive fighters of the 4th Air Group from Rabaul.

Allied counterattacks came swiftly. At midday on March 8, five Hudsons from Horn Island randomly attacked the ships in the Huon Gulf. Squadron Leader Deryck Kingwell, newly appointed as the commanding officer of 32 Squadron, enthusiastically claimed a hit on a transport, but his bombs caused only minor damage to *Yokohama Maru*. A handful of B-17s, also staging out of Horn Island, bombed the airstrip at Salamaua from thirty thousand feet and demolished two hangars, then continued north to Lae and dropped the rest of their bombs in the harbor area.

Thus far, the initial occupation of New Guinea had cost the Japanese virtually nothing. That changed in dramatic fashion on the morning of March 10 when American carrier planes caught Kajioka's fleet by surprise. Credit for the attack goes to Vice Admiral Brown, who sorely wanted another crack at Rabaul. In the days since his first attempt, Task Force 11 had been refueled and replenished off New Caledonia while Brown pressed his superiors for another opportunity. He requested two carrier groups and received *Yorktown*, supported by Task Force 17, under the command of Rear Adm. Frank Jack Fletcher.

Brown had planned to hit Rabaul on March 10, but when word came that Lae and Salamaua had been invaded, the scheduled strike was scrapped in favor of a surprise attack on the Japanese invasion force. Once again, Brown's hopes of hitting Rabaul evaporated.

The new strike plan was hastily crafted while the combined carrier groups steamed across the Coral Sea. Because the Japanese heavily patrolled the sea lanes between New Britain and New Guinea, the probability of pulling off a surprise attack from that direction seemed unlikely. By steaming around New Guinea to Port Moresby, however, Brown's carriers could deliver their planes to within 125 miles of the enemy fleet with little chance of detection.

The biggest challenge would be getting the heavily loaded planes over the Owen Stanley Mountains. Captain Ted Sherman, *Lexington*'s commanding officer, later wrote: "We had little information as to the height of the mountains, and it was doubtful that our sea-level torpedo planes could clear them. Our intelligence data was extremely meager. Our charts showed the coastline but no details of the interior. Furthermore, our chart of the Gulf of Papua was marked 'Surveyed in 1894' and 'Area contains many coral heads which grow from year to year and whose position is unknown.' It was not a very pleasant prospect for a navigator."

The day prior to the attack, Sherman sent *Lexington's* air group commander to Port Moresby and another pilot to Townsville to get "the dope" on the region. Their most important finding was the location of a pass through the Owen Stanleys at 7,500 feet, roughly in line with the attack route. For a few hours each morning the weather atop the pass was usually clear, but the rest of the day it was cloaked in clouds.

Early on the morning of March 10, *Lexington* and *Yorktown* began launching their planes for the first-ever joint attack by U.S. Navy carrier groups. The combined strike force, consisting of sixty-one SBD Dauntlesses, twenty-five TBD Devastators, and eighteen F4F Wildcats, crossed the beach in scattered formations and started the long climb over the mountains. By early afternoon, the American flyers were back aboard the carriers, jubilantly describing how they had caught the Japanese napping. They attacked the enemy ships with a vengeance, claiming two heavy cruisers, five transports, a light cruiser, and a destroyer sunk; a minelayer "probably sunk"; two destroyers and a gunboat "seriously damaged and possibly sunk"; and two additional vessels damaged. The successful raid was later hailed by President Roosevelt as "the best day's work we've had." Medals were doled out like candy, with no less than fifteen Navy Crosses and nine Distinguished Flying Crosses issued to various participants.

As might be expected, the damage actually incurred by the Japanese was significantly less than claimed. The transports got the worst of it, with three out of five sunk and another beached. No warships were lost, but the light cruiser *Yubari* limped back to Rabaul with nine dead and fifty wounded aboard, and later underwent a complete refit. A seaplane tender and two destroyers received direct hits, and a minelayer suffered hull damage from near misses. The cost in personnel, on the other hand, had been steep. Among the transports alone the death toll was almost 350 men, with many additional casualties aboard the damaged warships.

The Japanese did not suspend SR Operation—another contingent of the South Seas Force strengthened Japan's foothold on New Guinea by capturing Finschhafen the next day—but the surprise attack by *Lexington* and *Yorktown* sent shock waves through the Imperial Navy. Inoue, stunned to discover that American carriers were in the area, henceforth insisted on carrier support whenever amphibious landings were made.

And in Japan, Admiral Yamamoto renewed his vow to lure the Pacific Fleet carriers into a decisive battle and crush them.

AT CLONCURRY, Major Carmichael scheduled the 40th Reconnaissance Squadron to hit Rabaul again. Their most recent attempt, on March 13, had been a dismal failure: only one bomber out of five participants had reached the target area. Carmichael decided to lead the next mission personally. To improve his chances for success, he brought in Master Sgt. Durwood Fesmire, widely considered the best bombardier in the 19th Bomb Group.

Following the usual profile, four B-17s flew up to Port Moresby on the afternoon of March 17 to prepare for the mission. They took off at dawn the next day to attack shipping in Simpson Harbor, but once again there were nagging problems. En route to the target at thirty thousand feet, Lt. "Dubby" DuBose and his crew struggled with a recalcitrant bomber. Both starboard engines ran poorly, and when the gunners tested their weapons they found only the twin-fifties in the tail were operational. All of the others had gummed up, their firing mechanisms frozen in the rarified air. Rather than turn back, DuBose elected to continue to the target, convinced that Japanese fighters could not climb high enough to bother them.

The B-17s reached Simpson Harbor and released their bombs, but soon thereafter DuBose and his crew encountered more trouble than they'd anticipated. The navigator, Lieutenant Steinbinder, later described their adventurous return flight.

> Just as we closed the bomb bay doors the ship began to shake like a leaf in a cyclone & the #4 engine broke into flames, showering the fuselage with molten aluminum. We shut off the engine and tried to feather the prop but couldn't. Finally we gave up. The three other ships left us. We flew on three engines for five minutes, losing altitude slowly but surely. Suddenly out of the clear blue sky 4 Zero fighters attacked us, two of them from below and 2 from the sides. They made their initial passes without getting any fire from us, as we had only 2 guns working. Suddenly one came under us strafing our belly and came up in full view of the rear gunner. He put in a burst & saw the ship smoking & falling away. The

others each made a few more passes but at a respectful distance, all their shells falling short. Can't understand why they didn't use their nose cannon [sic]. This fighting took up thirty-five minutes and they left us. We were down to 22,000 ft. and losing altitude faster than before. We tried feathering the #4 engine again. Without any rhyme or reason the darn thing started up again and shook the plane so badly that we all expected the wing to be torn off. We all donned parachutes and life vests as we were out to sea and prepared to jump. However, by cutting the throttle the engine merely kept the prop turning, which suited us very well. Pistons and pieces of aluminum, however, kept flying about. One large piece flew into the upper turret blister. Had our crew chief been in the upper turret it would surely have brained him. He, however, was lying down with a raging fever.

DuBose turned eastward to give Gasmata a wide berth and then pointed the B-17 south until they reached the tip of New Guinea. By the time he finally headed west toward Port Moresby, the detour had sapped precious fuel. Steinbinder calculated they would run out of gas thirty minutes short of home base. Updating their position, ground speed, and fuel status every ten minutes, he discovered that their fuel economy had begun to improve slightly.

Somewhere off the coast of New Guinea, the propeller on the tortured outboard engine fell off and twirled downward into the sea. A few minutes later the crew radioed Port Moresby to report that they were inbound, only to receive a warning not to land: an enemy air raid was in progress. Lacking the fuel to loiter, DuBose ignored the warning. "We couldn't wait," Steinbinder wrote, "so we flew in anyway."

Fortunately, the Japanese attackers departed only moments before the damaged B-17 arrived at Seven Mile airdrome. DuBose landed safely, cleared the runway, and was starting to taxi on two engines when the bomber ran out of gas. Grounded until repairs could be made, DuBose and his crew remained at Port Moresby while Carmichael led the other three B-17s back to Townsville.

Upon reaching Australia, Carmichael and Sergeant Fesmire disagreed on the results of the attack. The other bombardiers had been briefed to toggle their bomb loads on the leader's cue, but Fesmire thought they had dropped prematurely. He waited until he had a cruiser in his sights yet was humble enough to admit that his bombs merely exploded close to the warship, causing no damage. Carmichael, however, claimed the cruiser had been sunk, and confronted Fesmire about not dropping with the others. The sergeant replied that those bombs had only killed "a few fish," but Carmichael continued to insist that they had sunk the cruiser. A squabble ensued. Out of pride Fesmire held his ground for a while, but he was too heavily outranked to sustain the argument. Finally he blurted, "All right! They sunk the damn cruiser!"

Credit for the warship was officially awarded to Carmichael's crew, but Fesmire was correct: the Japanese suffered no such loss on March 18. In fact, no Japanese vessels were even damaged, for the essential reason that high-altitude bombing almost never succeeded against shipping. Over Rabaul, many a bombardier was fooled by the Davapia Rocks, known to locals as the "Beehives," which jutted from the middle of Simpson Harbor. From five miles up they looked just like a vessel, especially when the wind and tides created the illusion of a wake.

BACK AT PORT MORESBY, Lieutenant DuBose decided he was unwilling to leave his valuable B-17 at the mercy of the next Japanese air raid. The crew removed everything they could unbolt to lighten the bomber, after which DuBose climbed aboard and risked taking off using the three good engines. He and a minimal flight crew got airborne and took the B-17 to Townsville, leaving Lieutenant Steinbinder in charge of six crewmen and three thousand pounds of U.S. Army equipment. They would have to stay at Port Moresby and wait for a ride back to Australia.

The accommodations at Seven Mile airdrome were terrible—even worse than at Cloncurry—and the stranded Americans went four days without shaving or changing their clothes. Steinbinder felt like "a bum," but thanks to the unexpected delay, he and the other crewmen were rewarded with a unique opportunity. In the company of hundreds of Aussies, they were among the few Yanks to witness a minor miracle.

CHAPTER 12

The Last Outpost

A S THE WAR IN THE Southwest Pacific entered its fourth month, Vice Admiral Inoue continued to focus his attention on New Guinea. It was obvious to both sides that whoever controlled the world's second largest island would dominate the region. By the middle of March 1942, the Japanese held Lae, Salamaua, and Finschhafen, giving them control of the northeast coast. As soon as improvements to the airdrome at Lae were completed, Imperial Navy aircraft merely had to zoom over the Owen Stanley Mountains to attack Port Moresby. The outlook for the Australian garrison was bleak.

The conquest of New Guinea received enthusiastic coverage in the Japanese press. One newspaper boasted: "Port Moresby is already on the verge of collapse as a result of repeated bombing by the Nippon Navy air corps. The present [efforts] of Nippon Army and Navy detachments completely sealed the fate of New Guinea."

Such propaganda had been published virtually every day since the beginning of the Pacific war, and by the spring of 1942, military personnel and civilians alike were brimming with overconfidence. The effect, later called *senshobyo* (literally, "victory disease"), was most apparent in the actions of military planners. Often displaying complete disregard for the capabilities of Allied forces, they tended to spread their forces thinly over large areas, sometimes extending them far beyond their lines of supply. (A prime example of *senshobyo* would occur in early April, when Vice Admiral

Inoue and Major General Horii received orders to commence the second stage of the Southern Offensive. Instead of concentrating their resources on one objective, they planned simultaneous operations against Port Moresby and Tulagi, hundreds of miles from Rabaul in opposite directions. Even as that operation got underway, Admiral Yamamoto and the Combined Fleet staff began war-gaming the next offensive, the invasion of Midway.)

At Rabaul and Lae, meanwhile, the 24th Air Flotilla was stretched to the limit as Rear Admiral Goto's airmen softened up Port Moresby. The land-attackers of the 4th Air Group flew a grueling schedule of long patrol flights every day, weather permitting, in addition to a steady diet of bombing missions. Port Moresby was raided twice on March 10 by a total of eighteen *rikko*; then five Zeros conducted a strafing attack on March 13, and the following day nine *rikko* hit Port Moresby again while eight other medium bombers, escorted by a dozen fighters, attacked the Allied airdrome on Horn Island.

The pace did not let up. On March 15 nine *rikko* bombed Madang on the northeast coast of New Guinea, after which the 4th Air Group shifted its attention to Tulagi, hitting the anchorage and seaplane base for two consecutive days. Next, the land-attackers returned to Port Moresby for raids on March 19 and 20 before finally taking a much-needed rest. By then, the airmen and ground personnel had been conducting nonstop operations for almost four weeks.

However, despite the 4th Air Group's effort to destroy Allied air power at Port Moresby, American B-17s continued to reciprocate by periodically hitting Rabaul. Rather than collapsing, the last outpost on New Guinea frustrated the Japanese with its resiliency.

FOR THE GARRISON at Port Moresby, the respite taken by the 24th Air Flotilla came as a huge relief. The young militiamen of the 30th Infantry Brigade, whose average age was just eighteen, had deployed to New Guinea with only minimal training. Since then they had endured conditions that would practically drive a man insane. Osmar White, a newspaperman who arrived in mid-February with four other accredited war correspondents, despised New Guinea's climate.

> Every afternoon and every night it rained. Every night hordes of black, voracious mosquitoes came singing hungrily out of the grass. Every dawn

hordes of black, voracious flies came in buzzing thirstily. They slept in clots and festoons on the rafters of the mess. Assaults on them with insecticide at night would bring down a squirming carpet that covered the packed earth floor, but it never appreciably diminished their numbers.

Conditions were slightly better down at the waterfront. The Catalina squadrons enjoyed decent accommodations and food in the RAAF mess, but the frequency of their long, hazardous missions led to extreme fatigue. Sometimes the airmen flew on consecutive nights, yet they went about their business with quiet determination. George Johnston, another of the war correspondents who covered the fighting in New Guinea, was in awe of the aircrews' stamina. "Repeatedly I saw men come in after 13-hour patrols, snatch a bite of food and a few hours' sleep, then roar off again over the reef on another job that would keep them in the air for 14 hours," he wrote. "I saw them, almost staggering from want of sleep, falling into bunks while the squadron's incomparable ground staff 'bombed up' for another trip scheduled for take-off a few hours later."

North of town at Seven Mile airdrome, the living conditions were much worse. Japanese air attacks had demolished all of the permanent buildings, which meant the only shelter from the savage sun consisted of tents and other temporary structures. Aircrews and ground personnel lived in primitive camps scattered among the ugly, scrub-covered hills surrounding the runway. Clouds of mosquitoes brought the inevitable malaria and dengue fever. Sanitation was virtually nonexistent. Latrines, as the saying went, consisted of nothing more than "a shovel and a walk." The direct result of this casual approach to hygiene was repeated outbreaks of dysentery, gastroenteritis, and other intestinal ailments.

As bad as the living conditions were, the monotonous diet of army rations did nothing to improve the men's health or their morale. John Steinbinder, who endured several layovers at Seven Mile, wrote sarcastically: "We have a great variety of food here. For breakfast we have hash, potatoes, hardtack, and coffee; for lunch, hash, potatoes, bread, and tea; for dinner, hash, potatoes, rice, peaches, and coffee, with choice of hardtack or bread."

During daylight hours, maintenance personnel and construction crews toiled under the blazing sun, keeping one eye skyward for the next enemy raid. At any moment a flight of Zeros might swoop down undetected, for there were too few warning posts in the mountains between Lae and Port Moresby. The early detection network, such as it was, depended entirely on radio reports based on visual sightings, some of which came from the Japanese side of the mountain range. Probably the most daring coastwatcher on New Guinea was thirty-three-year-old Flt. Lt. Leigh G. Vial, known by his call sign: "Golden Voice." Assisted by local villagers who periodically delivered supplies to his primitive camps, he observed the Japanese from the hills overlooking Lae, frequently providing the only advance warning of an incoming raid.

Even when timely warnings were received, most of the Aussies remained at their posts after the sirens began to wail. Major General Basil M. Morris, the senior Australian officer at Port Moresby, issued a directive stating that the men were to keep working until the bombs began to land within two hundred yards, at which time "officers would be permitted to order their men to take shelter." As if on a dare, the men habitually waited until the last possible second before sprinting to the nearest underground bunker or slit trench. The latter type of shelters were more exposed than a solid bunker, but they offered some protection from the most-feared Japanese bombs, the 60-kilogram fragmentation devices called "daisy cutters," which exploded into hundreds of jagged shards.

In addition to the poor living conditions and enemy air attacks, the airfield environment itself was tiresome. Sometimes the runway was hard-packed and dusty, other times slick with mud. And it was almost always under construction as workmen attempted to lengthen it toward Bootless Bay. Heavy rains turned the taxiways into muddy bogs, and aircraft frequently became mired while attempting to maneuver around bomb craters or other obstacles. On several occasions, nervous pilots got stuck while taxiing at high speed to avoid an incoming raid. The airdrome lacked adequate hardstands and revetments, which meant that all of the planes were vulnerable. Those that ran off the taxiways were usually torched by strafing Zeros.

Despite the detrimental conditions and frequent attacks, the garrison and ground crews soldiered on. Their primary motivation came from the knowledge that Port Moresby was the last outpost between the Japanese and Australia. The government was already talking about conceding the northern half of the continent if New Guinea fell, a threshold that became known as the "Brisbane Line." Australians were deeply concerned, not realizing that the Imperial Army lacked enough divisions for such a monumental invasion.

Perhaps the most discouraging situation at Port Moresby was the lack of fighter defense. For weeks the garrison had been promised a squadron of Kittyhawks, the Commonwealth's name for the American-built Curtiss P-40E Warhawk, but delay after delay ensued, and no fighters materialized. In frustration, the troops began to joke sarcastically about "Neverhawks" and "Tomorrowhawks." Finally, an announcement came that the squadron would arrive on March 20.

At the designated time, four fighters approached Seven Mile. A large welcoming committee rushed to the runway, cheering wildly, throwing hats in the air, and waving towels over their heads. But elation turned abruptly to panic as the fighters zoomed down and opened fire. Men scrambled in all directions as yet another strafing attack by enemy Zeros began. Although the raid caused little damage, the uncanny timing of the 4th Air Group was a cruel joke.

THE PROMISED FIGHTERS really did exist. Formed in early March at Townsville, 75 Squadron received an allotment of P-40Es set aside by the U.S. Army. Ground personnel and a few pilots were drawn from 24 Squadron, which had been operating Wirraways from Garbutt Field and Horn Island since evacuating from Rabaul, but most fliers were transferred from other squadrons across Australia. Six pilots were combat veterans, including five with experience against the Germans in the North African desert. The soon-to-be commanding officer, Sqn. Ldr. John F. Jackson, was officially credited with downing six Axis aircraft while flying Hurricanes and Tomahawks. Squadron Leader Peter Jeffrey had scored five victories with the same outfit, 3 Squadron. Even more impressive, both in name and combat record, was Flt. Lt. Peter St. George Bruce Turnbull, with nine Axis planes to his credit. But only one pilot in the new squadron had ever faced the Japanese. Bruce Anderson, a veteran of 24 Squadron, had unsuccessfully attempted to intercept Kawanishi flying boats over Rabaul in January. Later that month, during the heavy carrier attack that preceded the Japanese invasion, he had crashed on takeoff, injuring both legs. After convalescing in an Australian hospital, he rejoined the squadron at Townsville.

Trained in great haste, 75 Squadron encountered trouble almost from the beginning. The first fifteen Kittyhawks were scheduled to reach

Townsville on March 7, but during a transit flight from New South Wales, ten of the fighters encountered terrible weather that resulted in the loss of three aircraft and two pilots. Over the next two weeks, training mishaps wiped out three more fighters, leaving only eighteen available for operations in New Guinea.

On the morning of March 21, after an overnight stop at Horn Island, the Kittyhawks were prepped for the long flight to Port Moresby. Peter Jeffrey led four fighters up a few hours ahead of the rest, reaching the New Guinea coast at approximately1400 hours. After orbiting south of the harbor while their identity was positively established, the Kittyhawks proceeded toward Seven Mile. But not everyone got the word that friendlies were approaching, and a machine-gunner opened fire at the fighters during their final approach. Other trigger-happy defenders joined in, their accuracy alarmingly good. All four Kittyhawks were damaged, two of them severely, and a bullet missed Jeffrey's head by less than an inch.

But the near-disaster was quickly forgotten. Soon after the Aussies landed, a lone Japanese reconnaissance bomber appeared over Seven Mile. The crew of the Type 1 *rikko*, piloted by CPO Heihatchi Kawai of the 4th Air Group, may have anticipated a routine mission when they left Rabaul that morning, but they were in for a surprise.

John Steinbinder, still stranded at the airdrome, was one of the few Americans to observe the ensuing action, which he later described in his diary: "Just after the P-40s landed, a Japanese reconnaissance ship came over and proceeded dropping bombs. 2 P-40s took off and cut off its retreat and then began a dogfight the likes of which I'll perhaps never again see."

Steinbinder's view from the ground was limited, but what he recorded was accurate. Flight lieutenants Wilbur L. Wackett and Barry M. Cox jumped into the two airworthy Kittyhawks and took off to bushwhack the reconnaissance plane, which snooped around Port Moresby almost every afternoon at about the same time. While they were scrambling, a quick-thinking RAAF communications officer ordered the radioman on duty to hold down his transmitter key—a simple but effective method of "jamming" the frequency—which prevented Kawai's crew from reporting the presence of the Australian fighters. The outcome was witnessed by hundreds of men including Steinbinder, who evidently thought the fighters were American: "Our P-40s made 5 passes at this bomber," he wrote, "before the darn thing finally blew up in mid-air."

The twin-engine Mitsubishi not only burst into flames in view of practically everyone on the ground, its meteoric plunge to the ocean was regarded as a miracle. The garrison, having taken the enemy's aerial punches on the chin for two months without fighting back, went into a frenzied celebration. One exuberant witness was Osmar White: "We onlookers fell on one another's necks, howling hysterically with joy," he wrote. "For miles around, men found they had business at the airfield. They came roaring up the road on lorries, cheering and laughing. They stopped, poured out of the vehicles, and stood staring with a mixture of awe and disbelief at the fighters on the ground."

The cheers and backslapping continued when the remaining fourteen Kittyhawks arrived. Almost immediately, John Jackson began to plan an attack against the nearest Japanese base, Lae airdrome. Reconnaissance photos taken earlier that day showed numerous planes lined up along the strip, and Jackson was eager to go on the offensive.

Ten Kittyhawks were available the next morning for the mission. If Jackson had any personal worries prior to his first combat against the Japanese, one may have been the fact that his own younger brother was scheduled to participate. Flight Lieutenant Leslie D. Jackson, nine years younger, was untested in combat but eager to match his brother's score.

As the Kittyhawks began taking off, Plt. Off. John LeGay Brereton swerved to avoid a parked Hudson and ran off the runway at high speed. His fighter caught fire and was eventually destroyed, but not before Brereton was freed from the cockpit.

Now down to nine fighters, Jackson led the attackers in a thrilling climb over the sharp peaks of the Owen Stanley Mountains. As the Kittyhawks weaved among the clouds, backlit by the early morning sun, at least one Aussie pilot was profoundly touched by the splendor of his surroundings. The cumulonimbus clouds resembled "glorious silver mountains" to Flg. Off. John W. W. Piper, who was awed by the vista and yet keenly aware that he would soon be attempting to kill people. To the twenty-four-year-old from Armadale, Victoria, the conflicting emotions were nearly overwhelming.

After crossing the mountains, the Kittyhawks separated into two groups and dived toward Lae. Peter Turnbull held four fighters overhead to provide top cover while John Jackson led the rest down to strafe the airdrome. His plan worked to perfection, catching the Japanese off guard.

The Kittyhawks executed a wide, sweeping turn over the Huon Gulf and attacked from seaward, out of the rising sun. Racing in at low altitude, Jackson and Piper targeted a row of Zeros parked neatly in the middle of the runway. Off to one side, Bruce Anderson, Barry Cox, and Flg. Off. John A. Woods aimed at another row of aircraft.

Each of the Kittyhawks had six Browning M2 .50-caliber machine guns in the wings. When the pilots pressed the trigger on their control stick, the collective firepower of thirty heavy machine guns cut a wide swath down the long rows of parked planes, igniting several blazes.

After the first pass, Jackson boldly swung his fighters around to strafe the airdrome from the opposite direction. The pilots maneuvered without mishap and roared back down the strip. Blinded momentarily by thick columns of black smoke, they fired into the parked planes a second time, Piper dipping so low that the wing of his Kittyhawk struck the propeller of a Zero. The impact ripped one of the machine guns from its mount and damaged a main structural spar, but the sturdy fighter held together.

But that second strafing run gave Japanese antiaircraft gunners time to man the batteries, and a pair of Zeros suddenly appeared. Flight Petty Officer 3rd Class Seiji Ishikawa and his wingman of the same rank, Yutaka Kimura, had departed from Lae an hour and twenty minutes earlier on routine patrol. Spotting the slender Kittyhawks, which they mistook for British Spitfires, the two Japanese dived toward the top cover element led by Turnbull. A third Zero, flown by FPO 3rd Class Keiji Kikuchi, managed to get airborne just before the airstrip was turned into a shambles by the strafers.

Seeing the aggressive Zeros, the Aussies flying top cover shed their belly tanks and engaged the enemy. Turnbull and Flt. Lt. John H. S. Pettit each fired at different planes, yet their bullets seemed to have no effect. Wilbur Wackett discovered that only one of his six guns was working, but he gave chase to a diving Zero without hesitation.

The son of Sir Lawrence J. Wackett, a pioneer of the Australian aviation industry, young Wilbur may have been feeling invincible after helping to shoot down the reconnaissance plane over Port Moresby the previous day. As he dived after the Zero, now some two thousand feet below him, he all but ignored a second enemy fighter that came into view. This was probably Kimura, who lined up on Wackett even as he maneuvered his Kittyhawk into a firing position behind the leader. A few heartbeats later,

Kimura pumped numerous rounds into the fuselage, engine, and cockpit of Wackett's fighter.

The Kittyhawk belched smoke, its Allison liquid-cooled engine mortally damaged. Wackett evaded further harm by diving into a cloud, but the engine quit soon after, leaving him to glide blindly downward. He came out the bottom of the cloud to find himself only a thousand feet above the Huon Gulf—too low to bail out—so he rode the silent Kittyhawk all the way down. Several miles out to sea, midway between Lae and Salamaua, Wackett executed a dead-stick splashdown. Shaken by the watery crash, not to mention the sight of a nearby shark, he inflated his yellow life preserver and swam clear of the aircraft.

Overhead, Bruce Anderson was also in trouble. Sometime during the second strafing run he was hit by light antiaircraft fire or bounced by a Zero. When last seen, Anderson was behind and below John Woods, who was himself no higher than three hundred feet. For a moment Woods thought he was being chased by an enemy fighter but then realized that Anderson was behind him, his Kittyhawk streaming smoke. Suddenly the mottled-green fighter rolled on its side and plunged toward a hill. Woods did not actually see it impact the jungle, but he knew beyond a doubt that Anderson was dead.*

No sooner had the remaining Kittyhawks turned for home than two Hudsons from 32 Squadron attempted a bombing run on Lae airdrome. Neither succeeded—the payload from one hit the water short of the runway while the shackles in the other failed to release—and both aircraft were hit by enemy gunfire. Petty Officer Kikuchi damaged one Hudson, piloted by Flt. Lt. Patrick R. McDonnell. Two crewmen were wounded, but the gunners, in turn, evidently shot Kikuchi's fighter out of the sky. His death in action was later recorded by the 4th Air Group.

Back at Seven Mile, the men of 75 Squadron were thrilled by the success of their first mission. Against the loss of Anderson and Wackett, the strafers reported the destruction of nine planes on the ground. The estimate was

---

*A number of historians have erroneously described Anderson as being captured at Lae and later executed at Rabaul. It's a simple matter of mistaken identity. Among the crew of an RAAF Catalina shot down on May 4, 1942, was Plt. Off. Francis O. Anderson, the navigator. He was executed at Rabaul six months later, along with the rest of his crewmates.

actually low, for once, and the raid earned a tribute from the Japanese in a postwar history: "Virtually the entire contingent of planes (nine Zeros and one land-based attack plane) were strafed on the ground and caught fire, and two Zeros were lost in the air. This was the first Allied raid against a Japanese base in which both fighters and bombers participated."

Despite the mission's success, the day concluded badly for 75 Squadron as two more Kittyhawks were destroyed during the afternoon in separate operational accidents. Both pilots were rescued; but with Brereton's crash on takeoff that morning plus the downing of Anderson and Wackett in combat, the squadron's accumulated losses came to five Kittyhawks.

The only good news came later with the recovery of Wilbur Wackett, who had staggered ashore barefoot nearly nine hours after ditching his Kittyhawk in the gulf. Friendly natives guided him on a four-day journey through the mountains to the village of Bulwa, where a detachment of New Guinea Volunteer Rifles was camped. Weeks later, sick with malaria, Wackett returned to Port Moresby after crossing the Papuan Peninsula almost entirely on foot. Curiously, Wackett reported that he had witnessed two Japanese fighters falling in flames on the morning of March 22. As a result, Peter Turnbull and John Pettit were each awarded an aerial victory, though Kikuchi's Zero was actually knocked down by the gunners of a Hudson.

THE DAY AFTER Jackson's surprise raid, in what was undoubtedly a measure of retaliation, nineteen Type 1 bombers from Rabaul attacked Seven Mile airdrome. The *rikko* arrived overhead at about 1330 on March 23 and dropped their bombs just as several Kittyhawks scrambled. Two fighters got stuck in the mud, and the rest took off barely ahead of the exploding bombs. Fifty minutes later, four Zeros swooped down and strafed the runway, destroying both of the mired Kittyhawks and damaging a third.

One of the Zero pilots, FPO 2nd Class Kyoichi Yoshii, doubled back for another strafing run. As the Kittyhawk pilots had learned the previous day, the element of surprise usually gave strafers one pass at relatively low risk, but making a second run raised the danger exponentially. The angry gunners at Seven Mile underscored the point. Yoshii's Zero, hit by ground fire, suddenly made a ninety-degree turn and smashed into a hill. His body, thrown clear of the wreckage, revealed that a bullet had struck him in the head. The Japanese would never consider that a pilot had been vanquished by the enemy; therefore, Yoshii's death was explained as a deliberate suicide dive into a gun emplacement.

Meanwhile, the Kittyhawks that had scrambled aloft were unable to intercept the fast, high-altitude bombers. The squadron's first attempt to defend Port Moresby was not merely disappointing but fruitless. Worse, the destruction of the two fighters stuck in the mud brought the squadron's losses to an unacceptable level.

As a matter of routine, notification of the accrued losses was forwarded up the chain of command to RAAF headquarters. Within hours, the high command granted permission to pull the squadron back to Horn Island if necessary. The choice was left entirely to Jackson.

A former rancher with an affable personality to match his big physique, John Jackson understood the importance of the situation. One way or another, his decision would impact the lives of hundreds, perhaps thousands of Allies. His men affectionately called him "Old John," partly because he had fought in North Africa, and partly because he was thirty-four, a family man. They trusted him, revered him, which ultimately made his decision easy. Knowing that 75 Squadron had already done wonders for the morale of the beleaguered garrison, and that pulling out would have a devastating effect on everyone, Jackson chose to stay. In electing to face the enemy head-on, he had absolutely no doubt that Port Moresby would be attacked more relentlessly than ever.

THE JAPANESE did not disappoint. During the last week of March the 4th Air Group raided Port Moresby no less than four times. For the airmen of 75 Squadron, the days were filled with alerts and periodic scrambles, some of which developed into heated combat. Two more pilots were killed by the end of the month, and aircraft losses to all causes reached eleven Kittyhawks. Inevitably a few fighters needed significant repairs, lowering aircraft readiness even further. On the morning of March 30, exactly five were available for combat duty.

The Japanese were poised to wipe out 75 Squadron. With just a small measure of additional effort they probably would have accomplished it, but the 4th Air Group suddenly halted operations for several days beginning on March 28. Although the break was temporary, it proved enormously beneficial for the Australians.

The reason for the unexpected hiatus was attrition. During the past month the 4th Air Group had lost seventeen Zeros and six land-attack planes to all causes, including five fighters destroyed in air-to-air combat. The irony was that Rear Admiral Goto did not realize how desperate the situation was at Port Moresby. Although his aircrews claimed to have destroyed fifty-six enemy planes during March (more than the total number of planes the Allies possessed in the region), Goto remained conservative with his attack plans. Just when the Australians were holding on by their fingertips, he gave them a reprieve. As a result, the Japanese missed their best opportunity to knock out Allied air strength at Port Moresby and completely dominate the skies over New Guinea.

CHAPTER 13

New Guinea Interlude

IN AUSTRALIA, SLIGHT GAINS in troop strength were finally being realized as ships from the United States offloaded thousands of personnel at the port cities of Sydney and Brisbane. For many Americans, the long journey had been unforgettable, if only because of the discomforts. The 80th Pursuit Squadron, for example, reached Brisbane after twenty-two days aboard a vintage passenger ship. According to the squadron's official history, the voyage had in no way resembled a pleasure cruise.

> There were approximately 2,500 troops aboard the *Maui*, which had served as a troop transport in World War I. Living conditions were poor. The men sleeping in the holds attempted to clean their quarters, but the *Maui* was an ancient craft and its holds defeated their efforts. No amount of scrubbing could remove the odor which clung to the *Maui* from its former service as a cattle boat. . . . Water was scarce and showers could be taken only when it rained. Personnel were given the choice of either drinking their daily cup of tea or shaving with it; most men preferred to shave with salt water. The shortage of liquids, however, was confined to water, the officers' bar being well-stocked.

Not all of the crossings were so uncomfortable. Elegant liners brought their share of men and material, such as *Queen Mary*, converted into a troopship and camouflaged with shades of gray paint. She docked at Sydney on March 28 carrying 8,400 soldiers and airmen, including the ground echelon of the 43rd Bomb Group (Heavy). The group operated four squadrons of B-17s, but the flight echelon was not scheduled to arrive for several months; therefore, the ground troops were assigned to maintenance depots where they fixed battle-weary aircraft and assembled new planes.

Fighters and other relatively small planes were shipped to Australia in crates, whereas most multi-engine aircraft were flown across the Pacific, a hazard-filled odyssey that took days to accomplish. On March 22, the first flight of sleek new Martin B-26 Marauders safely reached Archerfield Municipal Airport outside Brisbane after six days in transit from Hawaii. The following week, the inherent dangers of the ocean crossing were starkly illustrated when no less than three Marauders were lost—at least two due to storms—with only one crewmember recovered. Despite the tragedies, the 22nd Bombardment Group (Medium) was ready to move a squadron of B-26s up to Townsville on March 29 to commence training for combat operations. Three more squadrons would follow as soon as their flight echelons were in place.

At about the same time, 17 officers and 784 enlisted men of the 3rd Bombardment Group's ground echelon relocated from Brisbane to Charters Towers, an old mining town southwest of Townsville. The group possessed few aircraft until the following week, when a squadron of A-24 Dauntless dive-bombers arrived. Remnants of the Far East Air Force, 27th Bombardment Group (Light), the crews had seen action in the Philippines and Netherlands East Indies. Their senior officer, Lt. Col. John H. "Big Jim" Davies, assumed overall command of the group at Charters Towers and assigned the Dauntlesses to the 8th Bombardment Squadron.

On the last day of March, a contingent of eight A-24s led by Capt. Floyd W. "Buck" Rogers moved up to Port Moresby. Two of the Dauntlesses were damaged on landing, but the crews received an enthusiastic welcome as the first American squadron based in New Guinea. The honor wore off quickly, however, as Rogers came down with dengue fever. One of the A-24s was apparently plagued with mechanical problems, resulting in the availability of only five aircraft for the squadron's first mission the following day.

Six Kittyhawks of 75 Squadron escorted the five A-24s, led by 1st Lt. Robert G. Ruegg, over the mountains to Lae. Finding the airdrome socked in by clouds, Ruegg swung his dive-bombers south to Salamaua, considered a secondary airdrome by the Japanese. The Dauntlesses dropped five 500-pound general-purpose bombs on the structures adjacent to the runway, reportedly starting fires amid the wreckage. Otherwise damage was limited. On the positive side, no Japanese planes tried to intercept the raiders.

Flying a solo reconnaissance over Lae on the morning of April 4, John Jackson daringly descended to five hundred feet and roared down the strip, strafing planes and men. Encouraged by the results, he decided to lead another fighter sweep against the airdrome that afternoon. Surprisingly, the Japanese had taken no precautions to shelter their aircraft. The five participating Aussies found a row of bombers lined up along the north side of the airstrip, mirrored by another row of fighters on the south. The outcome was all too predictable. Several of the exposed planes burst into flames, sending up columns of black smoke that could be seen from a distance of twenty miles.

Just as predictably, retaliation came the next morning. In a coincidence of numbers, seven Type 1 bombers escorted by four Zeros attacked Seven Mile airdrome and were intercepted by seven Kittyhawks. Les Jackson was credited with shooting down a Zero in flames (the 4th Air Group acknowledged a corresponding loss), but the bombers were successful, blowing up vital stores of gasoline and ammunition.

Despite the aggravation caused by the raid, the general outlook at Port Moresby improved dramatically that afternoon as a steady stream of combat planes landed at Seven Mile. By sundown, the dispersal area was packed with more aircraft than the garrison had ever seen at the airdrome: six B-25 Mitchells, nine B-26 Marauders, six P-39 Airacobras, and three B-17 Flying Fortresses. Judging from the unprecedented number of bombers, it was obvious that something big was about to happen.

For the Allies at that point in the Pacific war, "big" was a relative term. A plan had been devised to attack two locations on New Britain simultaneously: the Marauders and Flying Fortresses would hit Rabaul while the Mitchells pounded the airdrome at Gasmata. Scheduled for the morning of April 6, the dual raids represented the most ambitious event yet attempted from New Guinea. Even the airmen were keyed up. John Steinbinder, back with his regular crew, was uncharacteristically nervous.

"Don't know why, but I feel that this is going to be disastrous," he wrote in his diary. "I must be getting hysterical or something. I'm afraid I've been on the ground too long."

Trying to grab a few hours of sleep in the oppressively warm night, Steinbinder and his fellow crewmembers stretched out on cots or even on the wings of their fully armed and fueled bombers. They were restless, prepared to take off on a moment's notice should the Japanese attack, but the night was quiet.

Shortly after midnight the crews were roused from their makeshift beds to eat breakfast and attend final briefings. The B-17s began rolling down the runway at 0200, and the B-26s took off an hour later, the idea being that the Marauders, with their superior speed, would make up most of the difference and hit Rabaul in coordination with the Flying Fortresses. The last to take off were the B-25s, whose target was the airfield at Gasmata.

The dual missions, almost completely overlooked by historians, represented some significant benchmarks. Foremost was the fact that both the B-25 Mitchell and the B-26 Marauder made their combat debuts over New Britain on April 6. The coincidence of the two most famous American medium bombers of World War II fighting their first action on the same day over the same Pacific island has rarely, if ever, been pointed out.

More importantly, at least to the Japanese, the mission on April 6 represented the first attack on Rabaul by Allied medium bombers.

THE SIX MITCHELL BOMBERS en route to Gasmata were hot. Not as in overheating, or fast, but stolen. Or so the legend goes. As of a few days earlier, the 3rd Bomb Group's only aircraft were the dive-bombers absorbed from the old Far East Air Force. The other squadrons had been promised B-25s for weeks, but none had arrived. The situation improved, however, when someone discovered twelve brand-new Mitchells parked at Archerfield near Brisbane.

Curiously, the bombers wore serial numbers that identified them as property of the Netherlands East Indies Air Force. They were, in fact, the first B-25s delivered out of a contract for 162 Mitchells purchased by the Dutch from North American Aviation. Ferried across the Pacific just before the Netherlands East Indies capitulated, the twelve bombers were regarded as orphans by the 3rd Bomb Group. Following the age-old rule of "finders-keepers," the group requisitioned them on short notice, and later took four more without authorization, generating numerous tales about how the planes were "stolen" from the Dutch.

The Dutch flags on the B-25s had been painted over by the time "Big Jim" Davies led them toward Gasmata on April 6. To conserve fuel for the eight hundred-mile round trip, each aircraft carried eight 300-pound high-explosive bombs, about half the rated bomb load. Roaring over the enemy airstrip at five thousand feet, three B-25s attacked the northeastern area of the airdrome and placed twenty bombs in the runway area. The other two Mitchells attacked the southeast quadrant, but their bombs were dropped early in the face of heavy antiaircraft fire. At least one B-25 was damaged by shrapnel from an air burst, but no crewmen were wounded and all aircraft returned safely to Seven Mile.

THE FORTRESSES of the 40th Recon Squadron did not enjoy such good results on April 6. The plan called for the B-17s to bomb Vunakanau airdrome ten minutes before the B-26s arrived over Simpson Harbor, but the concept was overly optimistic. On virtually every previous mission the squadron had encountered a significant problem, either with the weather or mechanical troubles, and this event was no different. Two of the three B-17s turned back for various reasons, leaving Lt. "Dubby" DuBose to press on alone. He made it to Rabaul without incident, flew two dry runs over Vunakanau to coordinate the timing with the expected arrival of the B-26s, and then dropped his bombs on the third pass.

By that time the crew could see enemy fighters taking off. In addition, as navigator John Steinbinder later put it, bursts of antiaircraft fire were "breaking all about," so DuBose prudently turned toward Port Moresby. The left outboard engine sputtered and quit a few minutes later, making the lone B-17 vulnerable to enemy fighters. The Japanese did not attack, however, and the return flight to Port Moresby was completed on three engines. Upon arrival the crew claimed the destruction of two aircraft parked at Vunakanau, but the Japanese recorded no corresponding losses.

THE FIRST MISSION by B-26s did not fare much better. The crews of the 19th Bombardment Squadron/22nd Bombardment Group, previously based at Langley Field, Virginia, had spent the better part of a year overcoming several glitches with the new aircraft. Designed for speed, the Marauders boasted two of the most powerful aircraft engines currently available, the Pratt & Whitney R-2800 eighteen-cylinder radial. The bomber's wings were thin and relatively short, prompting wisecrackers to nickname it the "Flying Prostitute." (As the saying went, the engines appeared to have no visible means of support.)

But no one joked about the Marauder's unusually high landing speed. The combination of its low-drag fuselage, small wing, and tricycle landing gear (the B-26 employed a nose wheel instead of a tail wheel) was unforgiving. The B-26 required careful handling, especially when operating on short runways. Takeoff speeds were high when fully loaded with fuel and ammunition, and there was an unnerving tendency for the propellers on early models to suddenly over-speed if the pilot was careless with pitch control settings. Several fatal crashes marred the group's initial training, the low point coming just two days after the war began when the group's commanding officer and his entire crew were killed in a takeoff mishap. As the number of fatal accidents increased, the B-26 began to acquire more unattractive names such as the "Widow Maker" and the "Flying Coffin."

The Marauder men may have felt they had something to prove, but the challenges they faced could hardly have been greater. Like the crews of Major Carmichael's squadron that flew early missions from New Guinea, the 22nd Bomb Group entered combat with no experience in the Southwest Pacific region and little understanding of its inherent dangers. In support, the RAAF contributed some of its most experienced people to the effort. Among them was Sqn. Ldr. Thomas McBride Price, who had led the first Catalina raid on Rabaul. For the first Marauder mission on April 6, he flew in the copilot's seat of *Liberty Belle*, piloted by 1st Lt. Albert J. Moye.

Of the nine B-26s that staged up to Port Moresby, eight were considered operational for the mission and began taking off at 0300 into an inky black sky. Heavy rain squalls made it difficult to get the formation joined up; subsequently two Marauders returned to Port Moresby after failing to find a suitable pass through the mountains. The remaining six aircraft crossed the Solomon Sea and followed the southern coast of New Britain to St. George's Channel, a circuitous route that took longer than expected. By the time they approached Simpson Harbor, nearly an hour had elapsed since DuBose's solo attack.

The Japanese were ready: seven A5M fighters had scrambled from Lakunai airdrome, and the antiaircraft batteries were fully manned.

Approaching Rabaul from the east, the B-26s dropped nineteen bombs over Simpson Harbor, then reversed course and egressed over the same route. Their wide, sweeping turn exposed them to the ring of anti-aircraft guns for much longer than if they had simply continued straight ahead, but, miraculously, the only damage was sustained by *Liberty Belle*. Shrapnel from a nearby burst pierced the fuselage, slightly wounding the radio operator.

Over St. George's Channel a Marauder belatedly released another four bombs, bringing the total dropped to twenty-three. Only one hit was claimed, but with it, the Marauder crews were credited with sinking a transport. That the Japanese suffered no such loss on April 6 is hardly surprising.

Retreating back down St. George's Channel, the Marauders had no trouble outdistancing the few A5Ms that gave chase. But not all of the B-26s escaped danger. Well away from Rabaul, *Liberty Belle*'s right engine suddenly quit, whereupon Moye and his crew realized they were quickly running out of fuel. Perhaps a fuel line had been nicked by shrapnel from the antiaircraft shell, or the crew might have mismanaged the fuel system; either way the Marauder was in real trouble.

Turning due south toward the Trobriand Islands, Moye set the trim for single-engine operation. This required additional power on the good engine, consuming what little remained of the fuel. Just north of Kiriwina Island the left engine quit. Unfortunately the Marauder's operating manual contained scant information to procedurally guide the pilot through a dual engine failure, and Moye nearly lost control of the cross-trimmed bomber. Instinctively, he put the plane into a dive, maintaining enough airspeed to keep the wings level.

Too low for the crew to bail out, the Marauder ended its descent in a violent splashdown that broke the fuselage in two. Both sections sank in less than two minutes. The flight engineer, Staff Sgt. Samuel K. Bourne, never surfaced, but the rest of the crew swam clear of the sinking wreckage. Banged up from the ditching, they struggled to stay afloat with only one life raft between them.

At that moment, a Catalina of 11 Squadron was nearing the outbound limit of a long patrol from Tulagi. Pilot Officer Terence L. Duigan and his crew happened to be near Woodlark Island when the radio operator picked up a Morse code signal regarding the downed B-26. Alerted to be on the lookout, the Aussies almost missed Moye and the other survivors, who had reached dry land with the aid of local natives. Luckily one of the Marauder crewmen had a Very pistol and fired three flares in quick succession. Noting their position, Duigan touched down in a nearby lagoon, taxied deftly between some coral reefs, and brought the Catalina in close. He was astonished to see one of his own commanders, Squadron Leader Price, being hauled aboard with the others. Little did any of them realize that Duigan had just pulled off the first air-sea rescue by an RAAF flying boat.

AFTER COMPLETING the raids against Rabaul and Gasmata on April 6, most of the American bombers refueled at Port Moresby before returning to their respective bases in Australia. One exception was Lieutenant DuBose and his B-17 crew, who experienced a delay as described by Steinbinder, the navigator. "After refueling we had to wait for the B-26s to clear the field," he wrote in his diary. "While we were waiting, the Japs bombed Moresby."

Sitting in the Plexiglas nose of his B-17, Steinbinder had a front-row seat as the first bomb from the retaliatory strike exploded five hundred feet away. He later noted that "the other 69 bombs hit the hills as we tried to get off the field," but the B-17 didn't quite make it out of harm's way. While trying to taxi in the midst of all that excitement, DuBose dropped one of the main wheels into a bomb crater, and two whirling propellers were damaged when they struck the ground.

Fighters from 75 Squadron intercepted the raiders, but the Aussies had little success against the high-level bombers. Flying Officer Edmund J. Johnson, one of the replacement pilots, made a dead-stick landing in a swamp after his engine was disabled by just two bullets. Les Jackson attacked a pair of Zeros head-on, and his engine was likewise put out of commission, forcing him to crash-land on a coral reef. His Kittyhawk came to rest in just six feet of water, at which point Jackson climbed from the cockpit onto one of the wings. When some of his squadron mates appeared and circled overhead, he danced a little jig to signal that he was okay. Seeing this, John Jackson radioed to base that a "kite" was down, not recognizing his own brother on the Kittyhawk's wing. "The pilot's okay— jumping about," he added. "Seems a happy sort of chap."

Johnson and Jackson both escaped injury, but the interception cost 75 Squadron two more Kittyhawks. The good news that day came from the relative successes achieved by the bombers over Rabaul and Gasmata. Almost imperceptibly, there had been a shift in the balance of power. The Allies were still pathetically weak, but their ability to send more than a dozen bombers against the Japanese was perceived as a major improvement. And the momentum continued to build as two more B-26 squadrons became operational. Compared to the paucity of missions completed by the B-17s, the Marauders fairly burst into action, hitting Rabaul no less than nine times over the next seventeen days. Usually the results echoed the first effort—lofty claims for damage compared with little actual harm done to the enemy—but there were exceptions.

Just before noon on April 9, eight Marauders attacked Simpson Harbor and Vunakanau airdrome. Half, loaded with 500-pound general purpose bombs, attacked shipping from 4,500 feet, scoring a near miss on a docked merchantman and a possible hit on a copra warehouse. The other four Marauders conducted a low-level attack on Vunakanau, scattering dozens of 100-pound demolition bombs across the airdrome from a mere five hundred feet. In fact, the bombers were too low: all four received shrapnel damage from their own bombs. But their ordnance hit several parked bombers and started a large fire in a munitions warehouse. The returning aircrews were credited with destroying nine aircraft on the ground, a whopping exaggeration, but there's no denying that the mission was a success. Rear Admiral Masao Kanazawa, commander of the 8th Base Force, described the raid as "severe." He also noted details of the destruction in his diary: "At Vunakanau, 30 casualties from the 7th and 10th Establishment Squads, with one dead at the airfield under a torrent of exploding torpedoes. Conspicuous signs of defeat in the air war."

Kanazawa's profound words about defeat indicate that the Japanese were humiliated by the attack, as though they had not anticipated the Allies' ability to land such a solid punch in broad daylight. In the Malaguna Road stockade, Lark Force POWs heard about the destruction at the airdrome, including rumors that corpses were stacked high in a hangar. "[T]wo truckloads of bodies were seen entering the town en route to the crematorium," noted Capt. David Hutchinson-Smith of the 17th Antitank Battery. "I personally saw the trucks returning to Vunakanau with blood smeared over side boards and wheels, and with shrapnel holes in canopy and body."

The next Marauder raid, on April 11, was less successful. Eight bombers took off from Port Moresby at 0900, but one turned back because of mechanical trouble. The remaining aircraft were divided among three different targets. Four B-26s, all from the 33rd Bombardment Squadron, split into pairs to attack Vunakanau and Lakunai airdromes. The two that bombed Vunakanau released forty 100-pounders from the relatively safe altitude of 2,500 feet and observed no direct hits. The other two bombers dropped their ordnance on the runway and revetment area at Lakunai, reportedly starting a major fire, but the actual damage was minimal.

During the attack run over Lakunai, the Marauder piloted by 1st Lt. Louis W. Ford was rocked by three antiaircraft bursts. Shrapnel hit the right engine, punctured the fuel tank in the left wing, severed hydraulic lines, and ignited vapors in the auxiliary fuel tank mounted in the bomb bay. The latter quickly became a blowtorch, and Ford tugged on the tank's release handle in the cockpit to drop the flaming container. It wouldn't budge. The B-26 seemed destined to explode, but two crewmen climbed into the bomb bay and physically kicked the gas tank free. Although the immediate threat was gone, the bomb bay doors were stuck in the open position because the hydraulic lines had been cut. Faced with multiple in-flight emergencies, Ford safely reached the coast of New Guinea and belly-landed in a field of kunai grass near Tufi. The crew survived, but it took them forty-seven days to reach Port Moresby.

Meanwhile, the four Marauders from the 19th Bomb Squadron targeted shipping in Simpson Harbor. They dropped a dozen 500-pounders and hit nothing but seawater; nevertheless the crews were electrified by the sight of an "aircraft carrier" that had gone unnoticed until they started their bomb runs. *Kasuga Maru*, a converted liner, was moored near Lakunai airdrome while offloading a cargo of Zeros. The Marauders were jumped, in turn, by three Zeros that had been delivered by a different ship. Each side claimed one victory, but neither actually scored any hits.

Returning to Port Moresby, the Marauder crews reported the presence of the *Kasuga Maru* in Simpson Harbor, and an effort to sink it was organized immediately. Three Marauders, loaded with the few remaining 500-pounders at Port Moresby, took off at daybreak on April 12. Four others flew in from Australia during the early morning hours, refueled, and then took off from Seven Mile at 0930 to find the carrier. The first group got through and attacked the carrier (mistakenly identified as *Kaga*), dropping nine bombs. One hit was claimed along with four near misses, but the ship suffered no damage.

The second element of Marauders, minus one aircraft that had returned to base because of mechanical trouble, failed to find the carrier in Simpson Harbor. Risking heavy antiaircraft fire, the crews bombed random targets instead. Only later, while departing toward the east, did they stumble upon *Kasuga Maru* out in St. George's Channel. By that time, however, all of their bombs had been dropped.

And so the record of underwhelming achievements continued. It seemed that no matter what the Allies tried, they could not attack Rabaul without something going haywire.

CHAPTER 14

Wild Eagles

WHILE NEW AMERICAN squadrons were slowly being established in Australia, the first weeks of April were an important time for Japanese units at Rabaul. The most notable event was a major restructuring of the Imperial Navy on April 1, highlighted by the creation of several new air groups. Rear Admiral Goto's 24th Air Flotilla was transferred to the Central Pacific and replaced by the 25th Air Flotilla, led by mustachioed, aristocratic-looking Rear Adm. Sadayoshi Yamada. A naval aviator for twenty-five years, Yamada had commanded the aircraft carriers *Soryu* and *Kaga* earlier in his illustrious career. His new assignment was accompanied by some welcome news: the Tainan Air Group, one of the Imperial Navy's most famous fighter units, would soon be joining his forces at Rabaul.

Organized six months earlier on Formosa (present day Taiwan), which the Japanese called Tainan during World War II, the air group had already seen extensive combat. During the first weeks of the Southern Offensive, they flew missions over the Philippines; then in January the group moved south to Balikpapan for operations over the Malay Peninsula. Only a few weeks later, as the Southern Offensive progressed rapidly into the Netherlands East Indies, the group moved again—this time to the fabled island of Bali. When orders to transfer into the 25th Air Flotilla came at the beginning of April, the pilots and ground personnel boarded the cargo liner *Komaki Maru* for the 2,500-mile voyage to Rabaul.

Considering the scope of operations in the Southeast Area, the addition of the elite fighter group was certain to generate publicity for Yamada's new flotilla. When it came to dramatizing air battles or the achievements of airmen, Japanese periodicals were little different from those in the West, and Rabaul even had its own cadre of staff correspondents attached to naval headquarters. Hardly a day went by without a newspaper story about the latest exploits of the "Navy Wild Eagles." Coined early in the war, the term became a popular literary device, not unlike the use of "Leathernecks" to describe American marines. Naval aviators were referred to as umiwashi (sea eagles) and army airmen as rikuwashi (land eagles), but the papers nearly always called them "wild eagles," evidently to maximize the dramatic impact of the articles.

On paper, Yamada's new flotilla was impressive. The Tainan Air Group (forty-five Type 0 fighters), 1st Air Group (twenty-seven Type 96 land attack aircraft), and 4th Air Group (reformed as a land attack group with thirty-six Type 1s), constituted the backbone of the combat force, while the Yokohama Air Group (twelve Type 97 flying boats) provided long-range reconnaissance and patrols. A separate command, the Special Duty Force, utilized the aircraft transporter *Mogamigawa Maru* to move planes between Rabaul and the advance bases.

At the beginning of April, however, the 25th Air Flotilla's strength was nowhere near prescribed levels. Lakunai airdrome housed just fourteen Zeros and eleven obsolescent Type 96 fighters, several of which needed repairs. The *rikko* units actually possessed only sixteen Type 1s (about half needing repair) and nine aging Type 96 bombers at Vunakanau; and the Yokohama Air Group had eight serviceable flying boats in Simpson Harbor. Fighter strength improved when the aircraft transporter *Goshu Maru* delivered twelve Zeros on April 7, and *Kasuga Maru* arrived five days later with another twenty-four Zeros. The aircraft and pilots from the fighter component of the old 4th Air Group, which was no longer a composite unit, were absorbed into the Tainan Air Group while the latter was en route from Bali.

When *Komaki Maru* docked at Rabaul after two weeks at sea, many of the air group personnel were sick. The idea of being a fighter pilot no longer seemed glamorous to FPO 2nd Class Saburo Sakai, who had experienced a miserable voyage.

More than eighty of us were jammed into the stinking vessel, which crawled sluggishly through the water at twelve knots. For protection we were given only one small 1,000-ton sub chaser. . . .

The ship creaked and groaned incessantly as it wallowed along in its zigzag pattern. Every time we passed the wash of the escorting sub chaser we heeled over, rolling drunkenly. Inside the vessel conditions were torturous. The heat was almost unbearable; I did not spend a single dry day during the entire two weeks. Sweat poured from our bodies in the humid and sultry holds. The smell of paint was gagging, and every single pilot in my hold became violently ill. . . .

At last the ship chugged its way into Rabaul Harbor, the main port of New Britain. With a gasp of relief I staggered from below decks to the pier. I could not believe what I saw. If Bali had been a paradise, then Rabaul was plucked from the very depths of hell itself. There was a narrow and dusty airstrip which was to serve our group. It was the worst airfield I had ever seen anywhere. Immediately behind this wretched runway a ghastly volcano loomed 700 feet into the air. Every few minutes the ground trembled and the volcano groaned deeply, then hurled out stones and thick, choking smoke. Behind the volcano stood pallid mountains stripped of all their trees and foliage.

Docking at the Government Wharf on April 16, 1942, *Komaki Maru* disembarked its weary passengers. Sakai, whose widely published autobiography later made him the most famous pilot in the Imperial Navy, was seriously ill with malaria or dengue fever when he arrived. He remembered the ship as a rusty old bucket, but *Komaki Maru* was actually a large, modern vessel compared to most Japanese merchantmen of the day. Launched in 1933 by the Kokusai Line, the 8,500-ton ship featured several first-class cabins and had called at American ports before the war. But upon its transfer into the Imperial Navy, it received substandard maintenance. After more than a year of South Seas operations with little upkeep, the ship seemed "decrepit" to Sakai.

No matter, *Komaki Maru* had safely delivered one of the navy's crack fighter units to Rabaul. When the next Allied attack occurred, the Tainan Air Group would be ready.

THE MORNING OF April 18 found a large work party of Australian POWs at the Government Wharf, where they labored to unload cargo from the newly arrived *Komaki Maru*. The ship carried an extensive list of hazardous material, including high-octane aviation fuel, bombs, ammunition, and aircraft parts for the Tainan Air Group. Shortly before noon the prisoners were ordered ashore. Guards marched them to a grassy spot, where they sat for a simple meal of rice.

The timing of the break could not have been more advantageous. Without warning, two B-26s appeared over the rim of the caldera to the southwest. The Marauders stayed low, hugging the contours of Tunnel Hill as they raced toward Simpson Harbor at 250 miles per hour. The B-26 flown by 1st Lt. Richard W. Robinson veered to the right, heading toward Lakunai airdrome; the other, piloted by 1st Lieutenant George F. Kahle, Jr., made straight for the Government Wharf and *Komaki Maru*.

In full view of the prisoners and hundreds of Japanese, four 500-pound bombs detached from the bomb bay of the low-level Marauder. The first exploded in the water just ahead of the ship's bow; the next two were direct hits, one on the forward main deck, the other aft; and the fourth landed just astern of the vessel. The *Komaki Maru* shuddered under the impact of the two hits, which ignited the cargo of aviation fuel. "A few seconds later," recalled an Australian eyewitness, "the ship was an inferno and the roar of the flames almost drowned the screams of the Japanese trapped aboard."

Overhead, Kahle closed his bomb bay doors and accelerated from the target area. Across the harbor, Robinson scattered 100-pounders on the dispersal area of Lakunai airdrome while his gunners strafed targets of opportunity, including a moored Kawanishi flying boat. The sky all around the two Marauders erupted with angry black bursts from shore emplacements, but to no effect. As a Japanese soldier later noted: "Our antiaircraft guns and machine guns fired fiercely but were unable to score."

Two patrolling Zeros also gave chase, though their attempt was in vain. The B-26s not only boasted the most powerful radial engines available but were fitted with four-blade propellers, giving them a slight speed advantage that even the Zero pilots had to grudgingly acknowledge. South of Rabaul, however, a third Marauder appeared from the opposite direction, flying *toward* Rabaul about a thousand feet below the Zeros. Piloted by 1st Lt. William A. Garnett, commanding officer of the 33rd Bombardment

Squadron, the B-26 had taken off almost an hour behind schedule due to complications at Port Moresby.

Recently selected for promotion to captain, Bill Garnett was popular with his men and highly regarded as an administrator. But he did not fly often, nor did he currently have his own bomber or even a regular crew. A few weeks earlier, he had wrecked his B-26 (and a citizen's house) during a landing mishap in Australia. Tapped to lead the Rabaul mission, Garnett borrowed a plane and then pieced together a crew. Some of the men had plenty of flight experience, including the radio operator, thirty-one-year-old Tech. Sgt. Theron K. Lutz of New Jersey. Others were rookies. Corporal Sanger E. Reed, a nineteen-year-old mechanic, had volunteered for the mission—his first combat sortie—and served as Garnett's engineer/tail gunner. The crew's trouble began early. As the six Marauders parked at Port Moresby went through start-up procedures on the morning of April 18, Garnett could not get either engine running. He flooded the carburetors, and then drained the batteries while cranking the electric starters. Young Reed watched in silence. "I was the engineer," he said, "but in those days a corporal did not make suggestions to captains that were having trouble. You kept your eyes down and didn't make any noise. He ran the batteries down, so then we had to pull the props through by hand to clear them."

Because of the delay, Garnett delegated the lead to another pilot, and the rest of the Marauders departed. Finally, after getting an off-duty pilot to start the engines, Garnett and his crew got airborne some fifty minutes late. The original plan called for the formation to take a wide detour around the northern end of New Britain and then turn to attack Rabaul from the northwest. Garnett apparently reasoned that if he approached Rabaul directly from the south, he could erase much of the time deficit. He was unaware that three Marauders had already turned back because of a massive weather system over the Solomon Sea. The two that pressed on, flown by Kahle and Robinson, had not followed the planned detour either. Instead they flew straight to Rabaul, dropped their bombs, and were racing for home when Garnett approached them from the opposite direction.

Kahle and Robinson flashed by Garnett, a thousand feet over his head. Fast on their heels came the pursuing Zeros, which subsequently broke away from the retreating Marauders and went after Garnett's bomber instead. Corporal Reed, manning the .50-caliber machine gun in the tail, watched the enemy fighters close the gap. "We couldn't get away," he later recalled. "Garnett tried to dive fast enough to get away from them, but the first plane caught up with us."

Flying the lead Zero was twenty-four-year-old Lt. j.g. Jun-ichi Sasai, commander of the 2nd *Chutai* in the Tainan Air Group. The son of a navy captain, he was a rising star in the Imperial Navy and had earned the nickname "Gamecock" because of his determination. Now, with two victories already to his credit, he approached Garnett's bomber from above and behind. The advantages of speed and altitude favored Sasai, but Sanger Reed, the Marauder's young tail gunner, fired first. He saw the Zero emit smoke, but Sasai may have simply pushed the throttle to full power, for his Zero had sustained no damage.

In the Plexiglas dorsal turret of the B-26, Cpl. Reese S. Davies aimed his twin "fifties" to the rear and opened fire at Sasai, but after discharging just two rounds, the guns fell silent.

Standing at one of the .30-caliber waist guns in the fuselage, Sergeant Lutz heard the two rounds go off and wondered if the turret guns had jammed. The more plausible explanation is that Davies was killed or incapacitated when Sasai opened fire. There is no doubt that the *chutai* leader's shooting was accurate: Sasai's bullets and explosive shells ripped into the right engine of the Marauder, probably puncturing a fuel tank. The engine burst into flames and the fire spread rapidly across the wing, prompting someone in the cockpit to activate the bailout alarm.

Lutz moved aft to warn Reed, who was now shooting at the second Zero. "Lutz was pounding me on the back and telling me to bail out," Reed remembered. "I realized then that the alarm bell was ringing. I pulled the pin on the gun tripod and pushed it ahead, and started to climb out over it. When I got part way out, I could see that our right engine and wing were on fire. At this time I saw the front escape hatch go flying over my head. So, somebody was trying to get out the front. As I tried to get out, my foot got caught on the tripod, and I couldn't get back in because of the slipstream. Sergeant Lutz reached down and jerked my foot loose and away I went—my first parachute jump, and my last."

Reed's chute popped open and he began to rotate slowly. He caught brief glimpses of the Marauder, almost completly engulfed in flames, as it plummeted into the sea near the shoreline. No one else bailed out except Lutz, who followed Reed by jumping from the tail gun position.

Drifting down into a coconut grove, Reed sustained nothing more serious than a few scratches. While brushing himself off, he looked up and saw Lutz descending toward St. George's Channel. After hiding his parachute under some bushes, Reed ran to the water's edge in time to see Lutz swimming around a small promontory toward the opposite shore of a bay. Reed hurried along the beach toward Lutz's position, but as he rounded the promontory he came face to face with a Japanese patrol. There was no point in trying to evade them, so Reed raised his hands, becoming the first American airman captured in the New Guinea region.

The Japanese sent natives in an outrigger canoe to pick up Lutz, who soon joined Reed on the beach. The two captives were then marched to what Reed described as "a Japanese rest camp," probably near Vunapope. The information is supported in the diary of an unnamed Kempeitai officer: "An enemy plane was shot down near Higashisaki. No. 9 Company captured a signal sergeant and engineer corporal who had parachuted from their plane." (The Japanese word *Higashisaki*, meaning "East Point," identified the tip of the Gazelle Peninsula. The 9th Infantry Company was an element of Colonel Kuwada's 3rd Infantry Battalion, encamped near Vunapope.)

Within an hour, a Buick sedan adorned with Japanese flags arrived at the camp. A Kempeitai officer jumped out and made the Americans stand at attention. "He had a riding crop and proceeded to beat the piss out of us," remembered Reed. "When his arm got tired he'd switch hands and keep beating on us, the whole time yelling and screaming. Of course, we couldn't understand a word he was saying."

Lutz and Reed later discovered why the officer was so agitated. Thirteen miles to the north, the *Komaki Maru* burned uncontrollably. Its cargo of ammunition began to explode, adding to the wholesale destruction. At least eleven of the ship's crew perished along with eleven members of the Tainan Air Group who were still aboard, and some thirty-one were wounded. Army casualties, although not recorded, were heavy according to Captain Hutchinson-Smith.

No one could get near the ship to fight the conflagration, which became even more intense when oil from the ship's ruptured fuel tanks ignited. Fanned by the wind, the burning slick spread across the surface of the harbor, forcing other ships to move to safer anchorages.

Long into the night, the fires and explosions continued unabated. A Japanese observer noted, "The noise caused by the explosion of the projectiles and the rise of flames sky-high in the darkness made a gruesome scene." The most spectacular explosion occurred shortly after 1900 hours, when the bombs stored deep in the hull erupted with a blast "that seemed to crumble heaven and earth." Flaming debris rained down onto storage sheds along the wharf, setting those buildings afire. "All at once," wrote the unidentified witness, "the situation was critical, because there were considerable provisions and ammunition within, and all around the vicinity there were mountains of [stockpiled] gasoline and oil. The ammunition exploded repeatedly, fuel fires flared up, and the area was a sea of flames."

By some miracle not a single POW was hurt. However, several made the mistake of displaying their glee in front of the Japanese. "They must all be very happy after seeing today's bombings," wrote one observer. "Among them were some who clapped their hands. All the members of my unit who heard this agreed that [we should] kill them off one after another."

Although no POWs were executed that night, an officer and an enlisted man were severely punished for laughing while the *Komaki Maru* exploded. First, the Japanese lined up all of the Lark Force officers on the parade ground, then forced them to watch as a dozen guards wielding stout wooden sticks pummeled the two offenders for thirty minutes.

WITHIN DAYS of the sinking, Vice Admiral Inoue began preparations for "MO" Operation, the dual invasions of Tulagi and Port Moresby. On April 21, with the Tainan Air Group and Rabaul's land-attack units at full combat readiness, the aerial campaign against Port Moresby resumed. The Japanese attacked more ferociously than ever, generally with at least one full *chutai* of Type 1 bombers escorted by fifteen or more Zeros. Despite a valiant effort by 75 Squadron, the onslaught exacted a steady toll on the defenders.

A midday fight over Port Moresby on April 24 was typical of the David-versus-Goliath encounters. A dozen Zeros, one of them flown by Saburo Sakai, another by Hiroyoshi Nishizawa, strafed Seven Mile airdrome. "We swooped down on six B-26 bombers, fifteen P-40s, and one P-39, all of which seemed to be evacuating the field," recalled Sakai. "We tallied two bombers and six P-40s as definite kills, with a probable for the P-39. After the one-sided air battle we continued up to Moresby [harbor], strafing and burning one anchored PBY."

To their great frustration, neither Sakai nor Nishizawa scored any victories on this occasion. And, contrary to Sakai's account, the Aussies put up only six Kittyhawks. Three were shot down or forced down, with one pilot killed in action.

Les Jackson and twenty-year-old Sgt. Robert W. Crawford were at five thousand feet when they saw at least three Zeros attacking a Marauder. They dived to intervene, and Jackson claimed a victory, but two of the Zeros performed rapid wingovers and got behind Crawford in the blink of an eye. The armor plating behind the seat undoubtedly saved Crawford's life, but he suffered minor wounds nonetheless—and his fighter was sieved with holes. When the rudder cables were shot away, he had no choice but to ditch offshore.

Pilot Officer Oswald J. Channon was leading the other four Kittyhawks at twenty-five thousand feet when one of the pilots spotted Zeros almost three miles below. Plunging downward from the cold upper atmosphere into warm, humid air, the Kittyhawks' canopies fogged up. The pilots zoomed back up to clear their windscreens, but Channon evidently became the victim of an opportunistic Zero. His P-40 was found later that day near a village, Channon's body still inside the wreckage.

Sergeant Michael S. "Mick" Butler was shot down when the oil cooler in his P-40 was punctured during a brief but intense dogfight. Butler made a forced landing that severely damaged the aircraft, but he lived to fight again. Meanwhile, the Zeros conducted several strafing attacks that destroyed a Catalina and two parked Marauders. Overall it was a costly day for Port Moresby's defenders.

AS THE MONTH of April wore on, the aerial punches and counterpunches intensified. Major General Brett assumed command of the Allied air forces on April 20, and during the next ten days American bombers conducted at least eight raids against Rabaul and Lae. The weary crews of the 40th Recon Squadron, the only heavy bombardment unit to hit New Britain thus far, finally received some help. The men and equipment of the 7th Bomb Group were absorbed into the 19th Bomb Group, whose squadrons were scattered all over northern Queensland. After a few weeks of training and refurbishing, the 30th Bomb Squadron at Cloncurry was ready to commence combat missions, with additional squadrons soon to follow.

The newcomers learned the hard way that New Guinea itself could be as hazardous as the enemy. On the afternoon of April 24, four B-17Es of the 30th Bomb Squadron landed at Seven Mile and refueled for their first Rabaul mission, scheduled for early the next morning. Taxiing commenced at approximately 0300, but the lead Fortress tilted into a muddy crater and became firmly stuck. The remaining B-17s took off at the prescribed time and began to join up while climbing in the darkness toward Rabaul, but the last of the three never rendezvoused. It had crashed into the upper slopes of Mt. Obree, instantly killing all eight crewmen. Back at Seven Mile, the mired Fortress was also destroyed despite the crew's best efforts to pull it free. Shortly after 0800, fifteen Zeros of the Tainan Air Group strafed the airdrome, and the Fortress went up in flames.

Two days later, an attack by nine Type 1 bombers and eleven Zeros caused mayhem in the dispersal area at Seven Mile, destroying three A-24s and a B-26. The following day, Flg. Off. Montague D. Ellerton of 75 Squadron took off for Townsville in a Kittyhawk that needed depot-level maintenance. A veteran of the fighting in North Africa, Ellerton was approaching the Australian mainland when he spotted a P-39 that had made an emergency landing on a wide stretch of beach. Thinking he could assist the American pilot, Ellerton attempted a conventional landing on the beach, but the Kittyhawk's wheels dug into the soft sand and flipped the fighter onto its back. Trapped upside down in the cockpit, the twenty-three-year-old Ellerton drowned in the rising tide.

By April 28, 75 Squadron was down to just five serviceable P-40s. John Jackson stood the alert duty that morning along with Barry Cox, Pete Masters, John Brereton, and Sgt. William D. Cowe. Two of the pilots, Cox and Masters, had just been released from the field hospital following severe bouts of dysentery. Still feeling ill, they flew anyway.

Shortly after 1100 hours, Leigh Vial radioed a warning that a Japanese raid was inbound from Lae. The pilots scrambled aloft, initially climbing southward to gain altitude before turning north toward the Japanese. Jackson spotted them first: eight Type 1 bombers at twenty thousand feet or above, plus eleven Zeros perched even higher. He swung the Kittyhawks eastward to gain more altitude and then turned to approach the bombers from below. Climbing steeply, the Aussies pushed the fighters to the very edge of their performance envelope.

Predictably, the Allison V-12 engines lost horsepower above sixteen thousand feet. The Kittyhawks' airspeed bled off rapidly, and Masters was barely making headway by the time he maneuvered into position to shoot at one of the bombers above him. As soon as he opened fire, the recoil caused his fighter to stall. Tumbling earthward in an inverted spin, he could hear Jackson "shouting epithets" over the radio.

Jackson, despite all of his experience, had also gotten himself into a stall. Against a superior number of agile Zeros, it was a terrible position to be in. For a few agonizing moments, his Kittyhawk hung almost motionless in the air, completely vulnerable to the Zeros and *rikko* gunners. Brereton and Cox, trying to stay on Jackson's wing, evidently stalled as well. Bullets suddenly pierced Brereton's fighter, wounding him. He got out of danger, but Jackson and Cox were not so fortunate.

No one knows exactly what happened. Both Kittyhawks were seen to fall uncontrollably. One came down in a screaming vertical dive, striking a hill behind Mount Lawes with such force that its engine was buried six feet deep; the other also dove straight down at tremendous speed but smashed into a swamp. The wreckage of the latter was not located for months.

Les Jackson, hospitalized with an intestinal virus, got up from his cot upon learning of the combat and went with the squadron doctor to the mountain crash site. Initially there was some uncertainty about whose remains had been collected by AIF troops at the scene, but Les didn't have to look. Upon learning that the troops had found a foot in a size ten boot, he knew it was John's.

THE NEXT DAY was Emperor Hirohito's forty-first birthday. All across Japan, and on every military post, airfield, and ship throughout the empire, the event was treated as a national holiday. At Lae, the men of the Tainan Air Group gathered for a special breakfast. "All sailors with any cooking experience joined the kitchen staff," remembered Saburo Sakai, "and prepared the best possible breakfast from the limited supplies available."

The flyers had just finished their meal when a strident bugle call warned of an incoming raid. High overhead, three B-17s released several bombs that exploded with unusually good accuracy among the planes parked at the airdrome. "Five Zeros lay in flaming wreckage," Sakai later wrote. "Four others were seriously damaged, riddled throughout with jagged bomb splinters." (The 25th Air Flotilla war diary confirms Sakai's statement, listing five Zeros as "burned out" on April 29.)

A few Zeros escaped damage, and two of Sakai's squadron mates took off to chase after the high-flying B-17s. Hours later FPO 1st Class Toshio

Ota returned, claiming that he had downed a B-17. But the 93rd Bomb Squadron, which conducted the mission, lost no Fortresses that day.

Infuriated by the interruption of their holiday, the Tainan pilots organized a counterattack. Jun-ichi Sasai led eight Zeros aloft to "return the Emperor's birthday greetings." Heading west toward Port Moresby, the fighters crested the craggy tops of the Owen Stanleys and then immediately nosed over, hugging the downhill slopes to avoid detection.

The attack worked to perfection. Swooping down on Seven Mile airdrome, the Zeros took the Australians by surprise. Eight snarling fighters—one skimming along just twelve feet above the ground—raced the length of the runway with their weapons spitting thousands of bullets. Men scattered in all directions as Sasai and his pilots doubled back for multiple runs. When they returned to Lae, they jubilantly reported burning a parked B-17, damaging three others, and also damaging a fighter. (The Allies acknowledged damage to a twin-engine Hudson and one Kittyhawk.)

Later that morning, a grieving Les Jackson took over 75 Squadron as the interim commanding officer. But the squadron was completely used up, and there were no serviceable planes for him to lead when a formation of Type 1 bombers attacked the airdrome that afternoon. The Australians could only watch in dismay as the enemy formation dropped a total of 108 daisy-cutters on the airfield. Afterward, four Zeros strafed the runway again.

Fortunately for the beleaguered outpost, Port Moresby lacked fighter defense for only one more day. On the morning of April 30, a large contingent of P-39D Airacobras approached the airdrome from the south. Hundreds of war-weary men came out to watch and cheer as twenty-six slender green fighters touched down one by one on the hard-packed runway. The flight was led by Boyd D. "Buzz" Wagner, a pipe-smoking Pennsylvanian who, at the ripe old age of twenty-five, was already a lieutenant colonel. His accelerated promotion was the reward for becoming the Army's first ace of the war, accomplished the previous December in the Philippines. Now assigned to the headquarters staff, he was sent to Port Moresby as the senior American fighter director. Knowing that 75 Squadron was used up, he was anxious to bring as many American fighters to New Guinea as he could get. The pilots, members of the 35th and 36th Pursuit Squadrons, 8th Pursuit Group, had barely gotten acclimated to Australia before they found themselves at the front lines. Now, as they climbed from the unique car-type doors of their Airacobras, they were completely unprepared for the blast of hot, humid air that washed over them. It was a rude New Guinea welcome.

In the meantime, the weary mechanics of 75 Squadron managed to patch up three Kittyhawks sufficiently to return them to service. Their effort, however, was merely symbolic. During the next attempt to intercept a Japanese raid on May 2, nineteen-year-old Sgt. Donald W. Munro was shot down and killed. Later that day, one of the two remaining Kittyhawks was wrecked in a takeoff mishap. The last available fighter flew briefly on May 3, but the pilot was forced to land just seven minutes after takeoff with an overheating engine. With that, 75 Squadron's defense of Port Moresby was finished.

By the slimmest of margins, the squadron had preserved Australia's last outpost. For a span of forty-four days, the men of 75 Squadron had faced the Japanese blitz alone. The cost: twenty-two Kittyhawks and the lives of twelve pilots, including the squadron commander. And then, just when the Australians had nothing left to fight with, Buzz Wagner showed up with his Airacobras, almost as if timing his arrival for dramatic effect.

The Airacobras did not by themselves save New Guinea, but there is no question that they made a positive impact on the situation at Port Moresby. Although the Japanese would maintain aerial superiority in the region for months to come, the dark days of terror and frustration, of diving for cover while praying for a miracle, were finally coming to an end.

CHAPTER 15

MO: The Offensive Blunted

DURING THE FIRST WEEK of May 1942, the Japanese continued to pound Port Moresby relentlessly in preparation for MO Operation. Losses accumulated on both sides, but no unit struggled more than the 8th Pursuit Group. Six Airacobras were lost during the first four days alone, with all six pilots either killed or missing in action. The shortcomings of the P-39 were plainly evident in combat against Zeros, yet the Americans fought aggressively. They had to. By this time, virtually everyone at Port Moresby knew the Japanese planned to invade.

Major General Horii had scheduled the assault to begin on May 9. His plan called for two battalions of the 144th Infantry Regiment, supported by the 55th Mountain Artillery Battalion, to land southeast of Port Moresby near the site of Kila Kila airdrome. Simultaneously, another battalion would debark northwest of Port Moresby and proceed directly inland toward Seven Mile airdrome. And, in yet another cooperative effort, troops of the 3rd Kure Special Naval Landing Force would encircle and capture the fixed defenses.

But the Japanese were unaware of one huge disadvantage. For months, Allied cryptographers had been steadily breaking down the primary code used by the Imperial Navy for encrypting messages. Known as JN-25, the code was never completely broken (at best, analysts deciphered perhaps fifteen percent of the messages), but by early April the experts knew a great deal about MO Operation. Analysts concluded correctly that both Port Moresby and the southern Solomons were the intended targets, and by the end of April they knew enough about the plan to formulate a detailed outline.

Much of the analysis was focused on Rabaul. Allied reconnaissance planes revealed that both Lakunai and Vunakanau airdromes were busier than normal, an indication that the 25th Air Flotilla was being strengthened. On May 1, a particularly large influx of land attack aircraft arrived at Vunakanau, including nine Type 1s and eighteen Type 96s. The former were replacements for the 4th Air Group while the latter belonged to the Genzan Air Group, a veteran unit formed in Korea. Renowned for their role in sinking the British warships *Prince of Wales* and *Repulse*, the Genzan flyers would be used mainly to support an intense schedule of long-range patrols from Rabaul with their older Mitsubishi G3Ms. Finally, additional Type 0 fighters were parked at Lakunai, having been pulled from the forward bases to augment Rabaul's fighter strength. This put Lae in a precarious situation, with only six Zeros operational as of May 4.

Aboard his new flagship *Yamato*, anchored in the Inland Sea at Hashirajima, Admiral Yamamoto fretted over the division of forces required by the separate assaults on Port Moresby and Tulagi. He was also troubled by Vice Admiral Inoue's request for additional carriers. Presently the Close Support Force consisted of four heavy cruisers, one destroyer, and one small flattop, *Shoho*. Displacing less than fourteen thousand tons, she carried only sixteen planes—four of which were old A5Ms. Yamamoto was reluctant to detach any of the fleet carriers from the Mobile Striking Force, but he knew that the Americans would try to stop the offensive with one or more carriers of the Pacific Fleet. Yamamoto's greatest desire was to draw the American carriers into the open and crush them; therefore he ordered Rear Adm. Chuichi Hara, commander of Carrier Division 5, to support the operation with Japan's newest fleet carriers, *Zuikaku* and *Shokaku*. Arriving at Truk on April 25, Hara's two flattops joined a pair of heavy cruisers and six destroyers to become the MO Striking Force, commanded by round-faced Vice Adm. Takeo Takagi.

As April drew to a close, Inoue received the go-ahead to commence the operation. He ordered the transports and warships of the Tulagi invasion force to begin their phase on April 29, and as soon as they departed Simpson Harbor, other ships began loading for the assault on Port Moresby.

Dockside workers, including hundreds of Australian POWs, struggled mightily to load eleven troop carriers and several large warships. Among the latter was the aircraft transporter *Mogamigawa Maru*, which carried the 5th Air Attack Force headquarters, personnel of the 4th Air Group and Tainan Air Group, occupation troops, maintenance supplies, fuel, and all the equipment necessary to establish a new base at Port Moresby. Clearly, Vice Admiral Inoue was confident of a decisive victory.

While the Australian POWs loaded the invasion fleet, Takagi's powerful striking force steamed south from Truk. On paper, the total forces available to Inoue were impressive: three aircraft carriers, six heavy cruisers, three light cruisers, thirteen destroyers, two large minelayers, thirteen transports, and a host of auxiliary ships. By design, however, the forces were divided among several widely scattered groups.

At Pacific Fleet headquarters in Hawaii, Adm. Chester Nimitz made a determined effort to thwart the operation. He could do little to assist the Australian garrison at Tulagi, but he was certainly capable of interfering with the Japanese fleet in the Coral Sea. On April 15 he sent *Lexington* and Task Force 11, now commanded by Rear Adm. Aubrey Fitch, to join *Yorktown* and Task Force 17 in the Southwest Pacific. The rendezvous was accomplished on May 1 near the New Hebrides, whereupon the warships commenced refueling from a pair of oilers.

In Melbourne, Lieutenant General Brett placed the Northeast Area on high alert in response to the Japanese threat and ordered a significant increase in the number of patrols over the Coral Sea. He also ordered more bombing raids on Rabaul and the advance bases at Lae, Salamaua, and Gasmata. In compliance, the 22nd Bomb Group scheduled a mission against Rabaul for the first day of May. Taking off from Reid River, a new airbase outside Townsville, the Marauders flew up to Port Moresby on April 30 with plans to launch the attack the next morning. But in yet another dismal effort, only three Marauders made it all the way to the target. The rest turned back early due to "a variety of electrical and hydraulic problems."

The weather over Rabaul was terrible, so the Marauders bombed the alternate target, Gasmata. Returning safely to Port Moresby, the crews were ordered to remain overnight while additional Marauders flew up from Townsville for another crack at Rabaul. Early in the morning on May 2, the B-26s departed hastily to avoid an incoming Japanese raid. One

Marauder did not get off the ground before the enemy attack commenced, but the remaining seven planes headed for New Britain.

The mission leader, 1st Lt. Christian I. Herron of the 33rd Bomb Squadron, had an older and vastly more experienced officer beside him in the copilot's seat. Although not qualified to physically fly the B-26, Charles Raymond "Bob" Gurney, a thirty-seven-year-old RAAF squadron leader, flew with Herron's crew to share his extensive knowledge of the region. Raised in New South Wales, Gurney had joined the air force in 1925 and later flew freight to the Morobe goldfields for Guinea Airways. Eventually he became a captain in Qantas Airlines, flying four-engine Empires between Sydney and Great Britain. Recently, he had been given command of 33 Squadron, which operated ex-Qantas Empires out of Townsville.

At some point during the flight to Rabaul, Herron became separated from the other Marauders, which pressed on without him. Thus, he not only reached Rabaul well behind the others but the Japanese were fully alerted. Despite the odds Herron made a daring solo attack. During his run over Simpson Harbor, one of the Marauder's engines was hit hard by antiaircraft fire, and Herron briefly sought shelter inside a large thunderstorm brewing over St. George's Channel. Inside the turbulent storm, however, he struggled just to keep the crippled bomber airborne. He ordered the crew to toss overboard anything that wasn't bolted down, which made the aircraft marginally easier to control; he then flew south almost three hundred miles, trying to get closer to friendly territory. Approaching the Trobriands, Herron instructed the radio operator to begin broadcasting their position and intentions to ditch. Gurney, knowing the Japanese would likely intercept the uncoded message, suggested a simple but clever deception. The radioman tapped out: "Making a forced landing where Francine used to live," which the staff at Port Moresby recognized. A woman of that name had lived on Kiriwina Island, the biggest in the Trobriand group. Now headquarters knew where to send a rescue plane.

But the B-26's flight did not end happily. Evidently hoping to save the airplane, Herron attempted a conventional wheels-down landing on a patch of flat terrain that "looked like a meadow." Unfortunately it was the wrong call. The B-26 was extremely tricky to handle on one engine, and because of its tricycle landing gear, not just any field would do. As a rule, pilots were trained to leave the wheels retracted for emergency landings on unfamiliar terrain. The rationale was simple: if the ground proved to be anything but smooth, the extended nose wheel could strike an unseen obstacle and cause the aircraft to flip. For that very reason, belly landings were considered safer and usually caused less damage to the aircraft. Furthermore, the emergency procedures section of the B-26 operating manual explicitly cautioned that the airplane would not "maintain altitude on one engine with the landing gear extended."

Nevertheless, Herron put the wheels down, necessitating an approach speed much higher than normal to maintain control of the crippled bomber. Not surprisingly, the appearance of flat, solid ground on Kiriwina was deceptive. It was actually a bog, much like the one on New Guinea where the "Swamp Ghost" came to rest. When the B-26 touched down and decelerated, the nose wheel plowed into the marsh. The front strut ripped loose, and the Plexiglas nose of the Marauder buried itself in the muck, causing the bomber to flip over onto its back. Moments later five of the crewmen emerged from a hatch in the bomber's belly. Shaken but unhurt, they struggled through waist-deep ooze to the crumpled nose. They found Gurney dead, but Herron was still alive, trapped in the upside-down cockpit as it slowly began to fill with swamp water. He called out, anxious to know if anyone was hurt. The survivors clawed desperately at the wreckage, trying to pull Herron to safety, but he drowned before they could reach him. Soon thereafter, a Catalina arrived from Port Moresby and flew the anguished crew back to base.

Other squadrons suffered even greater losses during the frenzied reconnaissance effort over the Coral Sea. The RAAF's Hudsons and Catalinas were in dire need of overhaul, but the constant demand for patrols and reconnaissance was too great to pull them off the line. The flying boats in particular showed the effects of too many missions. The hulls leaked badly after months of combat operations, and the crews operated in a state of near exhaustion. And yet, when the Japanese threatened to invade Port Moresby, the Aussies went out time after time to patrol the sea lanes and reconnoiter the enemy's bases. In a span of just five days, the Catalina squadrons launched almost twenty sorties from Port Moresby, Tulagi, and other advance bases. The flying boats achieved their objectives but at great cost: three were lost, two others were damaged, and eighteen airmen failed to return.

The first Catalina lost was piloted by twenty-six-year-old Flg. Off. Allan L. Norman of South Australia. Launching from Port Moresby at 0600 on

May 4, his crew headed for the Solomon Sea. A little more than six hours later, they reported an attack by enemy planes southwest of Bougainville. Nothing more was heard from the flying boat, which in fact had been badly damaged and forced down at sea. All nine crewmen were picked up by a Japanese warship and taken to Rabaul, where they were turned over to the 81st Naval Garrison Unit, an infantry force that conducted shore patrols and routine guard duties.

Two days after Norman's Catalina was forced down, Sqn. Ldr. Godfrey Hemsworth and his crew took off for a lengthy reconnaissance flight. Fourteen hours into the mission they came across a pair of Japanese destroyers southeast of Misima Island. Before the initial sighting report could be transmitted in full, a new message from the Catalina stated that the plane was under attack. Once again, nothing more was heard from the aircraft. No Japanese carriers were operating in the area, but the converted seaplane tender *Kamikawa Maru* was busy setting up an advance base at nearby Deboyne Island. Perhaps one of its floatplanes encountered the Catalina and shot it down. Although the circumstances are speculative, this much is known: Hemsworth and his entire crew were killed when their plane crashed near Misima. In a span of two days a total of eighteen airmen—including one of Australia's most experienced pilots—were lost while patrolling the Coral Sea.

The reconnaissance effort was not in vain. On the afternoon of May 3, Allied planes located the Tulagi invasion fleet in the southern Solomons. The sighting reports were received by Task Force 17, as were a few panicky messages from the Australian garrison at Tulagi. Rear Admiral Fletcher, well south of the Solomons, expected to rendezvous the next day with the former ANZAC squadron commanded by Rear Admiral Crace, but the reports prompted him to alter his plans.

Taking *Yorktown* north at high speed, Fletcher reached a position approximately one hundred miles south of Guadalcanal by dawn on May 4. Although too late to prevent the invasion of Tulagi, *Yorktown* launched twenty-eight SBD Dauntlesses, twelve TBD Devastators, and six F4F Wildcats to attack the enemy naval force. The raiders caught the Japanese totally by surprise, but from the Americans' point of view the results were disappointing. Problems with fogged-over bombsights and faulty torpedoes limited the damage to only a few confirmed hits, prompting Fletcher to launch two additional strikes. By the end of the day,

Yorktown's airmen had dropped twenty-two torpedoes and seventy-six 1,000-pound bombs; they also fired tens of thousands of machine gun rounds while strafing ships or shooting down a handful of pesky float-planes. Bullets proved nearly as effective as bombs and torpedoes against the lightly constructed vessels, but for all the ordnance expended, only the destroyer *Kikuzuki* was sunk outright. A large minesweeper, *Tama Maru,* was mortally damaged and sank two days later; two other warships suffered minor damage; and two small wooden patrol ships (former whalers used for minesweeping) were blown up by direct hits. The cost to the *Yorktown*: only three planes, with all pilots and crewmen rescued.

Fletcher's attack stunned the Japanese. At 25th Air Flotilla head-quarters in Rabaul, Rear Admiral Yamada scrambled to react. A raid against Port Moresby by G3Ms of the Genzan Air Group was called off and the planes were rearmed with torpedoes to strike back at the American task force.

But the Americans counterpunched first. Six Marauders took off from Port Moresby and attacked Vunakanau airdrome, dropping dozens of 100-pound demolition bombs on the runway area. They found the Japanese bombers parked in the southwest corner of the airfield, and the Marauder crews claimed the destruction of twelve to fifteen G3Ms. According to Japanese records, however, only five were actually hit—and all five were deemed repairable. Evidently, much of what the American airmen saw was the combination of several large fires as fifty drums of fuel, two gasoline trucks, and a utility vehicle went up in flames at Vunakanau.

Continuing to react to the threat posed by Fletcher's warships, Yamada ordered additional patrol planes to cover the Port Moresby Invasion Force as it got underway from Simpson Harbor on the afternoon of May 4. Australian POWs could not help but be impressed by the size of the fleet steaming out of the harbor. Counting nearly thirty ships, they began to refer to the spectacle as the "Day of the Armada." Civilian nurse Alice Bowman, held prisoner at Vunapope, watched in amazement as "a sleek Jap aircraft carrier" headed down St. George's Channel in company with four heavy cruisers.

The carrier was *Shoho*, centerpiece of Rear Adm. Aritomo Goto's Support Force. The flattop and its escorts from the 6th Cruiser Division had provided cover for the Tulagi operation the previous day, then made a quick dash to Rabaul to cover the departure of the Port Moresby Invasion

Force. Once the transports were safely away, the support force turned toward the last reported position of the American carriers. The invasion fleet, meanwhile, headed south for the Jomard Passage, which would lead them through the Louisiade Archipelago en route to Port Moresby.

Intent on finding these naval forces, the Allies launched dozens of reconnaissance flights from Queensland, Horn Island, and Port Moresby. At 1035 on May 4, a Mitchell crew from the 90th Bombardment Squadron reported "a carrier and two heavy cruisers" sixty miles southwest of Bougainville. Before they could send more details, the B-25 was driven away by enemy fighters. The next day, another B-25 from the 90th found the carrier, which turned out to be *Shoho*, and loitered overhead for more than an hour while the radio operator transmitted a homing signal. The idea was that B-17s would track the radio frequency and attack the carrier, but no friendly bombers responded.

At Port Moresby that evening, a crew from the 40th Recon Squadron prepared to continue the surveillance of the *Shoho*. "We are to go out tomorrow at 12:45 A.M. and locate an aircraft carrier & its escorts," John Steinbinder noted during his overnight stay. "Three B-17s came in tonight loaded with 600# bombs. We are to go out and spot [the carrier] so that we can radio its position and these 3 are to bomb it."

The B-17s, all from the 19th Bomb Group at Townsville, would augment the 40th Recon Squadron over the next several days. Their presence at the crowded airdrome was a calculated risk. The big bombers made easy targets for Japanese raiders, but the Allies were determined to put as many aircraft as possible into the skies over the Coral Sea.

The early morning mission went off as planned, although the recon Fortress did not take off until 0345 due to mechanical problems. By 0800 the crew found the *Shoho* in company with two destroyers, two cruisers, and a seaplane tender. "We circled above them at 14,000' and radioed their position back to Moresby," noted Steinbinder in his diary. Back at Seven Mile, the waiting B-17s rumbled into the air and headed for the coordinates given by Steinbinder. For a while, the lone Fortress continued to shadow the Japanese warships, but when a pair of fighters took off from the carrier's flight deck and climbed rapidly, the B-17 judiciously headed north "at full speed" to begin the next segment of its scheduled mission.

The B-17s from Port Moresby attacked *Shoho* in the vicinity of Bougainville, but just as with every previous attempt to bomb ships from high altitude, the Fortresses failed to record a single hit. The lack of success did not surprise Dick Carmichael. "We couldn't hit the side of a barn," he acknowledged later. "With the Norden bombsight, which is all we had at that time, on a clear day at twenty thousand, twenty-five thousand, or thirty thousand feet . . . a B-17 or B-24 is not going to make any hits on a ship maneuvering below, any kind of a ship."

The first attempt to sink *Shoho* had been a failure, but now the carrier's location was well known—and the next attack would have a much different outcome.

AT ALMOST EXACTLY the same hour, the crew of a Kawanishi flying boat sent an important message to Rabaul. They had allegedly sighted "one battleship, one aircraft carrier, three A-class cruisers and five destroyers" approximately 420 miles southwest of Shortland Island. The news thrilled Rear Admiral Yamada and his staff, who presumed *Yorktown* and Task Force 17 had been located. Fletcher had no battleships, but he did have three cruisers and six destroyers. The Japanese simply mistook the 9,950-ton *Astoria*, largest of the cruisers, for a battleship. At Vunakanau, ground crews again began loading torpedoes into G3Ms of the Genzan Air Group, but headquarters decided the American fleet was too far away, and the attack order was never issued.

By the afternoon of May 6, after casting about for two days in search of each other, the opposing forces had developed a relatively clear tactical picture. Yamada ordered the *rikko* units at Vunakanau to prepare for dawn searches and possible strikes against the American carriers. Aboard *Yorktown*, now in company with the *Lexington* task force, Fletcher deduced that the Port Moresby invasion fleet would pass through the Louisiade Archipelago. He ordered his combined forces—which also included Rear Admiral Crace's cruiser support group—to cut them off.

Daybreak on May 7 found the opposing sides sending out dozens of planes to reconnoiter the Coral Sea. Before long, the radio channels were filled with sighting reports. First, the crew of a Nakajima B5N from *Shokaku* found two American ships, the oiler *Neosho* and the destroyer *Sims*, approximately 160 miles south of the MO Striking Force. Somehow the airmen mistook the big oiler for a carrier, possibly because it was located approximately where Rear Admiral Hara expected to find the American flattops. Upon receiving the erroneous sighting report, Hara began launching strike planes from *Shokaku* and *Zuikaku* at 0800.

BUT TASK FORCE 17 was not where the Japanese anticipated. Instead, the carriers were more than three hundred miles to the west, approaching Rossel Island in the Louisiade Archipelago. Nearby, the cruiser support group under Rear Admiral Crace had just detached from the main force and was proceeding directly toward the Jomard Passage, where Crace planned to block any attempts by the invasion fleet to reach Port Moresby. His warships had hardly separated from Task Force 17 when a floatplane from the heavy cruiser *Furutaka* found them.

The floatplane's sighting report reached 25th Air Flotilla headquarters at approximately 0830, and amplifying information was received from two additional search planes soon thereafter. Yamada responded by ordering an immediate strike. Lieutenant Kuniharu Kobayashi led twelve Type 1 *rikko* armed with torpedoes aloft at 0950, followed by an escort of eleven Zeros. Slightly more than an hour later, nineteen Type 96 *rikko* carrying bombs took off and headed independently toward the last position given by the *Furutaka*'s floatplane.

Meanwhile, the crew of an SBD scout bomber from *Yorktown* had found *Shoho* about forty miles northwest of Misima Island at 0845. *Yorktown* and *Lexington* both began launching aircraft at 0926, and within forty-five minutes a force totaling ninety-three aircraft was on its way to attack the Japanese flattop. Ironically, there were now four different attack groups in the air—three Japanese and one American—each searching for distant targets.

The blue-gray planes of the U.S. Navy struck first. A trio of dive-bombers opened the attack on *Shoho* at 1110, and for the next twenty-one minutes the flattop was at the mercy of dozens of dive-bombers and torpedo planes. But no mercy was given. For the first time since Pearl Harbor, American forces had the upper hand on an enemy carrier. The Navy pilots literally smashed the diminutive *Shoho*, hitting the flattop with thirteen bombs and seven torpedoes. It sank at 1135, only four minutes after the captain gave the order to abandon ship.

AFTER A LENGTHY SEARCH, Lt. Cmdr. Kakuichi Takahashi, leader of the combined strike force from *Zuikaku* and *Shokaku*, reached the frustrating conclusion that the American carriers were not where the scout planes reported they would be. Only two ships had been found, a large oiler and a destroyer. The Nakajima Type 97s with their heavy torpedoes were getting low on fuel, so Takahashi directed them to return to their carriers along with the Zeros. He then turned his thirty-six Aichi Type 99 dive-bombers loose on the oiler and its escort.

The antiaircraft gunners aboard *Neosho* and *Sims* could not cope with so many attackers. At 1126 three bombs struck *Sims* in quick succession and broke her back. The destroyer sank quickly, stern first. Scores of sailors leapt into the water, but two powerful explosions from the ship's depth charges killed many of the struggling swimmers. A whaleboat picked up only fifteen survivors, all enlisted men, two of whom later died from massive injuries.

The much larger *Neosho* was pummeled by seven direct hits, and the pilot of a crippled dive-bomber deliberately crashed his plane into the mangled ship. Eight more bombs struck the water near *Neosho*, causing severe splinter damage, but the sturdy oiler refused to sink. Dead in the water, the oiler drifted for four days, her wretched survivors trapped on board. Help did not arrive until May 11, when the American destroyer *Henley* rescued what was left of the crew and then finished off the abandoned wreck with torpedoes.

HUNDREDS OF MILES to the west, eight B-17s lumbered into the air from Townsville to attack the Japanese invasion fleet. Major Edward C. Teats recalled, "We were to find the Jap convoy and hit it before sunset, if possible." It was a tall order. The enemy ships were more than seven hundred miles to the northeast, yet General Brett sent the heavy bombers in the hopes of accomplishing something positive for a change. Two B-17s turned back because of engine trouble, but the remaining six crossed the Coral Sea in pairs, each element separated by about five minutes. After several hours of flying, the first element sighted the Port Moresby Invasion Force. Bursting antiaircraft shells alerted the other two flights, and Teats looked down to see ships "maneuvering wildly in all directions, like an aggregation of excited water bugs."

Observing from the rearmost element, Teats noted that the first and second pairs of B-17s failed to score any hits. Presently his own bombardier, 1st Lt. M. D. Stone, selected a target and announced that he was ready to make his run. Teats turned to the specified heading and was about to switch the autopilot over to the bombardier's control when heavy flak began exploding directly ahead, precisely at their altitude. Shoving the yoke forward, Teats dropped the big Fortress several thousand feet "to mess up the Jap gunners' range," but the enemy gun directors quickly adjusted their aim. The effect, recalled Teats, was alarming.

> Neither before nor after have I seen such heavy and well placed antiaircraft fire as those cruisers and destroyers threw at us. We could see the orange flashes as the ships' batteries fired. Things grew hotter and hotter. The side-gunner reported some [bursts] close behind us, and then my wing man peeled off and took some distance because one burst was so close, the side-gunner thought the plane had been hit.
>
> The split-second the bombardier reported "bombs away," I made a sharp diving turn away to the left and at that same instant, the tail-gunner began to chatter excitedly through the interphone. [In] the turn, I saw a line of shell bursts on the level course we had just left, and later the tail-gunner reported that one burst really had our name on it. If we had not turned when we did, someone else might be relating this story . . . but it wouldn't be me. I knew that those Nip gunners were in the groove, and I also knew that they were getting close. The tail-gunner reported that the bursts started about a mile behind and each one came a little closer, directly on our level. By his report, we evaded by a split second either a direct hit, or one just as bad.

Teats credited the Japanese warships with "beautiful antiaircraft gunnery," but remarkably no B-17s were hit. In turn, there is evidence that the bombers scored either a hit or a near miss on at least one transport. The diary kept by Private Hisaeda, embarked in *Matsue Maru*, refers to one of the transports requiring damage repair.

MUCH LIKE THE "Navy Wild Eagles" from *Shokaku* and *Zuikaku*, Lieutenant Kobayashi and the land-attackers of the 4th Air Group were frustrated. By midday on May 7 they had failed to locate the American carriers, though they had actually gotten within seventy-five miles of Task Force 17. Suddenly headquarters ordered Kobayashi to turn west and search a new location. Finding no ships, the strike leader sent his Zero escorts back to Rabaul. Nearby, the bomb-carrying G3Ms of the Genzan Air Group also searched in vain for the American carriers.

By sheer coincidence, the Zeros headed for Rabaul stumbled upon Rear Admiral Crace's cruiser support group. During the morning, search planes from Rabaul had shadowed the warships from time to time, but no other aircraft had been seen overhead until the Zeros approached from astern at 1447. The fighters, described by one Allied source as "a formation of 10 or 12 single-engine monoplanes with retractable landing gear," flew past the ships on a parallel course a few miles to the west. Aboard the heavy cruiser *Australia*, eighteen-year-old Midn. Dacre H. D. Smyth counted eleven fighters (the correct number) and recalled that they turned away when some of the screening destroyers fired at them

The presence of the Japanese fighters greatly disturbed Crace, who was justifiably worried about the lack of air support for his warships. Only five months had passed since *Prince of Wales* and *Repulse* were overwhelmed off the Malay Peninsula, and his own formation was vulnerable to bombers and torpedo planes out of Rabaul. If fighters were in the area, the dreaded attack planes were not far off.

Oddly enough, the next aircraft to appear was a *Yorktown* dive-bomber, its crew lost. The pilot, a young ensign, radioed for directions to his carrier but was instead ordered to fly to Port Moresby. He was fortunate. Arriving as he did on the heels of enemy fighters, he might have been blown out of the sky by jumpy antiaircraft gunners.

No sooner had the Dauntless flown off than another formation of planes approached, this time from straight ahead—and this group was not friendly. The Zeros had reported the cruiser group's location to Lieutenant Kobayashi, who alerted the Genzan flyers nearby and then ordered his torpedo-carrying G4Ms to attack. He evidently planned to use the same strategy that had sunk *Prince of Wales* and *Repulse* the previous December, coordinating both formations to strike simultaneously from different directions. While the Genzan Air Group maneuvered southward to attack the warships from astern, Kobayashi led his *rikko* straight toward the enemy.

Down below, the six warships gathered into a diamond-shaped defensive alignment known as Formation Victor. The flagship, the ten-thousand-ton *Australia*, was in the center of the diamond with the American destroyer *Perkins* in the lead and two more destroyers on the outer flanks. Bringing up the rear were the heavy cruiser USS *Chicago*, outfitted with a new radar system, and the light cruiser HMAS *Hobart*. Plotters in the *Chicago*'s combat information center tracked the incoming planes while the formation plowed ahead, each ship taking ample separation from the others to allow for hard maneuvering.

Unfortunately for Kobayashi, the Type 1 *rikko* approached the Allied formation several minutes ahead of the bomb-carrying G3Ms, rather than simultaneously. Mistaking *Australia* for a British *Warspite*-class battleship, the torpedo bombers commenced their attack at approximately 1430. Descending in a tight V, they leveled off just above the wave tops and bored in from dead ahead at 250 miles per hour. Midshipman Smyth recalled seeing them "bunched together and flying very low" a few degrees off the *Australia*'s port bow. What he couldn't see were the huge Type 91 torpedoes, one inside the belly of each plane. Upon release, the eighteen-foot-long weapons would race beneath the surface at more than forty knots, making them difficult to evade.

In a coincidental case of mistaken identity, numerous sailors aboard the ships thought the Japanese attackers were Army Type 97 heavy bombers (Mitsubishi Ki-21s). The combat narrative published by the Office of Naval Intelligence observed that the features of the Type 97 "best fitted" the description of the attacking aircraft, and it was an understandable mistake. The two Mitsubishi designs were virtually indistinguishable when viewed from head-on, but the Ki-21 was not equipped to carry torpedoes.

The shipboard antiaircraft gunners cared little about the attackers' identity. Beginning with *Perkins*, the destroyers of the outer screen opened fire with 5-inch guns when the low-flying planes drew within 6,500 yards. Due to extraordinary luck or superb marksmanship, two *rikko* were shot down in quick succession—and Kobayashi's plane was the first to crash. Dividing into two elements, the remaining ten G4Ms roared past *Perkins* on both sides and headed toward the two biggest ships, the cruisers *Australia* and *Chicago*. Now inside the warships' defensive ring, the twin-engine torpedo planes faced a hailstorm of fire from all sides. Twisting and turning, each ship fired every gun that could be brought to bear. With remarkable bravery the Japanese aircrews maintained their discipline, closing to within fifteen hundred yards to drop their "fish," but due to the intensity and accuracy of the antiaircraft fire, only half managed to release their torpedoes.

On the bridge of *Australia*, Capt. Harold B. Farncomb gave instructions to the helmsman and with skillful maneuvering dodged two of the torpedoes by the narrowest of margins. Inside the hull, having just reached his battle station, Midshipman Smyth could hear the high-pitched whine of the motors as the torpedoes passed by. Several hundred yards aft of *Australia*, Capt. Howard D. Bode was equally adroit at maneuvering *Chicago* between the three torpedoes aimed at his cruiser. None hit, but *Chicago* did not escape without damage. Gunners in the torpedo planes strafed the upper decks of the cruiser as they flew past, wounding seven sailors, two of them mortally.

The shipboard gunners continued to blast away at the retreating planes, and two more Mitsubishis tumbled into the sea. In the aftermath, numerous gun crews claimed a share in the scoring. *Chicago* reported five enemy aircraft shot down, while other ships estimated between four and six torpedo bombers fell during the attack. The 4th Air Group indeed suffered a severe blow that afternoon, losing four planes and their crews over the task force. A fifth *rikko*, its senior radio operator dead and the pilot badly wounded, ditched on Deboyne Reef and sustained heavy damage. Another shot-up G4M proceeded directly to Lae and suffered additional damage upon landing. Thus, only six out of the original twelve torpedo bombers returned to Vunakanau. The attack had also been extremely costly for the 4th Air Group in terms of casualties, with thirty-one crewmen killed and at least two wounded—and not a single torpedo had struck its target.

Four minutes after the torpedo attack concluded, the nineteen G3Ms of the Genzan Air Group approached the cruiser force. Radar operators aboard *Chicago* tracked the formation as it closed from astern at an estimated eighteen thousand feet, but the twin-engine bombers weren't after the American cruiser. Instead they targeted *Australia,* releasing some twenty large bombs in a single salvo. Towering columns of spray tinged with black smoke erupted all around the cruiser, and for several agonizing moments the ship was totally obscured. Crewmen on nearby ships thought she had blown up, as did the Japanese. And then, almost like an apparition, *Australia* emerged from the spray and the smoke, her upper decks glistening with seawater. Unbelievably, not a single bomb had struck the 630-foot-long warship, though two exploded close enough to give her hull a good shaking.

In all, thirty-one aircraft from Rabaul had attacked Crace's cruiser force without scoring a single hit. Back at Vunakanau, however, the returning aircrews reported a completely different outcome to their superiors: "[O]ne *California* class battleship blown up; one *Warspite* class battleship received two torpedo hits, extensive damage; one *Augusta* class heavy cruiser sunk. Two torpedoes were fired against a *Canberra* class cruiser but results are unknown."

Only one element of the report came close to the truth—the acknowledgment that a pair torpedoes had been launched at one of the ships. The rest was a combination of careless observation and pure invention.

The warships of Crace's cruiser force had dodged every attack thus far, but they were not yet out of danger. Almost immediately after the G3Ms flew off, a new threat appeared from the north at high altitude. Three B-17s of the 40th Recon Squadron happened along just in time to see the G3Ms completing their bombing run. Mistaking the twin-engine planes for American medium bombers, the B-17s attacked *Australia* in the belief that it was a Japanese battleship. Fortunately for the cruiser, the bombardiers' record against shipping did not improve. Crace reported that the pattern of bombs landed "seven cables" (about 1,400 yards) from *Australia*, though they splashed uncomfortably close to the destroyer *Farragut*.

AT APPROXIMATELY 1500 hours, a new sighting report from a Japanese reconnaissance floatplane convinced admirals Takagi and Hara that the American carriers had been located. The reported position was roughly 350 miles west of *Shokaku* and *Zuikaku*, and though the afternoon was growing late, Hara thought they could pull off a strike before sunset. It could not be completed before darkness fell, so only the most experienced airmen were picked. They would not have the support of fighters, for the Zeros lacked direction-finding equipment and could not find their way back to the carriers in the dark.

The Japanese were not aware that the hastily conceived strike was based on bad information. Once again, the reconnoitering aircrew had made a grievous mistake. They had actually found Crace's cruiser support group again, not Task Force 17, which by coincidence lay cloaked beneath a thick overcast less than two hundred miles from the Japanese carriers.

For the handpicked crews of the Japanese dive-bombers and torpedo planes, the mission truly began to unravel when the *Lexington*'s radar detected the would-be attackers. *Lexington* and *Yorktown* launched additional Wildcats to join the existing combat air patrol, bringing the total number of fighters in the air to thirty. Lieutenant "Red" Gill skill-fully vectored several Wildcats to intercept the first radar contact: nine Nakajimas of the *Zuikaku* carrier attack unit.

Believing they were still many miles from the American task force, the Japanese airmen were taken completely by surprise. Within minutes, five torpedo planes plunged into the sea, carrying fifteen airmen to their deaths. Other formations received similar treatment. The Wildcats downed two more torpedo planes and one dive-bomber in the fading twilight, and another torpedo plane later ditched near its carrier. In sum, the fruitless effort cost the Japanese nine planes and eight veteran crews. Worse, it raised the day's total losses to at least twenty aircraft and one flattop.

Monitoring events aboard his flagship anchored in the Inland Sea, Admiral Yamamoto was dismayed by the news. That night his chief of staff, Rear Admiral Ugaki, wrote in his personal diary:

A dream of great success has been shattered . . .

Two enemy carriers still remain, while our torpedo bombers were annihilated. It will be risky to carry out an invasion attempt before destroying [the Allied forces]. Moreover, to make contact with the enemy tonight seemed impossible. In view of these [considerations], we suggested to the chief of staff, Fourth Fleet, that they put off the invasion of Port Moresby as the local situation warranted.

At Rabaul, Vice Admiral Inoue made a decision that would have seemed inconceivable just twenty-four hours earlier. The Allies were winning at this stage of the battle, having sunk *Shoho* and blocked the invasion fleet's path to Port Moresby. Deeply concerned about the safety of the convoy, Inoue followed the advice of Yamamoto's staff and issued a bulletin stating that the Port Moresby invasion was postponed for two days. He then detached two heavy cruisers from the MO Main Force to bolster the Striking Force and ordered the Port Moresby Invasion Force to withdraw temporarily to the north. There, in relative safety, the convoy was to await the outcome of the carrier battle that was certain to occur.

THE NEXT DAY, May 8, 1942, the American and Japanese carrier forces fought the first naval battle in history in which the opposing ships never made visual contact with each other. The outcome slightly favored the

Japanese. *Shokaku* was badly damaged by three bombs and withdrew to Truk with 109 crewmen dead and dozens more wounded. In exchange, *Lexington* was hit by two torpedoes and two bombs, and *Yorktown* sustained damage to her flight deck from one direct hit. *Lexington* seemed to have initially weathered the attack, but several hours later the vapor from ruptured fuel lines ignited deep inside her hull, and the beloved carrier was disemboweled by violent explosions. The day's action cost the Japanese some forty-two aircraft, a steep price that was partially offset by the returning airmen's enthusiastic reports. The "Wild Eagles" claimed that they sank *Saratoga*—which is only logical, as *Lexington* allegedly had been sunk in February—and also claimed a carrier of the *Yorktown* class as "probably sunk."

Vice Admiral Inoue was thrilled by the reports coming in from the MO Striking Force. He and his staff, believing that two American carriers had been sunk, congratulated themselves on yet another victory. Word was flashed to Admiral Yamamoto at Hashirajima and to Imperial General Headquarters in Tokyo, whereupon the Information Bureau consolidated the reports. The next morning, banner headlines announced the victorious news throughout Japan:

Crushing Blow Dealt Enemy Navies
Imperial General Headquarters, May 8 (5:20 p.m.):

Fleet units of the Imperial Navy operating in New Guinea waters discovered powerful units of the combined Anglo-American fleet sailing in the Coral Sea southwest of New Guinea on May 6, and attacking them on May 7, thunder-sank an American battleship of the California class, disabled a British heavy cruiser of the Canberra class, and badly damaged a British battleship of the Warspite class.

Continuing the battle on May 8, the Imperial Navy sank an American aircraft carrier of the Saratoga class and another aircraft carrier of the Yorktown class. The Imperial Navy is still continuing the attack.

Thanks in large part to the outrageous claims submitted by the *rikko* units at Rabaul, the citizens of Japan believed the Imperial Navy had sunk at least three capital warships and seriously damaged two others.

The exaggerations grew even larger five days later, when another banner headline boasted that *eight* Allied warships had been sunk or damaged in the Coral Sea. In reality, only the destroyer *Sims* had gone down immediately, while the *Lexington* and the *Neosho*, though horribly damaged, stayed afloat until American torpedoes ultimately sent them to the bottom.

Predictably, Imperial Navy losses were minimized by the *Johokyoku*. News releases revealed only that "a small aircraft carrier" had been sunk and "31 planes were yet to return." The *Shoho* was not publicly named, and the government further diminished its loss by describing the anonymous carrier as "a converted tanker."

Aboard his flagship, Yamamoto and the Combined Fleet staff were skeptical of the victory's supposed greatness. On the afternoon of May 8, expecting to hear that more attacks were being conducted against the remnants of the American fleet, Yamamoto learned that the damaged *Shokaku* had been withdrawn to Truk. The rest of the MO Striking Force, low on fuel, was reportedly moving northward to meet oilers, after which the warships would support the landings on Ocean and Nauru islands. The most troubling information of all was that Vice Admiral Inoue, lacking carrier support for the Port Moresby Invasion Force, had ordered the ships to return to Rabaul. The Combined Fleet demanded an explanation, but neither Inoue nor his Fourth Fleet staff responded. Their silence sparked anger aboard the *Yamato*, according to Rear Admiral Ugake:

> Not only did they not reply to our inquiry, they postponed the invasion of Port Moresby indefinitely. They were going to carry out the occupation of Ocean and Nauru Islands as scheduled and put the forces in defensive positions.
>
> Thereupon our staff officers became very angry and demanded that we send a strongly worded telegram to [Inoue's] chief of staff. They charged that the Fourth Fleet had fallen into defeatism after losing *Shoho*, [therefore] an order calling for exploitation of the battle achievement and destruction of the enemy remnant should be sent to them.

On the evening of May 8, Yamamoto ordered Inoue to annihilate the rest of the American ships. But compliance was no longer a practical option for the Fourth Fleet commander. The ships of the MO Striking Force were low on fuel, and *Zuikaku* possessed just twenty-one attack planes in operational status. Inoue could not refuse Yamamoto's order, so he instructed Vice Admiral Takagi to hunt for the American warships after refueling. The latter spent most of May 9 replenishing his force and then headed briefly into the Coral Sea. The next morning, his search planes found nothing more than the drifting *Neosho*. Early that afternoon, Takagi turned back toward Rabaul, where he eventually delivered some of *Zuikaku's* fighters.

Just like that, MO Operation fell apart. Yamamoto had no choice but to postpone the invasion of Port Moresby for a minimum of two months. And, in addition to all the other problems, the Imperial Army staff chose this time to express concerns over "the past weakness " of the South Seas Force and began proceedings to replace it with the Seventeenth Army. "We could carry [MO Operation] out now if we want," wrote Ugaki in his diary, "but it is no use as long as the command taking charge of the operation is not yet fully determined."

THE AUSTRALIAN POWs at Rabaul noticed a dramatic change in their captors. Prior to MO Operation some of the guards had boasted, "Japan take Moresby, then Australia, you go home." The bragging had alarmed the Aussies, who had been caught up quite literally in the Southern Offensive's remarkable victories. But now it was the Japanese who looked worried. They were silent, and some even seemed depressed. The reason became obvious on May 10 when most of the scattered naval forces returned to Simpson Harbor. "The ships that came into focus," wrote Alice Bowman, "were a battered and dirty replica of the fleet that had sailed so jauntily out of Rabaul less than a week ago." Among the warships she observed was a badly damaged aircraft carrier, undoubtedly *Shokaku*, which crept along the shoreline into Blanche Bay. Bowman observed that the carrier's flight deck was empty and its "pitted superstructure stood out starkly."

David Hutchinson-Smith also saw evidence of extensive damage among the ships. "How differently they returned and how our spirits soared," he recalled. "[S]ome were on fire, others down by the stern, some listing heavily to port, others to starboard . . . some only kept afloat by continuous pumping. Those of the 'invading' troops who returned were dazed, sick and shaken and very, very glad to be able to put a foot on dry land once more."

For the thousand-plus POWs of Lark Force and the two hundred civilian internees at Rabaul, the knowledge that the invasion had failed was a tremendous boost. Their only regret was that they could not openly celebrate, having learned from the bombing of the *Komaki Maru* that the Japanese hated more than anything to lose face.

THREE DAYS AFTER the Port Moresby Invasion Force returned, Admiral Yamamoto was granted an Imperial Rescript, his third since the beginning of the war. On this occasion the Emperor pronounced: "The air corps of the Combined Fleet, battling with high courage in the Coral Sea, inflicted a crushing defeat upon the American-British combined enemy fleet. We are deeply gratified." Understanding the proclamation for what it was—a political statement for the benefit of the people—Yamamoto responded in a manner described as "slightly ambiguous." He had good reason. Japan's top admiral was thoroughly frustrated, not only because the primary goal of MO Operation had failed, but also because his losses continued to mount. Before dawn on May 11, the American submarine *S-42* slammed two torpedoes into *Okinoshima*, flagship of the Ocean-Nauru invasion force. Damaged at Tulagi seven days earlier, the big minelayer had been repaired at Rabaul before undertaking the current operation. This time it was not so fortunate. While being towed near Buka the next morning, *Okinoshima* rolled over and sank. To make matters worse, the repair ship *Shoei Maru*, sent from Rabaul to aid the stricken minelayer, was attacked that afternoon by a different sub and sunk near Cape St. George.

The losses were not publicized, and the citizens of Japan continued to feed off the sensational stories presented by the *Johokyoku*. Two weeks after the battle in the Coral Sea, while the country prepared for its annual Navy Day celebrations, a nationwide radio broadcast was presented by the navy's senior public affairs officer. Speaking for more than an hour, Capt. Hideo Hiraide recalled the lopsided victories won by the Imperial Navy in World War I and praised the outcome of the Coral Sea event. "The Imperial Navy," he stated, ". . . emerged victorious, definitely sinking two of America's most formidable aircraft carriers and annihilating all their shipboard planes." Hiraide was contemptuous of the Allied commanders, calling them "incapable and unoriginal," and even accusing them indirectly of cowardice. "The only thing that impressed us . . . was the speed with which the enemy remnants fled."

Toward the end of his lengthy broadcast, Hiraide issued an ominous warning to the Australians: "Of all the belligerents, Australia is to be most pitied. The Sixth Continent, considered by many as a paradise, rose against us by banking on the worthless aid of the United States and Britain. This erstwhile paradise is about to be turned into shambles."

Like the emperor's latest rescript, the claims and threats uttered by Hiraide were nothing more than propaganda tools. Intoxicated by the early victories, the Japanese believed so completely in their own invincibility that they were easily convinced of a great triumph in the Coral Sea.

To this day, most historians give the Imperial Navy credit for a tactical victory after comparing the losses accrued by both sides. But they typically examine only the actions of May 7 and 8, during which the Japanese lost one small carrier compared to the Pacific Fleet's loss of a large carrier, a destroyer, and an oiler. Similarly, historians usually credit the Pacific Fleet with a strategic victory due to the postponement of the Port Moresby invasion. In the strictest sense, both points are valid; but a fair and balanced assessment of the battle can only be made by considering the *entire* operation.

First, the Japanese achieved only one of their goals: the occupation of Tulagi, which came at the cost of two warships and some wooden patrol boats on May 4. (In describing these losses in his diary, Rear Admiral Ugaki regarded the sinking of *Kikuzuki* and *Tama Maru* as "fairly big sacrifices.")

As for the so-called Japanese victory of May 7–8, the Imperial Navy paid dearly. In addition to the loss of *Shoho*, the fleet carrier *Shokaku* was put out of action for months, and neither she nor *Zuikaku* were available for Yamamoto's pivotal quest to crush the Pacific Fleet at Midway a few weeks hence. Additionally, the Japanese lost dozens of their best and brightest airmen in the Coral Sea, including an inordinate number from the carrier-based torpedo squadrons and the land-based 4th Air Group.

Finally, the goal of occupying Ocean and Nauru islands was abandoned—but not until two additional ships had been sunk. In all, while accomplishing only one out of the operation's three stated objectives, the Japanese lost six ships, nearly eighty planes, and scores of experienced airmen.

Yamamoto's most important prediction proved accurate. Months before the start of the Pacific War he proclaimed: "For a while we'll have everything our own way, stretching out in every direction like an octopus spreading its tentacles. But it'll last for a year and a half at the most. We've just got to get a peace agreement by then."

Yamamoto later revised the timetable, saying he could "run wild" for six months to a year, but even that was overly optimistic. Exactly 150 days after the attack on Pearl Harbor, the Imperial Navy was stopped cold in the Coral Sea. The Southern Offensive had been blunted.

Of even greater importance, the Japanese remained unaware that their JN-25 code had been compromised. They also failed to recognize the outcome of MO Operation for what it truly was: a warning.

CHAPTER 16

Guests of the Emperor

A WEEK PRIOR TO THE CLASH in the Coral Sea, the Imperial Navy took control of the POWs in the Malaguna Road stockade. The prisoners seemed to think they would receive better treatment from the navy than their army overseers had given them, but not everyone benefitted. Flight Officer Allan Norman and his Catalina crew, captured on May 4, were held by the 8th Base Force, responsible for the interrogation of new prisoners. Based on postwar evidence, the treatment of Norman's crew was much more brutal than the Lark Force soldiers and interned civilians had experienced.

In the aftermath of the Coral Sea battle, the main stockade was quiet for a few weeks. But in late May, the POWs were surprised to see Alfred A. Harvey, a plantation owner, brought in for questioning. Also arrested by the Japanese were Harvey's wife Marjorie, their eleven-year-old son Richard, Mrs. Harvey's brother, James S. Manson, and William H. Parker, a close family friend.

The small group was isolated from the main population, according to David Hutchinson-Smith: "The Japanese herded them in a small room opposite the guard house and allowed them out only to have ulcers dressed or to visit the benjo, and then only under close guard. They were not supposed to speak to anyone, but the lad was allowed out now and then and played ball with the guards, with whom he was apparently a favorite."

A few days after their arrest, the family was accused of espionage. The formal charge stated that they had "communicated with the enemy by radio telegraphy and fires," but no other details were provided. Alfred Harvey, who went by "Ted," had been a coastwatcher in 1940 and was issued a special crystal for his two-way radio. But early the following year the intelligence organization decided that the location of his radio was unsuitable and withdrew the crystal, telling Harvey his services were no longer required. Apparently this did not sit well with the fifty-seven-year-old planter. Ignoring repeated warnings from his superiors to stay off the air, he continually broadcast "all sorts of silly reports to Port Moresby" on commercial frequencies.

Harvey was probably his own worst enemy. Neither he nor his family represented any sort of threat to the Japanese, but the Kempeitai were constantly hunting for "Europeans" and two-way radios. In late March, the Imperial Navy established a *Minsei-bu* (civil administration bureau) to bring New Britain's native population under Japanese control. Thereafter, islanders were bribed or cajoled into revealing the locations where their former white "mastas" were hiding in the jungle. It was only a matter of time before the Harveys were betrayed.

Vice Admiral Inoue personally got involved in the case, convening a formal court martial to put the Harveys on trial. The proceedings were held in a vacant building in Chinatown with Capt. Shojiro Mizusaki, the commanding officer of the 81st Naval Garrison Unit, serving as president of the tribunal. Three other naval officers were named as prosecutors, but no legal representation was provided for the defense of the accused.

During the so-called trial, the Harveys underwent intense questioning for three days. An interpreter assisted them with presenting their answers, but the verdict was preordained. Found guilty of espionage, all five civilians were sentenced to death. Inoue approved the findings and passed the order for their execution down the chain of command to Captain Mizusaki, who, in turn, instructed his adjutant to "dispose of them by shooting."

On the appointed day in early June, the condemned Australians were placed aboard a truck that took them from Rabaul down the coastal road to Crater Peninsula. Not far beyond Lakunai airdrome, the vehicle stopped near the foot of Tavurvur volcano.

It was a desolate, foul place. A nearby pit called the "Malay Hole" had served as Rabaul's dumping ground for years. The air, already ripe with the stench of garbage, was further polluted with the rotten-egg smell of sulfur. No vegetation grew near the volcano, and the soil, consisting mostly of soft ash and pumice, was easily excavated. It was an ideal location for a burial ground, which was exactly why the Japanese selected it for a crematorium and "war cemetery."

A number of naval officers, including Mizusaki and his adjutant, Lt. Yoshio Endo, were already waiting at the site. They watched as sailors got the family down from the truck and lined them up in front of a pre-dug hole. Three other sailors, armed with rifles, were reportedly dejected at having to carry out the execution, especially against the likeable boy, Richard. "I remember hearing some seamen say it was a really miserable scene," recalled a member of the garrison unit. He believed it impossible that "a young boy could be guilty of any crime."

Richard stood between his parents, who held hands as the master-at-arms shouted commands to the firing squad. When the shots rang out, Richard became the youngest Australian executed during World War II. The firing squad was not dismissed until Manson and Parker were killed, after which a work party of native laborers backfilled the common grave.

AS THE NUMBER of bombing raids on Rabaul intensified, so did the consternation of the Australians held captive in the Malaguna Road stockade. Although no bombs had yet struck the camp or nearby work sites, every attack raised the possibility of a disaster. "The air raids, reconnaissance, bombing and strafing caused us no little worry," recalled Hutchinson-Smith. "There were 86 raids by the [Allies] during our stay and many a sleepless night we had when there was a bomber's moon."

A few months earlier, the POWs had been surprised when the Japanese granted permission to write letters to their families. It was an unusual offer, the more so because the Japanese promised to deliver the mail during a regular bombing attack on Port Moresby. The prisoners happily obliged, knowing their loved ones would find comfort in hearing that they were alive. Chaplain John May considered it a "remarkable gesture" on the part of the Japanese, but the captors almost certainly had ulterior motives. For one thing, they never revealed the existence of the

POW camp to the International Red Cross. Therefore, the letters likely served as a tool for informing the Allies that hundreds of Australians were in close proximity to military targets. To carry the logic one step further, the Japanese themselves would benefit if the Allies decided to restrict the area from future attacks.

The letters were dropped in khaki-wrapped bundles over Seven Mile airdrome on the morning of April 28. Each bundle wore a long streamer with instructions in English for delivery: "Any person who has received this package is cordially requested to send it over to the Army Headquarters of Port Moresby." Unfortunately, several bundles overshot the airdrome and were lost at sea, but four parcels with a total of 395 letters were delivered to headquarters and then forwarded to Australia.

Interestingly, the Allied response was to bomb Rabaul even harder than before, and one of the clearly visible targets was regularly identified as a "military camp." No apparent effort was made to minimize the risk to the POWs. As time wore on, the prisoners came to dread the raids for two particular reasons. The first was fear of being killed by their own side; the second was disgust with the deplorable condition of the bomb shelters.

For months, the *benjo* buckets (clay pots used as toilets) had been emptied into bore holes scattered around the stockade. Eventually every available space was tapped, including the parade ground. Torrential rains frequently backwashed raw sewage into low-lying areas of the camp, including the bomb shelters.Whenever the air raid sirens went off, which happened often, the prisoners were understandably reluctant to jump into the shelters.

Some men preferred to watch the air raids rather than take cover. The Marauders typically roared in low and fast, and were greeted by a hailstorm of antiaircraft fire. Hutchinson-Smith, an expert in the principles of artillery, often laughed to himself at the antics of the Japanese.

> We had a good demonstration at noon one day when we were working on a ship in the middle of the bay. Without warning, a [bomber] came in over Vulcan at about 2,000 feet. He flew on a straight course at that altitude, and did the [Japanese] let go! There were men firing rifles and revolvers, heavy machine guns, light machine guns, and multiple pom-poms. The noise was terrific and when the heavy AA opened up

the air vibrated; but on he went, passing over Namanula Ridge. As he did so, the after gun on a transport near our ship came into action. First the gunners forgot to remove the muzzle cover, had perforce to depress the gun to remove it, and then had to re-lay all over again. They were running around the gun chattering like monkeys and tripping over themselves. Finally when they were ready to fire, they depressed too far, fired a good 1,500 feet below the plane, and the blast blew away the front of their sandbag protection.

Even if a plane came over at 15,000 or 20,000 feet it would be the same performance, with everyone firing furiously. The amount of ammunition they wasted each time must have been colossal, and at night the pyrotechnics were well worth getting out of bed to see.

Two other POWs who quietly cheered the B-26s were Theron Lutz and Sanger Reed. The two Marauder crewmen were not interned in the main camp but instead found themselves in a separate enclosure surrounded by wire. "We never saw any other soldiers around except the guards," recalled Reed. "We were not in a big camp."

At first Lutz and Reed had the small Kempeitai compound to themselves, but after a few days they were joined by an Australian fighter pilot, Sgt. David S. Brown of 75 Squadron. Twenty-five years old, Brown had joined the squadron as a replacement fresh out of the training command. He was barely accustomed to the high-performance Kittyhawk (and in fact had already "pranged" one in a landing accident at Townsville), when he flew his first combat mission on April 11. While escorting an A-24 strike on Lae that morning, his fighter was disabled by intercepting Zeros. After bellying in on a tidal flat near Salamaua, Brown was taken prisoner and sent to Rabaul for interrogation. No doubt the Japanese were eager to learn more about the "British" squadron that was giving them so much trouble.

During the next few weeks the Kempeitai repeatedly singled out Brown, Lutz, and Reed for interrogation. Recently promoted from buck private, Reed could rightly claim to know almost nothing of interest to the Japanese. "At that time I looked about sixteen," he added. "I played dumb, and I really was dumb." The Kempeitai tried intimidation, including threats of execution, but it didn't work on Reed. "I remember one time having a sword held at my throat and being told, 'You lie,' and

I was lying. I thought that I had had it then but I just shrugged my shoulders and stuck to my story and got away with it."

To the frustration of the Kempeitai, Reed successfully maintained his facade of youthful ignorance. Lutz, on the other hand, told them plenty. But he was also clever. When the Japanese compiled the information given by the two Marauder men, the results looked important. In fact, the intelligence was considered so valuable that a report was "telegraphed immediately to Imperial General Headquarters." Actually, most of the contents were outdated or misleading. For example, the prisoners apparently stated that there were about two hundred P-39 fighters in Australia. This was fairly accurate if the P-400 export model was included, but while one captive claimed there were 150 of them in Townsville, the other said the fighters were scattered across the continent. The contradictory information served no real purpose.

Similarly, the report to Imperial General Headquarters listed "approximately 30 P-40s in Sydney and Melbourne, 36 bombers (B-26) in Townsville from the 22nd Bombardment Group, also 15 B-17s in Townsville." At first glance it would seem that Lutz had provided the enemy with sensitive information, but in reality he gave the Japanese figures having no permanent value. Lutz also talked at length about the 22nd Bomb Group's journey to Australia from the West Coast. The information was of great interest to the Japanese, but it was actually yesterday's news. Lutz also gave the Kempeitai false information, such as the notion that 150 P-39s would be attached to the 22nd Bomb Group.

If Lutz's intention was to give up just enough important-sounding information to keep himself and Reed alive, he succeeded brilliantly. First, he revealed nothing truly vital, such as intelligence about Port Moresby or the capabilities of the Marauder. More importantly, Imperial General Headquarters was so impressed with the information that Lutz and Reed were transferred to Japan. About three weeks after their capture, the two crewmen were put into a small boat that took them out to what Reed later described as an "aircraft carrier." This was almost certainly the former liner *Kasuga Maru*, converted into an escort carrier, which had arrived at Rabaul on May 7. The airmen were informed that the ship would take them to Japan, but a short time later sirens and whistles sounded throughout the ship, and the POWs were quickly escorted ashore. No attack came, but it was obvious the Japanese were taking no chances due to the battle taking place in the Coral Sea.

Lutz and Reed spent three more weeks in the Kempeitai compound before another attempt was made to move them. On May 26 they boarded the merchant ship *Naruto Maru*, which had arrived four days earlier with a load of ammunition. The two Americans saw Sergeant Brown on the wharf, but he did not board the ship with them. *Naruto Maru* departed for Japan later that day and docked at Yokohama after an uneventful week at sea. Lutz and Reed faced an uncertain future in Japan, including months of harsh interrogations at a secret intimidation camp run by the Imperial Navy. But both men survived the duration of the war and would learn years later that they had been most fortunate to leave Rabaul behind.

TWO DAYS PRIOR to the departure of Lutz and Reed, Marauders appeared over Rabaul for the last time. Six were scheduled to take part in the attack on Vunakanau airdrome, but in a familiar reprise, half of the assigned bombers either failed to get off the ground or turned back because of mechanical trouble. Only three aircraft of the 408th Bomb Squadron reached Rabaul on the morning of May 24, and they found much of the Gazelle Peninsula obscured by a layer of clouds. Locating a hole in the overcast, the trio dived down and attacked Vunakanau out of the northwest at just 1,500 feet. Heavy, accurate flak damaged two of the three B-26s over the target area, but they dropped their bombs and caused considerable damage of their own, burning down the Genzan Air Group's headquarters and damaging four land attack aircraft, one of them severely.

Although there was no interference from Japanese fighters, 1st Lt. Harold L. Massie realized within minutes that the right engine of his B-26, *Imogene VII*, had been mortally damaged. Feathering the prop, he kept the Marauder in the air long enough to reach Wide Bay. Once again the B-26 proved difficult to ditch on just one engine—the landing speeds were simply too high. *Imogene VII* hit the water hard, and two enlisted crewmen went down with the wreckage. The six survivors, helped to shore by native villagers with canoes, suffered an assortment of injuries. Corporal Dale E. Bordner, the radio operator, was unconscious; 2nd Lt. Marvin C. Hughes (navigator) lay in a native hut with a deep gash in one leg and cuts on his feet; Staff Sgt. Jack B. Swan (photographer) had a broken shoulder. The other three—2nd Lt. Eugene D. Wallace (copilot), 2nd Lt. Arthur C. King (bombardier), and Massie—had sustained an assortment of cuts and bruises.

What truly dismayed the survivors were the things they lacked: food, weapons, and adequate clothing. They had no flashlights, no matches, or any of the simplest tools for survival. All the men except Gene Wallace had discarded their shoes or boots in the water. For six men with one pair of shoes, the odds of survival were not just grim, they were downright alarming.

As the Marauder men would soon discover, the jungle would not feed them despite its lush growth. Eric Feldt, the director of the coastwatching network, likened the jungles of the Southwest Pacific to "a desert," and he had the collective experience of twenty years in the islands to prove it. "At its best," he wrote, "the food the jungle can supply is only enough to sustain life, and under a prolonged diet of jungle food, mental and physical vigor decline until there is no ability left to do more than barely support life itself."

The survivors' one stroke of luck was that they came ashore in Wide Bay, where some of the native villages still showed allegiance to their former white *mastas*. Learning to communicate with the natives using Pidgin English, the flyers heard about a man who looked like them and lived "nearby." Wallace had the shoes, so he hiked for three hours with native guides to meet Father John Meierhofer, a missionary from Salzburg, Austria, who ran the Roman Catholic mission at Kalai. Months earlier he had stubbornly refused to help the soldiers of Lark Force, but now he gave Wallace some disinfectant and bandages and told him about another white man who might help.

After three days' rest it was Massie's turn to set out. He was gone for two weeks but succeeded in locating Leslie John Stokie, thirty-nine, a hardy transplant from Victoria who had lived on New Britain for many years as a plantation manager and a territorial police officer. Returning to Wide Bay, Massie learned from the headman of the local village that food was running low. The Americans began a series of moves between other villages and John Stokie's hideaway, dividing themselves into small groups to lessen the demands on their hosts, never staying too long in one place. Gradually they worked their way inland, intending to cross New Britain at its narrowest point, the twenty-mile neck separating Wide Bay on the south coast from Open Bay on the north. Unfortunately the native foot trails became strenuously steep in the island's interior. They also passed through the domain of a mysterious warrior tribe, the Molkolkol, rarely seen but widely feared for their stealth and ferocity. Meanwhile the castaways were gradually becoming weaker. By late June they were on the verge of collapse, both physically and emotionally, and within a few weeks only two men still had the strength to walk. On July 27, Massie and Art King journeyed northward alone, hoping to find Stokie, but that was the last their crewmates saw of them.

The remaining four Americans didn't budge for weeks. They rested, hoping to conserve enough strength to survive in New Britain's inhospitable jungles, not realizing that their nightmare had just begun.

IN EARLY JUNE, rumors began to circulate through the Malaguna Road stockade that the Lark Force POWs were going to Japan. Many a nervous prisoner hoped the rumors were true, if only because the American bombing attacks were coming ever closer to killing them. The Australians had cheered the bombers at first; now they were deeply concerned for their own safety. "On [one] occasion," wrote Hutchinson-Smith, "a large number of men was employed in the copra shed at Toboi Wharf when it was strafed with incendiary bullets by low-flying aircraft. A few men were slightly wounded and scorched, but serious casualties were not sustained. There were other occasions when machine-gun and cannon fire sprayed the camp, and the notable June 4, 1942, when incendiaries landed in and around the camp, one penetrating the cookhouse roof and knocking the handle off the soup pot containing the next morning's breakfast!"

One of the strafing attacks was probably the work of *Suzy-Q*, a well-known B-17E piloted by Maj. Felix M. Hardison, commanding officer of the 93rd Bomb Squadron. Making a rare solo night attack on May 26, Hardison took advantage of a full moon and dropped his bombs on the wharf area from five thousand feet. He then circled around and descended to just one thousand feet so that his gunners could strafe ground targets. During the run, one or more of the B-17's gunners shot up "a military camp at the edge of town."

By some miracle, no prisoners in the Malaguna Road stockade were killed or even seriously injured by the Allied attacks. Nevertheless the Japanese decided to move them, though the reason had no apparent link to the close calls. Instead, according to captured documents and diaries, the POWs were moved to alleviate an acute food shortage that developed only a few months after the Japanese occupied Rabaul. Every week, the stronghold's population swelled by the thousands as the troop buildup continued—but there was not a corresponding increase in the delivery of food. The Japanese relied heavily on shipments of rice, which provided the vast majority of their daily diet. The rice was augmented with a small amount of fish and vegetables (primarily tubers, such as sweet potatoes) obtained from local villagers, but the supplements by themselves were not nearly enough to sustain tens of thousands of Japanese and their prisoners. The main problem was that the Japanese concentrated on the delivery of troops, weapons, and ammunition rather than food. The records of the General Shipping Transport Headquarters tell the tale: of the 1,750,000 shipping tons allotted to the Southern Offensive, more than 80 percent were reserved for troop movement. It is not surprising, therefore, that stockpiles of food ran low in less than four months. On May 16 a Japanese soldier wrote, "There is no food left to requisition and there is nothing good to eat nowadays."

To alleviate the issue, more than a thousand enlisted POWs and civilian internees were roused from their barracks in the pre-dawn hours of June 22. As they formed into ranks on the parade ground, the noise and activity awakened the officers in their separate hut. When the latter tried to exit from their long barrack, however, they found machine guns trained on both doors. The message was plain: Stay inside.

The prisoners assembled on the parade ground were in miserable condition. Virtually all showed signs of malnourishment, their khaki uniforms hanging from bony frames. Many were sick with malaria, dysentery, or beriberi. Those who could stand swayed on their feet while the guards counted them several times and then separated them into groups. Finally, at 0900, the prisoners were marched toward the main gate. Happy to leave, they moved forward "with cheerful grins and banter," waving to the officers as they shuffled past. Some of the sick leaned on the shoulders of their stronger friends; others were carried on improvised stretchers or even dragged on doors removed from the barracks.

In the officers' barrack, Chap. John May picked up his bible. Having been transferred to the main stockade from Kokopo two months earlier, he began to read Psalms in a loud, clear voice for the benefit of the troops: "They that go down to the sea in ships, that do business in great waters; These see the works of the Lord, and his wonders in the deep."

In a ragged line, 845 soldiers and 208 civilians marched down Malaguna Road toward the waterfront. Along the way, they passed throngs of onlookers interspersed with squads of machine gunners. At one of the main wharves, the prisoners filed aboard *Montevideo Maru*, a large cargo liner, and descended into its cavernous holds. After watching them board, Japanese soldier Jiro Takamura wrote in his diary: "Since there is insufficient food, [the prisoners] are to be sent to rear echelons. They left on a naval ship in the evening. Saw them off and watched the ship until it disappeared over the horizon." Four days later he added, "Seems all military [POWs] with the exception of officers were sent to Hainan Island."

Takamura was only partially correct. *Montevideo Maru* sailed on June 22 with its cargo of prisoners, bound for Hainan Island off the South China coast, but the men were never delivered to their new work camp. At 0229 on July 1, a torpedo fired by an American submarine, USS *Sturgeon*, slammed into the starboard side of *Montevideo Maru* as it exited the Babuyan Channel off the coast of Luzon. The explosion ripped open the aft two holds, igniting a secondary blast in the fuel tank. The ship sank in eleven minutes, giving the Japanese crew only enough time to launch three lifeboats, none of which contained POWs. All available evidence indicates that the entire contingent of prisoners and civilian internees drowned when *Montevideo Maru* went under.

Congratulating themselves for sinking a large enemy merchantman, the *Sturgeon's* crew had no idea they had caused the worst maritime disaster in Australian history.

FIVE DAYS AFTER the sinking, Captain Mizusaki visited the nurses imprisoned at Vunapope and instructed them to collect their belongings. "You are going to Paradise," he told them. Within hours, the eighteen women were escorted aboard *Naruto Maru*, which had recently returned from Japan.

A nearly identical scene unfolded at the main POW stockade in Rabaul, where the Australian officers were still held. Chaplain May,

Captain Hutchinson-Smith, Colonel Scanlan, and fifty-seven others were ordered to gather up their meager holdings. They, too, were taken aboard *Naruto Maru*, where the nurses greeted them with a happy uproar. For more than a week, the Australians shared a crowded hold while the ship traveled north to Japan. But at Yokohama, the men and women were separated again.

Like Lutz and Reed, the captives were destined to face three more years of deprivation. Conditions were truly miserable, especially as the war dragged on and food shortages became routine; nevertheless all of them survived the ordeal and were repatriated after the war.

They were the lucky ones.

CHAPTER 17

Fading Glory

T HREE WEEKS AFTER the Battle of the Coral Sea, Admiral Yamamoto led approximately two hundred warships—almost the entire strength of the Combined Fleet—out of Japanese waters to begin the next big operation. In terms of gross tonnage, it was the largest armada yet assembled in the history of naval warfare.

Emotions ran high. Not only had Yamamoto dreamed of this moment for years, his entire war plan was predicated on it. He was certain that the American carriers would come out from Pearl Harbor to face his bold offensive, which called for diversionary landings in the Aleutian Islands (AI Operation) in addition to the capture of Midway atoll (MI Operation). Here was the perfect opportunity to crush the Pacific Fleet, and for the first time since the war began, Yamamoto himself was sailing into battle.

As history knows so well, the admiral's dream was shattered. Once again Allied code breakers made the difference. The intelligence network's deduction of the Japanese plans enabled Admiral Nimitz to position three carriers for an ambush near Midway. In a dramatic battle that began on June 4, the Pacific Fleet sank four enemy carriers and a cruiser in exchange for the loss of a single flattop and one destroyer. The resounding victory belonged to Nimitz, not to Yamamoto.

News of the disaster sent shock waves through Imperial General Headquarters. Lieutenant General Shinichi Tanaka, chief of the Military

189

Operations Section, reputedly stated: "We have lost supremacy in the Pacific through this unforeseen great defeat." Although it was not a deathblow to the Imperial Navy, the disaster severely impaired its aeronautical branch. More skilled aviators were killed in one day than could be trained in an entire year. The combined losses from the Coral Sea and Midway battles included five aircraft carriers and more than four hundred planes, bringing the navy's offensive capabilities to a standstill.

Deeply shaken, Yamamoto accepted full responsibility for the defeat. The blame was not his entirely—the stunning reversal of fortune had been caused by carelessness and overconfidence at multiple levels—but by virtue of his position as commander of the Combined Fleet, he was accountable.

On June 10, as Yamamoto's fleet steamed back toward Japan, the Information Bureau issued a brief statement that two American carriers had been sunk at Midway in exchange for one Japanese carrier sunk and another damaged. It was one of the most egregious lies yet uttered by Tokyo. To prevent the truth from leaking out, the Imperial Navy immediately clamped a tight lid on the disaster. Almost every sailor and airman involved was reassigned, either to highly restricted bases in Japan or to the far-off South Pacific. Even the wounded were sent into seclusion. Captain Fuchida, a hero of Pearl Harbor and other early actions, was wounded aboard the carrier *Akagi* at Midway. Arriving in Yokosuka aboard the hospital ship *Hikawa Maru*, he was whisked to a naval hospital in the middle of the night and held in complete isolation, a form of captivity he likened to being a prisoner of war in his own country.

Weeks after the defeat, the Information Bureau presented its "official" version of events, again using Captain Hiraide in a national radio broadcast. "As you are well aware, our Navy units, raiding Midway on June 5, wrought terrible havoc on the remaining American aircraft carriers," stated Hiraide. "They sank an aircraft carrier of the *Enterprise* class, another carrier of the *Hornet* class, a heavy cruiser, and a destroyer, crushing the remaining American air force in the Pacific. Considerable significance is attached to the Midway and Aleutians operations in that our Navy, by crushing American Navy and air remnants in the Pacific, has brought pressure to bear on the United States mainland."

It was all smoke and mirrors. Tokyo had taken its fabrications to a whole new level, and the public was none the wiser. The better part of a decade would pass before the truth of the defeat was revealed to the Japanese people.

Thanks to the calm demeanor of Emperor Hirohito, Yamamoto and his staff began a gradual recovery from the disaster. Envoys from the Imperial Palace visited them aboard the battleship *Yamato* on June 16, bringing word that Hirohito was "not too concerned about the recent defeat; such things were to be expected in war."

The message of forgiveness was a tonic for Yamamoto, but in Tokyo, tumultuous debates raged throughout Imperial General Headquarters as army and navy planners argued over ideas for the next stage of the Southern Offensive. The fallout from Midway affected both services. A planned invasion of New Caledonia, Fiji, and Samoa, known as FS Operation, had been scheduled to begin in mid-July but was postponed for two months. Soon after that decision was made, the operation was abandoned altogether. Among the reasons for scrapping it: a newly published report from the Imperial Navy citing several problems in the South Pacific.

The ten-point position paper, submitted by the navy's Operations Section on July 7, revealed multiple concerns. First, the service frankly admitted that the New Guinea campaign had degraded "into a war of attrition." Navy leaders also acknowledged that they faced "a huge challenge" in replacing the four hundred plus aircraft lost during the Coral Sea and Midway battles. As of late June, land-based fighter units averaged only 54 percent of their full complement. Reconnaissance units were at 37 percent, medium bombers at 75 percent, and seaplanes at 80 percent. The Tainan Air Group, now divided between Rabaul and Lae, was a prime example. On paper, it had a nominal strength of more than fifty pilots and was allotted forty five Zeros; but from May through July of 1942, the air group averaged only about twenty combat-worthy fighters. The supply line for replacements was described as "very sluggish," namely because not enough new aircraft were coming from the factories. The monthly output of all naval aircraft was only slightly ahead of attrition levels, and the navy was particularly disappointed in the slow delivery of fighters—less than ninety aircraft per month in the spring of 1942.

Yamamoto and the Combined Fleet Staff should not have been surprised by the deficiencies. Mitsubishi Heavy Industries built the majority of its Type 0 fighters at the Nagoya Aircraft Works, a huge factory in the densely crowded port city of Nagoya. The plant had recently been enlarged to more than 1.6 million square feet and boasted a workforce of some thirty thousand people, but for all that, it did not produce complete airplanes.

Due to a combination of industrial congestion and inconceivable shortsightedness, the aircraft factory had been built miles from the nearest airfield. As a result, the plant was restricted to producing subassemblies rather than whole planes. The engine, wings, fuselage, and tail section all had to be transported *thirty miles* to an airfield big enough for assembly and testing. There were no rail lines available, and the streets of Nagoya were too narrow for large trucks. Horse-drawn wagons had been tried, but their speeds over the narrow, rough roads caused too much damage to the aircraft components. Thus, the Japanese resorted to using primitive oxcarts to haul the subassemblies of their modern fighter to Kagamigahara airfield. It took twenty-four hours for each team of lumbering oxen to cover the thirty miles through the crowded streets. No improvements were made to the roads, which deteriorated as production rates increased and more oxcarts were employed. Determined to build more Zeros, the Imperial Navy contracted with another aircraft manufacturer, Nakajima, whose plant eventually exceeded Mitsubishi's in monthly production; but even at their highest output, the two factories averaged only 140 fighters per month.

BY LATE JUNE, the leaders at Imperial General Headquarters had revised the entire strategy for the war in the South Pacific. Rather than extending their territory by invading far-off islands, they decided to strengthen their grip on the islands already occupied—namely the Bismarcks and the Solomons. Virtually overnight, the prevailing mindset among the military leadership reverted from an offensive strategy to a predominantly defensive one. As part of a fleet-wide reorganization, the Eighth Fleet was formed in mid-July. It was commanded by fifty-three-year-old Vice Adm. Gunichi Mikawa, headquartered at Rabaul, who would be responsible for operations in the Southeast Area, thus freeing the Fourth Fleet to concentrate its forces in the Central Pacific.

There was one exception to the defensive posture. The Japanese were not content merely to occupy the northeastern coastline of New Guinea—they wanted the whole island. By capturing Port Moresby, they could still force Australia out of the war. Conversely, as long as the Allies held Port Moresby, their attacks on Rabaul and its satellite bases would gradually intensify.

Having failed to capture Port Moresby by sea, Imperial General Headquarters began to investigate the feasibility of an overland assault against the Australian outpost. To some, the idea of sending a large infantry force across the Owen Stanley Mountains seemed preposterous. However, due to the Coral Sea and Midway losses there would be no carrier air support for another seaborne attempt, and the planners were anxious to try something different.

The outcome was called the Ri Operation Study. On June 12, Imperial General Headquarters issued Great Army Instruction No. 1180, which directed the Seventeenth Army to "immediately begin research, in cooperation with navy units in the area, for the feasibility of an overland attack on Port Moresby from the north coast of British New Guinea." Because the Seventeenth Army lacked its own planes, aerial support was provided by the 25th Air Flotilla in the form of reconnaissance flights over New Guinea and heavy pressure on Port Moresby. Seven large-scale bombing raids were conducted during the first three weeks of July, typically employing twenty or more *rikko* escorted by at least fifteen fighters. But rather than producing the desired knockout blow, the missions became more and more costly for the Japanese. Not only had Port Moresby survived the earlier onslaught of raids, it was now under-going significant expansion. Over the past few months, Australian and American engineers had completed several new airdromes, enabling more squadrons of P-39s and P-400s to move up from Australia. Although still outclassed by the Zeros, the American fighters intercepted the Japanese raids in ever greater numbers.

As with Seven Mile airdrome, the new fields were initially named for their distance by road from Port Moresby. The first, constructed by an Australian militia battalion, was called Five Mile. Its two parallel runways, each 6,000 feet long, were surfaced by American engineers. Farther from town, near the village of Bomana, Twelve Mile airdrome was completed in mid-May 1942. It had a hard-packed gravel runway of 4,500 feet, a length suited for fighters, medium bombers, and reconnaissance aircraft. Two miles farther out, Fourteen Mile was completed by American army engineers near the Laloki River. Its dirt runway, 5,300 feet long, was later resurfaced with pierced steel planking, commonly known as Marston mat. In August, engineers completed Seventeen Mile airdrome, carved out of a mostly wooded area north of the Waigani swamp. Crocodiles and other

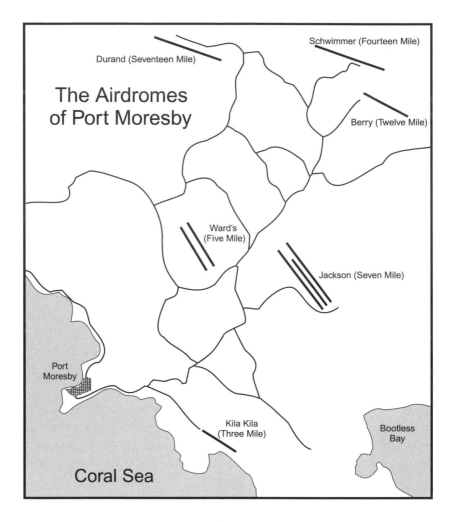

The Airdromes
of Port Moresby

Schwimmer (Fourteen Mile)

Durand (Seventeen Mile)

Berry (Twelve Mile)

Ward's
(Five Mile)

Jackson (Seven Mile)

Port
Moresby

Kila Kila
(Three Mile)

Bootless
Bay

Coral Sea

fearsome reptiles shared the wetlands, and one snake killed by airmen allegedly measured twenty-six feet in length.

All of the fields were constructed in haste. Their living conditions were deplorable, but the overall improvement in offensive and defensive capability was incalculable. The Japanese could see this for themselves. Despite the fact that the Tainan Air Group boasted more aces than any other air group in the Imperial Navy, they could not gain the upper hand. "As the months passed at Lae and the air battles grew in intensity, our supplies gradually diminished," recalled Saburo Sakai. "Despite the excellent fighting record of our own wing of Zero fighters, we found it impossible to pin down the Allies. They appeared in ever-growing numbers in the air. Coupled with their always persistent aggression, they proved a formidable force, indeed."

Losses among the Airacobra squadrons were heavy, but the relatively inexperienced American pilots held their own against the veterans of the Tainan Air Group. For one thing, the American pilots could afford to be a bit more reckless when fighting near their own airdromes. If shot down (presuming they suffered no debilitating wounds in air combat), they stood a much better chance of surviving than if they came down over enemy territory. During May 1942, the first month of combat for the Airacobra squadrons, twenty P-39s/P-400s were shot down with eleven pilots killed or missing in action. In June, twenty-three Airacobras were shot down or crash-landed while intercepting enemy raids, costing the lives of seventeen pilots. In comparison, the Tainan Air Group lost eleven Zeros and nine pilots in May, followed by the loss of five Zeros and four pilots in June. Although the Americans were losing more planes and pilots, replacements were available. This was not the case for the Japanese. As Saburo Sakai hinted, the Tainan Air Group was slowly being used up.

In addition to predominantly fighting over their own airfields, the American pilots held another potential advantage: motive. What Sakai referred to as "persistent aggression" by the Airacobra pilots was actually vengeance. The attack on Pearl Harbor had occurred only six months earlier, and retribution remained a powerful incentive for the Americans. In the most basic terms, they wanted to kill Japanese. The end result was that two of the Tainan Air Group's best attributes—superior aircraft and extensive combat experience—were whittled away by the sheer determination of their opponents.

CHAPTER 18

MacArthur's New Airman

DESPITE THE FAILURE of the 25th Air Flotilla to knock out Port Moresby, the Japanese proceeded with Ri Operation. Three transports, loaded with elements of the South Seas Force and escorted by Cruiser Division 18, departed Rabaul on the evening of July 20 for the Huon Gulf. The following afternoon, under cover of bad weather that minimized the effectiveness of Allied air attacks, the convoy reached its destination. Infantry of the Sasebo Special Naval Landing Force went ashore northwest of Buna, and a large contingent of army troops landed at Gona. Unopposed, they grabbed yet another vital segment of the New Guinea coastline.

The inability of Allied air power to prevent the latest Japanese landings was not surprising. Week after week, the crews of the 3rd, 22nd, and 19th Bomb Groups had applied pressure on the enemy, but the overall results were disappointing. Frequent mechanical problems, bad weather, supply shortages, and the sheer length of the missions kept aircrews and maintenance personnel on the threshold of exhaustion. As the months passed, the situation increasingly took its toll on men as well as machines. Squadrons struggled to provide enough aircraft for the scheduled missions, and many of the planes that could still be considered airworthy were barely holding together. If just one aircraft was slowed by a poorly performing engine, an entire formation might be compromised, especially on long missions. All too often raids were completed haphazardly, with bombers reaching the target (if at all) either singly or in pairs, almost always without fighter escort. The attackers were therefore subjected to the full brunt of the defending fighters, but for all the incurred risk, the raids rarely caused much damage. More often than not, the returning aircrews reported results far in excess of what they actually achieved.

Naturally, after flying long and hazardous missions that had no apparent effect on the enemy, the morale of the Allied flyers began to wane. To make matters worse, egotism and sour professional relationships in the upper levels of command trickled down to affect the airmen's performance.

The trouble began at the very top. Many U.S. Army aviators, particularly those with extensive time in uniform, believed that General MacArthur strongly favored the ground forces over air power. As evidence, they pointed to his participation in the 1925 court-martial of Col. William L. "Billy" Mitchell, a brilliant but strident activist for air power who was convicted of insubordination for his scathing criticisms of the armed services. MacArthur, one of the judges at Mitchell's court-martial, ruled in favor of conviction. Among those who subsequently harbored some resentment was George Brett, who had worked closely with Mitchell both during and after World War I.

Similarly, many aviators were critical of MacArthur's role in the Philippines debacle. Brett also belonged in this category. When MacArthur was beleaguered on the Bataan Peninsula, Brett had recommended to the army chief of staff that no more supplies should be expended on what was obviously a lost cause. MacArthur later became aware of Brett's position and decided he was disloyal. MacArthur also blamed Brett personally for the failed attempt to provide B-17s for his evacuation from Mindanao.

Conversely, Brett was harsh in his private criticisms of the supreme commander. "General MacArthur has a wonderful personality when he desires to turn it on," he wrote in July 1942. "He is, however, absolutely bound up in himself. I do not believe he has a single thought for anybody who is not useful to him, and I believe he detests the Air Corps through his own inability to thoroughly understand it and operate it as he does ground troops. There are rumors that he refuses to fly."

Brett had ample reasons for his rancor. When MacArthur reached Australia and traveled to Melbourne, Brett made several attempts to meet with him and was deliberately snubbed. During the next four months,

Brett met face to face with MacArthur only seven times. Brett was frequently stonewalled by MacArthur's chief of staff, the arrogant, acerbic Richard Sutherland, who was now a brigadier general. Although not an aviator, Sutherland had the habit of meddling with mission orders and other aspects of the air war he knew little about. He flaunted the power that came with his position as MacArthur's chief of staff, and many officers detested him for it. Brett went so far as to call him "a bully who, should he lose his ability to say 'by order of General MacArthur,' would be practically a nobody."

Brett outranked Sutherland and probably should have been more forceful with him. Instead, the two became embroiled in a war of words, firing retaliatory memos and directives from their respective offices. On June 3, for example, Sutherland directed Brett to explain why the P-39s and P-400s at Port Moresby were unreliable as escorts for bombing missions. Sutherland thereby revealed his lack of understanding about the dire situation in New Guinea, where the Airacobra squadrons were desperately trying to defend Port Moresby against daily attacks.

In the same memo, Sutherland questioned the low availability rate of the B-17s, but before Brett could address either grievance, Sutherland fired off another memorandum. This time he complained that "according to operations reports, no attack has been made upon the airdromes at Rabaul in compliance with Operations Instruction No. 8." But the reality was that Flying Fortresses had attacked Rabaul several times since May 29, when that particular instruction was posted. Sutherland, for all his posturing, appeared to be totally ignorant of the week's activities. On June 9 he sent Brett another memo that purportedly showed no B-17 raids on Rabaul, only reconnaissance flights. He ordered Brett to attack the stronghold "without further delay," unaware that Flying Fortresses had already hit the waterfront and storage facilities three times between the 2nd and 5th of June. The crews were doing their best with what they had, but Sutherland seemed more interested in discrediting Brett.

Sutherland was not the only one causing friction. Some of MacArthur's department heads, having accompanied him from the Philippines, regarded themselves as the heroes of Bataan. The group included Brig. Gen. Charles A. Willoughby (intelligence), Brig. Gen. Richard J. Marshall (deputy chief of staff), Brig. Gen. Hugh J. Casey (engineering), Brig. Gen. William F. Marquat (antiaircraft), and Brig. Gen. Harold H. George (air).

Their cliquishness was an affront to outsiders. "Marshall, Willoughby, Marquat and Casey . . . have talked a great deal but accomplished little," noted Brett. "They have an exaggerated idea of their own importance, and the impression I get is that they are controlled by Sutherland; [they] are, in fact, 'yes-men'. They are officious and have no proper sense of the need for cooperation with the forces operating under the Commander-in-Chief."

Among this group, Willoughby was probably the most unique. Born in Germany, he described himself as the son of a baron and behaved accordingly, but birth records in his home city of Heidelberg do not substantiate his claim. Alternately, he said he was an orphan. Whatever his true heritage, Willoughby served two stints in the army after changing his surname from Weidenbach to Willoughby. By the time he pinned on his star he'd cultivated a Prussian demeanor. He wore expensive tailored uniforms, even a monocle, and often expressed himself with a dramatic flair. Such traits might have been charming had Willoughby been a brilliant officer, but he was greatly overshadowed by MacArthur.

George was the most promising. A genuine fighter ace with five victories in World War I, he had earned a Distinguished Service Cross for combat valor. In the Philippines he performed well during the bitter but hopeless defense of the northern islands, particularly after General Brereton departed for Australia. Using the remnants of the Far East Air Force's pursuit group, amounting to hardly more than a handful of fighters, he harassed the Japanese for weeks. George is also credited with organizing approximately one thousand airmen into an infantry unit. Unfortunately, his life ended tragically while visiting Batchelor Field on April 29, 1942. Newly assigned as the aviation commander for the Northwest Area, George had just climbed from his twin-engine transport and was talking with a group of bystanders when a P-40 veered off the runway during takeoff and smashed into the parked plane. The spectacular collision caused only minor injuries to the P-40 pilot, but three bystanders were killed, including George.

The loss of the top airman in MacArthur's headquarters added to the discord in Australia. Brett and Sutherland feuded openly, and Brett's own chief of staff proved to be unpopular as well. He had selected AVM William D. Bostock, wanting a senior RAAF man as his deputy, but Brett underestimated the harmful effect of internal politics on his directorate system. Furthermore, he found his deputy's behavior annoying. "Bostock has a very poor personality," wrote Brett. "He always appears to be grumpy and discontented. He is rather arbitrary in his opinions, which of course will not work without adequate background. He is completely [against] General Headquarters and is unsympathetic towards everything they do."

By the summer of 1942, the bickering and the personality clashes had everyone on edge. MacArthur demanded absolute loyalty from his subordinates, but he did not have Brett's or even Sutherland's. The latter faked his loyalty in the interest of advancing his own career, but MacArthur never caught on. The one he resented most was Brett, who had arrived in Australia more than two months earlier and was treated almost like royalty by representatives of the Labor and Conservative parties. Brett had been unanimously recommended for supreme commander by the Australian and New Zealand service chiefs in late February, a month before MacArthur arrived, and that alone was enough to make him intensely jealous. Described as "an exceptionally sensitive man and excessively attentive to his personal destiny," MacArthur coveted the spotlight for himself. He probably did not despise Brett quite as much as Sutherland did, but neither did he attempt to mediate the feud between his two subordinates.

With so much finger pointing and professional jealousy infecting the leadership in Australia, it's almost miraculous that the Allies were able to conduct *any* sort of campaign against the Japanese. Brett did the best he could, but the mediocrity of the air war reflected badly on him. It became painfully clear to many people that Brett simply wasn't tough enough to handle the demanding job. Colonel Burdette M. Fitch, the adjutant general at MacArthur's headquarters, described Brett as "a rather easy-going Air Force officer who was probably a better flyer than administrator."

HALFWAY AROUND the world, General Marshall and the Joint Chiefs of Staff were increasingly aware of the trouble brewing in Australia. Over the past few months MacArthur had sent numerous "eyes only" messages to Marshall and Gen. Henry H. "Hap" Arnold, commanding general of the U. S. Army Air Forces. The two men also received an objective briefing from Brig. Gen. Ross G. Hoyt, recently returned from Australia, who was of the opinion that "either Brett or MacArthur must go."

Marshall was not eager to recall Brett, with whom he shared a friendship as well as an alma mater, Virginia Military Institute. But the secretary of war, Henry L. Stimson, had lost confidence in Brett months earlier and leaned on Marshall to replace him. In late June, MacArthur sent yet another message complaining of the critical need for more planes, parts, and people, describing the efficiency of his air units as "only average." He reminded Marshall that the supply problems had been "reflected constantly in reports made by Gen. Brett to Gen. Arnold and by occasional radios by myself." Convinced that the time for change had finally come, Marshall sent a reply to MacArthur on June 29 that read: "Desire your views and recommendations on possible replacement of Brett by General Frank Andrews."

Intentionally or not, Marshall's message gave MacArthur carte blanche to openly criticize Brett—and that is exactly what he did. The verbose reply erased all doubts about MacArthur's frustrations:

I would prefer Andrews to Brett and believe a change here would strengthen the air component. I know both men intimately and have no doubt whatever that Andrews, while not naturally as brilliantly gifted as Brett, possesses those elements of basic character which constitute a better fighting commander under battle conditions. Brett is unquestionably highly qualified as an air technician and in air administrative duties of a productive or supply character; he is an unusually hard worker but his very industry leads him to concentrate at times upon unimportant details which tend to obscure a true perspective of more important matters; he is naturally inclined toward more or less harmless intrigue and has a bent, due perhaps to his delightful personality, for social entertainment and the easy way of life; he is unpopular with the Australian administration who resent his lack of forthrightness and he does not command the confidence of the younger and fighting elements of the air corps here. I would rate his service during the past three months under my command as only average. His relationship with the navy component is poor. His relations with my headquarters have been personally most cordial but professionally he has been evasive. Although Brett has a very large staff I do not consider it particularly competent. This may be due to his inability to select and place the right men in key positions or possibly he is unable to properly coordinate them. Andrews is a type of commander who needs a competent Chief of Staff and Operations Officer. In case the change is made I suggest that he be permitted to bring these two staff officers with him and that men of corresponding rank here be returned with Brett.

Marshall had his answer. It was obvious that MacArthur wanted Brett replaced, but a new problem arose when Marshall's first nominee turned down the job. Lieutenant General Frank M. Andrews, a renowned advocate of strategic bombing and a longtime ally of Marshall's, had no intention of working under MacArthur. Andrews, then in charge of the Caribbean Defense Command, considered the offer as more of a demotion than an opportunity.

On July 6, Marshall offered two new candidates for MacArthur's consideration: Brig. Gen. James H. Doolittle, the hero of the raid on Tokyo a few months earlier, and Maj. Gen. George C. Kenney, presently in command of the Fourth Air Force on the West Coast. MacArthur answered promptly:

> I know intimately all commanders named . . . and rate them all superior. I would much prefer Kenney to Doolittle not so much because of natural attainments and ability but because it would be difficult to convince the Australians of Doolittle's acceptability. His long absence in civil life would react most unfavorably throughout the Australian Air Force. I therefore recommend Kenney and would be glad to have his order issued as soon as possible.

MacArthur's arguments against Doolittle ring false. Doolittle was known worldwide for his many aeronautical achievements, so the Australians did not need to be convinced of his acceptability. Doolittle was about to receive a Medal of Honor for his role in the Tokyo raid, and the suggestion that the RAAF would disapprove of Doolittle's "long absence" from the military was preposterous. MacArthur didn't care what the Australians thought; he wanted an American-led effort in the SWPA and would do whatever was necessary to support his own ambitions.

The real reason MacArthur didn't want Doolittle was because Doolittle was far too famous. He was a superstar, one of the world's most renowned aviators. He had set numerous speed records, won the world's three biggest air racing prizes (the Schneider, Bendix, and Thompson trophies), and personally developed much of the technology and methodology used in instrument flying. His impact on aviation was extraordinary. Doolittle would have done the Allied cause a great service in Australia, which he proved later by leading the Eighth Air Force in Europe. But MacArthur didn't want him in Australia because he might steal the spotlight.

Compared with Doolittle, few people outside the U.S. Army had heard of George Churchill Kenney. Even his citizenship was obscure. He considered himself an American but was born in Yarmouth, Nova Scotia. Both of his parents were Canadian citizens, not vacationers as he claimed, and Kenney spent his first ten or eleven years in Nova Scotia. On the other hand, his family could trace its heritage to some of the earliest settlers of New England. Moreover, the Kenneys moved to a suburb of Boston around the turn of the century. After high school Kenney studied engineering at the prestigious Massachusetts Institute of Technology but dropped out after three years because of financial concerns. He still found steady work in civil engineering and gained experience in all types of construction—from bridges to railroads to office buildings. He and a partner started a successful business, wherein Kenney discovered his knack for problem-solving.

When the United States entered World War I, Kenney wrote to the War Department and requested aviation training. By early June he was back at M.I.T. for ground school, after which he completed basic flight training at Mineola, New York. He then sailed to France and underwent additional training before receiving an assignment to the 91st Aero Squadron, a reconnaissance outfit that specialized in photographic missions during the last months of the war. Kenney was highly decorated after making several flights deep into enemy territory, earning both a Silver Star and a Distinguished Service Cross, the latter pinned on by Billy Mitchell. Kenney also scored two confirmed aerial victories, but he was much more concerned about the high mortality rate among his own squadron mates: only one in four of the 91st's original cadre of pilots survived the war.

After the war Kenney enjoyed a steady rise through the ranks, displaying a talent for innovation gleaned from the lessons of combat and his previous experience as an engineer and businessman. He was the first to mount a machine gun inside the wing of an airplane (a pair of .30-caliber guns in a De Havilland in 1922) and is generally credited with the invention of the parachute bomb. He was also blessed with an abundance of energy as well as confidence, attributes that offset his small physical stature. According to biographer Thomas Griffith, Kenney stood "five feet, five and a half inches tall," but that half-inch lends an optimistic note to the measurement. In photographs, Kenney almost always appeared significantly shorter than the individuals around him. His face, highlighted by a fleshy lower lip and a prominent scar on his chin, enhanced the bulldog image.

Described by *Time* magazine as "a cocky, enthusiastic little man who can inspire his flyers with his own skill for improvisation," Kenney was exactly the man MacArthur needed in the Southwest Pacific. While en route to Australia, he worked on new ideas with his aide, Maj. William G. Benn of Shamokin, Pennsylvania. Caught up in discussions over techniques for low-level bombing against ships, the two men decided to test a little-known method called "skip bombing," first tried by the British. Borrowing a Marauder during a layover at Fiji, they loaded it with inert bombs and made repeated passes against coral outcroppings.

With his engineering background and years of aviation experience, Kenney was no stranger to hands-on testing. He later described his first skip-bombing trials with Benn:

> It was quite evident that it was going to take quite a bit of experimental flying to determine the proper height for release of the bomb and how far from the [enemy] ship it should be released. From this first experiment it looked as though 100-feet altitude and a distance of about 400 yards would be somewhere near right. We bounced some bombs right over the targets, others sank without bouncing, but finally they began skipping along just like flat stones. Benn and I both agreed that we would have to get some more firepower up in the nose of the bomber to cover us coming in on the attack if the Jap vessels had very much gun protection on their decks, but it looked as though we had something. The lads at Fiji didn't seem to think much of the idea but I decided that as soon as we got time . . . I would put Benn to work on it. He was really enthusiastic about it, particularly after we began to score some good "skips" against the coral knobs.

During the month of July, meanwhile, MacArthur had moved his headquarters from Melbourne to Brisbane, where he settled into an office building formerly occupied by the Australian Mutual Providence Society. When Kenney and his aide arrived in the city on July 28, they were first escorted to Lennon's Hotel, said to be the finest in Brisbane.

After checking into Flat 13 (which he considered a lucky number), Kenney met with Richard Sutherland and heard his "tale of woe" about the state of the Allied air forces. Kenney knew Sutherland well—ten years earlier they had been classmates at the Army War College—and although he admired Sutherland's intelligence, he was well aware that Sutherland antagonized almost everyone he worked with.

On his second day in Australia, Kenney visited briefly with his predecessor, George Brett, then went up to the eighth floor of the AMP Building to call on his new boss. Ushered straight into MacArthur's office, Kenney noticed that the supreme commander "looked a little tired, drawn, and nervous." There was good reason: MacArthur had just been informed that the Japanese army was landing at Buna, on the coast of New Guinea. Not only was this a fresh crisis, but an unfortunate coincidence. MacArthur had planned to establish a defensive perimeter around Port Moresby by building new airfields at Buna. An Australian garrison was already in position at Milne Bay, and the operation to land American engineers at Buna, code named Providence, had been scheduled for August 10. The Japanese simply beat him to it. Despite the serious situation, MacArthur devoted at least two hours to a personal meeting with Kenney, thus demonstrating his belief in the importance of air power. Not that he was pleased with the performance of the existing units. To the contrary, for the first half of the meeting MacArthur ranted nonstop, unloading a litany of complaints. Kenney listened attentively and later outlined MacArthur's diatribe in his diary.

> Listened to a lecture for approximately an hour on the shortcomings of the Air Force in general and the Allied Air Force in the Southwest Pacific in particular. [MacArthur] said, among other things, that he believed that the Air Force could do something; that so far he could not see where they had done anything at all; that the whole thing was so badly botched up that he believed his staff could run it better than the Air [Force] had done. He had no use for anyone in the organization, from Brett down to the grade of colonel. He claimed that Brett was disloyal to him, that Royce was a scatterbrain and that all the rest of the generals should never have [made field grade] in the first place. He said they were all made by the underhanded submitting of their names to Washington without his approval. He informed me that he expected me to be loyal to him.

As soon as I got a chance to say anything, I told him frankly that I had been sent out here to take over the air show and that I intended to run it; that as far as the question of loyalty was concerned, if for any reason I found that I could not work with him or be loyal to him I would tell him so and do everything in my power to get relieved. He grinned and put his hand on my shoulder and said, "I think we are going to get along all right."

Instinctively knowing which buttons to push, Kenney had thawed MacArthur's frosty shell of mistrust in a matter of minutes. Perhaps his small stature was a contributing factor, but it was probably Kenney's infectious blend of intelligence and energy that won over the supreme commander. For another hour they chatted about the war. MacArthur did most of the talking, during which he outlined an important operation scheduled for early August. Although it would take place in the southern Solomons, outside his command area, he had pledged full support and needed Kenney's recommendations. Kenney responded that he could not give any recommendations until he knew exactly what he had to work with and pledged to leave immediately for an inspection tour of the forward bases. He would then return to Brisbane and present a clear answer.

Before leaving the city, Kenney spent several hours with General Brett observing his directorate system. Brett offered Kenney the use of his personal aircraft, an early-model B-17D, which Kenney gladly accepted. The Flying Fortress, originally named *Ole Betsy*, was in tiptop shape. One of the first B-17s to see combat in the Philippines, it had received heavy damage during a mission over Borneo and was subsequently rebuilt in Melbourne, receiving a complete tail assembly cannibalized from another B-17. The unique repair inspired the next pilot to rename it *The Swoose* after a popular big-band tune, "Alexander the Swoose (Half Swan, Half Goose)." Permanently withdrawn from combat status, the B-17 was later sent back to Melbourne for a more thorough engine overhaul, at which point Capt. Frank Kurtz, Brett's pilot, selected it as the general's personal transport.

Kenney took off aboard *The Swoose* at 2300 on July 29 and landed four hours later at Townsville to pick up three important passengers. Waiting for him were Brig. Gen. Ennis C. Whitehead, USAAF, who had arrived from the States a month earlier; Maj. Gen. Ralph G. Royce, USAAF, commander of air operations in the Northeastern Sector at Townsville;

The first attack on Rabaul was made by Navy Type 96 land attack aircraft (Mitsubishi G3M "Nells") from Truk on January 4, 1942. Although nearly obsolete by Japanese standards, the bombers were untouched by Australian antiaircraft guns or interceptors. *Ron Werneth*

The only "fighters" in the RAAF inventory at the beginning of the war were CAC-1 Wirraways, copied from the North American AT-6 trainer with a few minor improvements. During the hopeless defense of Rabaul, 24 Squadron lost eight out of ten Wirraways. *Australian War Memorial*

A Type 99 carrier bomber (Aichi D3A "Val") from *Shokaku* approaches
Rabaul on January 20, 1942. The attack that day by more than one hundred
carrier-based planes knocked 24 Squadron out of commission. A follow-up
raid two days later destroyed the Australian coastal defense guns. *Maru*

A Type 97 carrier attack aircraft (Nakajima B 5N "Kate") was shot down by the militia antiaircraft battery on January 20 and crashed on the slopes of a nearby volcano. The Aussie gunners also damaged several attackers; two were ditched at sea and a third crashed while attempting to land on its carrier. *Ron Werneth*

Wing Commander John Lerew, who led poorly equipped 24 Squadron at Rabaul, found his superiors only slightly less troublesome than the Japanese. He routinely sent messages laced with sarcasm, but his courage in battle was unmatched. *Josephine Lerew via Lex McAulay*

The first American raid on Rabaul was conducted February 22–23, 1942, by B-17 Flying Fortresses of the 14th Reconnaissance Squadron, temporarily assigned to the U.S. Navy. The author's uncle, Lt. John Steinbinder, flew forty-three combat missions as a navigator in the squadron (later redesignated the 435th RS), including a dozen missions over Rabaul. *Margaret Gamble Steinbinder*

Workhorse of the RAAF, the Catalina flying boat was slow and ungainly but could carry 4,000 pounds of bombs over great distances. Less than twenty-four hours after Rabaul fell, Catalinas of 11 and 20 Squadrons made the first of many night raids on Simpson Harbor. *Michael Claringbould*

Fast and well armed, the Navy Type 1 land attack aircraft (Mitsubishi G4M "Betty") saw action throughout the Pacific. In combat the Betty caught fire easily, and the units at Rabaul suffered devastating losses. Elements of Air Group 705 are pictured here over Simpson Harbor in 1943. *Maru*

Long stretches of boredom were common during reconnaissance flights and even attack missions, which took many hours to complete. Here, the starboard-side gunner in a Betty uses chopsticks to eat a boxed "aero lunch" while keeping watch on the world outside. *Osaka Mainichi*

When two waves of Bettys attacked the USS *Lexington* task force almost four hundred miles from Rabaul on February 20, 1942, Lt. Edward "Butch" O'Hare singlehandedly thwarted the second wave, earning the Pacific war's first Medal of Honor. He is pictured (left) shaking hands with his CO and mentor, Lt. Cmdr. John "Jimmy" Thach, in front of an F4F Wildcat. *National Archives*

Dead heroes. Commander Takuzo Ito (top, left) directed the 4th Air Group's attack on *Lexington*. After O'Hare damaged his bomber, Ito and his crew died in a failed attempt to crash into the carrier. Also aboard the plane was Lt. Cmdr. Yogoro Seto (top, right). A separate suicidal ramming attempt by Lt. Cmdr. Masayoshi Nakagawa (bottom, left) likewise failed to hit the ship. The Betty piloted by Lt. Akira Mitani (bottom, right) fell in flames to O'Hare's guns. *Osaka Mainichi*

With its two outboard engines idling, a B-17E of the 19th Bomb Group waits to taxi while P-39 Airacobra fighters take off from Seven Mile airdrome in mid-1942. Throughout the war, Port Moresby served as the primary staging base for Allied air groups in the Southwest Pacific. *Michael Claringbould*

Fighter pilots of RAAF 75 Squadron wear a casual assortment of combat gear. For a critical span of forty-four days, the lone squadron held off relentless Japanese attacks against Port Moresby. In the process, virtually all of their Kittyhawk fighters were destroyed or put out of commission. *David Wilson*

Allied antiaircraft guns were sparse at Port Moresby during the early months of the war. Eventually, large-bore guns, such as this 3-inch weapon of the 94th Coastal Artillery, were installed in protected emplacements to defend against Japanese bombers. *MacArthur Memorial*

Built for speed, the streamlined B-26 featured the most powerful radial engines then available. This Marauder of the 22nd Bomb Group was photographed at Townsville, Queensland, in the spring of 1942, when American planes wore highly visible red and white rudder stripes. *Michael Claringbould*

The combat debut of both the B-25 Mitchell and the B-26 Marauder took place in the Southwest Pacific on April 6, 1942. Here, a sleek Marauder of the 22nd Bomb Group has just bombed the Japanese airdrome at Lae on the coast of New Guinea. *MacArthur Memorial*

A Model 21 Zero (A6M2) of the Tainan Air Group is being warmed up at Lakunai airdrome in mid-1942. With a roster of aggressive aces, Japan's most famous fighter unit destroyed dozens of Allied aircraft in the air and on the ground. *Hajime Yoshida*

Maintenance on a Model 21 Zero is performed in the shadow of Tavurvur volcano, which belches smoke across Matupit Harbor from Lakunai airdrome. Note the perfunctory application of palm-frond camouflage. *Henry Sakaida*

A primitive hangar at Lakunai shows evidence of blast damage from Allied attacks. Curiously, the Zero parked inside is heavily camouflaged with palm fronds, but there are no trees anywhere nearby. *Henry Sakaida*

Flight Petty Officer Saburo Sakai, his face bloody and swollen, is surrounded by members of the Tainan Air Group at Lakunai on August 8, 1942. Partially paralyzed and blinded in one eye, he completed a 650-mile flight from Guadalcanal after a machine-gun bullet creased his skull. *Henry Sakaida*

When his regular bomber suffered an engine failure on the eve of a big mission to Rabaul, Capt. Harl Pease Jr. and his crew took a worn-out B-17E instead. Shot down over New Britain on August 7, 1942, Pease was posthumously awarded a Medal of Honor. *MacArthur Memorial*

After the war it was learned that Pease and one of his crewmen had bailed out and were taken prisoner. Two months later, Warrant Officer Minoru Yoshimura of the 81st Naval Garrison Unit oversaw the execution of Pease and seven other captives, who were bayoneted at the edge of a common grave. *Australian War Memorial*

High-altitude bombing rarely succeeded against ships. Kenney's former aide, Maj. William Benn, perfected skip-bombing tactics with B-17s of the 63rd Bomb Squadron. The missions, usually conducted on moonlit nights, achieved far better results. *Author's Collection*

Head of V Bomber Command during the second half of 1942, Brig. Gen. Kenneth Walker was one of the army's top proponents of high-altitude daylight strategic bombing. His convictions were often at odds with the low-level tactics favored by General Kenney, who also preferred night attacks against heavily defended Rabaul. *Douglas Walker*

Ordnance men prepare to "bomb up" *Yankee Doodle Dandy*, a B-24 Liberator of the 90th Bomb Group (Heavy) in a revetment at Port Moresby. The group's early combat history was marred by bad luck, with an inordinate number of accidents and non-combat-related losses. *90th Bomb Group Association*

Blazing tropical heat, poor living conditions, and combat stress put a big strain on morale. But the top American airman in the Southwest Pacific, the diminutive Gen. George Kenney, awarded hundreds of medals to inspire his men. *James Harcrow*

Kenney also instigated a system to give combat crews a week's relaxation in Australian cities. This cartoon pokes fun at the crew of a B-17 that has just returned from R&R in Sydney—with the men in worse shape than before. *43rd Bomb Group Association*

Major Paul "Pappy" Gunn, a salty, self-taught mechanical genius, reworked underperforming twin-engine bombers like the Douglas A-20 and North American B-25 into extremely potent low-level attackers that devastated Japanese shipping. *Larry Hickey*

On January 5, 1943, against Kenney's orders, Walker led twelve bombers to Rabaul in broad daylight. His B-17F, *San Antonio Rose*, was photographed mere hours before Japanese fighters shot it down. The crew was never recovered, and Walker received a Medal of Honor. *Justin Taylan*

A large stockpile of fuel goes up in flames after a raid on Port Moresby during Operation I-Go. Although the blaze was spectacular, the collective damage caused by Yamamoto's last offensive was relatively light and failed to make an impact on the Allies. *Author's Collection*

Admiral Isoroku Yamamoto (center), commander of the Combined Fleet, transferred his headquarters to Rabaul in early April 1943 for Operation I-Go. He and his staff, including Vice Adm. Matome Ugaki (right), honored the aircrews by observing the departure of each attack. *Henry Sakaida*

Yamamoto informally salutes a Zero fighter taking off from Lakunai airdrome. *Henry Sakaida*

and William S. Robinson, an Aussie billionaire industrialist with important political connections. After refueling, *The Swoose* took off again for Port Moresby. It would be a night without sleep as the VIPs got acquainted while crossing the Coral Sea. They touched down at Seven Mile airdrome at 0700, whereupon Kenney got his first taste of the already warm and humid air of New Guinea. *The Swoose* roared aloft again, heading for Horn Island to stay out of harm's way.

Visiting the front lines on just his second full day in the theater, Kenney impressed the men at Port Moresby. They had lost faith in Brett, who rarely visited and had no concept of how awful the conditions at Port Moresby had become. Kenney later wrote: "[Brett] didn't get up there very often; I think he was up there maybe twice. They didn't have much equipment and weren't getting any more equipment; they weren't getting spare parts when their airplanes began falling apart. Brett didn't get up to [see] them, and he didn't check and find out what they needed and see that they got it. Their food was terrible stuff, and he wouldn't do anything about that. They were getting malaria pretty badly, and there was nothing done about that."

Kenney was disgusted with just about everything he saw on the tour. Joined by Brig. Gen. Martin F. "Mike" Scanlon, the ranking American at Port Moresby, Kenney spent the day visiting the base with Royce and Whitehead. During the briefing for a bombing mission, Kenney was appalled by the lack of organization. The preliminaries were conducted by an Australian officer who simply declared that the objective was Rabaul, giving no specific targets. Kenney later wrote, "I found out afterward that nobody expects the airplanes to get that far anyhow, and if they do, the town itself is a good target."

A meteorologist spoke next. His estimates of the weather conditions over Rabaul were based on historical data rather than real-time analysis. Kenney observed that no one was designated to lead the formation, mainly because the bombers were not expected to stay together en route to the target—and no one seemed to care. The only thing the crews fretted about was their bomb load. "The personnel are obsessed with the idea that a bullet will detonate the bombs and blow up the whole works," Kenney noted. "If enemy airplanes are seen along the route, all auxiliary gas and bombs are immediately jettisoned and the mission abandoned."

Thoroughly displeased with bomber operations, Kenney next inspected the fighter squadrons and found them no better. After touring the fighter area for a few hours with Lt. Col. Richard A. Legg, commanding officer of the 35th Fighter Group, Kenney wrote, "His organization is lackadaisical, maintenance is at a low ebb, and while he is short of spares there is no excuse for only six P-39s out of forty being constantly available for combat."

Kenney also investigated the camp areas. "Throughout the Moresby area the camps are poorly laid out and the food situation is extremely bad," he later wrote. "There is no mosquito control discipline and the malaria and dysentery rates are forcing relief of a unit at the end of about two months' duty."

Now Kenney knew why MacArthur was displeased. Nobody seemed to be doing anything about the appalling conditions at Port Moresby, though Kenney did find a few subordinates—none above the rank of major—who were actually attempting to improve things.

After a quick assessment of the overall situation, Kenney immediately began to make changes. First, he told Whitehead to remain at Port Moresby to "look after the fighters" and implement some new policies. He directed that an American staff officer attend every mission briefing; also, every bombing mission would have a specific primary target assigned along with at least two alternates. Finally, he instructed Whitehead to inform Legg that if he didn't snap out of his lethargy, he'd be replaced.

Accompanied by Royce, Kenney returned to Townsville on August 31 and spent the day looking over the base—the most important in Australia. It was the center of operations for an increasing number of air groups at widely scattered locations, including a brand-new airfield at Mareeba, 180 miles to the northwest near Cairns. Kenney flew to Mareeba the following day and met with Dick Carmichael, recently promoted to lieutenant colonel, who had taken over the 19th Bomb Group. The move to Mareeba had been beneficial for the group. The base was 400 miles closer to Port Moresby, which shortened the missions considerably, and the wooded landscape surrounding the airfield was far more pleasant than the hot, fly-infested outback.

Despite the improvements, the airmen were exhausted and morale remained low. And, as Kenney soon discovered, an even bigger problem affected daily operations: the supply system was terribly inefficient. It astounded him to learn that eighteen of the B-17s at Mareeba were grounded for lack of engine parts and tail wheels, all because of bottlenecks in the supply line. Orders for replacement parts were sent via Townsville to Charters Towers, which had limited stocks, so the paperwork had to be forwarded to the main supply depot at Tocumwal, twelve hundred miles away in New South Wales. A month would sometimes elapse before a reply came, which too often was negative: either the part was unavailable or the requisition form had not been filled out properly. The snafus galled Kenney, who realized that hidebound desk jockeys were responsible for the disruptions. Arming himself with a detailed requisition list, he told Carmichael to cancel all missions except essential patrols and get ready for a maximum effort scheduled for a few days hence.

Kenney flew back to Townsville on the morning of August 2 and relieved Royce, then continued to Brisbane and went right back to work. He telephoned Maj. Gen. Rush B. Lincoln, commander of air services in Australia, and gave him the list of desired spare parts, which were to be airlifted to Mareeba as soon as possible.

Next, as promised, Kenney debriefed MacArthur on his trip to the forward area.

> I told him frankly what I thought was wrong with the Air Force set-up in both Australia and New Guinea and discussed the corrective action that I intended to take immediately. I asked him to give me authority to send home anyone that I thought was deadwood. He said, "Go ahead. You have my enthusiastic approval." I then discussed the air situation and told him that I wanted to carry out one primary mission, which was to take out the Jap air strength until we owned the air over New Guinea. That there was no use talking about playing across the street until we got the Nips off our front lawn.

MacArthur gave Kenney unconditional approval to implement his plan. More importantly, he promised not to micromanage Kenney's troops. He didn't care what the men looked like or what they did as long as they "would fight, shoot down Japs, and put bombs on the targets."

CHAPTER 19

Medal of Honor: Harl Pease Jr.

PRIOR TO MIDWAY, the staff at Imperial General Headquarters realized the importance of establishing an airfield in the eastern Solomon Islands. The capture of Tulagi in early May had given the Japanese a fine anchorage for warships and flying boats, and the addition of an airdrome would strengthen the defensive perimeter around Rabaul. It would also serve as a point for launching attacks against Allied bases in New Caledonia and the New Hebrides. But there were no suitable construction sites in the immediate vicinity of Tulagi for an airdrome large enough to accommodate land attack aircraft as well as fighters.

However, just twenty-three miles to the south lay the large island of Guadalcanal, which featured a broad plain near its northern coast. Home to thousands of Melanesian natives for untold generations, the island had been "discovered" by the Spanish in 1568, whereupon a member of the expedition named it in honor of his hometown. For hundreds of years the name appeared as *Guadalcanar* on most nautical charts, but the spelling was corrected after the island became part of the British Solomon Islands Protectorate. In the decades before World War II, segments of the coast had been developed for copra production. Lever Brothers, makers of popular English soaps, established plantations along the northern shore and were joined by Australian interests such as Burns, Philp & Company. The latter also operated a rubber plantation, and an enterprising rancher grazed a herd of cattle on the grassy plain, thereby providing a supply of fresh beef to nearby islands.

The Japanese investigated the island's potential almost immediately. Two weeks after settling in at Tulagi, the commanding officer of the Yokohama Air Group reported that Guadalcanal offered good attributes for an airfield. Engineers and staff from the 25th Air Flotilla and 8th Base Force departed from Rabaul in a flying boat on May 25 and visited Guadalcanal two days later to confirm the report. Slightly over a mile inland, just east of the Lunga River, they located a site for an airfield.

On June 1, Rear Admiral Yamada sent a letter to his immediate superior, Vice Adm. Nishizo Tsukahara (commander of the Eleventh Air Fleet, headquartered on Tinian), requesting the establishment of an airfield at Guadalcanal. Copies were also telegrammed to the staffs of the Combined Fleet and Imperial General Headquarters, resulting in two more inspection trips. Vice Admiral Inoue conducted the last trip in person on June 19, flying down from Rabaul to visit the site. At about the same time, small parties of naval troops from Tulagi set up tent encampments on Guadalcanal. They built a wharf and burned the kunai grasses off the plain; they also shot some of the cattle and ransacked plantations, which had been abandoned by their owners before Tulagi fell.

In late June the fast transport *Kinryu Maru* departed from Truk in company with several other cargo ships and an escort of five destroyers. Arriving off Guadalcanal on July 6, the transports offloaded the 11th and 13th Establishment Units along with tons of construction equipment: approximately one hundred trucks, four heavy tractors, six mechanized road rollers, two generators, an ice-making plant, and a pair of narrow-gauge locomotives with a dozen hopper cars. Construction of the airstrip began on July 16 and proceeded quickly with the help of Melanesian muscle. (The Japanese issued a declaration that all native men between the ages of fifteen and fifty must work for them. The islanders' only compensation was a vague promise of "identification as a civilian" at some future time.)

Although most of the plantation owners had evacuated the island, a few courageous individuals stayed behind to spy on the Japanese. Recruited previously into Eric Feldt's coastwatching organization, they observed the airfield construction from hilltop hideouts and sent trustworthy natives to infiltrate Japanese work gangs. At great risk, the coastwatchers reported each new development by radio, providing Allied commanders with invaluable intelligence about the progress of the enemy airfield. Periodic reconnaissance missions supplemented the coastwatchers' reports. Photo runs over Tulagi by the former 40th Reconnaissance Squadron (redesignated the 435th Bombardment Squadron in May) commenced on June 18. Three weeks later the "Kangaroo Squadron," as it was nicknamed, began conducting daily photographic missions over the area. Two Marine Corps officers, Lt. Col. Merrill B. Twining and Maj. William McKean, accompanied the 435th's mission on July 17. Observing the work on the Guadalcanal airfield, Twining remarked, "I hope they build a good one. We are going to use it."

Twining knew what he was talking about. Even before the Japanese began work on the airfield, the U.S. Joint Chiefs of Staff had decided on a bold plan to wrest control of the southern Solomons from the enemy. The recent naval battles had revealed that Japan's vaunted forces could be defeated, and the Joint Chiefs capitalized on the opportunity for America's first offensive. On July 2, less than seven months after Pearl Harbor, they produced an outline titled "Joint Directive for Offensive Operations in Southwest Pacific Area." The two-page document named a single objective: the conquest of the Bismarcks and New Guinea.

The plan was ambitious, but the Joint Chiefs broke it down into three separate tasks. The first was the "seizure and occupation of [the] Santa Cruz Islands, Tulagi and adjacent positions"; the second called for the capture of the upper Solomons and the northeast coast of New Guinea; and the third was the occupation of Rabaul and other key positions in the Bismarcks and New Guinea. No timeline was given. The plan would obviously require years to accomplish.

The Joint Chiefs moved swiftly to initiate the first task, named Operation Watchtower. The amphibious assault on Tulagi, initially scheduled for August 1, was delayed six days when the airfield on Guadalcanal was discovered. MacArthur lobbied hard to oversee the operation—the eastern boundary of his area of command, longitude 160 degrees east, cut through Guadalcanal almost precisely at Lunga Point—but he was also dealing with the Japanese invasion of Buna in his own backyard.

As it turned out, the Joint Chiefs already had Admiral Nimitz in mind to command Operation Watchtower. Due to his recent victory at Midway he was a bona fide superstar, not only within the navy but across the entire country. More importantly, he possessed the naval and amphibious forces needed for the offensive, including a division of marines currently being trained at Wellington, New Zealand. Determined to keep the operation a one-man show, the Joint Chiefs arbitrarily moved the boundary of the Southwest Pacific Area to longitude 159 degrees east, thereby placing Guadalcanal and Tulagi within the South Pacific Area (SOPAC), one of three subdivisions of the vast Pacific Ocean Areas under the supreme command of Nimitz.

MacArthur objected vigorously but was pacified when the Joint Chiefs promised to shift command to his jurisdiction for the second and third tasks outlined in the Joint Directive. With that reassurance, he pledged to assist with whatever support he could provide.

It was at this juncture that George Kenney arrived in Australia. After visiting Port Moresby, he discussed with MacArthur the possible roles the heavy bombers could play in the forthcoming operation. Tulagi and Guadalcanal were about nine hundred miles due east of Port Moresby—too far for B-17s with a load of bombs—so Kenney planned to hammer Rabaul instead. He informed MacArthur that he had called a temporary halt to all B-17 missions so that the 19th Bomb Group could make needed repairs and rest its airmen prior to a maximum effort. "When I told [MacArthur] that I planned to put between 16 and 18 B-17s on Vunakanau on 6 August," Kenney later wrote, "he looked as though he was about to kiss me."

At daybreak on August 4, The Swoose took off for the United States with General Brett aboard, and Kenney took over as the commander of Allied Air Forces, Southwest Pacific Area.* The following day he flew to Mareeba to impress upon Dick Carmichael the importance of the mission to Rabaul. In his journal, Kenney noted that a B-17 reconnaissance flight

---

*As the first B-17 to return from combat, The Swoose conducted a public relations tour of the United States. Pilot Frank A. Kurtz Jr., a bronze medalist in the 1932 Olympics, later became the most decorated pilot in the army air forces. His daughter Swoosie, named for the famous airplane, became a well-known actress. As for The Swoose, it remains the oldest surviving B-17 and the only D model in existence. After thirty years in storage, it is being fully restored at the National Museum of the U.S. Air Force in Dayton, Ohio.

over Rabaul that morning had found "100 bombers and fighters lined up on Vunakanau airdrome."

Oddly, Kenney had recorded an even higher number the previous day: "Information shows Jap concentration of approximately 150 airplanes, most of them bombers, at Vunakanau airdrome." The source of Kenney's information is unknown, but the Japanese had nowhere near that many planes at Rabaul. Whether the figures were an honest mistake or one of Kenney's grandiosities, he hoped to suppress the enemy's ability to launch counterattacks against the Guadalcanal invasion fleet. Urging Carmichael to have nineteen or twenty B-17s available for the strike, Kenney informed him that he expected his group commanders to personally "lead their groups in action."

Unbeknownst to Kenney, Carmichael had not complied with his instruction to halt all bombing missions, possibly because Kenney was not officially Carmichael's boss when he issued the instruction. On August 2, the day after Kenney's first visit to Mareeba, Carmichael sent five B-17s to attack shipping near Buna. The Fortresses were intercepted by nine Zeros of the Tainan Air Group and jettisoned their bombs prior to reaching the target, rendering the mission useless. That didn't stop the aggressive Japanese from shooting down one B-17 and damaging another, costing the 19th a valuable Fortress and the lives of nine crewmen.

THERE WAS GOOD REASON for the concentration of aircraft at Rabaul, and it had nothing to do with Guadalcanal. Having recently put a large force ashore at Buna, the Japanese decided to extend their domination over the Papuan Peninsula by expanding southeastward toward Samarai. Unaware that the Allies were developing a new base at Milne Bay, Vice Admiral Yamada sent a reconnaissance plane over the area on August 3. When the *rikko* crew discovered the freshly built airfield, the Japanese were horrified. The Allies had obviously been working on it for weeks, and to the Japanese the new airdrome posed "a great threat." Rear Admiral Yamada ordered all aircraft of the 25th Air Flotilla to gather at Rabaul, such that by August 6 he had amassed thirty-two land attack aircraft at Vunakanau, nineteen Zero fighters and one reconnaissance plane at Lakunai, and five flying boats in Simpson Harbor. Yamada's force also benefited from the arrival of a new air group that same afternoon.

Slated to move to Port Moresby after the conquest of New Guinea was achieved, the 2nd Air Group was a composite carrier unit consisting of fifteen new Zero Model 32 fighters (Mitsubishi A6M3s) and sixteen Type 99 carrier bombers. The planes were delivered to Rabaul by the escort carrier *Yawata Maru*, which launched its full deck-load a short distance from New Britain. Upon landing at Lakunai, the air group was placed under Yamada's command. At sunrise the next morning, he would send the entire flotilla against Milne Bay.

Meanwhile, from their base at Tulagi in the southern Solomon Islands, three flying boats of the Yokohama Air Group patrolled their assigned sectors on the afternoon of August 6. Due to reduced visibility caused by heavy rain, they failed to detect the American invasion fleet as it approached Guadalcanal.

DURING THE AFTERNOON and evening of August 6, every operational B-17 in the 19th Bomb Group headed for Port Moresby, but Kenney did not get the twenty aircraft he'd hoped for. Due to maintenance issues and recent combat losses, only sixteen were considered operational. Conflicting accounts credit the 28th and 30th Bomb Squadrons with contributing between seven and ten aircraft, while the 93rd Bomb Squadron provided the balance. During the flight from Mareeba to Port Moresby, the B-17 flown by Captain Harl Pease of the 93rd suffered an engine failure less than an hour from New Guinea. Knowing that Seven Mile airdrome had inadequate repair facilities, Pease elected to return to Mareeba on three engines. After a flight of nearly a thousand miles, the malfunctioning B-17 was right back where it started.

Of all the pilots in the 19th Bomb Group, nobody had a stronger desire to participate in the big raid than Harl Pease. Raised in Plymouth, New Hampshire, the only son of a prominent family, he'd earned a degree in business management from the University of New Hampshire in 1939. He had served with distinction with the 19th since the beginning of the war, but there is little doubt he was troubled by one glaring failure: he had attempted to rescue MacArthur at Del Monte Field in March but was denied the opportunity due to the pitiful condition of his B-17. It didn't matter that MacArthur blamed George Brett for the screwup, and it didn't help that practically everyone in the 19th considered Pease one of their best pilots. His name was associated with the failed rescue attempt. Being a part of the great raid on Rabaul would go a long way toward erasing that stigma.

Pease was determined to participate, but all of the 93rd Bomb Squadron's combat-worthy planes were now at Port Moresby. Nevertheless he looked over the remaining bombers, and one stood out. Bureau number 41-2429, an early model B-17E, wore an unusual camouflage paint scheme and a catchy name: *Why Don't We Do This More Often*. Chronologically the bomber was practically new, having rolled off the Boeing assembly line only seven months earlier. But now, because of the rigors of combat, she was an old plane; a relic, beyond war-weary. A survivor of the Philippines, she had flown numerous missions over the past seven months, and her engines were tired. She also had a history of electrical failures and had recently aborted several missions. The squadron's engineering officer, Lt. Vincent Snyder, had restricted the Flying Fortress from further combat duty.

But 41-2429 also had a redeeming quality—a legitimate claim to fame—and Pease was undoubtedly aware of it. A few days after his own failed attempt to rescue MacArthur, *Why Don't We Do This More Often* had carried the general to safety with Capt. Bill Lewis at the controls. The serendipity of finding the bomber at Mareeba was hard to ignore. The old gal was still flyable too; she just wasn't supposed to go into combat. However, in his capacity as the operations officer for the 93rd Bomb Squadron, Pease didn't need anyone's approval to fly the B-17 to Port Moresby. Loading up the crew, which included his copilot, Sgt. Frederick W. Earp of the RAAF, Pease crossed the Coral Sea for the third time that day, and arrived at New Guinea in the middle of the night.

Upon reaching Seven Mile airdrome at 0100, Pease encountered opposition. Vince Snyder, who was piloting a B-17E named *Queenie* on the mission, objected vehemently when Pease showed up at the proverbial eleventh hour with a "defective plane." Snyder had a valid argument. Not only had he declared the bomber unsuitable for combat, but an electric fuel pump was now inoperative in the B-17, and Pease's crew had to borrow a manual pump from Maj. Felix Hardison's bomber, *Suzy-Q*.

Seeking an ally, Pease turned to Hardison, the commanding officer of the 93rd Bomb Squadron. Hardison knew that every bomber was needed and agreed to let Pease join the mission. However, when Snyder requested that the newcomer be assigned to the center of the formation for protection, Hardison declined. Individual positions had already been designated, and the B-17s were parked accordingly. That didn't matter to Pease. He would take the last available slot on the outside of the formation, flying on the wing of his best friend, Capt. Edward M. Jacquet. In the meantime, Pease and his bone-tired crew cared only about resting a few hours before the big event got underway.

At 0730 on August 7, the first Flying Fortress rumbled into the air, but the mission started to go sour almost from the beginning. As one bomber accelerated down the dirt strip, it veered suddenly off the runway and cracked up on a pile of rocks. Miraculously, the bombs did not detonate. The crew, walking away with only minor injuries, reported that a runaway supercharger had caused the airplane to go out of control.

The remaining fifteen bombers formed up over New Guinea without incident. Seated in a 28th Bomb Squadron B-17E, Dick Carmichael led the formation toward Rabaul at twenty-two thousand feet. But soon more trouble cropped up, forcing two B-17s to abort, one with an engine malfunction, the other with electrical failure. The formation had been reduced to thirteen planes, but ironically, *Why Don't We Do This More Often* kept pace.

AT DAWN ON August 7, the 25th Air Flotilla was poised to take off for the planned strike against Milne Bay. But the event was suddenly disrupted by frantic, plain-voice radio calls from Tulagi and Guadalcanal. A massive assault by American ships, planes, and marines was underway against both locations. Recovering from his shock, Rear Admiral Yamada sent three *rikko* to find the American fleet. Shortly thereafter, Vice Admiral Tsukahara transmitted a message from Eleventh Air Fleet headquarters on Tinian, urging the 25th Air Flotilla to "destroy the enemy invasion forces with all its might." Tsukahara then boarded a flying boat and headed for Rabaul to personally take command of the naval forces in the Southeast Area.

Yamada ordered the units at Vunakanau and Lakunai to shift their targets to the Tulagi-Guadalcanal area. This generated considerable excitement among the aircrews, especially the pilots of the Tainan Air Group. The distance to Guadalcanal was approximately 650 statute miles, and Zeros had never before been called upon to fly such a tremendous distance for combat operations. The fourteen-cylinder Sakae radial engines were thrifty, but the fighters would need every ounce of fuel in their 330-liter detachable belly tanks to complete the mission. For that reason, against established doctrine, the pilots were instructed not to release the tanks prior to engaging enemy aircraft.

Because of fuel consumption, the newly arrived Model 32 Zeros of the 2nd Air Group would not be used for the mission. Some of the improvements in the new version—shorter wings with squared-off tips and a larger, more powerful radial engine—made the Model 32 faster and more maneuverable than its predecessor but at a significant reduction in range. Thus the 2nd Air Group's fighter component would remain at Rabaul to provide aerial defense.

The Type 99 dive-bombers were another matter. Although they, too, lacked the range to complete the round trip, Yamada decided their offensive potential justified the cost of sending them on a one-way mission. The navy had established a floatplane base in Shortland Harbor, but it was doubtful the dive-bombers would make it even that far on the return trip. Therefore, Yamada ordered the seaplane tender *Akitsushima* and one of the new Type 2 flying boats to take up positions southeast of Shortland Island, where the carrier bombers were most likely to ditch.

Beginning at 0950, eighteen Zeros of the Tainan Air Group took off from Lakunai, though one later turned back because its landing gear would not retract. Approximately fifteen minutes later, twenty-seven Type 1 *rikko* of the 4th Air Group roared aloft from Vunakanau, and at 1045, nine Type 99 dive-bombers of the 2nd Air Group took off from Lakunai on what was certain to be their final flight.

By the time the American B-17s approached Rabaul an hour later, the fifty-three Japanese warplanes were well on their way to Guadalcanal.

DICK CARMICHAEL'S thirteen heavy bombers had been pushing northward for better than three hours. After bouncing through the intertropic frontal system and weaving between towering clouds, they found the conditions somewhat better over northwestern New Britain. Visibility improved even more as the formation, still at twenty-two thousand feet, reached the designated Initial Point and turned southeast for the bomb run. Grouped in a V of Vs, with the Fortresses of the 28th Bomb Squadron in the lead, the formation resembled a broad arrowhead pointed toward Rabaul. In the lead ship of each three-plane element, the bombardier hunched over his Norden bombsight. During the fifteen-minute run-in to the target, the pilots "slaved" the autopilot to the bombardier's control. There weren't enough bombsights available for every plane, therefore only the lead aircraft of each element carried one. The other bombardiers simply dropped their bombs on the leaders' cue.

Hoping to avoid early detection, the formation maintained radio silence throughout the flight, but the Japanese had a good warning system in place. The navy operated several radars, including two long-range sets near Tomavatur Mission. Usually working in tandem, they provided 360-degree coverage out to a distance of ninety miles. The radars were augmented by observation posts and listening stations scattered across New Britain, the latter equipped with large, tuba-shaped horns designed to collect and amplify the sound of approaching planes. Given plenty of advance warning, numerous interceptors were airborne when the Fortresses approached Rabaul.

The first *Rei-sens* attacked just as the B-17s opened their bomb bay doors, several minutes before reaching the drop point. Estimates by American crewmen that twenty fighters intercepted them were fairly accurate. Lieutenant Yoshio Kurakane led fifteen Model 32 Zeros of the 2nd Air Group into action, joined by Johji Yamashita with eleven Model 21 Zeros of the Tainan Air Group. The fighters made effective frontal attacks, spraying 7.7mm bullets and 20mm cannon shells as they slashed between bombers at closing speeds of almost five hundred miles per hour. After diving clear of the Fortresses' guns, they zoomed back to an advantageous altitude before initiating another attack.

Inside the bombers, gunners spun their turrets or pivoted their hand-held weapons back and forth, squeezing off bursts, trying to fire ahead of the onrushing Zeros. The interior of a Flying Fortress was all metal—a simple framework of aluminum covered by a thin outer skin—which for the crew was like being on the inside of a giant drum. The entire plane shook from the recoil of the machine guns, and the pounding gunfire reverberated loudly. Acrid smoke drifted through the fuselage, accompanied by the clatter of hot brass shell casings against the metal floors. The steady throb of the Wright Cyclone engines and the rush of the slipstream through the bomb bays and gun ports became background noise, punctuated at times by the bang of enemy cannon shells or the eerie zing of deadly shrapnel. Bullets rattled against the outer skin and buzzed through the fuselage with the sound of angry bees. Men cursed and ducked instinctively at the near misses, or grunted softly when their bodies were torn by unseen objects traveling almost the speed of sound.

Aboard Vince Snyder's *Queenie*, a 20mm shell took out the oxygen system. The air at twenty-two thousand feet was thin, and hypoxia began to affect the crew within minutes. Feeling woozy, Snyder struggled to maintain his position on the wing of *Suzy-Q*.

Down below, dozens of antiaircraft batteries opened up, joined by dozens of guns aboard the ships in the anchorages. Fortunately for the bombers, the shells burst above and behind the formation, which continued without wavering. When the lead bombardier "pickled" his bombs, the others dropped too, sending a total of ninety-six bombs of various sizes whistling toward Vunakanau airdrome. Crews later reported that their aim was true: the bombs exploded on the runway and nearby dispersal areas.

The Zeros attacked even more vigorously as the formation turned away from the target and headed southward. Aboard Carmichael's bomber, a side gunner was killed and another gunner wounded. The oxygen system was also shot out, and Carmichael keyed the command channel of his radio to inform Hardison that he was dropping to a lower altitude. When the lead B-17 started down, Hardison followed in *Suzy-Q*. Behind them, trying to maintain position on Hardison, the groggy Vince Snyder reacted to the abrupt change by putting *Queenie* in a "crash dive." He almost collided with *Suzy-Q*, and the sudden maneuvering caused a domino effect among the trailing B-17s. Pilots took evasive action to avoid ramming into each other, which broke up the formation. With the defensive integrity of the formation gone, the Fortresses at the rear were the most vulnerable. Captain Jacquet's B-17E, *Tojo's Jinx*, suffered two casualties with one gunner killed and another wounded, and other B-17s absorbed varying degrees of damage.

But it was Pease, at the tail end, who caught the full force of the Zeros' aggression. The combat doctrine of the Japanese was to always fight offensively. Whatever type of aircraft they faced, their preferred tactic was to single out one plane and overwhelm it. Thus, when *Why*

Don't We Do This More Often lost an engine and fell behind, the Zeros pounced like wolves on a wounded caribou.

In *Tojo's Jinx*, Ed Jacquet "hollered and screamed for the formation to slow down to protect Harl." Later he learned that no one heard his radio call. Aboard *Queenie*, Pvt. Edward L. Troccia saw Pease's bomber "going down with both inboard engines on fire." And in another B-17, Capt. John D. Bridges observed Pease's auxiliary fuel tank drop in flames from the bomb bay. He used his intercom to ask the upper turret gunner: "Where's Pease? What happened to Pease?" But the gunner, still banging away at Zeros with his twin machine guns, was too preoccupied to respond.

All of the B-17s carried a four-hundred-gallon auxiliary fuel tank in the bomb bay, and according to Dick Carmichael, the tank mounted in *Why Don't We Do This More Often* lacked a self-sealing liner. That alone would have been reason enough to restrict the bomber from combat. In a 1980 interview Carmichael stated: "Unfortunately, [Pease] had one of those old . . . auxiliary tanks. . . . He had one that was not the bulletproof type. He had [one of] those metal tanks. I guess nobody knew it, maybe he didn't pay much attention to it, or at least he didn't change it. We had to have a bomb-bay tank to get to Rabaul and back. So I think that's what did him in on the way back. He was hit and caught afire."

Despite heavy damage and the fire in the bomb bay, *Why Don't We Do This More Often* stayed in the air a remarkably long time. It finally came to grief forty nautical miles south of Rabaul, most of it torn apart on impact, though one large section of the fuselage landed in the Powell River a few miles upstream from Tol plantation. Native villagers found it in the water with three bodies floating nearby. On a subsequent visit the corpses were no longer there, having either been washed downstream or scavenged by crocodiles. Part of the cockpit was later discovered some distance from the river with the bodies of the copilot and the radio operator still inside. Pease's crew numbered nine men according to most accounts, which meant that four were unaccounted for.

DESPITE THE LOSS of Pease's crew and the other combat casualties, George Kenney was ecstatic about the apparent success of the mission. Gunners in the B-17s claimed to have shot down seven Zeros, and the bombardiers scored a "bull's-eye" on Vunakanau airdrome. Or so Kenney believed. Relying on earlier intelligence estimates and an intercepted enemy message, he was convinced that the attack had destroyed dozens of enemy planes. His autobiography, written years later, exaggerated almost every facet of the mission. Kenney wrote that eighteen heavy bombers conducted the strike and shot down "eleven of the twenty Jap fighters that participated." He also wrote that 150 aircraft were parked "wingtip to wingtip on both sides of the runway at Vunakanau" and implied that reconnaissance photos taken afterward showed at least 75 had been destroyed. For evidence he referred to the intercepted message, transmitted from Rabaul on the afternoon of the attack, in which Rear Admiral Yamada reported that he had thirty land attack aircraft operational for the following day. Misinterpreting the report, Kenney took it to mean the Japanese had "only" thirty bombers remaining.

In reality, the raid had caused only superficial damage. Within hours of the attack, the airdrome was repaired sufficiently for the *rikko* of the 4th Air Group to land after their raid on American ships at Guadalcanal. Twenty-two bombers came back (four had been shot down and one ditched at sea), and another subsequently cracked up while landing. The losses were offset by the arrival of nine Type 1s of the Misawa Air Group, rushed from Tinian on the afternoon of August 7 to augment Yamada's offensive firepower. (Two more *chutais* of Type 1s, totaling eighteen aircraft, were scheduled to arrive the following day.) After factoring in the combat losses, the nine additional bombers gave Yamada a total of thirty-five medium bombers at Rabaul, a net gain of three aircraft. Thus his statement that thirty planes were operational on August 7 is absolutely plausible. Undoubtedly several aircraft that had participated in the strike against Guadalcanal needed repairs for battle damage or mechanical issues.

In fact, Yamada's message proved that not a single Japanese plane had been destroyed on the ground at Vunakanau. When the Fortresses attacked, virtually all of the land attack aircraft were heading toward Guadalcanal or conducting searches. As for fighter units, the Japanese combat logs show that no Zeros fell in action over Rabaul, though approximately a dozen were damaged.

The raid, which cost the 19th Bomb Group two Flying Fortresses and eleven men killed or missing, caused no real harm to the Japanese. Despite the fact that the B-17s hit nothing but dirt, the attack did yield benefits for Kenney, who later boasted: "The Marines landed at Guadalcanal with practically no opposition. Tulagi was also taken, but with a little more fighting. There was no Jap air interference." How could he have overlooked the fifty-three Japanese planes that attacked from Rabaul? How could he have overlooked the nine American navy aircraft shot down in the vicinity of Guadalcanal by Rabaul-based Zeros? Kenney's claim was a gross exaggeration. Nevertheless he was the new star of the SWPA, receiving congratulatory messages from MacArthur and others, which he passed on to the 19th Bomb Group.

There were additional benefits for the B-17 men. For one thing, Kenney's exhilaration over the mission's apparent success was infectious. He singlehandedly boosted the morale of his "boys," telling them they'd done an outstanding job, and to prove it he handed out a boxful of medals. Before the mission, Carmichael had told Kenney that no one in the 19th Bomb Group had been decorated in months—which probably had something to do with the group's abysmal combat record. Luckily for them, Kenney believed that "little bits of pretty ribbon had helped in World War I; maybe they would help in this one, too." The cherry on top came from MacArthur, who told Kenney, "Don't forget to pass out as many decorations as you think fit."

Kenney didn't hold back. Dick Carmichael was awarded a Distinguished Service Cross, the nation's second-highest award for heroism in armed conflict. Several other participants received the Silver Star, the nation's third highest award for valor. Among them was a lead bombardier who had fired his nose gun at the attacking Zeros, then moved to the bombsight, dropped his bombs, and returned to the nose gun to shoot at more Zeros. He wasn't wounded, but did essentially what was expected of any bombardier under combat conditions.

After doling out a slew of lesser medals and some Purple Hearts, Kenney wrote a recommendation for a Medal of Honor. Privately he thought Harl Pease had "had no business in the show," but he presumed that Pease's B-17 had crashed with no survivors. Kenney deemed his sacrifice worthy of the nation's highest award, and MacArthur heartily endorsed the recommendation. Approval followed quickly. Congress made it official on November 4, and four weeks later President Roosevelt presented the medal to Pease's parents in a ceremony at the White House.

Ironically, the presumption that Pease and everyone aboard his bomber had perished was wrong. Pease and Master Sgt. Chester M. Czechowski, the tail gunner, bailed out of the B-17 before it crashed. A third crewman may have followed.* As Pease and Czechowski floated down in their parachutes, one or more Zero pilots deliberately opened fire, and Pease was shot through the lower leg. Unable to evade on the ground, he and Czechowski were captured within a day or two. Both were taken to the Malaguna Road stockade around August 10, whereupon Pease requested medical attention. One of the Japanese laughed and said, "We don't treat American airmen!"

Fortunately for Pease, a civilian prisoner possessed some basic medical supplies, and under his daily treatments Pease made a gradual recovery. But he never learned about the Medal of Honor. By the time Congress voted to approve the award, the situation at Rabaul had changed drastically.

---

*In December 1948 a team of U.S. Army investigators visited Pease's bomber and were informed by a native named Nini that "he had observed the plane falling and before it exploded he saw a parachute floating down." He led the team to the site, where a few bones were found along with a wallet and "a trinket with a crown on it." Although no identification was made, circumstances suggest that the ill-fated jumper was the eighth crewman.

CHAPTER 20

The Personification
of Evil

THE CAPTURE OF Captain Pease and Master Sergeant Czechowski in early August brought the number of military prisoners at Rabaul to approximately two dozen aviators. At least ten were Australians, including Kittyhawk pilot David Brown and the nine-man crew of Allan Norman's Catalina.

Four other captives were from a 3rd Bomb Group B-25 that ditched near Salamaua on May 23. The Mitchell bomber had been forced down by Zeros of the Tainan Air Group, but the crew survived thanks to the skill of 1st Lt. Henry A. Keel, who made a textbook water landing in the Huon Gulf. After exiting the plane, Cpl. Louis E. Murphy avoided capture by swimming hard toward the open gulf, but Keel and three others were picked up by a Japanese boat crew and taken to naval headquarters at Salamaua. The sixth member of the crew has never been accounted for.

Murphy floated alone in the Huon Gulf for nearly forty-eight hours before the currents pushed him ashore. Found by local natives, he was carried to an encampment of New Guinea Volunteer Rifles, who had been hiding in the hills since January. While resting under their care, Murphy was joined by the crew of a Mitchell shot down during a disastrous raid on May 25. Out of eight B-25s that attacked Lae without fighter escort, five were shot down and a sixth crash-landed with battle damage.

By the time Murphy returned to Port Moresby, Keel and the other captured crewmen were almost certainly at Rabaul. Little is known of their experiences in captivity on New Guinea, except that the senior naval officer provided them with Japanese clothing because they were "only partly clad" when picked up. One crewmember, a sergeant, had been wounded on May 23, and Keel was reportedly ill when he reached Rabaul. Both men were hospitalized under the care of Lt. Chihiro Yamaguchi, a navy physician, but their condition did not improve.

About five days after Keel and the unnamed sergeant entered the hospital, the commanding officer of the 81st Naval Garrison Unit learned that both men were "in a bad way." Captain Mizusaki conferred with Rear Adm. Keisuke Matsumaga, chief of staff of the 8th Base Force, who ordered the two Americans executed. The following day, they were taken to the usual site at the foot of Tavurvur volcano. Doctor Yamaguchi accompanied the pair, later claiming that he "administered what comfort he could," but his attempts at kindness counted for little. The master at arms of the 81st Naval Garrison Unit, WO Kunihei Fujisaki, decapitated both prisoners.

The other two captives from the B-25, thought to be Lt. Durwood R. Reed (copilot) and Sgt. Thomas Marsh, RAAF (lower turret gunner), remained in the custody of the 81st Naval Garrison Unit, and by early August they were joined by at least five new prisoners. Among them was Lt. David S. Hunter, the first American fighter pilot captured in the region. (Another P-39 pilot, Lt. Edward D. Durand, was shot down over Lae on April 30. There have been persistent rumors that he was captured, and within his own squadron it was considered "common knowledge" that the Japanese had executed him on New Guinea, but no confirmation of either his capture or his death has ever been established.)

Hunter, who flew a P-400 export variant of the Airacobra in the 80th Fighter Squadron, had been shot down during a strafing mission over Gona on July 22. Postwar interrogations with various Japanese guards indicate that he was hospitalized at Rabaul for "burns or light wounds . . . and was getting well." After his release from the hospital he was placed in a camp run by the Kempeitai, presumably the same enclosure where Sergeant Brown was held.

Two other newcomers were Harold Massie and Arthur King, who were in terrible condition. Ten weeks had passed since Massie ditched their damaged B-26 in Wide Bay, south of Rabaul. Since that time he had been desperately scrounging for food with his crewmen until only he and King remained strong enough to walk. Barefoot, the two men set off for Open Bay on July 27, hoping to meet up with coastwatcher John Stokie on New Britain's north coast. But before they could find him they were captured, probably after walking into a village inhabited by pro-Japanese natives.

Two Australian coastwatchers were also among the new prisoners at Rabaul. The remarkable story of Cecil Mason and Roy Woodroffe had begun months earlier, when they were among a half-dozen coast-watchers stationed on New Ireland and its neighboring islands. During the first months of the war the men were left alone, mainly because the Japanese were too preoccupied with fortress-building to search for indi-viduals hiding in the jungle. After the *minsei-bu* was established on New Ireland at the end of May, the Japanese became more concerned about the coastwatchers' presence. Using a combination of coercion and bribes, the Japanese subjugated the native islanders, and the coastwatchers gradually lost their influence over all but a few loyal friends.

Thirty-year-old Cornelius "Con" Page, a planter in the Tabar Islands east of New Ireland, could see for himself that the Japanese were slowly closing in. His home, a plantation called Pigibut, was raided only five days after the fall of Rabaul. Headquarters at Townsville had urged him to bury his radio and move to safety, but Page stubbornly refused to leave. A twen-tieth-century Robinson Crusoe, he'd "gone native" years earlier, taking an island girl named Ansin Bulu as his common-law wife. Page answered to no authority but his own: he was the lord of his little tropical island.

In March 1942, the navy awarded Page a commission as a sublieu-tenant in the reserves, the idea being that if he were captured he might be treated as a prisoner of war rather than as a spy. Officials even sent a naval cap and epaulets with the next supply drop, a gesture without precedent in the Royal Australian Navy, but the symbols of rank were both too little and too late to bolster Page's sagging reputation. Within a few months virtually all of the natives except Ansin Bulu had turned against him. Page finally agreed to be picked up, but the aging American submarine sent to rescue him suffered a breakdown and had to withdraw to Brisbane.

On June 8, troops of the Kure No. 3 Special Naval Landing Force raided Page's island, Simberi. They hunted him down for three days, even using dogs and armed natives, but Page somehow eluded them all. The sailors did succeed in capturing Ansin Bulu before returning to their base at Kavieng, so Page, realizing the Japanese would return with reinforcements, sent an emergency signal to Townsville on June 12. His one chance of rescue, he advised, would be to have a flying boat pick him up on the west side of the island. A Catalina took off from Cairns on the evening of June 16 and made a careful inspection of the island at very low altitude, but nothing was seen of Page.

In the meantime, John S. Talmage, a veteran of World War I who owned a plantation on a nearby island, had joined Page in the hopes of being rescued. Unfortunately for both men, a platoon of SNLF returned to the Tabar Islands on June 14 aboard the auxiliary minesweeper *Seki Maru No. 3*. The naval infantry chased Page and Talmage from island to island for six days before finally running them to ground on June 20. The sailors seemed impressed with the coastwatchers. One wrote in his diary: "With the use of wireless, they have broadcast the movement of our troops to Port Moresby and Australia. These spies were devastating to us."

Page and Talmage were taken to the Kavieng jail on June 21, whereupon the SNLF went in search of two other coastwatchers holed up on New Ireland. Alan F. "Bill" Kyle, a veteran of the Great War and a former administrator in the Namatani agricultural district, and Gregory W. Benham, a warrant officer in the district police, had become coastwatchers by default. After the Japanese invasion in January, both men passed up opportunities for evacuation, willfully staying behind in order to coordinate rescues for other parties.

The organizer of the coastwatching organization, Lt. Cmdr. Eric Feldt, particularly hoped to rescue Kyle, his closest friend. An aging S-class sub was sent to pick up Kyle as well as Benham, but although it surfaced off New Ireland for two nights in a row, neither man was found.

Learning that more submarines had arrived in the Southwest Pacific, Feldt traveled to Brisbane for a conference with Rear Adm. Ralph Christie, USN, commander of submarine operations in the theater. Feldt explained the value of the coastwatchers and appealed for one more attempt to save the stranded men, adding that he had an agent available to put ashore. Christie approved the plan, and on July 8 the *S-43* departed Brisbane carrying Cecil John Trevelyan Mason, a thirty-nine-year-old flight officer in the RAAF.

After making a slow, careful transit of the Coral Sea, the S-boat reached New Ireland on July 18. The next night, Mason paddled ashore in an inflatable boat and questioned a local islander, then noticed that the native wore a Japanese arm band. The man was obviously collaborating with the enemy. His answers were evasive, and he refused to divulge any helpful information about Kyle or Benham. (Both men, it turned out, had been captured less than twenty-four hours before the first sub was to pick them up.)

Thwarted on New Ireland, Mason rendezvoused with the *S-43*, which then moved seventy miles east to Anir Island. There, Mason hoped to contact yet another coastwatcher, leading telegraphist Roy Woodroffe, RAN. Mason went ashore on the night of July 21 but was subsequently captured along with Woodroffe. Unaware of this, the sub's crew elected to remain offshore for several consecutive nights while attempting to contact Mason. After ninety-six frustrating hours, the *S-43* departed for Brisbane.

The string of bad luck on New Ireland and nearby islands was one of the darkest hours for Feldt's coastwatching program. Not only were all of the early volunteers swept up by the Japanese occupation, the agent sent to rescue them was also captured. The Japanese extracted all the information they could get from Benham, Kyle, Page, and Talmage, then took them to Nago Island in Kavieng Harbor for execution. Page and Talmage were killed on or about July 21, followed by Kyle and Benham on September 1.

For unknown reasons, Mason and Woodroffe, along with two natives who had been captured with them, were transported to Rabaul. They were already in the POW compound, therefore, when Pease and Czechowski arrived during the second week of August. Approximately a month later the prisoners were joined by Father George W. Lepping, a newly captured Roman Catholic priest, who noted a disparity in the treatment of POWs and internees. Years later he wrote: "The military prisoners were held in much tighter security than the missionaries and other civilians, being handcuffed and roped to their beds at night."

During daylight hours the prisoners were allowed to mingle. Although talking was supposedly forbidden, Lepping and the others "found ways around that." Harl Pease entertained them with stories of the 19th Bomb

Group's adventures in the Philippines and Java. He explained how the B-17s flew at night using celestial navigation, and he invented humorous nicknames for the guards based on their physical traits and personalities. Self-assured, a natural leader, Pease earned the admiration of his fellow prisoners. The guards also liked him, according to Father Lepping. "The Japanese looked up to Pease because they were in awe of the B-17. The Fortresses were semi-gods to them, and to have a Captain of a 'Boeing,' as they called them, was something to be remembered."

THE CAMP GUARDS may have admired Pease but they had no control over his fate. In late August, the 81st Naval Garrison Unit began to periodically eliminate small groups of prisoners and civilian internees. The first such event occurred on August 29, when six Australian civilians captured the previous month near Kokopo were led away under the guise of a work party. Two German priests saw the men taken from the camp. Later that day the prisoners' possessions were brought back and buried, but the six Australians were never seen again.

At approximately this same time, a Chinese civilian named Timothy Mak, a former clerk at the Burns, Philp & Company store in Rabaul, observed a truck carrying eleven or twelve captured officers heading toward Lakunai airdrome. Mak wasn't able to identify the prisoners, nor did he witness what happened to them, but he was later informed that they had been executed. He "seemed sure" that some of the prisoners were American airmen and believed they were killed in retaliation for a bombing raid on Rabaul.

The latter detail adds credibility to his statement. Shortly after 1000 hours on August 29, eight Flying Fortresses struck the dispersal area at Vunakanau airdrome. Little is known about the damages caused by the raid, but the Japanese were troubled, especially because of the heavy losses they had endured at Guadalcanal during the past few weeks. Mak's observation adds to the likelihood that the Allied prisoners he saw on August 29 were executed as a reprisal. Two of the aviators may have been the remaining members of Keel's crew, Sergeant Marsh and Lieutenant Reed, but their bodies were never recovered.

ANOTHER GROUP of prisoners was led away from the compound on the morning of October 8. Father Lepping watched as guards of the 81st

Naval Garrison Unit handed out picks and shovels to Pease, Czechowski, Massey, and King, as well as to the two Australian coastwatchers, Mason and Woodroffe. Captain Mizusaki, the English-speaking commandant, told the POWs that they were going to work on a new airdrome near Kokopo. He then pointed at Lepping and said, "You go tomorrow." Before Pease and the rest of the work party left the camp, the other prisoners took up a collection and provided them with spare articles of clothing. But that afternoon, recalled Lepping, the tools and extra clothing were returned. "We never saw the six men again," he wrote.

After the war, WO Minoru Yoshimura, a platoon leader in the 81st Naval Garrison Unit, provided detailed testimony about the executions of Pease and the other POWs. The six men of the so-called "work party," along with the two native islanders who had been captured in July with Mason and Woodroffe, were transported to the crematorium near Tavurvur crater. Several officers were already in attendance, including Mizusaki and his adjutant, Lt. Shiro Nakayama. Yoshimura was also somewhat surprised to see a young army doctor arrive aboard a motorcycle with a sidecar attached.

The prisoners, wearing blindfolds and with their hands tied behind their backs, were lined up at the edge of a large hole that had been dug beforehand by native laborers. Yoshimura issued commands to several recruits to bayonet the eight prisoners, but several of the sailors were timid or hesitant with their thrusts. Only one of the POWs and the two natives fell into the hole; the other five captives lay on the ground, writhing in agony.

At this, the medical officer moved forward, saying something to Yoshimura about singling out the healthiest survivors. Yoshimura later stated:

I asked him what he was going to do. He did not reply, but laughed and produced some medical instruments. I then realized he was going to carry out a dissection and had possibly obtained permission from Lieutenant Nakayama or 8 Naval Base Force, so I ordered the sightseers who had crowded around to disperse and those who had work to do to go back to their unit. This doctor then cut the jugular vein of the suffering prisoner of war before opening his abdomen. He then took some dark-looking object out, which . . . he handed to the NCO. He then quickly stepped over to the next prisoner of war who was still alive and writhing on the ground, so the doctor cut his jugular vein, opened him up and took a dark-looking object out. This whole process took about 5 or 6 minutes. The doctor was wearing surgical gloves. I saw the doctor, NCO and driver get on their autobike afterward; the NCO was carrying a shallow white tray containing whatever objects they had removed from the two prisoners of war.

As soon as all the prisoners of war were placed in the hole I gave the coup de grace by stabbing each one in the throat.

For all its gruesomeness, the testimony given by Yoshimura was fairly objective, making his description of the doctor's demeanor all the more chilling. Possibly this was Chikumi, the same medical officer who had dissected Capt. John Gray in February. If so, the doctor may well have been a psychopath.

The Japanese military in World War II had a reverence for cold steel. On the island of New Britain alone, literally hundreds of Allied prisoners were murdered with bayonets or katana swords. And the systematic killings continued. On November 4, 1942, exactly six months after their capture in the Coral Sea, Allan Norman and the other members of his crew were taken to the usual place near Tavurvur crater. Two other Australians—one unidentified, the other probably Sergeant Brown of 75 Squadron—accompanied the Catalina crewmen. The Japanese blindfolded them, bound each man's arms and legs with wire, and then forced them to kneel at the edge of a common grave. All eleven men were decapitated by members of the 81st Naval Garrison Unit.

OF ALL THE Allied aviators and coastwatchers known to have been captured in the Southwest Pacific in 1942, only those who were transported to Japan for further interrogation, namely Sergeant Lutz and Corporal Reed, survived. Likewise, Bob Thompson and four other crewmen of his downed Catalina were fortunate that an Imperial Navy cruiser plucked them from the sea and took them straight to Japan.

Otherwise, none of the military prisoners held by the 81st Naval Garrison Unit at Rabaul were allowed to live. By the end of the year, the soft volcanic soil near Tavurvur held dozens of corpses in common graves.

And in the years to come, many more would be added.

CHAPTER 21

A Shift in Momentum

GEORGE KENNEY HAD BEEN a busy general for the past few months. On August 7, the day of the big raid on Rabaul, he sent a message to Washington requesting authorization to form a numbered air force—an all-American one at that. General Marshall had already shared with Kenney that "he didn't think much of mixing nationalities in the same organization," and Kenney agreed. After barely a week in Australia, he had already made up his mind that the multinational directorate system established by his predecessor, General Brett, was ineffective. His request for a new organization was approved by Marshall on August 9, and the Fifth Air Force was officially activated at Brisbane on September 3.

Kenney used the intervening weeks to select the principal members of his staff. He admired the leadership and organizational abilities of Brigadier General Whitehead, who was still at Port Moresby, and named him deputy commander. A new headquarters, the Advance Echelon, or ADVON, was created to give Whitehead direct control of day-to-day operations in New Guinea. The assignment suited both men perfectly. Kenney, who still commanded all Allied air forces in the SWPA, would run the Fifth Air Force administratively from Brisbane while Whitehead managed combat operations from his new headquarters at Port Moresby.

Kenney's top priority was to build up the bomber force. When he arrived in Australia and told MacArthur that his first goal was to "knock out the Jap air strength," he was referring primarily to Rabaul. The stronghold was *the* major source of enemy air power in the region. Every Japanese plane and airman arrived at Rabaul from points north—either directly from Japan, via Truk, or via the Central Pacific. Some planes and crews remained at Rabaul, but most were shuttled immediately to New Guinea or the Solomons. A bomber man at heart, Kenney intended to neutralize Rabaul and its satellite bases using established methods of bombing as well as new innovations, including low-level parafrag attacks and skip bombing.

His choice to lead this force, known as V Bomber Command, was easy. Brigadier General Kenneth N. Walker had arrived in Australia with Whitehead back in July. Kenney had known both men for twenty years and was impressed with their style and ethics. As he later put it, they possessed "brains, leadership, loyalty, and liked to work." The forty-four-year-old Walker, one of the youngest generals in the air force, was a zealous proponent of strategic air power. His name was practically synonymous with high altitude formation bombing, for he had been a principal member of the team that developed the tactics and techniques currently in use.

Kenney's choice for V Fighter Command was likewise easy. He had heard plenty of praise for the performance of Lt. Col. Paul B. "Squeeze" Wurtsmith at Darwin, where his 49th Fighter Group stoutly resisted numerous Japanese attacks. Summoned to Kenney's office in Brisbane, Wurtsmith made a good first impression. "He looked like a partially reformed bad boy," wrote Kenney. "He believed in himself, was an excellent thief for his group, took care of his men, and they all followed him and liked him." Wurtsmith was informed that he was being given the fighter command. If he failed, Kenney would send him back to the States "on a slow boat." But if he succeeded, Kenney promised him a general's star—a jump of two ranks.

When it came to motivating people and getting results, Kenney had few peers. MacArthur had given him carte blanche to clean house, and he quickly got rid of personnel he considered "deadwood." Many an underperforming senior officer—especially those who had served under Brett—were posted back to the States. Kenney replaced them with people whose abilities he admired: problem solvers, tactical experts, and, most importantly, men with a desire to smash the enemy.

Now that he had his own air force and a cadre of talented individuals, George Kenney kick-started the aerial program that had languished since the opening days of the Pacific war. Initially, however, he was sidetracked by the enemy's campaign to invade Port Moresby by crossing the Owen Stanley Mountains. The fighting in New Guinea was fierce, both on the ground and in the air, as battles raged around Buna, Kokoda, and Milne Bay during the second half of 1942. In addition, Port Moresby itself continued to suffer frequent heavy raids from Japanese units stationed at Lae and Rabaul.

Despite the distractions, Kenney tried to send B-17s to Rabaul as often as possible. After the big strike on August 7, several follow-up raids were conducted in the hopes of disrupting Japanese counterattacks against Guadalcanal. Six bombers attacked Rabaul on August 9, causing little appreciable damage for the loss of two more B-17s. One was shot down with no survivors over New Britain; the other crash-landed on a coral reef near the New Guinea coast, and all crewmen got out safely. Eight Fortresses returned to Rabaul on August 12, this time to hit Simpson Harbor. Prior to reaching the target they met stiff opposition from Zeros but still dropped forty-eight 500-pounders. The bombs supposedly "sank or badly damaged at least three transports," but only one ship, the seven-thousand-ton oiler *Matsumoto Maru*, sustained minor damage.

Two days later, a brand-new B-17E of the "Kangaroo Squadron" took off shortly after 0600 on a reconnaissance mission over Rabaul and Kavieng. Named *Chief Seattle from the Pacific Northwest*, the bomber had been paid for entirely by the citizens of Washington, many of them schoolchildren, who raised more than $280,500 during a bond campaign sponsored by one of Seattle's newspapers. The popular effort, culminating with a special christening ceremony, generated enormous publicity for the B-17. But a happy ending was not to be. Piloted by Lt. Wilson L. Cook, a veteran of forty-five missions, *Chief Seattle* failed to return from just its second mission. That evening, squadron member John Steinbinder wrote in his diary: "My roommate [Lt. Hubert S. Mobley] and crew left this morning to attempt shadowing empty ships as they left Buna. They haven't returned yet. I'm afraid they were caught or something. I sure hope they return somehow."

Steinbinder and the other members of the 435th Bomb Squadron would not see their comrades again. No distress calls or any other messages were ever received from *Chief Seattle*, and more than sixty-five years later, the fate of the bomber and its crew remains a mystery.

§

RABAUL WAS HIT twice more in August, including the aforementioned mission on the 29th that may have led to the retaliatory murder of a dozen prisoners. In contrast there were only five raids in all of September, mainly because MacArthur's forces were compelled to counter the Japanese offensive in New Guinea. By mid-September, enemy troops on the Kokoda Trail had pushed across the Owen Stanley Range to within thirty miles of Port Moresby. They were even closer to the airstrip being built at Laloki, where the construction workers were extremely nervous. Rumors that Japanese troops infiltrated the camps at night prompted many of the work crews to carry side arms, and those who lacked a weapon were anxious to obtain one. Sergeant Carthon P. Phillips, a crewmember in the 30th Bomb Squadron, had an unexpected encounter after landing at Laloki on September 12.

> I no sooner got down off the ladder and started getting my gear together when this black fellow came running across from a cleared area a good two hundred yards away. As he kept coming toward our B-17, I got to thinking: "What in the hell is he doing?"
>
> He ran up and had a roll of Australian pounds worth some two hundred dollars in his hand. He said, "Sergeant! I'll give you this whole roll for your forty-five."
>
> I said, "Man, you're crazy. I can't sell it to you. We'd both get in trouble."
>
> He said, "Oh, yes you can—I'll give you this whole thing for it. The Japs are coming in on us at night and I want to be able to shoot one."

The proximity of enemy troops to Port Moresby had everyone concerned. Kenney concentrated on attacking the Japanese supply convoys and beachheads with the Fifth Air Force as well as the RAAF, but the efforts were usually piecemeal. On September 14, just as the fighting on the Kokoda Trail reached a critical stage, the commander of SOPAC requested help for his predicament on Guadalcanal. Vice Admiral Robert L. Ghormley wanted the Fifth Air Force to "beat down the Jap air strength at Rabaul" so that he could land a convoy of reinforcements and supplies. MacArthur conferred with Kenney, who, in turn, called Ken Walker and told him to send his B-17s. Kenney knew the last-minute change of plans would be unpopular—the bombers had already been loaded for a mission against Buna—but the marines on Guadalcanal were in "real trouble."

Once again the 19th Bomb Group undertook a series of hazardous raids against Rabaul. By this time the crews could practically conduct the two-day missions in their sleep. Port Moresby was still being bombed on a regular basis, which meant the routine of safeguarding the B-17s had not changed. The crews flew from Australia to Seven Mile airdrome, where they gassed up before conducting the thousand-mile round trip to Rabaul and back. Various squadrons of the 19th flew three exhausting raids beginning September 15, but the missions yielded negligible results.

General Walker accompanied the third mission, led by Major Hardison of the 93rd Bomb Squadron. Four B-17s departed from Port Moresby at 2300 on September 17 for an early morning attack on Rabaul. Walker typically carried a portable oxygen bottle so that he could move freely about the aircraft and observe all of the crewmen, from the tail gunner to the bombardier. "Wandering all over the place like that isn't healthy," his aide later told a reporter, "but the general figures he can't tell the boys how to go out and to get shot at unless he's willing to get shot at, too."

On this occasion Walker was none too pleased with the effort. It was bad enough that only four B-17s participated in the mission; the conclusion was even worse as the bomber piloted by Lt. Claude N. Burcky became lost in foul weather. Hours after their expected landing time, the crew radioed that they were low on fuel and bailing out. An RAAF Catalina spotted the wreckage two days later on the west coast of the Cape York Peninsula, more than four hundred miles southwest of Port Moresby. Burcky and seven other crewmen were picked up, but the navigator was never found.

FOR THE JAPANESE, the Allied invasion of Guadalcanal on August 7 presented a huge crisis. That evening, aboard the flagship *Yamato*, Rear Admiral Ugaki reflected on the deep concerns of the Combined Fleet Staff. He noted in his diary that the United States had "employed a huge force, intending to capture that area once and for all." To his credit, he immediately grasped the principal goal of the American offensive. "Unless we destroy them promptly, they will attempt to recapture Rabaul, not to speak of frustrating our Moresby operation."

In direct response to the situation on Guadalcanal, Admiral Yamamoto moved his headquarters from Japanese home waters to the South Pacific.

His flagship arrived at Truk lagoon on August 28 and did not venture out again for eight months. The presence of the super-battleship was merely symbolic. Despite the fact that several decisive naval battles were fought in the waters around Guadalcanal during that period, the world's most powerful warship remained inside the anchorage, little more than a floating hotel for the Combined Fleet Staff. Rabaul, not Truk, was the hub of frenetic activity during the Guadalcanal and New Guinea operations, but Yamamoto stayed aboard his flagship, sending staff members to observe the forward areas and liaise with subordinate commands.

For example, about two weeks after *Yamato* dropped anchor at Truk, Rear Admiral Ugaki flew to Rabaul for meetings with various army and navy representatives. Prior to landing on the afternoon of September 10, the chief of staff's aircraft made an aerial tour of the harbor, during which Ugaki was impressed by the sight of Tavurvur, the active volcano. He then began a series of meetings with the staffs of the Eighth Fleet, Eleventh Air Fleet, and Seventeenth Army. On his third day at Rabaul, Ugaki "closeted" himself in the Eleventh Air Fleet headquarters to monitor the progress of a counteroffensive against the marines on Guadalcanal. That night, September 12, a powerful force of more than three thousand Japanese troops began a two-day push to overwhelm American positions from the south, but they were stopped at Lunga Ridge by elements of the 1st Raider Battalion. (This became known as the Battle of Edson's Ridge, named for the commander of the 1st Raider Battalion, Lt. Col. Merritt A. Edson.) Although greatly disappointed by the operation's failure, Ugaki remained outwardly circumspect. In contrast, the Seventeenth Army command seemed completely stunned by the setback, and Ugaki took it upon himself to bolster their morale.

After several days of observation, Ugaki had gained a clear understanding of the challenges facing the Japanese at Guadalcanal as well as New Guinea. He was unimpressed with the army staff, and to make matters worse, all of the units at Rabaul were embarrassed by a spectacular mishap that occurred during his visit. At about 1300 hours on September 14, Ugaki was attending a conference when the rattle of machine-gun fire echoed across the caldera. But there was no enemy attack in progress; instead, an accident near the waterfront had ignited a munitions stockpile, and the commotion Ugaki heard was caused by exploding ammunition. Within moments a chain reaction of detonations touched off additional stockpiles of ordnance. Bombs and torpedoes exploded with spectacular force, spreading destruction in a rapidly expanding circle. Suddenly the entire township was in jeopardy. Ugaki and Vice Admiral Tsukahara, along with their staff officers, abandoned the headquarters building and took cover in an air-raid shelter. In the commercial cold storage facility, three-quarters of a mile away from the explosions, civilian internee Gordon Thomas felt the ground shudder, and a few moments later the windows were blown in.

The accident was not unlike the botched demolition by Lark Force engineers in January but on a much larger scale. Over the past eight months Rabaul had received literally hundreds of shiploads of bombs, torpedoes, artillery shells, small-arms ammunition, and drums of gasoline and oil. Most of the war materiel was stockpiled near wharves and jetties so that it could be quickly forwarded to the combat areas, but the Japanese had taken no precautions despite the obvious dangers posed by air raids. Ugaki himself noted that munitions were "piled up without any order." Thousands of drums of petroleum products were stored haphazardly, and many had been sabotaged by Australian POWs working as stevedores. (Captain Hutchinson-Smith wrote with undisguised glee that whenever possible, the caps on the drums were loosened "to allow the precious liquid to trickle out.")

Although the exact cause of the disaster was never determined, a widely supported theory suggests that it began when a fuel dump in the eastern part of Rabaul caught fire. Accumulated spillage that had seeped into the drainage ditches subsequently flared up, sending a river of flames toward the waterfront. The expanding fire touched off the ammunition stockpile, and the mayhem began. In this instance, heavy explosions rocked the township for the next twelve hours. At daybreak, while touring the scene of devastation at the waterfront, Ugaki vowed to punish the people who should have safeguarded the munitions.

IN AUSTRALIA, meanwhile, General Kenney had come to the conclusion that high-altitude bombardment, at least in its present form, was not working in the Southwest Pacific. There simply weren't enough bombers available to effectively blanket any given target. He was especially disappointed with the results of anti-shipping strikes and gave more consideration to low-level attack methods. Recently, Douglas A-20s of the 3rd Bomb Group had used parafrag bombs against the airdrome at Buna with excellent effect, but blowing up parked planes was much easier than hitting a moving ship. Furthermore, it took a heavy bomb to cause significant damage to a warship. Convinced that the answer lay in skip-bombing, Kenney released Major Benn from duties as his aide and sent him to Torrens Creek, a new airfield in Queensland, where a squadron of B-17s fresh from the States had recently settled.

Kenney planned to activate the 43rd Bombardment Group (Heavy), whose ground personnel had arrived in March aboard HMS *Queen Mary*. The group lacked aircraft and flight crews until mid-August, when a dozen B-17Fs landed at Torrens Creek. Pulled from submarine patrol duties in the Panama Canal Zone, the crews had picked up new bombers in California and were assigned to the 63rd Bomb Squadron, temporarily attached to the 19th Bomb Group for combat training. They were still serving that function when Benn reported to Torrens Creek in late August.

Lieutenant Roger E. Vargas, a navigator in the squadron, recalled his first meeting with Kenney's erstwhile aide. "I happened to be the officer-of-the-day when Major Benn arrived at Torrens Creek. He came in and asked me where I was from. I told him we had come from Panama, and mentioned to him that we had new B-17s and well-trained crews but we were not being used properly. He said, 'I'm going to be taking over your squadron, and we'll be doing things differently.'"

Just how differently was soon revealed, as Benn began to train his crews in the art of skip-bombing. He had tried it in a B-26 at Fiji, but taking the huge, four-engine B-17 down to mast height was a radical departure from anything the men had tried before. "He talked us into all kinds of things," remembered one pilot. "After Benn got there, we never flew above seven or eight thousand feet except to get over the Owen Stanley Mountains. He really had a lot of different tactics to hit shipping."

Benn had inherited a squadron of eager crews. His star pupil was Capt. Kenneth D. McCullar, a hotshot pilot from Courtland, Mississippi, who possessed in spades the qualities writer Tom Wolfe would later call the "right stuff." The aggressive McCullar was handsome, marvelously skilled at flying, and popular with his men. He also loved gambling, to the point that when he picked out his new B-17 in California, he selected one based on the last two digits of its serial number—21. Naturally he named it *Black Jack*.

§

THREE WEEKS AFTER Benn took over the 63rd Bomb Squadron, General Kenney arranged to watch a demonstration of skip-bombing at Port Moresby. Benn had worked out the physics, and the crews practiced with inert bombs on the SS *Pruth*, a British merchantman that had run aground on a reef almost twenty years earlier. Much of the ship's superstructure was gone, salvaged for scrap, but the rusting hulk provided an excellent target. Partially awash yet impossible to sink, it withstood repeated hits while the crews perfected their techniques.

On this occasion, Kenney watched as McCullar brought his Fortress down to just two hundred feet above the wave tops. A single bomb dropped from the belly of the B-17, skipped off the water "like a stone," and smacked into the side of the ship. Kenney was thoroughly impressed as McCullar made nine more runs against the *Pruth*, tallying a total of six hits.

Despite the success of the static demonstration, Kenney realized that Benn's squadron was not quite ready to attempt low-level attacks against the Japanese. In the meantime, he shared ideas with Ken Walker on how to improve the results of anti-shipping strikes. It was all too apparent that the odds of hitting a moving vessel from high altitude were practically zero. The Japanese ship-handlers merely had to observe the bombs as they tumbled from the aircraft and then turn out of the way. Even the near misses seemed to have little effect on the enemy. Kenney believed the problem was the result of using delayed-action fuses. With a delay of as little as 1/10 second, the bomb plunged too deep to be effective. An instantaneous fuse detonated the bomb on impact with the water, sending shards of steel in every direction. Kenney was certain "that an instantaneous explosion near a vessel, up to perhaps fifty yards away, would push fragments into it, killing Japs, cutting steam and fuel lines and maybe setting fires." Walker did not agree with the idea, but Kenney ordered him to "try it for a while" so that they could gauge the results.

Walker's objection underscored a widening chasm between the two generals. Both men worked tirelessly to defeat the Japanese, but they differed personally as well as professionally. Walker had all the attributes of an officer and a gentleman. Above average in height, athletically built, he dressed with style, entertained with flair, and was an accomplished dancer. Not surprisingly, women found him attractive. He was twice divorced, with two sons from the first marriage and one from the second. Kenney, in contrast, was a head shorter than Walker and more of a bulldog, both in appearance and personality. He was also a combat veteran of World War I, unlike Walker, who was considered something of an outsider because he had neither attended West Point nor flown in France. Those who had were cliquish. The army's upper establishment was the domain of West Pointers, so Walker pushed himself, working harder and longer than his peers. And, like many compulsive workers, he became moody and impatient when conditions were stressful.

But there was also a positive element to Walker's situation, for he could empathize with the frustrations of the lower ranks. In many ways he became their champion. Ordered to Port Moresby to run the Advanced Echelon for a few weeks, both to gain experience and give Whitehead a rest, Walker made a point of improving the men's living conditions. Personable with the troops, he dressed down by wearing an open-neck khaki uniform, frequently typed his own reports, and habitually waited with the men in long chow lines. Such actions were beneficial for morale, but what truly made a difference was Walker's habit of accompanying crews on combat missions. He averaged almost a mission per week, including several over Rabaul, and was recognized for his efforts with the receipt of a Silver Star in August. The citation read, in part: "The large amount of first-hand information gained by General Walker has proved of inestimable value."

IN LATE SEPTEMBER, as the dual battles for control of New Guinea and Guadalcanal raged eight hundred miles apart, a meeting of Allied commanders was arranged at Noumea, near the southern tip of New Caledonia. Kenney flew from Brisbane accompanied by Richard Sutherland, who represented MacArthur for the high-level conference. Ghormley and Nimitz were also in attendance, while the army contingent numbered half a dozen generals including Hap Arnold. The agenda focused on the continuing crisis on Guadalcanal, which meant that Kenney would be asked again to help. "The Navy wanted me to make mass raids on Rabaul airdromes and shipping as a primary mission," he later confirmed. Kenney agreed to "try to burn the place down," but he also reminded the attendees that his air units were already stretched thin while "knocking off Jap convoys to Buna, maintaining air control over New Guinea, and helping out our ground forces."

The enemy advance on the Kokoda Trail had been halted by American and Australian infantry, and the half-starved Japanese were in full retreat back toward Buna. But the high command was not giving up. Convoy after convoy departed from Rabaul with reinforcements, and most reached Buna unscathed thanks to a seasonal pattern of heavy storms over the Coral Sea. The lousy weather not only protected the convoys en route to New Guinea, it gave the Japanese an opportunity to increase the tempo and volume of shipping in Simpson Harbor.

This was a matter of necessity. The Japanese were being beaten on Guadalcanal as well as on New Guinea, and the surviving forces desperately needed reinforcements and supplies. Thus, in addition to the convoys sent to Buna, heavily armed cruisers and destroyers were dispatched almost daily to Guadalcanal. They sped down the natural passage through the Solomon Islands known to Americans as "the Slot," timing their arrival at Guadalcanal for soon after nightfall. The warships would unload "rice, bullets, and soldiers" and then shell the marine positions before heading back to Rabaul. The nocturnal actions were so regular that an American correspondent referred to the convoys collectively as the "Tokyo Express." Although a misnomer, the nickname caught on.

Elsewhere, the Japanese retreat from the Owen Stanley Mountains was good news for V Bomber Command. For the first time since the Pacific war began, Port Moresby was deemed safe enough to house B-17s full time. Most squadrons remained in Australia with their maintenance units, but a handful of Fortresses from 30th Bomb Squadron moved up to Fourteen Mile airdrome for temporary duty. The new field was dusty, primitive, and plagued with mosquitoes, and the living conditions were terrible, especially the food. Nevertheless the physical demands on aircraft and crews alike were greatly reduced thanks to the shorter duration of the missions. After just a few weeks, the contingent from the 30th was relieved by the 63rd Bomb Squadron. Major Benn thought his crews were nearly ready to try skip-bombing in Simpson Harbor, but the squadron had been experiencing chronic trouble with its delayed-action fuses. When the next mission was scheduled, Benn tried a different tactic.

Six Fortresses took off from Port Moresby in the wee hours October 2 and reached Rabaul before sunrise. Throttling back to reduce noise, they descended to 2,500 feet or less, then separated and went after individual targets. There were plenty of vessels to choose from. Lieutenant James T.

Murphy, flying a B-17F named *Pluto* (naturally with a depiction of the Walt Disney pooch adorning the nose), aimed for what he later described as "the biggest ship I had ever seen." After a twenty-second attack run, during which Japanese antiaircraft fire became intense, the bombardier released four 1,000-pounders. "The bombs went exactly as we'd hoped—one hit the ship directly, with the other three very close to it," Murphy wrote. "Major fires broke out all over the ship."

Three other pilots attacked shipping with similar results, according to Murphy. Captain Folmer J. Sogaard hit a "destroyer," while Ken McCullar and Capt. Byron L. Heichel each hit smaller merchant vessels. "The results were fantastic," Murphy later wrote. "At 2,000 feet, we just couldn't miss! Four ships were sunk that night." Murphy's enthusiasm evidently got the better of him, for the 43rd Bomb Group's official history states only that two merchant ships were set afire and a direct hit was scored on a destroyer, and stops short of claiming any vessels as sunk. Furthermore, the exhaustive postwar analysis conducted by the Joint Army-Navy Assessment Committee (JANAC) revealed that no damage was sustained by any noncombatant ships on October 2. But the Fortresses did achieve something. The old cruiser *Tenryu*, launched in 1918, was hit by a bomb and suffered thirty dead.

Three days after the anti-shipping strike, elements of the weary 19th Bomb Group were back over the airdromes at Rabaul. Six Fortresses of the 30th Bomb Squadron took off from Port Moresby on the afternoon of October 5 to hit Vunakanau, and the 28th Bomb Squadron sent eight B-17s to attack Lakunai. Despite the promising number, only three of the latter group actually reached Rabaul due to poor weather. The target area was obscured by clouds, and results of the attack were not observed.

South of Rabaul, the Fortresses of the 30th Bomb Squadron fared even worse. Finding Vunakanau obscured by clouds, the B-17s made one orbit to set up a second bomb run and were jumped by more than two dozen Zeros. The Japanese pilots, among the most aggressive yet encountered, made repeated and well-coordinated attacks against the front of the formation, where the B-17s' defensive fire was weakest. After fighting off the first wave of fighters, the Fortresses released their bombs over Vunakanau and were turning southward when a second wave of Zeros hit them. Bullets and cannon shells pierced several bombers. The B-17 flown by Lt. Earl L. Hageman had its right inboard engine knocked out, then lost the left inboard engine when the next wave of Zeros struck. Diving from the formation, Hageman was last seen headed for some clouds with eleven Zeros in pursuit. Neither he nor his eight crewmen were ever heard from again.

The other five B-17s "took a beating," with several casualties among the crews. The worst case was Plt. Off. Allan J. Davenport, a twenty-two-year-old RAAF navigator whose leg was nearly severed, evidently by a 20mm shell. Unfortunately the crew got lost for hours in the awful weather, and soon after they landed at Port Moresby, Davenport died.

In Brisbane, Kenney "got his dander up" after hearing about the mission. Not only had the effort been costly in exchange for minor damage to the enemy, there were reliable reports that Ken Walker had been aboard one of the B-17s. "I can always hire a 10 dollar a week man to sweep the floors," Kenney chastised. "No more combat missions."

The following day, MacArthur called Kenney into his office to discuss another big effort against Rabaul, again in support of Guadalcanal operations. Kenney later recalled: "I had already planned to do something about that place. For the past couple of weeks the Japs had been unloading supplies and troops there. They might be building up for a reinforcement of their forces in the Solomons or maybe around Buna. The shipping had not been a good target, as the Jap vessels had been coming in just before dark, unloading at night, and leaving before daybreak. The airdromes in the Rabaul area were well beaten up and the Jap air strength was low."

Kenney's vow to burn down Rabaul began with the positioning of three dozen B-17s from Mareeba to Port Moresby on October 8. The planned mission called for total efforts by both the 19th and 43rd Bomb Groups, which would coordinate their attack to follow a preliminary raid by RAAF Catalinas. Thirty-six Fortresses were scheduled to participate, making it the largest Allied bombing effort yet attempted in the Pacific. A follow-up attack was also planned for the night after.

But the initial event almost didn't go off. After receiving a forecast of foul weather between Port Moresby and Rabaul that afternoon, Walker cancelled the mission. In his defense, three weeks earlier he had flown a night mission over Rabaul and saw firsthand the hazardous conditions created by the powerful storm system that routinely thwarted flights over the Solomon Sea. Kenney wasn't convinced, however, as biographer Martha Byrd later explained: "When he learned that Walker had canceled the first of the two planned strikes, Kenney consulted a different weatherman, got a favorable forecast, and overruled his bomber commander."

Kenney's instincts were correct. The weather was not a factor, and the preliminary raid by the RAAF exceeded all expectations. Flying all the way from Cairns, four Catalinas from 11 and 20 Squadrons arrived over Rabaul at 2050 on October 8. Ordered to "light up the town and harbor perimeter," the heavily laden flying boats carried an amazing payload. As they crossed over the township at several thousand feet, the Cat-boats dropped twenty demolition bombs, ten small fragmentation bombs, and sixty incendiaries. Approximately half of the incendiaries fell into the residential area north of Simpson Harbor, starting numerous fires. Six heavy bombs landed in the commercial district and ignited one of the many stockpiles of ammunition or fuel the Japanese had imprudently placed throughout the town, and an enormous fire flared up. The flames were still visible from sixty miles away as the Catalinas made their way back to Australia.

The Flying Fortresses, representing four different squadrons, began taking off just prior to midnight. Six bombers dropped out for various malfunctions, but the remaining thirty aircraft gathered at a marshalling point one hundred miles south of Rabaul. Grouped in elements of two or three planes each, they headed toward the target in a strung-out line at altitudes ranging from 4,500 feet to 11,000 feet. Even in the darkness, the crews could see Rabaul from many miles away. The fires started by the RAAF eight hours earlier burned brightly, casting a reddish glow over the township.

The attack commenced at 0400, and for nearly two hours the heavy bombers made individual passes over Rabaul. Japanese antiaircraft positions reacted by shooting wildly, while the searchlight crews tried to pinpoint B-17s. The night sky was turned into a bizarre montage of arcing tracer rounds and brilliant fingers of white light, punctuated by the staccato flashes of exploding antiaircraft shells. Inside the bombers, pilots whose vision was adjusted to the soft red glow of instrument lights were temporarily blinded. To the men in the trailing B-17s, the view up ahead was spectacular. One pilot likened the scene to "a colossal fireworks display."

Although the sudden loss of night vision and the intense pyrotechnics created a nerve-wracking experience for the Americans, the bombardiers took advantage of the fires illuminating Rabaul to release an impressive amount of ordnance. Ninety 500-pounders, more than two hundred

300-pounders, and fifty-five incendiary clusters followed the path of the bombers from west to east, blasting a swath of destruction across the township. Bombs damaged the coaling jetty on the western shore of Simpson Harbor, hit the Malaguna Road encampment, exploded stockpiles of fuel or ammunition in the Bayloo district (centered around a large Chinese construction business), and demolished several buildings in Chinatown.

The following day, listeners tuned to Radio Tokyo heard the announcer complain that a bomb had struck a hotel in Rabaul, killing fifty "Geisha girls." The Allies would have been incredulous to learn that the enemy had indeed transported some *three thousand* conscripted prostitutes to Rabaul in early 1942. Known as "comfort women," most were Koreans and Formosans taken from their homes or hired under false pretenses, then forced to provide a sexual outlet for the troops. The army and navy each maintained three "special purpose houses" in Rabaul, and the 3rd Infantry Battalion set up a brothel at Vunapope in a monks' dormitory (after first evicting the Brotherhood of the Sacred Heart).

AT LEAST ONE PERSON on the ground at Rabaul actually celebrated the destructive night raid. The previous day, when Captain Mitzusaki of the 81st Naval Garrison Unit took Harl Pease and five other prisoners out for execution, he had pointed at Father George Lepping and said, "You go tomorrow."

Mizusaki may have been toying with the priest, but Lepping believed he was about to be killed. For the remainder of the day, he received an outpouring of sympathy from his fellow prisoners. However, the situation changed after dark. "During the night the American B-17s came over and bombed Rabaul for hours," Lepping recalled. "The Japanese gave us permission to seek shelter in a small dugout. While the Commandant was running for a dugout he was struck in the leg by shrapnel."

Miraculously, no prisoners were hurt during the raid, but Mizusaki was evacuated aboard a hospital ship. A new commandant took over the next day, and the planned execution of Father Lepping was soon forgotten.

FOUR HOURS AFTER the raid, a crew from the 435th Bomb Squadron took photographs of the damage. The results confirmed numerous bomb hits and showed the supply dump near the Bayloo construction company still in flames. But the photos came with a price. Four Zeros attacked the B-17, killing the tail gunner and severely wounding the Australian copilot, Sgt. David R. Sinclair, whose left lung was punctured by a 7.7mm bullet. Even more disturbing, the photos revealed that Simpson Harbor was full of ships: a whopping twenty-six transports, two subs, a sub tender, a cruiser, four destroyers, and two minelayers. Similarly, seventy-two fighters and six twin-engine aircraft crowded Lakunai airdrome.

Obviously, Kenney's speculation about Japanese air strength was inaccurate. A few units—particularly the fighters of the Tainan Air Group and the land attackers of the 4th Air Group—had been depleted by heavy losses at Guadalcanal, but replacements came quickly. Vice Admiral Tsukahara moved the headquarters of the Eleventh Air Fleet to Rabaul in August and was busy funneling whole air groups to the Southeast Area. In one remarkable move, fourteen Zeros of the 6th Air Group flew all the way to Rabaul from Japan. Guided by two bombers, the Zeros made refueling stops at Iwo Jima, Saipan, and Truk before arriving at Lakunai airdrome on August 21. The island-hopping journey, which spanned nearly three thousand miles, was considered "without precedent" for single-engine aircraft in the Imperial Navy.

Other units were likewise shifted to the Rabaul area. The 26th Air Flotilla, consisting of the 6th Air Group (fighters) and the Misawa and Kisarazu Air Groups (land attack), arrived in August. The land attack component of the 21st Air Flotilla was ordered to move south from the Philippines on August 27, and the fighter component of the 24th Air Flotilla was sent from the Central Pacific to Rabaul. For operational control, the flotillas were given additional designations. Rear Admiral Yamada's 25th Air Flotilla became the 5th Air Attack Force, the 26th Air Flotilla under Vice Adm. Seigo Yamagata became the 6th Air Attack Force, and the 21st Air Flotilla became the 1st Air Attack Force, headquartered at Kavieng with approximately twenty Type 1 land attack aircraft.

Thus, as the reconnaissance photos taken on October 9 indicated, the airdromes at Rabaul were full of planes. Available air strength included approximately fifty medium bombers, eighty Zeros (equally divided between A6M2s and the newer A6M3s), twenty dive-bombers, eight flying boats, and three reconnaissance planes. Nevertheless, the night attack on the township was deemed so successful that another effort was scheduled immediately. Fires were still raging as seven RAAF Catalinas attacked at

0330 on October 10, scattering more than a dozen large fragmentation bombs and five hundred small incendiaries across the town. Thirty minutes later, eighteen Fortresses dropped almost two hundred demolition bombs and thirty-eight incendiary clusters along the waterfront from the Toboi Wharf all the way around the harbor to Sulphur Creek, as well as in the commercial district. Simultaneously, three B-17s hit Lakunai airdrome with sixteen modified 300-pound bombs, a new innovation that Kenney employed "to annoy the Nips."

In his memoir, Kenney described the bombs' lethal effects:

> To cut up aircraft on the ground we had wrapped these bombs with heavy steel wire, and dropped them with instantaneous fuses on the end of a six-inch pipe extension in the nose. They looked good. The wire, which was nearly one-quarter inch in diameter, broke up into pieces from six inches to a couple of feet long, and in the demonstration it cut limbs off trees a hundred feet away which were two inches thick. The noise was quite terrifying. The pieces of wire whirling through the air whistled and sang all of the notes on the scale and wailed and screamed like a whole tribe of disconsolate banshees.

To what degree the bombs fitted with "special extension instantaneous fuses" terrorized the Japanese is not directly known, but an impressive fire was observed in the dispersal area after the attack. Overall the second raid contributed to the widespread destruction caused the previous day. Rear Admiral Ugaki, back aboard *Yamato* in Truk lagoon, noted in his diary that casualties at Rabaul amounted to 110 dead and wounded.

Kenney was pleased to declare the raids on consecutive nights a major success, and MacArthur sent him a glowing message about the "fine performance over Rabaul." When Kenney next met with Ken Walker, on October 12 in Brisbane, the latter was allegedly in a sulky mood because his orders to cancel the first mission had been countermanded. Walker hated to be proven wrong. Kenney could not resist teasing him about it, but after twisting the proverbial dagger, he applied a bit of diplomacy by describing the enormous pressure he was under to take out Rabaul. This reportedly had the intended effect on his subordinate's bruised ego.

§

THE 19TH BOMB GROUP conducted two additional raids on the Rabaul airdromes in mid-October, but the crews had to force themselves to concentrate. Rumors had been circulating for weeks that they would be sent home, an event that was all but confirmed when Kenney, accompanied by Walker, held awards ceremonies at both Townsville and Mareeba on October 15. Altogether they decorated more than 250 personnel of the group. "By the time I got through," Kenney wrote, "I had worn most of the skin off the thumb and forefinger of my right hand. It was a great show."

The 19th's relief had been pending since late September, when General Arnold toured the SWPA on a visit from Washington. Kenney had asked for a replacement group, explaining that the men of the 19th were "beaten down psychologically." Kenney sought fresh crews from the States who were eager to fight. Richard Carmichael, though not a veteran of the group's early campaigns, was a popular commander with the 19th and had led them long enough to appreciate their difficulties. He especially admired what they had accomplished with the early C and D models of the B-17, which he called "a bastard mixture of airplanes," but he could also understand Kenney's desire to exchange the group for better airplanes and fresh crews.

The 19th could not return to the States, however, until adequate replacements were available. Kenney was delighted when General Arnold agreed to send over the 90th Bomb Group (Heavy), currently based in Hawaii. Their arrival in Australia, planned for November, would give Kenney four squadrons of Consolidated B-24D Liberators. He was unconcerned about the logistics of maintaining two different types, knowing that most of the new B-17 groups were being sent to Europe anyway. "I was not particular," he later wrote. "I'd take anything."

In the meantime, the punch-drunk 19th Bomb Group and Bill Benn's 63rd Bomb Squadron would have to handle all of the heavy bombing assignments for a few weeks until the remaining three squadrons of the 43rd Bomb Group—the 65th and 403rd at Torrens Creek and the 64th at Iron Range, a new field in northern Queensland—became operational. The "Kangaroo Squadron" would also continue to fly single-ship reconnaissance missions over New Guinea, the Bismarcks, and the northern Solomons. The long-distance flights were hazardous but vital, providing the only reliable intelligence regarding the enemy's concentrations of shipping and aircraft. Photos of Rabaul taken on October 20 and 22, for example, revealed more than seventy ships in the anchorage. As a direct result, Benn was ordered to conduct the mission he had been anticipating for weeks: the first skip-bombing attack by American aircraft.

The mission profile called for an initial wave of B-17s to attack Rabaul from conventional altitudes to distract the Japanese antiaircraft gunners. Seven Fortresses of the 19th Bomb Group accomplished this at 0145 on October 23, dropping twelve tons of bombs on Simpson Harbor with no direct hits observed. Approximately an hour after they departed, Benn approached with seven B-17s from the 43rd Bomb Group. He rode as an observer in one of the Fortresses until they neared the target area, at which point he tapped the copilot, Lt. Charles L. Anderson, on the shoulder. "Andy, why don't you move over and let me sit in the copilot's seat," he said, "and I'll decide when to drop the bombs." After weeks of training, Benn was determined to call the shots himself for the inaugural attack.

Four of the B-17s attacked the harbor area from several thousand feet, again to distract enemy gunners, while the remaining three crews initiated the skip-bombing methods they had practiced so diligently. After picking out individual targets, the pilots descended to about two thousand feet and maneuvered to set up their first attack. Flying at right angles to the intended bombing path, they watched the moon's reflection on the surface relative to the position of the target, thereby judging the moment to execute a ninety-degree turn inbound. On completing the turn, they chopped power on all four engines and glided down to about two hundred feet above the water. Some pilots allowed a few extra feet, compensating for the "pucker factor" of taking such a huge bomber almost to the surface. Regardless of the exact altitude, each of the Fortresses flew an attack profile that Boeing's engineers had never imagined. These were the original stealth bombers, dropping quietly out of the night sky and leveling off well below the terrain surrounding the great caldera. The aircraft were invisible to the Japanese lookouts, yet the B-17 crews could clearly see their targets. "We had good moonlight," recalled Anderson, "so we could see the ships."

The first attack was made by Benn's aircraft, piloted by Lt. Franklyn T. Green. Aiming for a light cruiser outside of Simpson Harbor, they dropped a heavy bomb and crossed over the warship's superstructure mere feet above the radio mast. The passing shadow of the bomber apparently shocked the Japanese gunners into action, but the B-17 was already a hundred yards past them when their guns lit up the night sky. Next, Green attacked a five-thousand-ton cargo ship, after which he climbed for a conventional attack on a fifteen-thousand-ton merchant ship inside Simpson Harbor. Direct hits were claimed against all three vessels, and both of the merchantmen allegedly sank. The cruiser was last observed in flames, sinking by the stern. Ken McCullar, already credited with sinking or damaging four ships with *Black Jack*, claimed two direct hits on a destroyer. Finally, the Fortress flown by Capt. Carl A. Hustad made a successful attack, hitting a ten-thousand-ton vessel that was subsequently reported on fire.

Altogether, the skip-bombers and the high element claimed four direct hits, nine "very close near misses," and four near misses that allegedly sank a cruiser, a destroyer, and two large noncombatants while damaging a transport and a "small cargo vessel." But as so often happened, the results of the first skip-bombing effort were not as effective as the crews presumed. Based on Japanese records and the postwar JANAC findings, only two ships were hit on October 23. Both were submarine chasers, 160 feet in length and displacing slightly more than four hundred tons each. They could easily account for the "cruiser" and "destroyer" claimed by the bomber crews, especially considering the vagaries of the moonlight and the adrenalin rush of combat, but neither ship sustained serious damage. As for the claims totaling more than thirty thousand tons of cargo shipping, there is no evidence that any noncombatants were hit, let alone damaged.

Of course, the JANAC report would not be revealed until after the war. In the absence of any other evidence, Kenney eagerly chalked up the claims as legitimate and summoned his former aide to Brisbane. Benn arrived that afternoon and was escorted straightaway to the eighth floor of the AMP Building, where General MacArthur personally pinned a Distinguished Service Cross on his uniform. Kenney beamed with pride. Benn was his protégé, and it was no secret that Kenney regarded the major's squadron as "the hottest outfit in the whole air force."

CHAPTER 22

New Identities

A S READERS HAVE undoubtedly discovered, the system used to identify Japanese aircraft at the beginning of World War II was unwieldy and confusing. A full identification combined two main components: A) the official military designation based on the plane's primary role and the Imperial year it entered service and B) the alphanumeric project code applied by the manufacturer.* The result was a bewildering array of names that all sounded alike, such as the Navy Type 96 carrier fighter (Mitsubishi A5M), Navy Type 96 attack bomber (Mitsubishi G3M), Army Type 97 heavy bomber (Mitsubishi Ki-21), Navy Type 97 carrier attack bomber (Nakajima B5N), and Navy Type 97 flying boat (Kawanishi H6K). The method was challenging enough for intelligence personnel, but Allied airmen became even more tongue-tied when they tried to reconstruct events after snatching blurred glimpses of planes in combat.

---

*The Imperial year, or Koki, was based on the year Emperor Jimmu founded Japan (660 BC in the Gregorian calendar), almost 2,600 years before World War II. Generally the last two digits of the year were used when referring to military equipment, such as the Type 99 carrier bomber, which entered service in the year 2599 (1939). From the year 2600 onward only the last digit was used; hence the nomenclature of the Type 0 carrier fighter and Type 1 land attack aircraft.

By the middle of 1942, as both the number and variety of Japanese planes increased, a much simpler identification method became necessary. The answer was a system of short, unforgettable code names. These came into practice shortly after Capt. Frank T. McCoy Jr., an intelligence officer in the 38th Bomb Group, was placed in charge of the Air Technical Intelligence Unit in Australia. McCoy and his team of enlisted men—Tech. Sgt. Francis M. Williams and Cpl. Joseph Grattan—set out to create a list of names that was both simple and effective. One of their first important decisions was to create two categories, using male names for fighters and female names for just about everything else (though refinements were made to the latter category).

McCoy, from Tennessee, drew upon his Southern heritage for several of the early code names. Blessed with a good sense of humor, he applied hillbilly nicknames to variations of the most famous of all Japanese fighters, the Mitsubishi Zero. The prevalent model (A6M2) became "Zeke," while "Rufe" was given to the Nakajima-built floatplane version (A6M2-N), encountered for the first time at Tulagi in the Solomons. When an upgraded variant of the Zero with nonfolding square wingtips entered combat in mid-1942, McCoy's team thought it was an all-new fighter and named it "Hap" as a tribute to the top American airman, Gen. H. H. Arnold. Usage of the code name continued for approximately one year until it was learned that Arnold took exception to it, whereupon the nickname was revised to "Hamp."

Ironically, some of the new code names were slow to catch on. "Zero" was already so iconic that airmen continued to use it to describe almost any fighter they faced in the Southwest Pacific. Even the obsolete, fixed-gear Mitsubishi A5M was often misidentified as a Zero, although by the time it received its own code name ("Claude," after an Australian friend of McCoy's), none were still serving on the front lines. Adding to the confusion, a new Imperial Army fighter that appeared at Rabaul in late 1942 looked remarkably like the Zero. The Nakajima Ki-43 *Habayusa* (Peregrine Falcon) was nicknamed "Oscar" by McCoy's team, but on numerous occasions the nimble fighters were misidentified as Zeros.

Japanese bombers were generally easier to identify. McCoy's team took delight in choosing code names that were not only unique but had interesting connections to real people. The name selected for the Imperial Navy's predominant land attack aircraft, the Mitsubishi G4M, was inspired by a well-endowed acquaintance of Sergeant Williams. The pair of gun blisters that bulged from the aircraft's fuselage reminded him of a big-breasted nurse he knew from Bridgeville, Pennsylvania, and so the bomber became known famously as "Betty." The venerable Mitsubishi G3M was nicknamed "Nell" for the wife of an intelligence officer in Melbourne, and an Australian army sergeant inspired the code name of the Aichi D3A "Val" dive-bomber. "Kate" was chosen for the Nakajima B5N carrier bomber, the Kawanishi H6K flying boat became "Mavis," and its successor, the massive H8K flying boat, was code-named "Emily."

From its homespun beginnings, the use of the code names expanded rapidly, gaining such widespread acceptance that all of the American armed forces adopted the program by the end of 1942. McCoy and his team constantly updated the list, which eventually grew to 122 names including all of the known aircraft in the Imperial Army and Navy inventories, and even some that were merely suspected of being developed. To this day, the use of the code names remains almost universal.

WHILE MCCOY and his team developed their list of names in the fall of 1942, the Eleventh Air Fleet at Rabaul tried desperately to dislodge the American invaders from Guadalcanal. The great distances involved—each round trip was the equivalent of 1,300 highway miles—gave the Japanese airmen no margin for error. This hard lesson was driven home on the very first day of the offensive, when fifty-three aircraft from Rabaul counterat-tacked the American fleet. Nine Aichi D3A "Val" dive-bombers took part despite the fact that their range barely exceeded 900 miles. Rear Admiral Yamada sent them anyway, instructing the pilots to attack the American troopships and then attempt water landings near Shortland Island, where a seaplane tender and a flying boat would serve as rescue pickets. Without fighter escort, the nine courageous crews attempted to fulfill their mission, but scored only a single hit on the destroyer *Mugford* with a 60-kilogram bomb. (Material damage to the destroyer was minor, but casualties proved relatively high with twenty-one crewmen killed.) In exchange, five of the Vals were shot out of the sky by U.S. Navy Wildcats. The remaining four ditched as planned near the Shortlands, but only three crews were rescued, bringing the 2nd Air Group's losses to nine aircraft and six crews.

The experiences of the 4th Air Group, which sent twenty-seven Mitsubishi G4M Bettys to attack the transports and warships anchored off Lunga Point, were similar. Each plane carried a payload of two 250-kilogram and four 60-kilogram bombs which were dropped in a massive salvo against the stationary ships; much to the disgust of the Japanese, however, none of the 156 bombs struck a vessel. The ultra-long mission was wasted. Even worse, four Bettys were shot down, a fifth bomber crash-landed on Buka Island, and yet another cracked up while landing at Vunakanau airdrome. In all, the group's losses for the day totaled six aircraft and twenty-eight crewmembers.

The *Rei-sen* fared better. The pilots of the Tainan Air Group accounted well for themselves, downing nine Wildcats, but the unit's popular torch-bearer, Saburo Sakai, was critically wounded. Spying what he thought was a covey of Wildcats, Sakai stumbled into a formation of SBD Dauntlesses and was caught in a heavy crossfire. Machine-gun bullets shattered the canopy of his Zero, and a .30-caliber round struck the metal frame of his flight goggles just above his right eye. The slug creased his skull rather than entering his brain, but the eye was permanently blinded. Bleeding profusely, temporarily paralyzed on the left side of his body from the bullet's impact, Sakai somehow held his fighter in the air for the 650-mile flight back to Rabaul. Fortunate to have survived, he remained out of action for almost two years.

Unlike Sakai, the great majority of Japanese airmen whose planes were damaged over Guadalcanal did not return—and the losses accrued rapidly. On the morning of August 8, Rear Admiral Yamada again tried to smash the American invasion fleet, this time with aerial torpedoes. Supported by nine *rikko* of the Misawa Air Group that had arrived the previous afternoon, Yamada was able to muster twenty-six Bettys and fifteen escorting Zeros. Three of the former turned back because of mechanical problems, but the remaining aircraft attacked the American ships at noon.

Within a matter of minutes, the entire *rikko* doctrine was turned on its ear. Intense, accurate antiaircraft fire from the warships of the screening force brought down no less than eight Bettys, and only one torpedo actually hit a vessel, resulting in moderate damage to the destroyer *Jarvis*. The worst harm was caused by Lt. j.g. Takafumi Sasaki, who deliberately "body-crashed" his flaming Betty into the transport *George F. Elliott*. The fires that ensued became uncontrollable, resulting in the demise of the ship the next day.

Of the fifteen remaining Bettys, four more were shot down by Wildcats, leaving eleven battle-damaged planes to face the daunting flight back to Rabaul. Less than half made it. Six went down en route, with only one crew recovered. Two escorting *Rei-sen* also failed to return. The shock to Yamada at losing eighteen Type 1s and two Zeros must have been great.

For the airmen at Vunakanau, the results of the two-day effort were especially devastating. Quite possibly, no other aviation unit in the Imperial Navy experienced a worse run of bad luck than the 4th Air Group. In February, when the *Lexington* task force approached Rabaul, the group lost fifteen planes and more than 100 airmen; next, during the Battle of the Coral Sea in early May, they lost six aircraft and 31 crewmen while attacking Rear Admiral Crace's cruiser support group; and now, two consecutive long-distance missions to Guadalcanal had cost the land-attack unit another twenty three Bettys and more than 150 elite aviators.

Two aspects of the 4th Air Group's combat history were particularly troubling. The most astounding was the minimal damage caused to the enemy. Over the span of three major battles, while sacrificing forty-four aircraft and some three hundred crewmembers, the attackers had hit exactly one American ship with a torpedo, and gunners shot down a couple of navy Wildcats. The greatest single achievement belonged to Lieutenant Sasaki, but only because he made a suicidal dive into a transport.

The other disturbing element was the tendency of the Type 1 aircraft to burst into flames. The lack of protection for the fuel tanks was clearly to blame, and *rikko* crews began to refer to their planes derogatorily as the "Type 1 lighter" or "one-shot lighter."

No one in the 4th Air Group suffered more acutely than Capt. Yoshiyotsu Moritama, who had commanded the unit since its inception in February. After the debacle over Guadalcanal on August 8, he composed a heartfelt "draft of his views" for his superiors. Moritama began:

> At the battle of offshore New Britain on February 20, at Coral Sea on May 7, and the First Battle of the Solomons on August 7 and 8: three times we encountered major U.S./British task forces, their combined fleet, and a large convoy of transport vessels. Every time we pressed the enemy hard, expending all our might with the determination to kill or die, we achieved great results, showed our naval air group spirit and ability, fully demonstrated our traditions, and thus won honor. However, we also lost

valuable lives each time, large numbers of experienced brave warriors who should otherwise have been successful in their future. Although this is a rule of war, this is truly a regrettable matter. As the direct leader of the unit, I am strongly aware that I am to blame for it, and humbly accept the responsibility.

In the main body of his draft, Moritama pleaded for changes. "[The] aircraft that we are currently using must be improved and strengthened drastically," he wrote. He also urged better coordination between surface units and air groups. It was his belief that the only path to victory lay in "collaborated operations between air and sea units with no hesitation to die."

Ironically, the men of the 4th Air Group—or what was left of it—became heroes in Japan. According to the claims submitted to Combined Fleet headquarters by Rear Admiral Yamada, the air units from Rabaul had crushed the enemy fleet at Guadalcanal on August 7 and 8. In his diary, Chief of Staff Ugaki noted the alleged results: "two light cruisers and ten transports sunk, one large cruiser set on fire, one medium cruiser seriously damaged and listing heavily, two destroyers and one transport set on fire, and four planes shot down. This should be called a great result."

The basis for Yamada's incredible exaggeration can only be surmised. Meanwhile, the Combined Fleet received a new report that "five enemy cruisers were sunk by a sudden night assault." This information was much closer to the truth. On August 7, a powerful Eighth Fleet cruiser group commanded by Vice Admiral Mikawa had sortied from Rabaul to attack the American amphibious force. The warships sheltered near Bougainville on the eighth while awaiting nightfall, then slipped down "the Slot" in the darkness and surprised the outer screen of Australian and American warships. In a vicious few minutes off Savo Island, Mikawa's ships sank four cruisers in exchange for relatively minor damage to two vessels. With the exception of the surprise attack on Pearl Harbor, the battle was one of the worst defeats in the history of the U.S. Navy.

Seizing on the initial reports of the two separate actions, the Combined Fleet Staff allowed themselves to be misled. "Putting the [results] together," Ugaki wrote, "we believe that all the warships and half of the transports have been sunk, and the fate of the battle has now been settled." Even so, the staff at Truk remained cautious while awaiting confirmation of the reports. Having experienced blatant exaggerations before, Ugaki urged the staff to "be ready for any change of plans."

The same could not be said of Imperial General Headquarters or the *Johokyoku*. In a nationwide radio broadcast on August 10, the chief of naval information declared that the American offensive had "ended in a fiasco." Newspaper headlines the next day boasted that twenty-eight Allied warships and transports had been sunk or damaged at Guadalcanal. Four days later, alleging that the results were based on "verified reports," the press raised the figures to twenty-nine warships and eleven transports sunk or otherwise destroyed. Friendly losses warranted only a brief explanation: "21 planes of the Imperial Navy crashed themselves against enemy warcraft." This, too, was a blatant exaggeration, but it served to venerate the fact that so many land attack aircraft had not returned from the mission.

The Allied losses, especially when compared to the total number of ships involoved, were not as disastrous as the Japanese claimed. In addition to the four cruisers sunk off Savo Island, transport *George F. Elliott* was scuttled as a result of the fires started on August 8. The destroyer *Jarvis*, hampered by the aforementioned torpedo damage, was caught in the open sea on the afternoon August 9 by a large force of *rikko*. The captain's decision to try to reach Australia for repairs led to a rare occurrence— the loss of a warship with all hands. Steaming slowly about 130 nautical miles southwest of Tulagi, *Jarvis* was attacked by thirteen Bettys of the Misawa Air Group escorted by fifteen Zeros. Mistaking the warship for an *Achilles*-class cruiser, the airmen from Rabaul put two more torpedoes into *Jarvis*—but not before the destroyer's guns shot down two attacking Bettys and damaged several others.

Although the loss of six ships was far less than the Japanese claimed, the U.S. Navy had suffered a severe blow. Even more problematic, especially from the standpoint of the marines on Guadalcanal, Vice Admiral Fletcher withdrew his carrier task force on August 8. In addition to fretting over the loss of more than twenty Wildcats during the first two days of operations, he cited the need to refuel his ships in safer waters. As a result of Fletcher's decision, the commander of the amphibious fleet also withdrew his ships from Guadalcanal, leaving the marines on their own. The absence of the ships was interpreted by the Japanese as further evidence of a great naval victory, giving them the impression that the Americans on Guadalcanal were weak and demoralized.

The story of the prolonged, bitter struggle that ensued is now legendary. For the Japanese, Guadalcanal became a veritable meat grinder. Tens of thousands of soldiers, most delivered by fast warships from Rabaul, either died from combat or succumbed to disease and starvation. Similarly, the Eleventh Air Fleet launched attacks almost daily from Rabaul, weather permitting, but the losses accrued at an appalling rate. Only the surface units of the Eighth Fleet enjoyed occasional success, particularly in night actions, yet they could not break the Allies' toehold in the Solomons.

By late September, the strain of the mounting losses over Guadalcanal was contributing to the poor health of Vice Admiral Tsukahara, commander of the Eleventh Air Fleet. Suffering from a combination of dengue fever, malaria, and "a stomach and intestinal ailment," he was sent home to Japan for recuperation. His replacement, Vice Adm. Jinichi Kusaka, arrived at Truk on October 7 for briefings with the Combined Fleet Staff. Raised in Ichikawa Prefecture, Kusaka had spent the past several years in administrative positions, most recently as director of the naval academy. During his time at Etajima, which followed his posting as director of the bureau of education, Kusaka had grown accustomed to the trappings and privileges of flag rank. Sometime after his arrival at Rabaul on October 8, he was pleased to discover that there were thousands of horses on New Britain. (The South Seas Detachment had brought 4,500 animals and even a veterinary detachment with the original invasion fleet in January.) The fifty-three-year-old admiral typically started his day with an early morning ride, often accompanied by one or more of his staff officers. Refined, with a slender build and pleasant features, Kusaka also had a habit of napping after lunch, even when the war was in full swing at Rabaul.

SHORTLY AFTER Kusaka's arrival, a major expansion of the aviation presence in and around Rabaul commenced. To support the ongoing battles for Guadalcanal and New Guinea, the Japanese decided to concentrate as many aircraft as possible in the Southeast Area. To make room for additional land- and carrier-based naval air groups, improvements were made to the existing airdromes and construction of several new fields was initiated.

Work on the first new airdrome on New Britain began as early as October 1942, when portions of two coconut plantations east of Kokopo were cleared. Progress was slow, for the Japanese had no bulldozers.

Army tanks were used to push down trees, but much of the effort to clear away the debris was done by POWs and labor gangs. Eventually the field boasted a 4,350-foot concrete runway near the shoreline of St. George's Channel. The Allies called it Rapopo, borrowing the name of the nearest plantation.

The field at Kavieng, New Ireland, was also expanded, though it was too far from Guadalcanal—approximately 780 statute miles—to support the battle directly. Therefore, the Japanese turned their attention to an existing airstrip on Buka Island, across a narrow passage from the big island of Bougainville. The Japanese had dawdled with improvements since occupying the island in March. Built before the war by the RAAF, the field was deemed unsuitable for major expansion when first inspected by the Japanese in mid-July, but it became much more important when Guadalcanal was invaded three weeks later. Construction personnel installed a power plant and underground fuel tanks, added defensive works, and surfaced the 2,300-foot runway with bitumen, a mixture of crushed coral and asphalt.

Simultaneously, surveyors began laying out a new airfield on the southern tip of Bougainville, near a village called Buin. (The Allies knew the location as Kahili in reference to a smaller but closer native village.) The engineers hoped to have the field ready to handle a *chutai* of Zeros by the third week of September, but excessive rain and harassing attacks by American planes caused delays. Declared operational approximately a month behind schedule, the field was plagued with problems. Rear Admiral Ugaki noted in his diary on October 25 that "every time it rained heavily, about ten planes were damaged due to skidding."

While the new strip at Buin was being completed, the Japanese conceived a plan to build an advance base at Munda Point on New Georgia Island. By late October the American air presence at Henderson Field (named in honor of Maj. Lofton R. Henderson, killed at Midway) had been reduced by attrition, leading the Japanese to believe they could build the new field in secrecy. To disguise its location on the western coast of New Georgia, workers completed most of the perimeter areas first. They labored beneath gigantic screens made by wiring the tops of palm trees together, which created the illusion of intact coconut groves. Despite the clever concealments, the airfield's presence was reported to Guadalcanal by coastwatcher Donald G. "Danny" Kennedy, a New

Zealander. Reconnaissance flights also revealed extensive small-boat traffic and piles of crushed coral at the construction site. The Allies tried to intervene, but the Japanese had gotten a significant headstart and managed to complete the airfield in early December.

Venturing even closer to Guadalcanal, the Imperial Navy also constructed a seaplane base at Rekata Bay, Santa Isabel Island, practically on the Allies' doorstep. Located only 155 miles northwest of Henderson Field, Rekata Bay served as a forward base for Mitsubishi F1M ("Pete") float planes as well as A6M2-N "Rufes." In addition, it provided a ditching location for aircraft that sustained combat damage over Guadalcanal.

WHILE THE JAPANESE improved existing airfields and built new ones, the Allies were doing the same on New Guinea. By late 1942 the number of bases at Port Moresby had almost quadrupled. The airdromes, named for their distance from town, included Three Mile, Five Mile, Seven Mile, Twelve Mile, Fourteen Mile, and Seventeen Mile. There was even a Thirty Mile strip used occasionally for fighter dispersal and emergency landings. The proliferation was such that new names were in order, simply to avoid potentially dangerous situations involving the takeoff and landing patterns associated with each runway. On November 10, all but the original Kila Kila airdrome (Three Mile) were renamed to honor dead warriors.

Seven Mile, still the biggest field and the hub of aerial operations at Port Moresby, was officially renamed Jackson Field as a tribute to "Old John" Jackson, killed in action while leading 75 Squadron during the desperate defense of Port Moresby. Five Mile was renamed Ward's Airdrome (also known as Ward's Strip), honoring the Australian whose battalion had begun construction of the field in mid-1942. Lieutenant Colonel Kenneth H. Ward was killed in action during the Kokoda Trail campaign in late August.

Compared to the deeds of Jackson and Ward, the criteria for some of the other selections were obscure. Twelve Mile was named for Maj. Jack W. Berry, lost on August 4 when his P-39 crashed at sea shortly after taking off from Port Moresby. Lieutenant Charles Schwimmer, 8th Fighter Group, 36th Fighter Squadron, was one of three Airacobra pilots who failed to return from a strafing mission against Lae on May 4, but for unknown reasons he was singled out as the namesake of Fourteen Mile. Another

P-39 driver, Ed Durand, was the first American fighter pilot lost in action over the New Guinea region. Shot down during a fighter sweep over Lae on April 30, he was rumored to have been executed by the Japanese, and Seventeen Mile airdrome was renamed in his honor. Finally, Thirty Mile was renamed Rogers Airdrome for the popular Maj. "Buck" Rogers, commanding officer of the 8th Bomb Squadron, 3rd Bomb Group, whose A-24 dive-bomber was one of several shot down during a disastrous mission against Gona on July 29.

The new field at Milne Bay, which supported the campaign against the enemy strongholds on the northeastern coast of New Guinea, also deserves mention. Completed during the fall of 1942, it was named for Sqn. Ldr. Charles R. Gurney, killed when his B-26 flipped upside down in a swamp on Kirawina Island after a bombing mission against Rabaul.

BY LATE OCTOBER, despite heavy losses in men and materiel, the Japanese still dominated the territory. More importantly, Imperial General Headquarters' commitment to winning the war in the Southeast Area had not diminished. A new plan to retake Henderson Field, scheduled for late October, received the fullest cooperation of Admiral Yamamoto. It was still his dream that Vice Adm. Chuichi Nagumo's carrier fleet would smash the Pacific Fleet in a decisive battle. The opposing forces collided north of the Santa Cruz Islands on October 26, resulting in a tactical victory for the Japanese. Nagumo's bombers and torpedo planes sank a carrier (USS *Hornet*) and a destroyer, while also inflicting serious damage on another carrier (USS *Enterprise*) and two additional destroyers. In exchange, the Japanese received crippling damage to carriers *Shokaku* and *Zuiho*. Of far greater importance was the loss of nearly 150 naval aviators. The toll was so great, in fact, that two undamaged carriers sailed back to Japan due to the lack of adequate aircrews.

At Truk, the Combined Fleet Staff was informed that Nagumo's planes had sunk a "*Saratoga*-type" carrier, a "*Yorktown*-type" carrier, two "new type" carriers, a battleship, and one unidentified warship. In addition, the Japanese had allegedly damaged a battleship, three cruisers, and a destroyer. It appeared that Yamamoto's goal of destroying U.S. sea power in the South Pacific had finally been fulfilled. Although the operation's goal of capturing Henderson Field failed, the navy was pleased to claim an overwhelming victory at Santa Cruz.

As a result of their presumption that the Allied forces were greatly diminished, the Japanese initiated yet another offensive against Guadalcanal. But there was one important difference: due to the damage sustained by Nagumo's carrier forces, aerial support for the next campaign would depend almost entirely on the Eleventh Air Fleet at Rabaul. A secondary difference, one not immediately apparent to the Allies, was a fleet-wide reorganization of the Imperial Navy. On November 1, the once proudly used names for aviation units were replaced with a standardized numeric system that identified groups by aircraft type and mission. The Tainan Air Group, for example, lost its fabled identity in favor of a bureaucratic number, becoming simply Air Group 251. After the shuffling, the forces available to Vice Admiral Kusaka included eleven air groups and two group detachments, divided among several flotillas. At Kavieng, the 1st Air Attack Force averaged about fifteen to twenty Zeros and twenty-five to thirty Bettys in operational status. The 5th Air Attack Force at Rabaul and Lae usually had twenty-five to thirty fighters ready at any given time, and the 6th Air Attack Force (Rabaul and Buin) typically had fifteen to twenty Zeros and thirty to forty Bettys in readiness. Additional aircraft included the Type 99 dive-bombers of Air Group 581, based at Buin, from which the Vals had adequate range to reach Henderson Field and return.

The Japanese air campaign against Guadalcanal resumed on November 11 as the Eleventh Air Fleet attempted to soften up Allied positions prior to the next big push. But the army's portion of the shared offensive was doomed from the start. The transport force, carrying ten thousand soldiers and many tons of supplies, was attacked relentlessly on November 14 by nearly every Allied combat plane on Guadalcanal. Six of eleven transports were sunk or deliberately beached, and only a small fraction of the ammunition and food was delivered.

The air campaign fared no better. Lieutenant Commander Fumio Iwatani, who served with the land attack units, later provided a remarkable glimpse of the struggle from the Japanese perspective.

[It] was impossible for us to continue this affluent operation as long as our logistical strength was weak. Historically we were told that the chances of victory in war are 70/30. It was taught to us that even when we were gasping under heavy damage, the enemy was also suffering. Therefore, we should press the enemy even harder, with our all might, and grab the victory. However, facing an enemy seemingly immortal to damage, we felt utterly incapable of keeping up. In the face of this war of attrition, our replacement troops, which were sent to us several times, disappeared like bubbles. The food and arms supply for [soldiers on] Guadalcanal became increasingly difficult to provide, despite our best effort, and people started to call Guadalcanal "starvation island."

In late November, recognizing that the Seventeenth Army was no longer capable of conducting effective operations on Guadalcanal as well as New Guinea, Imperial General Headquarters created the Eighteenth Army to take over the New Guinea campaign. To coordinate and administer the two armies, a new supervisory command, the Eighth Area Army, was established at Rabaul. Lieutenant General Hitoshi Imamura, placed in command of the new headquarters, paused at Truk during his journey from Japan and met with the Combined Fleet Staff. The outcome of their conference on November 21 was the difficult but necessary decision to give up the battle for Buna.

Lieutenant General Hatazo Adachi, commander of the newly created Eighteenth Army, also visited the Combined Fleet to discuss his forthcoming role. During supper that night in the wardroom of *Yamato*, Admiral Yamamoto made an astonishing prediction, telling Adachi that in all likelihood his soldiers would "never come back alive" from New Guinea. Yamamoto then smiled and said: "I, too, will not be able to go back home unless Guadalcanal is recaptured, so I am depending on your army."

The commander in chief's words were not only frank, but prophetically accurate.

CHAPTER 23

Heavy Bomber Blues

S HORTLY BEFORE GENERAL KENNEY headed overseas in the summer of 1942, he arranged for the shipment of fifty P-38 Lightnings from his previous command, the Fourth Air Force, to Australia. The first batch of twenty-five disassembled fighters arrived at Brisbane in mid-August, whereupon Kenney ordered his aviation support specialist, Brig. Gen. Carl W. Connell, to personally oversee the reassembly of the aircraft. Kenney also instructed Connell to obtain contracts with local sheet metal fabricators for the manufacture of ten thousand 150-gallon external drop tanks, which would greatly extend the Lightnings' range.

The combat debut of the P-38 in the Southwest Pacific was eagerly anticipated. Already something of an icon among fighters, the twin-engine Lightning was a big, unorthodox aircraft. The pilot sat in a central pod between the in-line engines, which were mounted in long, streamlined booms that tapered back to twin vertical stabilizers. Twice the size of a Zero, the P-38 boasted a powerful armament package of four .50-caliber machine guns and one 20mm automatic cannon in its smooth, pointed nose. The pair of sixteen-cylinder, turbo-supercharged engines produced a total of 2,300 horsepower, enabling speeds of almost four hundred miles per hour. (A photoreconnaissance version, modified to hold a pair of vertical cameras in place of the standard weapons package, was even faster.) But the excitement that accompanied the arrival of the new fighters soon gave way to frustration. The reassembled P-38s were plagued by an embarrassing array of defects, including missing parts, leaks in the fuel tanks and intercoolers, and faulty electrical power inverters. Due to the time required to correct the problems, the first squadron would not become operational until mid-November.

In the meantime, Kenney looked forward to bolstering his heavy bomber force when the B-24s of the 90th Bomb Group arrived in Australia. But once again there were vexing problems. The fledgling group, formed in July, was presently attached to the Seventh Bomber Command in Hawaii. Oddly, the group commander had developed an aversion to the B-24, perhaps due to unflattering comments made publicly by Charles Lindbergh, the famed trans-Atlantic aviator, who questioned the safety of the big bomber. Immediately after arriving in Hawaii, Lt. Col. Eugene P. Mussett and one of his squadron commanders voiced displeasure with their Liberators and demanded B-17s. Catching wind of the conflict, General "Hap" Arnold advised both Kenney and the Seventh Air Force commander that an "acute problem" existed within the 90th Bomb Group's leadership. Within days, Mussett and the squadron commander were replaced.

Under the new leadership of thirty-eight-year-old Col. Arthur W. Meehan, a West Pointer, the B-24s crossed the Pacific in early November. Considering the many inherent dangers of the five-thousand-mile journey, particularly the lack of navigational aids, it was a significant accomplishment that none of the forty-eight planes was lost. However, soon after the Liberators arrived in Australia, a rash of nose gear failures required the temporary grounding of the whole group. Replacement parts from the States proved faulty, so Australian machine shops were called upon to manufacture the needed items.

On November 13, three squadrons of B-24s moved to Iron Range, a brand-new airdrome on the remote Cape York Peninsula in northern Queensland. Having spent the past months in the splendor of Hawaii, the crews were dismayed to find primitive conditions at their new base. The two runways were not yet surfaced, and the living facilities consisted of tent cities.

Despite the unfavorable conditions, or perhaps because of them, Colonel Meehan scheduled the group's first combat mission just two days later. The crews were green as grass, barely trained, but they were enthusiastic. Copying a trend that was spreading like wildfire throughout the army, they customized the billboard-sized noses of their Liberators with a vast spectrum of nicknames and colorful artwork. The B-24s were named for regions and girls and almost everything in between: *Big Emma*, *Little Eva*, *Texas Terror*, *Cowtown's Revenge*, *Hellzapoppin*, *Moby Dick*, and dozens more.

On the evening of November 14, Meehan positioned nine Liberators at Port Moresby. The next morning, eight took off in the early hours to bomb the Buin-Faisi anchorage off the southern coast of Bougainville. No enemy ships were hit, and the inaugural mission cost the group two Liberators. One, damaged by antiaircraft fire, cracked up off New Guinea during a ditching attempt that went awry, and eight of the ten crewmembers perished. The other B-24 crash-landed on a beach near Iron Range with no casualties.

Determined to lead by example, Meehan ordered an even more ambitious strike the very next night. In hindsight, his choice of targets was ill advised. He planned to attack Rabaul, the most heavily defended bastion in the South Pacific, commencing with a night takeoff from the yet-unfinished strip at Iron Range. Fifteen crews from the 319th, 320th, and 400th Bomb Squadrons would depart at regular intervals beginning at 2300, and proceed individually at specific power settings designed to bring them together at approximately 0400 near Rabaul.

But large-scale operations are never easy, especially when conducted at night by an inexperienced unit working from an unfinished airdrome. Meehan got airborne on time in *Punjab*, piloted by Maj. Raymond S. Morse, commanding officer of the 320th Bomb Squadron, but immediately thereafter confusion set in. Due to poor airfield lighting and the absence of ground communications, several Liberators got out of position as they attempted to line up in the darkness. The crew of *Big Emma*, forced to abort the mission for mechanical reasons, pulled off to the side and parked among other non-participating bombers. Because there were no revetments, the planes were lined up dangerously close to the runway. Long minutes elapsed, and the next bomber did not take off until 2314, creating a sense of urgency among the remaining crews. To make matters worse, the whirling propellers of each departing Liberator kicked up a "Kansas-size dust storm," making the dim runway marker lights virtually impossible to see.

The combination of problems created a recipe for disaster. The eleventh Liberator to accelerate down the runway, *Bombs to Nippon*, piloted by Lt. Paul R. Larson of the 400th Bomb Squadron, veered off center and clipped the nose of *Big Emma*. Going out of control, Larson's B-24 impacted two other parked bombers with a sickening crash, and its 2,800 gallons of high-octane gasoline burst into orange-and-yellow flames. Moments later the payload of bombs exploded, wiping out Larson and his entire crew. An unlucky lineman, perched atop one of the parked bombers to observe the take-off, was also killed. Debris was scattered everywhere, forcing the closure of the runway and stranding the last four bombers waiting to take off. It was just as well, for two of the idling B-24s had sustained damage from the accident.

The mission itself was no less disastrous. Of the ten Liberators that took off prior to Larson's crash, only five reached Rabaul due to stormy conditions. Ultimately, only one B-24 dropped its bombs over the wharf area, causing no damage to the Japanese.

Later that morning, the news turned even worse. One by one, nine Liberators straggled back to Iron Range to find the cleanup from Larson's crash still underway. But there was no sign of *Punjab*; in fact, nothing had been heard from the crew since their departure. Ten men had flown off into the night sky, never to be seen again. The most bizarre element of *Punjab*'s disappearance was the fact that Major Morse, a former B-17 pilot who had replaced the squadron commander sacked in Hawaii, was convinced he would die. Two weeks previously, just as he was about to board a B-24 for the trip across the Pacific, someone had offered to help him with his belongings. Morse declined, claiming "he had no gear (except a bottle of whiskey and a change of underwear) because he expected to die and didn't want anyone to have to send all his stuff back to Hawaii." But not even Morse could have foreseen that his first mission would be his last.

The loss of four aircraft and thirty men in two combat missions stunned the 90th Bomb Group. General Kenney, who was in New Guinea to oversee a new counteroffensive against Buna, ordered Ken Walker to restrict the group from combat "until they had learned more about night flying and navigation and had done some practice bombing and gunnery." But this put Kenney in a bind. The 19th Bomb Group, having completed its final bombing mission over Rabaul on October 28, was now back in the States. With the B-24s temporarily out of combat, Kenney's only heavies were the Fortresses of the 43rd Bomb Group. Therefore, after barely a week of remedial training, the B-24s resumed combat operations. Colonel Ralph E. "Zipper" Koon took command of the group, which primarily conducted reconnaissance missions.The next attempt to bomb Rabaul came on December 7, the one-year anniversary of the Pearl Harbor attack. But the weather was "abominable," and none of the crews that reached the target area were able to pick out worthwhile targets.

Unfortunately, the group's run of bad luck continued. Eleven Liberators either fell out of the sky or never returned to base in just the first six weeks of operations. Most of the losses were the result of accidents or malfunctions, not combat, and the number of casualties was astounding: eighty-four crewmembers either dead or missing. Understandably, the group's morale plummeted.

One of the most unsettling losses occurred the day after Christmas, when another fifteen-bomber raid was attempted on Rabaul. In a tragic replay of the group's first effort in mid-November, a Liberator crashed while taking off. The right outboard engine of *Heavenly Body*, piloted by Lt. Roy B. Kendrick of the 400th Bomb Squadron, apparently failed just as he lifted off from Iron Range on the rainy night of December 26. Slicing to the right, the heavily loaded B-24 crashed into the woods off the end of the runway, and the inevitable fire touched off three massive explosions. One badly wounded crewmember was found alive among the wreckage, but he died less than two hours after rescuers dragged him from the flames.

Thirteen aircrews were still waiting in line to take off. Badly shaken by the horrendous crash, they were given the option of standing down from the mission, and several elected not to fly. Those that chose to continue, led by "Zipper" Koon, were ninety minutes behind schedule as they took off over the burning pyre of Kendrick's aircraft.

CHAPTER 24

Medal of Honor: Kenneth N. Walker

THE UNFORTUNATE LOSSES suffered by the 90th Bomb Group represented only one of several concerns facing Ken Walker during the closing weeks of 1942. Tasked with keeping pressure on the Japanese, both in New Guinea and the northern Solomons, he fretted almost daily over the lack of heavy bombers. He also experienced personal frustrations resulting from a series of disagreements with General Kenney. The two men usually got along, but on a number of specific issues their egos clashed.

Walker had dedicated his career to the application of strategic daylight formation bombing, which made it difficult for him to accept some of Kenney's innovations, such as skip-bombing and the use of parafrag bombs. One result was that he resisted when Kenney asked for a trial period using bombs fitted with instantaneous fuses against enemy shipping. Walker was supposed to be the bombing expert, and his strategies had been highly regarded in Washington. But in the Southwest Pacific, the situation was much different than Walker had expected. Kenney had his own agenda, and he also had the wholehearted support of his former aide, Major Benn, who now commanded the squadron involved in testing the fuses. Perhaps even more annoying, from Walker's point of view, was the fact that Benn had a direct line of communication with Kenney.

According to one of the 63rd Bomb Squadron's pilots, Benn exercised the privilege routinely. "I shared a tent with Benn in Australia," recalled James C. Dieffenderfer. "He'd go to the communications shack every night and teletype back and forth with Kenney. They'd plan missions and discuss what they were going to do."

There is little doubt that such cronyism created problems for Walker and probably fostered resentment as well. He was an outsider again, while Benn and Kenney shared their own private plans and ideas. After using instantaneous fuses for only a few anti-shipping strikes, Walker reverted to using delayed-action fuses for subsequent missions. Benn, well aware that Kenney had ordered a significant test period, placed himself in the crossfire by ignoring Walker and continuing to use the instantaneous fuses whenever his squadron was scheduled for a mission.

The showdown came in Australia on October 15. All three men participated in a series of awards ceremonies, whereupon Kenney learned that Walker "had been giving Bill Benn the devil for not obeying orders." Digging a little deeper into the controversy, Kenney discovered that Walker had stopped using the instantaneous fuses, which made his criticism of Benn seem hypocritical.

Kenney tried a diplomatic solution. First, he reminded Benn that Walker was his boss—and his orders were to be obeyed. Next, he informed Walker that he wanted a month-long trial using the instantaneous fuses. If he heard any more about delayed-action fuses being used, he would rescind Walker's privilege of specifying the settings. For the next month Walker adhered to the orders, but when Kenney returned to Port Moresby on November 19, Walker approached him again about using delayed-action fuses.

Although the variation between an instantaneous fuse and a 1/10-second delayed fuse might seem miniscule, Kenney was eager to show that the effects could be remarkably different. Arranging a demonstration, he and Walker watched as several bombs with instantaneous fuses were dropped near the hulk of the SS *Pruth*. All of the bombs missed, striking the water at distances of twenty-five to seventy-five yards from the ship. The two generals then rode a motor launch out to the reef where they transferred into a smaller boat to be rowed in close to the old wreck. As they moved alongside the rusted ship, Kenney triumphantly pointed out fresh gashes in the hull, some of them impressively large. The evidence was overwhelming: the bombs with instantaneous fuses had exploded on contact with the water, sending shrapnel from the casings in every direction. Even when the bombs missed by a wide margin, the jagged shards caused serious damage.

"Okay," Walker conceded. "You win."

Kenney allegedly savored his victory by making Walker row the boat back to the launch. If true, the embarrassment must have infuriated Walker, but he "thawed out" at Brigadier General Whitehead's quarters in Port Moresby after a few cocktails.

Despite the fact that the dispute over fuses had been settled, Kenney apparently began to question Walker's suitability and considered sending him back to Washington. He admired Walker's determination and tireless work ethic but also regarded him as "stubborn, oversensitive and a prima donna." Furthermore, Kenney was concerned that Walker, being "keyed up all the time," would not hold up under the stresses he constantly placed on himself.

Born in a remote New Mexico town in 1898, Ken Walker had spent most of his life with a chip on his shoulder. He was an only child whose father left when Ken was very young, and the abandonment had a lasting impact on his formative years. One of his own sons would later write: "My father was raised by his mother in a hardscrabble environment, and perhaps much of his personality was shaped by . . . the need to protect his mother and take on anyone who posed a threat."

As an adult, Walker was focused on his military career and the development of strategic bombing. One acquaintance remembered him for his "near total involvement with himself and his ideas," which may explain Walker's occasional defiance of General Kenney. On October 5, for example, Kenney told him in no uncertain terms to stop participating in combat missions. But Walker, ever the hands-on leader, continually ignored the verbal order.

In his defense, Walker was not the only general flying over enemy territory. During a return visit to Port Moresby on December 16, Kenney learned that both Walker and Ennis Whitehead had recently participated in separate, hair-raising missions. Whitehead had been aboard a B-25 that returned from a reconnaissance flight with a big hole in one wing from an antiaircraft shell, and Walker flew as an observer in a B-17 that clipped a tree while barge-hunting along the New Guinea coast, ripping off a three-foot chunk of the left wing.

Kenney chided both men, telling them once again "to stop flying combat missions." He was worried not only about losing them in combat but by what they would suffer if captured. "We had plenty of evidence that the Nips had tortured their prisoners until they either died or talked," he later wrote. "After the prisoners talked they were beheaded anyhow, but most of them had broken under the strain. I told Walker that frankly I didn't believe he could take it without telling everything he knew, so I was not going to let him go on any more combat missions."

Several days after Kenney's visit, Walker ordered another strike against Rabaul. For the past several weeks, his heavy bomber groups had been focused primarily on attacking convoys in the waters between New Britain and New Guinea. Consisting of heavily armed warships, the convoys were also protected by Zeros, resulting in intense air-sea battles and the loss of several heavy bombers. During one particularly costly week ending in early December, the 43rd Bomb Group lost four B-17s and their crews in exchange for one Japanese destroyer sunk and three damaged. Determined to hit the enemy's supply line where it would hurt the most—at the main terminal—Walker scheduled a major effort against Rabaul for the night of December 26.

The plan called for both the 43rd and 90th Bomb Groups to take part, but the crash of Roy Kendrick's B-24 at Iron Range that rainy night affected the latter group's participation. Of the fifteen Liberators scheduled to take part, all but a few dropped out after the accident. The situation was nearly as bad at Port Moresby, where the 43rd Bomb Group had only six Fortresses available for the mission. Surprisingly, the small number of B-17s achieved one of the group's most successful attacks to date. Led by Maj. Edward W. Scott Jr., the B-17s were officially credited with sinking one transport—but they actually sank two and also damaged a destroyer.

Scott released four bombs while attacking a large merchant vessel anchored just off Lakunai airdrome. His crew reported that the ship, later identified as the 5,859-ton *Italy Maru*, briefly caught fire, though none of the crewmembers could offer additional details. A reconnaissance photo taken several hours later showed the ship on its side, and credit for the sinking was duly awarded.

Other crews also scored but did not observe the results directly. An army cargo ship named *Tsurugisan Maru* was sunk that night, and the destroyer *Tachikaze* was badly damaged by a direct hit on the bow. The warship's captain, Lt. Cmdr. Yasumi Hirasata, was among those killed. The successful attacker was probably *Double Trouble*, a B-17F whose crew reported making four runs on a "cruiser." (One of the more creatively named bombers in the Fifth Air Force, the B-17 wore *Double Trouble* on the left side of the nose, and *Ka-Puhio-Wela*, the Hawaiian phrase for double trouble, on the opposite side.)

At Truk, the damaging raid got the attention of the Combined Fleet chief of staff, Matome Ugaki, who had been promoted to vice admiral the previous month. He noted in his diary that "B-17s obstinately attacked Rabaul last night" and also expounded on the problems the raids were causing: "For some time we've keenly felt the need of devising some effective countermeasures against B-17s. Against their tactics of coming to attack at daytime without being discovered, or attacking at night, dropping parachute flares, we hardly could do more than fold our arms. If our losses add up in this way, finally we would be unable to do anything but live in caves, or retreat. Now we must study this hard."

Ugaki could not have known that his projections would come true. More than two years after his speculation, the Japanese garrison began tunneling an extensive and elaborate network of caves in the volcanic soil around Simpson Harbor.

AS THE YEAR 1942 drew to a close, Allied reconnaissance flights revealed that Simpson Harbor was again crowded with ships. The hard-luck 90th Bomb Group did not fly another attack mission during the last few days of 1942, but seven Fortresses from the 43rd Bomb Group bombed Rabaul at approximately 0530 on December 30. Led by Major Scott and Captain McCullar, the crews made individual bombing runs at five thousand to six thousand feet. McCullar scored a direct hit on an unidentified vessel that caused a "large flash followed by fire and black smoke." Another crew claimed a nearly identical result, perhaps not by coincidence.

Jim Murphy, flying a B-17F named *Snoopy*, dropped down to skip-bomb two transports and claimed that he sank both with a single attack run, a feat he later described at length in his memoir. Murphy was officially credited with sinking one eight-thousand-ton vessel, while the second ship, which he estimated at ten thousand tons, was downgraded to a "probable." (The only loss to the Japanese that night was *Tomiura Maru*, a small cargo ship that sank on the opposite side of Simpson Harbor from where Murphy described his action. Most likely it was the victim of Ken McCullar's crew.)

The following night, New Year's Eve, six B-17s attacked Lakunai airdrome. Each Fortress carried a bomb load of eight 500-pounders wrapped with wire. "That package was the most positive method we had to ensure destruction of everything within a hundred yards," wrote Murphy, who was taking part in his second Rabaul mission in as many days. The returning crews reported secondary explosions on the airdrome, but Japanese records show no corresponding damage. Whether or not the wire-wrapped bombs caused much destruction, the year ended noisily at Rabaul, with dozens of big explosions.

AT TRUK, Admiral Yamamoto was probably not in a celebratory mood as he contemplated the end of 1942. Having opened the year with a string of brilliant victories, his naval forces were reeling. The concerns shared by many Japanese were expressed by Yamamoto's right-hand man, Vice Admiral Ugaki, in his diary. "The year 1942 is going to pass tonight," he wrote. "How brilliant was the first-stage operation up to April! And what miserable setbacks since Midway in June! The invasions of Hawaii, Fiji, Samoa, and New Caledonia, [the] liberation of India and destruction of the British Far Eastern Fleet have all scattered like dreams. Meanwhile, not to speak of capturing Port Moresby, but the recovery of Guadalcanal . . . turned out to be impossible."

The Allies were unaware of just how devastating the failed operations had been for the Japanese. Within days, Yamamoto would order KE Operation, a naval mission to evacuate the remnants of the units on Guadalcanal by warship. Ultimately some thirteen thousand emaciated troops would be rescued, but by the time the operation concluded in early February 1943, the Japanese had left nineteen thousand dead on Guadalcanal. Another thousand, mostly laborers, had been captured.

In terms of deprivation, New Guinea was even worse. Between late July and mid-August 1942, the Japanese had landed more than twelve thousand troops in the Buna area for the push across the Owen Stanley Mountains. When that effort was thwarted on the Kokoda Trail in September, the starving survivors gradually withdrew to a narrow defensive pocket near Buna. Another five thousand reinforcements were delivered from Rabaul, but the persistent Allied air attacks on the convoys eventually forced the Japanese to use submarines for delivering supplies.

As cargo vessels, the subs were completely inadequate. Although twenty tons of supplies were delivered on the nights of December 19 and 20, the Seventeenth Army chief of staff appealed for more food just four days later. The soldiers, he wrote, were "only keeping themselves alive by eating tree buds, coconuts, and seaweed." Later it was discovered that some Japanese had resorted to cannibalism.

The failed Buna campaign cost the lives of approximately twelve thousand men, including that of Major General Horii. On November 19, while scouting the coastline of New Guinea in a native canoe, he and two staff officers were swept out to sea by a sudden squall. The canoe swamped, drowning the conqueror of Rabaul and his chief of staff.

And yet, despite the costly setbacks at Buna and Guadalcanal, the Japanese were still arguably stronger than the Allies in the Southwest Pacific. The Imperial Navy completed its new airdromes on Bougainville and New Georgia, and in mid-December, Eighteenth Army units landed at Madang and Wewak on the north coast of New Guinea. Construction battalions built a network of airdromes for Imperial Army air regiments, thus reinforcing the western flank of Rabaul. For every advance by the Allies, the Japanese put up additional roadblocks.

EVIDENCE THAT the Japanese still held the advantage was photographed at Rabaul on December 30. No less than twenty-one warships occupied the anchorages, along with approximately seventy merchant vessels totaling an estimated three hundred thousand tons. "When the Jap accumulates that much tonnage," wrote General Kenney on the first day of 1943, "it means trouble for me shortly."

It is likely that Kenney also received Ultra intercepts revealing enemy plans for the deployment of a vital convoy to New Guinea. (A term first coined by the British, "Ultra" became the catch-all name for message intercepts in World War II. The highest security classification then available was Most Secret, but message decoding was considered even more specialized, or *ultra*-secret.) Separately, intelligence analysts noted a sharp increase in enemy air patrols over Lae and the Huon Gulf, a strong indicator of the convoy's intended destination. Hoping to "break the movement up at the source," Kenney told Walker to plan an all-out attack against Simpson Harbor. Only essential reconnaissance flights were to be conducted during the next few days so that the heavy bomb groups could perform much-needed maintenance.

According to Kenney's memoirs, Walker was instructed to schedule the attack for January 5, at dawn. Two days prior to the mission, Walker approached Kenney to request a change: he wanted to hit Rabaul at midday instead.

Walker was evidently worried about the participation of the 90th Bomb Group, a logical concern considering the group's string of bad luck, particularly during night operations. Recently, the group had implemented a program of rotating one squadron to Port Moresby for a week at a time while the other three squadrons operated from Iron Range. In order for the Australia-based Liberators to hit Rabaul at dawn, they would have to take off in the middle of the night and then rendezvous with the participants from Port Moresby—a daunting and potentially hazardous maneuver to attempt in the darkness. Walker wanted to delay the takeoff until after daybreak, reasoning that a noon attack would enable better concentration of defensive firepower and also yield a tighter bombard-ment pattern. Having spent his whole career advocating these tactics, Walker was anxious to implement them.

But Kenney was not persuaded. Convinced that the "Nip fighters" would fiercely contest the bombers at midday and ruin their accuracy, he told Walker to stick with the original plan. Kenney explained that he "would rather have the bombers not in formation for a dawn attack than in formation for a show at noon."

If Kenney's memoirs are accurate, Walker received clear orders, but he did not follow them. Something even stronger than the fundamentals of duty and honor—perhaps stubbornness, or deeply rooted convictions, or just the fact that he was tired of losing arguments to Kenney—compelled Walker to defy his boss. He delayed the takeoff time, but did not inform Kenney. Moreover, when the strike plan was distributed to the participants the day prior to the mission, the most successful heavy bombing squadron in the theater was not included in "the show." Despite the fact that Kenney had ordered "a full-scale bomber attack," his favorite squadron was excluded from the mission.

For more than sixty-five years, members of the 63rd Bomb Squadron have wondered why.

The whole truth will probably never be uncovered, but pilot Jim Dieffenderfer, a peripheral observer during the planning stages of the mission, later shared some compelling insight. When Walker revealed his intention to bomb Rabaul at midday, Bill Benn objected. "You're going to lose two airplanes," he advised Walker. "You shouldn't try going into Rabaul at high noon. It's best to keep bombing it at night."

There can be little doubt that Walker resented the major's critical opinion, especially after losing the dispute over bomb fuses. Benn represented the opposition, with direct support from Kenney. Dieffenderfer believes that Walker reacted personally, retaliating in the only way he could, by saying, "Fine, we just won't take your squadron," or words to that effect.

Walker's frustration can only be surmised, but he was obviously aware that a number of recent disputes had not gone his way. The fact that Bill Benn was Kenney's protégé probably did not matter any longer. Walker had already made up his mind to defy Kenney by attacking Rabaul at midday, and faced little additional risk in denying Kenney's favorite squadron a role in the mission. Walker may have also surmised that his tenure as head of V Bomber Command was growing short. If so, the forthcoming mission represented his last opportunity to showcase the strategies he had championed for years. Thus, his decision to violate orders would have been a relatively easy one. As the old saying goes, it's easier to seek forgiveness than permission.

Whatever was said between Walker and Benn, the animosity carried over to the afternoon of January 4. Although Benn's squadron was not going to participate in the mission, he attended the briefing conducted by Walker. So did Jim Dieffenderfer, who later recalled that Benn did not sit quietly.

I don't think Benn and Walker got along very well. I sat in on the briefing before that mission with Benn, who had somehow gotten word that our squadron wasn't going. During the briefing, Walker gave the time that the planes would arrive at such-and-such a place. Benn looked in his little notebook and said, "General, you're going to be about eight minutes early." Walker got his navigator and said, "Go check that out." The navigator came back after a few minutes and said, "Sir, he's right; we were a little bit off." How Benn knew that, I don't know. But he also knew that Walker wasn't supposed to go on the mission.

The crews scheduled to fly reacted to Walker's plan with a buzz of consternation. Frederick Wesche III of the 64th Bomb Squadron recalled: "When this was announced [that the attack] was going to be done in broad daylight at noontime, as a matter of fact at low altitude, something like 5,000 feet over the most heavily defended target in the Pacific . . . most of us went away shaking our heads. Many of us believed that we wouldn't come back from it."

The absence of the 63rd Bomb Squadron meant that Walker could not launch the total effort Kenney had asked for. To further complicate matters, bad weather in Australia interfered with the plan. The B-24s at Iron Range were unable to take off due to heavy rain, leaving Walker with only the aircraft at Port Moresby: six Liberators and six Fortresses. Twelve bombers were not nearly enough for him to adequately prove the tactics he espoused, but the mission got underway as planned on the morning of January 5, 1943.

Independent of the main strike, three B-17s took off at dawn to attack Lakunai airdrome with the intention of suppressing enemy fighters. One Fortress aborted because of mechanical trouble, but the other two reached Rabaul at approximately 0900. Finding it socked in by a low overcast, they loitered overhead for approximately thirty minutes and conducted three dry runs without dropping their bombs. The delay provided ample time for a dozen A6M3 Hamps of Air Group 582 to take off and climb toward the two bombers.

At 0930 the Fortresses pickled their bombs in the vicinity of Vunakanau. Curiously, the crews reported interception by "Me-109s," though there were no German fighters in the region. The crewmen were probably seeing their first Nakajima Ki-43 Oscars of the Japanese Army Air Force, which strongly resembled Zeros in appearance as well as agility. The primary difference was the Oscar's limited armament: a pair of 12.7mm (.50-caliber) machine guns mounted in the engine cowling.

A patrol of Oscars from the 2nd *Chutai*, 11th Flying Regiment, which had arrived at Rabaul only three weeks earlier, intercepted the B-17s first. Soon after the action got underway, one fighter was shot down in full view of everyone on the ground. According to the diary of an unnamed soldier embarked on *Clyde Maru*, the Japanese were "infuriated" by the sight.

Subsequently a swarm of army and navy fighters ganged up on the Fortress flown by Capt. Jean A. Jack, 403rd Bomb Squadron. They attacked head-on, knocking the B-17's ball turret out of commission on the first pass. A sharp-shooting Zero pilot also severely damaged the left wing. His bullets and cannon fire disabled the outboard engine and tore through the main spar, damaging the engine controls and oil cooler. The left fuel tank was punctured, and holes appeared in the side of the radio compartment. Jack was unable to feather the damaged engine, which vibrated badly as the crew fought off persistent fighter attacks for thirty minutes. Finally, a hundred miles south of Rabaul, the Japanese broke off their pursuit.

Realizing that his shot-up Fortress would never make it to Port Moresby, Jack headed southwest and searched for signs of habitation among the small islands off New Guinea. Near the D'Entrecasteaux Islands he spotted an islet with native huts visible near the beach and safely ditched the Fortress just offshore.

THE MAIN STRIKE got underway at approximately 0800 as crews manned their bombers and commenced preflight routines. Walker, listed officially as the command pilot, was a passenger aboard a B-17F named *San Antonio Rose*, piloted by Maj. Allan Lindbergh, commanding officer of the 64th Bomb Squadron. Also riding as an observer was Maj. Jack W. Bleasdale, executive officer of the 43rd Bomb Group. With two passengers aboard in addition to her regular crew, *Rose* lifted off from Jackson airdrome at 0848, followed by the rest of the assigned aircraft.

By the time the raiders neared Rabaul some three hours later, the undercast had cleared. Conditions for bombing were ideal, but during the long flight the bombers had become separated into two distinct groups, diminishing their potential strength. The first to reach the target were the Liberators. Led by Maj. Philip J. Kuhl, commanding officer of the 319th Bomb Squadron, the six B-24s approached Simpson Harbor precisely at noon. Crewmen could clearly see enemy aircraft scrambling from the airdromes down below, but aside from bursts of antiaircraft fire, there was little interference as the bombardiers selected individual targets and initiated their bomb runs at eight thousand feet.

From the air, the results of the attack looked impressive. Lieutenant William L. Whitacre, a pilot in the 319th, reported "at least three ships hit in the harbor and left burning." In another Liberator, the bombardier claimed to have definitely sunk a ten-thousand-ton merchant vessel.

Within minutes, however, the Liberator crews encountered a series of aggressive frontal attacks by approximately fifteen interceptors. Again there were Oscars mixed in with Imperial Navy *Rei-sen*, but all enemy fighters were reported as "Zeros" due to the Americans' unfamiliarity with the Ki-43. Several B-24s received minor damage from gunfire and antiaircraft shells, although no casualties were reported among the crews. In return, gunners aboard the Liberators claimed two fighters destroyed, one of which may have been Sgt. Maj. Haruo Takagaki, a veteran of the China campaign with fifteen victories. His Ki-43 fell in flames, but unlike the navy pilots who scorned parachutes out of principle, Takagaki wore one that day and successfully bailed out.

Ten minutes behind the B-24s, Walker's six B-17s separated before bombing individual targets. The crews claimed four or five direct hits against shipping but had little time to observe their handiwork before the fighters were on them. Fred Wesche, who had been concerned that the daylight strike would be a suicide mission, later gave the following account:

> [W]e went over the target and all of us got attacked. [My plane] was shot up. Nobody was injured, fortunately, but the airplane was kind of banged up a little bit. We had to break formation over the target to bomb individually and then we were supposed to form up immediately after crossing the target; but no sooner had we dropped our bombs than my tail gunner says, "Hey, there's somebody in trouble behind us." So we made a turn and looked back and here was an airplane, one of our airplanes, going down, smoking and . . . headed for a cloud bank with the whole cloud of fighters on top of him. There must have been about fifteen or twenty fighters. Of course, they gang up on a cripple, you know, polish that one off with no trouble.

The stricken aircraft was *San Antonio Rose*. As the rest of the B-17s withdrew southward over New Britain, the damaged Fortress lost altitude, its left outboard engine trailing smoke. Japanese fighters continued to attack relentlessly, causing it to fall even farther behind. When last seen, *San Antonio Rose* was heading into a cloud with four or five fighters still in pursuit.

The remaining crews returned to Port Moresby and submitted their reports. Altogether, ten vessels were allegedly hit by bombs, and various gunners received official credit for the destruction of seven enemy fighters. In light of the collective claims, the participating squadrons portrayed the mission as highly successful. However, the effort sought by General Kenney—the destruction of the Lae convoy—had been a total bust.

The Japanese had hardly been fazed. Updated intelligence estimates placed as many as eighty-seven ships at Rabaul on January 5, yet only ten of those vessels—five destroyers and five transports—made up the important convoy. Thus, it would have been virtually impossible for the bombardiers to know which ships to target.

An even greater irony was uncovered decades later by researcher Richard Dunn. His astounding collection of Japanese documents and diary excerpts provides ample evidence that the convoy departed from Rabaul at noon Japan Standard Time, which correlates to 1000 hours in the time zone utilized by the Allies. Consequently, the convoy wasn't even in the harbor when Walker's aircraft attacked at 1200: the ships had departed some two hours earlier.

The bombers did succeed in sinking *Keifuku Maru*, a small Imperial Army ship of less than six thousand tons that was unloading cargo just off Kokopo. Two other merchant ships were damaged, as was the destroyer *Tachikaze*, hit by a bomb for the second time in as many weeks. Aircraft losses amounted to three Ki-43s shot down, with at least one pilot rescued.

The American crews recounted what they knew of the missing B-17, which wasn't much. When *San Antonio Rose* failed to return by late afternoon, it became obvious that the crew was down somewhere. Word spread quickly that General Walker's plane was missing in action.

George Kenney reacted angrily when he learned that his bomber commander had defied him—and not just once, but twice. "Walker off late," he wrote in his daybook. "Disobeyed orders by going along as well as not starting his mission when I told him." Later, when he heard that Walker's plane had failed to return, Kenney ordered all available reconnaissance planes to search the islands along the route to Rabaul. The order was superfluous. Walker was held in high esteem by many airmen among the bomber groups, and no one needed to be told to search for the general or the other missing crewmen.

That evening, Kenney was informed that Walker's plane had been located on a coral reef in the Trobriand Islands. Still perturbed, he told General MacArthur that he intended to punish Walker with an official reprimand and send him to Australia "for a couple of weeks."

MacArthur agreed in principle but then suggested, "If he doesn't come back, I'll put him in for a Medal of Honor."

The next day, the Fates had a surprise in store for both Kenney and MacArthur. The downed airmen were plucked from a small island fifty miles south of the Trobriands but turned out to be Jean Jack and his crew. There was some embarrassment for Jack, who later admitted that while his rescuers were pleased at finding him, they were "quite disappointed when they found out his crew wasn't General Walker's."

The search for Walker and the men of *San Antonio Rose* continued. On January 6, a B-24 flown by Lt. George M. Rose took off from Port Moresby on a dedicated search and failed to return. The mystery of the plane's disappearance has never been definitively solved, but the combat log of Air Group 582 indicates that Hamps of the 2nd *Chutai* intercepted and shot down a lone B-24 over Wide Bay on the morning of January 6. The area would have been a logical place for Lieutenant Rose and his crew to search for the missing B-17.

In the meantime, other reconnaissance aircraft had discovered the enemy convoy bound for Lae. Among the bombers that shadowed the vessels on January 6 was a Liberator piloted by Lt. Walter E. Higgins, who decided to make a solo bomb run. But his B-24 was damaged by shipboard antiaircraft fire and then attacked by a whole *chutai* of Zeros, which forced Higgins to ditch near a small island south of New Britain.

B-24s were prone to breaking apart during ditching attempts, and in Higgins's case the bomb bays caved in when the Liberator contacted the water, causing the death of two crewmen. The 90th Bomb Group's history of bad luck was extended by the loss of two Liberators and twelve crewmen that day.

The hunt for Walker's aircraft and crew was now broadened to include the two additional bombers that went missing on January 6. This soon led to another odd twist. While conducting a search on January 7, Lt. James A. McMurria of the 90th Bomb Group, 319th Bomb Squadron discovered several crewmen stranded on a small island. Hoping to identify the crew, he dropped supplies along with a note that gave simple instructions. If part of Walker's crew, the men were to proceed to the north end of the island; if part of Higgins's, they were to head south. The men headed north, but when the rescue team arrived the next day, they found Higgins and his crew rather than Walker. Again there was some embarrassment, but Higgins maintained that his deception was not intentionally sinister; he simply concluded that assistance would be dispatched more quickly for a general and took his men to the north end of the islet to expedite their rescue.

Despite days and weeks of searching, no trace was found of Walker or *San Antonio Rose*. Kenney and MacArthur returned to Brisbane on January 9, having seen the Buna campaign to its successful conclusion, and MacArthur officially announced on the 11th that Walker was missing in action. A wizard at putting a positive spin on bad news, MacArthur issued a statement that pushed the limits of credibility. Walker, he said, "led a bombardment group which successfully attacked enemy shipping in Rabaul harbor. In this attack from nine to eleven enemy ships were destroyed." In MacArthur's world, it never would have done to state the truth: that Walker had led exactly twelve bombers over Rabaul and sank one ship.

Later that month Kenney wrote a letter to Walker's sons, Douglas and Kenneth Jr. His words of were full of encouragement, suggesting that the general might still be found, but Kenney had no doubt about the outcome. He was convinced that Walker would never be found, and his hunch proved correct. Over the past six and a half decades, no scrap of wreckage or the remains of any crewmembers have been located.

Nevertheless, intriguing questions still linger. Sketchy reports that two or more crewmen parachuted from the plane and were subsequently captured by the Japanese have circulated for years. One source was Bishop Leo Scharmach, the vicar of Vunapope. A witness to the sinking of the *Keifuku Maru*, he later shared what he knew of the raid in his memoirs.

> The attacking planes had their casualties also. At least one of them was shot down. Some of the surviving airmen were co-prisoners with some of our missionaries in Rabaul. To these the pilots related the story behind the daylight raid. An American general, who was leading the flotilla, had insisted on this venture against much contrary advice. When over Rabaul, his plane was hit, but did not crash in the vicinity. Possibly it came down in the jungle.

Five months after Walker was declared missing, a B-17 of the 43rd Bomb Group was shot down near Rabaul by an Imperial Navy night fighter. The crew's sole survivor, captured by the Japanese, was shown documents naming Major Bleasdale as an alleged POW. The few details that Lt. Jose L. Holguin was given made it sound as though General Walker had been killed or mortally wounded aboard the aircraft and thus had no chance of bailing out. Circumstantially, a comment by Scharmach supports Holguin's story. "We do not know if [the general] survived," wrote the bishop, "but we are sure the Japanese never heard about him . . . otherwise they would have triumphantly boasted about it."

The name of another crewmember, Capt. Benton H. Daniel, copilot of *San Antonio Rose*, was supposedly seen by a Catholic missionary, but nothing to substantiate the claim, or any of the other aforementioned details, has ever been uncovered. All of the stories were based on hearsay, and it's even possible that the information given to Holguin was a deceptive ploy on the part of the Japanese, provided in the hopes of eliciting information from him.

Whatever happened that day, the one definitive summation is that Ken Walker did not return. Had he been rescued, he would have faced sanctions for two counts of disobeying orders. Instead he died in battle, and General MacArthur made good on his promise to recommend him for a Medal of Honor.

The paperwork moved rapidly through channels until a review board questioned whether Walker's actions were considered "above and beyond the call of duty." It was an interesting dilemma. The Silver Star awarded to Walker in August had used the same words, citing his "disregard for personal safety, above and beyond the call of duty," which means the phrase was not exclusive to the Medal of Honor. However, Maj. Gen. George E. Stratemeyer, chief of air staff under General Arnold, responded to the query by writing: "It is the considered opinion of Headquarters, Army Air Forces that the conspicuous leadership exemplified by Brig. Gen. Kenneth N. Walker on the specific mission as cited by General MacArthur does constitute action above and beyond the call of duty."

The words that set Walker apart from the other men lost aboard *San Antonio Rose* were "conspicuous leadership." The mission had accomplished very little—and Walker had defied Kenney's orders by participating—but his decision to lead the small force of unescorted bombers over Japan's mightiest bastion was indeed gallant. He intended to set an example. As he hoisted himself through the belly hatch of *San Antonio Rose* that tropical morning, a Medal of Honor would have been the farthest thing from his mind.

CHAPTER 25

Blood in the Water

THE PARADOX OF THE January 5 attack on Rabaul was not that it failed to affect the Japanese convoy, or that Walker received a Medal of Honor. The greatest irony was the insignificance of the American effort: twelve bombers, no fighter escort.

Only two days later, the Japanese launched more than *eight times* as many aircraft from Rabaul to attack Port Moresby. Considering the high costs of the recent battles for Guadalcanal and Buna, it was an astonishing show of force. The Eleventh Air Fleet put up sixty fighters and forty-four medium bombers in an attempt to knock out the Allied airdromes.

But there was more irony to come. Halfway to Port Moresby, the armada was stymied by an impassable storm. The remarkable effort went for naught. Had the weather been favorable, a well-coordinated attack by 104 aircraft might have overwhelmed the defenses at Port Moresby, causing severe setbacks for Kenney and his air forces. As it was, the foul weather favored the Allies, and the Japanese returned to Rabaul in frustration.

That same day, Allied bombers attacked the enemy convoy bound for Lae. During the clash, off the south coase of New Britain, dozens of fighters battled fiercely over the convoy. While Oscars and Zekes dueled with Warhawks and Lightnings, the bombers sank 5,400-ton *Nichiryu Maru* off Gasmata on January 7 and set fire to *Myoko Maru* the following day in the Huon Gulf. Despite the loss of the two ships, an estimated four thousand troops of the Okabe Detachment, 51st Infantry Division were successfully put ashore at Lae.

Imperial General Headquarters considered the operation a major success. But some Japanese, such as FPO Hisashi Igarashi of Air Group 705, were concerned about the intensity of the Allied air attacks. "I heard one or two out of five vessels sank," he wrote in his diary. "Now the U.S. has the mastery of the air over the most of New Guinea (except a small area around Lae). Just several months ago we had the mastery, but to our regret we retreated enormously and the situation reversed. I don't know what strategies and tactics are being developed. Yet, looking at the reality at the front, I am really irritated."

Igarashi's concerns were mostly justified—the Allies had regained control of the southern region of the Papuan Peninsula—but the recent occupation of Madang and Wewak by the Imperial Army ensured that Japan would control the northern area of the New Guinea coast for many months to come.

ON JANUARY 23, exactly one year after the Japanese invaded New Britain, the Buna campaign was declared officially over. Halfway around the world in Casablanca, Morocco, the Southwest Pacific was a hot topic among Allied planners at a landmark conference. Code-named Symbol, the meeting marked the fourth time since the beginning of the war that President Roosevelt and Prime Minister Churchill met to discuss strategy. Many of the Allies' top military leaders also attended, including the Combined Chiefs of Staff from both the United States and Great Britain.

Although the main thrust of the conference was to reinforce the "Germany first" policy, Admiral King and General Marshall lobbied hard for an increase in the resources earmarked for the Southwest Pacific. The battle for Guadalcanal was already winding down, and the two service chiefs were adamant about maintaining the Allied initiative. Prior to the conference, King had conducted an analysis of the total resources being employed in the war effort by all Allied countries. His conclusion, though never independently verified, surprised the Casablanca attendees: 85 percent of the resources were being funneled to Europe, leaving the vast Pacific area—including China, Burma, and India—with the meager balance. King and Marshall argued that this number should be increased to thirty percent to capitalize on the victories at Buna and Guadalcanal.

Otherwise the Japanese might regroup and launch yet another campaign, which could force the United States into "withdrawing from commitments in the European theater." This rattled the British sufficiently that they agreed to let their American counterparts run the Pacific war as they saw fit, as long as obligations in Europe and Africa were met.

The final conference report, submitted to Roosevelt and Churchill by the end of January, called for "limited offensive measures" against the Japanese to begin in the coming year. At first glance the phrase seems fairly innocuous, but in fact it represented a monumental shift in Allied strategy. The capture of Tulagi and Guadalcanal, the first task outlined in the Directive for Offensive Operations issued six months earlier by the Joint Chiefs of Staff, was rapidly coming to a conclusion. The Joint Chiefs were hopeful that Rabaul could be captured by the end of 1943.

This was MacArthur's cue to prepare for the second and third tasks listed in the original directive, as previously agreed upon. The past thirteen months of warfare had given him a new appreciation for the importance of air power, which meant that Kenney and the Fifth Air Force were assured of playing a crucial role in the forthcoming operation. As directed by the Joint Chiefs, the next task called for "the seizure and occupation" of the remaining Solomon Islands as well as the portions of New Guinea held by the Japanese, including Lae, Salamaua, Finschhafen, Madang, and Wewak.

The task *in toto* may have seemed insurmountable, but MacArthur and his planners broke it down into logical elements. When circled on a map, the various islands and strongholds resembled stepping stones that formed two distinct pathways. The first, anchored at newly acquired Guadalcanal, extended up the chain of the Solomon Islands to the northwest; the second began at Port Moresby, headed up the coast of New Guinea, and then crossed the Bismarck Sea to the Admiralty Islands. Both pathways led toward Rabaul, the ultimate goal. Until it was recaptured or otherwise neutralized, the Japanese would continue to dominate the Southwest Pacific—and the road through the Philippines to Tokyo would be closed.

The outline of MacArthur's strategy, called the Elkton Plan, was simple. While MacArthur's forces advanced toward Rabaul from bases in New Guinea, Vice Adm. "Bull" Halsey, who had replaced the pessimistic Vice Admiral Ghormley in October, would simultaneously move up the Solomons. Each of the enemy-held objectives already boasted at least one existing airfield, the capture of which would enable Allied fighters to provide forward air support while naval and amphibious forces proceeded to the next stepping stone on the way to Rabaul. When all of the strategic points were in Allied hands, Rabaul would literally be surrounded.

THE PENDING ADVANCE in New Guinea was especially important to George Kenney. Throughout the previous year his air operations had predominantly been defensive in nature, designed to counter each of the Japanese offensives. But the roles shifted dramatically after the Japanese failed to capture Port Moresby and retake Guadalcanal. Throughout 1943 and beyond, the Allies would be almost exclusively on the offensive, with no turning back.

On a personal level, the beginning of 1943 was difficult for Kenney. Following the disappearance of Ken Walker on January 5, he assigned Ennis Whitehead additional responsibilities as the temporary head of V Bomber Command. Needing a full-time replacement for Walker, Kenney requested Brig. Gen. Howard K. Ramey, who arrived from Hawaii on January 18. After sitting with him for a full day of briefings, Kenney felt reassured that Ramey was the right choice. "I expected that his good steady hand would straighten out a lot of troubles," Kenney wrote. He did not identify the specific problems, but low aircraft availability and combat fatigue were two issues that grew worse by the day.

That evening, however, the assorted difficulties became unimportant. Kenney received news from Port Moresby that Bill Benn had failed to return from a midmorning reconnaissance flight. Whitehead expressed concern that Benn, flying a 3rd Bomb Group B-25C named *Algernon IV* to scout the New Guinea coast, had come to grief in the Owen Stanley Mountains when the weather turned ugly. Kenney didn't want to believe that Benn, "a superior pilot," would have failed to maintain a safe altitude during instrument conditions, but that is exactly what happened. Benn had flown blindly into a valley and slammed into the mountainside. A privately funded visit three decades later by Benn's great-nephew revealed that *Algernon IV* had crashed only five hundred feet below a pass. Heavy thunderstorms in the area likely contributed to the accident, which killed all seven men aboard the B-25.

In addition to the loss of his favorite airman, Kenney had to contend with the aforementioned issues of unsatisfactory aircraft availability and fatigue among the aircrews. Both conditions were serious. As of late

January 1943, V Bomber Command consisted of only five groups, much as it had throughout the previous year. Of the two heavy bomb groups, the 43rd had fifty-five B-17s assigned, but on any given day approximately twenty were being overhauled. No more than half of the remainder, a net of about seventeen bombers, were considered combat-ready on a daily basis. Of those, another 25 percent were used for reconnaissance flights, leaving the group with about thirteen bombers available for a bombing mission. Similarly, the 90th Bomb Group typically yielded only about fifteen combat-ready B-24s out of the sixty assigned.

The two medium bombardment groups were even weaker. The 22nd Bomb Group had been in combat for ten months, and although there had been no long-range missions to Rabaul since May 1942, the group had lost at least thirty Marauders during the ensuing months. The air battles over Lae and other New Guinea strongholds had been particularly costly. At the beginning of 1943 the group possessed just twenty-eight bombers, all in "extremely bad condition," prompting General Whitehead to send the entire group to Australia for an extended rest. Meanwhile, the 38th Bomb Group had arrived in the Southwest Pacific in August with only half its assigned squadrons. Several months later, two squadrons still remained in the South Pacific Area, and the two at Port Moresby had a shortage of B-25s, about ten less than their normal complement.

Finally, the 3rd Bomb Group (light) had conducted a steady diet of combat operations over New Guinea since early April 1942. The 8th Bomb Squadron, originally equipped with A-24 dive-bombers, had suffered the most notable losses, including an infamous mission against a convoy near Buna on July 29 from which only two Dauntlesses out of seven returned. Eleven men were dead or missing, including Maj. "Buck" Rogers and the popular operations officer, Lieutenant Virgil Schwab. After that disaster, the Dauntlesses were withdrawn. The group subsequently operated A-20s and B-25s with "conspicuous success," though fifteen A-20s were lost during the second half of the year. In the meantime, two squadrons equipped with B-25s were currently undergoing new training while their bombers were being modified as low-level gunships.

Despite the lack of heavy bombers, General Ramey managed to send several small-scale raids against Rabaul during the second half of January. All were conducted at night. The mission that had cost the lives of Walker and his crew served as a stark reminder of the dangers inherent in attacking the bastion in broad daylight. The only exceptions were the much-needed reconnaissance missions, which of necessity overflew Rabaul when the sun was high so that the crews could observe and photograph enemy activity.

The flip side of bombing at night, of course, was the difficulty of finding targets, not to mention hitting them. Thirteen night raids were conducted against Rabaul in January, but the Japanese lost only one small vessel, the 1,722-ton *Tetsuzan Maru*. Sunk on the night of January 21, it was evidently the victim of skip-bombing attacks by Lt. John Murphy and Maj. Ed Scott. The only known encounter with Japanese fighters occurred five nights later, when two enemy planes were briefly observed and the B-17 flown by 1st Lt. William M. Thompson Jr. returned with "an elevator partly shot off and bullets in both gas tanks." The fighters were probably Zeros of Air Group 204, which occasionally attempted night intercepts in coordination with searchlight batteries.

Despite the fact that the Japanese lacked true night fighters, the nocturnal strikes on Rabaul were anything but easy. As a Fifth Air Force summary put it: "The weather was generally bad, the equatorial front treacherous, [and] searchlight and antiaircraft activity more than annoying."

IF THE SHORTAGE of bombers was troubling, at least the numbers were tangible, giving Kenney and his commanders something to work with. The same could not be said of the increasingly disruptive problem of combat stress. It was a slippery issue. Military doctors did not completely understand it, and there was little empirical information available to explain its causes or suggest possible cures. Major James T. King, the 43rd Bomb Group's flight surgeon, was in equal parts fascinated by the symptoms of combat stress and concerned about its consequences. After conducting an unofficial study for several months, he wrote a point paper to alert the Fifth Air Force about its dangers.

> In our group, after the crew has flown from 100 to 130 combat hours or from 10 to 15 missions, they begin to notice that they are losing their natural zest and eagerness for combat flying. As the condition develops, there are manifestations of mental, emotional and physical tiredness, and changes in personality. Variably there is a preoccupation, moodiness, brooding, moroseness and irritability. The flyer is usually

tense and appears to always be worried. He notices that he is unable to rest adequately and has trouble sleeping. When he does sleep, he is frequently awakened by dreams and nightmares. The next morning he finds that he is just as tired as when he went to bed. Instead of taking one day to recover from a combat mission, it takes three or four. There is weight loss on an emotional basis. As an experienced squadron commander put it, he could recognize the condition at a glance by the haggard, hangdog expression in [men's] eyes.

Not surprisingly, King found that the primitive living conditions and bad food compounded the negative effects of combat stress on the airmen. He personally observed sleepwalking episodes as well as "hypnagogic hallucinations," a medical term for the odd, semiconscious behavior of men literally falling asleep on their feet.

King was especially fascinated by the proclivity of combat stress to infect entire crews. "A rather outstanding characteristic of stress is its contagiousness," he wrote. "[I have] repeatedly observed some member of a crew come down with the symptoms, and then in a matter of days the remainder of the crew will exhibit more or less the same thing."

The phenomenon also spread beyond the flight crews. "There is a noticeable dejection in ground personnel," King noted, "and essential ground services begin to deteriorate." When that happened, the normal stresses associated with flying could become self-fulfilling. Planes that received shoddy maintenance work experienced a higher rate of engine failure and other major system malfunctions, placing the already stressed-out crew in additional peril.

As a flight surgeon, King was most concerned when he observed the symptoms in pilots: "The stressed pilot sees the gyrocompass drifting and it takes a second or two to realize it. The automatic reflex to right the plane is gone, and he actually has to stop and think about what he must do. Then it takes a few seconds to carry it out and he does it poorly. Often he will turn the wrong way. This sort of thing destroys his confidence in the instruments, which makes for additional strain, which makes for poorer coordination and a further delay in reaction time. This vicious cycle may well end with the ship spinning in or flying into a mountain."

Every time a plane went missing, which happened with disturbing regularity, the cycle of stress gained a tighter grip on every man in the group. Ralph K. DeLoach, a pilot in the 43rd Bomb Group, recalled that several crews simply disappeared. "They just went out and that was the end of it. There was never another word. So there was stress and strain. A crew would go out and not come back, and we never had any idea of whether the cannibals had put them in their pots . . . or whether the sharks had eaten them, or whether the Japanese had captured them."

There was no practical cure for combat stress, and pilots diagnosed with an acute case were considered a liability. King advocated simple avoidance. He believed strongly in the ounce-of-prevention method, which included giving the crews something to look forward to: periodic leave in a comfortable rest area and a realistic chance of going home after completing an established number of missions. His recommendations were largely ignored, however, mainly because there weren't enough planes and crews available in the Southwest Pacific.

So the tired crews kept going. Rarely did more than a few days go by without a plane being declared missing. "We lost a lot of airplanes in the swampy areas and up in the mountains," agreed James L. Harcrow, another pilot in the 43rd Bomb Group. "I got in a big thunderstorm one night near the Owen Stanley Mountains, and we went up and down. We'd lose about three or four thousand feet, and then go shooting up. I think we went over the mountains on our back. The navigator seemed to think so—but the copilot and I were quite busy. When we finally recovered and came back to Port Moresby, the navigator got out of the airplane and kissed the dirt, saying 'Boy, I'm happy to be home.'"

Too many crews were less fortunate. The slopes of the Owen Stanley Mountains are strewn with dozens of wrecked aircraft, many of them still undiscovered. It is no coincidence that most of the crashes, such as the one that killed Bill Benn and his crew, were caused by pilot error and bad weather.

THE MONTH OF February brought little change in the routine. Rabaul was harassed by a few bombers almost every night, mostly by the 43rd Bomb Group with occasional participation by Liberators of the 90th. Between missions, the ground crews toiled to make repairs and keep the worn-out bombers airworthy. "I had to have seven airplanes available," recalled Jim Dieffenderfer, who doubled as his squadron's engineering officer. "We would load up with bombs and try to get twelve planes if we could."

The missions were divided among the squadrons to spread the workload. Crews flew a combat mission about every third or fourth night, usually taking off between 2300 and 0100. Flight profiles were deliberately simplified because of darkness, with little emphasis on maintaining formation. The trip to Rabaul took about three hours, according to Dieffenderfer.

> We took off from Moresby and went down the coast, climbing as fast as we could, then made a 270-degree turn to the right, which got us high enough to get over the Owen Stanleys. We went up the coast to the east of New Britain, then cut across Wide Bay to Rabaul. If it was overcast at our [estimated time of arrival], we would circle. If nothing happened, we'd go another ten minutes and circle again. Pretty soon the Japanese would start shooting at us. That's how we found them, about half the time. Once we located them, we'd go in one at a time.
>
> We would fly over and drop half our bombs, then go back about five minutes later and drop the other half. So every mission was actually two passes over the target. The Japanese didn't know how many airplanes we had, and we wanted them to think that we had a lot more than we did. The planners gave us a time to be over the target so that we didn't run into each other. We would pull out and watch the next guy go through the barrage of ack-ack. It was like a fireworks show. We'd watch him go through it, and pretty soon it was our turn to go through it again. It was exciting. Not anything you looked forward to, but that's what we were told to do and that's what we did.

On February 9, the same day the Guadalcanal campaign was officially declared over, General Kenney gave the go-ahead to begin a series of strong night attacks. He credited Whitehead with engineering a plan to "really take Rabaul apart," hoping to duplicate the successful raids flown in October. The profile called for the first wave of bombers to "burn out the town," paving the way for subsequent waves to attack the airdromes and shipping. Due to a spell of bad weather, the first opportunity to carry out this plan did not come until the night of February 14–15.

Kenney's favorite bombing outfit led the way. Recent changes had affected the 63rd Bomb Squadron—Bill Benn was sorely missed, and Ken McCullar had left to take over the 64th—but many of the old hands were able to participate. Lieutenant Dieffenderfer and the maintenance troops outdid themselves, getting thirteen Fortresses ready for the mission. The bombers began taking off from Jackson airdrome before midnight on the 14th, but one turned back because of mechanical trouble. The rest, led by Maj. Ed Scott, who had taken the reins of the squadron in November, continued toward Rabaul. He guided them through "electrical storms" in his B-17F, *Cap'n & the Kids*, while the group commander, Col. Roger M. Ramey (no relation to Brigadier General Ramey) flew as an observer aboard *Double Trouble/Ka-Puhio-Wela*.

Arriving over Rabaul at 0340, the first wave of Fortresses spent forty-five minutes making individual runs over known areas where fuel and munitions were stockpiled. Their diverse payloads, designed to start fires and spread them, consisted of flares, 300-pound demolition bombs, 100-pound "daisy cutters" wrapped with wire, 20-pound fragmentation bombs, and hundreds of incendiaries. An estimated three-fourths of the bomb loads landed in the target area, starting one massive petroleum-fed blaze and several smaller fires. An hour after the 63rd did their part, ten Fortresses of the 65th Bomb Squadron hit the downtown areas of Rabaul and Kokopo, starting more fires and destroying two searchlights. Two more attack waves, consisting of eight B-17s and four Liberators, brought the effort to a total of thirty-four heavy bombers. Altogether they dropped an estimated 98,000 pounds of bombs over Rabaul and Simpson Harbor, including 3,700 incendiary devices. There was no interception by Japanese fighters, and only three B-17s received minor damage from antiaircraft fire.

Other than the obvious fires, the results of the attack were not observed by American crews because of the darkness, but Japanese sources indicate that damage in certain parts of Rabaul was significant. A postwar history compiled by the Imperial Navy mentioned "considerable loss of ground installations and personnel," while a separate document described the event as a "big raid" responsible for setting fire to fifteen planes, destroying a large food stockpile, and burning up "lots of oil drums as well as ammo dumps."

For the men on the ground, the unusually heavy raid was both noisy and frightening. Petty Officer Igarashi, based at Vunakanau with Air Group 705, was impressed by the "loud sound of antiaircraft guns and bombing like thousands of lightning strikes."

After the mission, Colonel Ramey issued a personal commendation to the men of the 43rd Bomb Group, praising their effort in what he described as "one of the largest and most successful raids ever accomplished in the Pacific Area." The 63rd Bomb Squadron received a few days of rest, but two other squadrons from the group attacked Rabaul the following night with a total of seventeen Fortresses. Igarashi considered the second attack even worse than the first, though his perceptions may have been influenced by the onset of illness, probably dengue fever or malaria: "I had a terrible headache and fever," he wrote. "I felt beaten physically and emotionally. I tossed and turned to ease the suffering, but nightmares kept possessing me with no break." Considering Igarashi's misery, the noise of exploding bombs must have been difficult to endure.

COLLECTIVELY, THE TWO heavy bomber raids in mid-February 1943 burned up some stockpiles and aircraft at Rabaul, but the overall damage was far from debilitating. The stronghold was simply too vast, too well stocked, for such attacks to cause a major setback. Kenney himself knew there was still considerable room for improvement: an official Fifth Air Force assessment described the effort to bomb enemy shipping as "less than satisfactory," and that was putting it kindly. Thus far, the only technique that had shown promise was skip-bombing. Unfortunately, the character-istics that made B-17s ideal for long-range attack—namely their tremen-dous range and payload—did not translate favorably for skip-bombing in broad daylight. The sheer size, lack of maneuverability, and relatively low speed of the heavy bombers made them too vulnerable at low level.

The same was not true of smaller, twin-engine aircraft. In late 1942, thanks to a combination of happenstance and ingenuity, two U.S. Army models underwent modifications that changed the course of attack aviation.

The first of these, the Douglas A-20 Havoc light bomber, began its evolution by default. When the 89th Bomb Squadron/3rd Bomb Group received its first A-20s at Charters Towers in August 1942, the aircraft were supposed to be equipped with four fixed, .30-caliber machine guns in fuselage blisters and three additional machine guns in flexible mounts. But the guns had not been installed, and to make matters worse, the A-20's fuel capacity allowed a combat radius of only 250 miles. There were few Japanese targets within that distance, even when staging from Port Moresby. Seeking improvements, the 3rd Bomb Group turned to a middle-aged engineering officer who had joined them earlier that year under unusual circumstances.

One of the most innovative men in the Fifth Air Force, forty-three-year-old Major Paul I. "Pappy" Gunn had worked his way out of an impoverished youth in the Ozark Mountains. Blessed with an innate ability to understand anything mechanical, Gunn trained as an aviation mechanic in the U.S. Navy and later earned his wings as an enlisted pilot. Retiring as a chief petty officer after a twenty-year career, he became the operations manager and chief pilot for the Philippine Air Lines in 1939. When the Japanese attacked two years later, the U.S. Army Air Corps commandeered his planes and commissioned him as a captain. Soon thereafter, Manila fell, but Gunn was out of the country to transport a planeload of aviators to Australia. His wife and four children became prisoners, giving him the incentive to wage a private war against the Japanese. Stuck for all practical purposes in Australia, Gunn was well-acquainted with "Big Jim" Davies and attached himself to the 3rd Bomb Group at Charters Towers.

Gunn was renowned, as we would now put it, for "thinking outside the box." Perhaps more than any other individual in the Southwest Pacific, he possessed the raw genius to conceptualize an entirely different role for the A-20 than its designer had intended.* Gunn discarded the notion of using the A-20 as a conventional bomber and envisioned a low-level attacker, primarily a gunship, which negated the need for a bombardier. By eliminating that position and all of the associated equipment, plenty of space became available in the nose of the aircraft for mounting four fixed, .50-caliber machine guns. Gunn replaced the .30-caliber guns in the fuselage blisters with a single .50-caliber machine gun on each side, giving the A-20 a total of six forward-firing heavy machine guns. And with the power turret behind the cockpit locked forward, two more "fifties" were available. The bomber's combat range was increased by installing two fuel tanks totaling nine hundred extra gallons in the forward bomb bay, and honeycomb racks mounted in the rear compartment enabled the A-20 to carry forty or more small parafrag bombs.

Gunn personally conducted much of the flight-testing to ensure that important factors such as center of gravity (a critical component of safe flight) and structural integrity had not been compromised. The changes

---

* The A-20 was but one of many famed combat planes designed by Edward H. Heinemann during his career with Douglas. Others include the SBD Dauntless, A-26 Invader, A-1 Skyraider, A-3 Skywarrior, and A-4 Skyhawk.

were true field modifications, done completely outside normal channels without the hindrance of bureaucratic red tape. In a remarkably short time, the A-20s were transformed into potent attackers.

The success of the modifications set the stage for the next big project. It stood to reason that if alterations to a light attack aircraft like the A-20 were so successful, similar improvements would yield even better results in a sturdy medium bomber. General Kenney seemed to take credit for conceiving the idea himself. "I sent word to Pappy Gunn at Brisbane to pull the bombardier and everything else out of the nose of a B-25 medium bomber and fill it full of fifty-caliber guns, with 500 rounds of ammunition per gun," he wrote in his postwar autobiography. "I told him I wanted him then to strap some more on the sides of the fuselage to give all the forward firepower possible. I suggested four guns in the nose, two on each side of the fuselage, and three underneath. If, when he had made the installation, the airplane still flew and the guns would shoot, I figured I'd have a skip-bomber that could overwhelm the deck defenses of a Jap vessel as the plane came in for the kill with its bombs."

The truth was that Gunn had made preliminary drawings of a B-25 gunship in June 1942, fully two months before Kenney arrived in Australia. Regardless of who designed the package, Kenney kept his hand in the selection process. It was his prerogative to choose which squadron would receive the newly modified attack planes, for the crews would require intensive training. For that purpose, Kenney singled out another promising young pilot.

Captain Edward L. Larner, an A-20 driver in the 89th Bomb Squadron, had already received a promotion along with a Silver Star from Kenney during the Buna campaign. Larner had a reputation for taking his airplane lower than anyone else on strafing missions. On one occasion he'd banged up his aircraft by flying through the tops of palm trees; on another he returned with visible evidence that the tail had made contact with the ground. This was exactly the type of aggressive pilot Kenney adored. He cut Larner loose from the 89th Squadron and instructed him to "help Pappy with testing, and learn to like the airplane." Larner returned from the temporary assignment two weeks later, whereupon Kenney gave him another promotion, placed him in command of the 90th Bomb Squadron, and told him to train the squadron in the art of low-level attack.

Over the next two months, the crews acquired twelve modified B-25 strafers and adapted to the new techniques. Accustomed to conventional bombing profiles, they learned to attack at mast height without a bombardier. The old SS *Pruth* served them well, absorbing hundreds of inert bomb strikes and thousands of rounds of machine-gun fire.

Larner and his pilots developed an effective attack profile wherein the B-25s approached the target ship in pairs. At three miles from the target they descended to one thousand feet; then, to throw off enemy antiaircraft gunners, they separated while performing violent evasive maneuvers at full throttle, simultaneously dropping to five hundred feet. While one aircraft strafed the ship from end to end with its ten machine guns, the other made a combination strafing and bombing attack from abeam the vessel.

By the end of February, other squadrons were also participating in coordinated rehearsals against the old wreck. The A-20s and B-25s of the 3rd Attack Group worked on their unique low-level tactics, and the newly equipped RAAF 30 Squadron practiced strafing with its brutish, twin-engine Bristol Beaufighters. Sleekness and beauty were not attributes of the big two-place fighter. With its fat radial engines jutting slightly ahead of the cockpit, the "Beau" was the fighter community's equivalent of a hulking boxer, complete with a flattened nose. Appropriately, the Beaufighter packed a mighty punch. Four 20mm automatic cannons were mounted in the lower fuselage and six .303-caliber machine guns in the wings, enabling the aircraft to pulverize almost any target, from tanks to aircraft to lightly armored warships.

The A-20s and Beaufighters had their advocates, but Kenney placed all his chips on the modified B-25s. Referring to them as "commerce destroyers," he was anxious for an opportunity to send them against an enemy convoy. He did not have long to wait.

IN LATE FEBRUARY, only two weeks after the Guadalcanal campaign was declared officially over, Lieutenant General Imamura and Vice Admiral Kusaka initiated plans for a major operation to reinforce Lae with thousands of troops. The movement would require one or more large convoys, but the Japanese had several reasons to be confident. The convoy known as 18 Operation had successfully delivered four thousand troops to Lae in early January, despite the loss of two ships. A month later, the Imperial Navy had snatched almost eleven thousand soldiers from Guadalcanal with night runs by fast warships. Later still, a convoy got through to Wewak without interference. Emboldened by these successes,

Imamura and Kusaka decided to send Lieutenant General Adachi and six thousand troops of the Eighteenth Army to Lae in early March.

But the commanders at Rabaul, as well as their superiors at Imperial General Headquarters and the Combined Fleet, remained ignorant of the Allies' ability to decipher their radio traffic. At the end of the third week of February, several messages pertaining to the forthcoming operation were intercepted and partially decoded, providing the Allies with significant details of the plans. General Kenney learned of the operation on February 25. He later characterized the intelligence as "rather sketchy," an inaccurate assessment given the fact that one message from Kusaka's headquarters to the Combined Fleet gave the arrival of the Imperial Army's 51st Division at Lae on March 6 and another contained an estimate of the number of transports required. Flying up to Port Moresby on February 26, Kenney personally took charge of planning an all-out effort to smash the convoy.

The one important variable that Kenney and his staff had to deduce was the enemy's route. "Whitehead and I went over all of the information at hand," he wrote, "and tried to guess how we would run the convoy if we were Japs." Plotting all of the known convoy movements between Rabaul and Lae over the past four months, Kenney and Whitehead discovered that the Japanese used two basic routes. The shortest skirted the south coast of New Britain before crossing the Solomon Sea to the Huon Gulf; the other wandered along New Britain's north coast, then turned south though the Vitiaz Strait, and finally curved around the Huon Peninsula at Finschhafen. The latter route not only took longer but was disadvantaged by natural chokepoints that forced the convoys to steam within confined areas. Simple logic suggested that the Japanese would prefer the shorter route south of New Britain. However, when Kenney and Whitehead consulted their meteorologists, they learned that the weather over the Solomon Sea was forecast to be clear during the period in question, whereas the forecast for the Bismarck Sea was "very bad." That sealed it for Kenney. He believed the Japanese would follow the longer northern route, despite its drawbacks, in order to hide the convoy beneath the stormy weather.

On the last day of February, Kenney gave Whitehead detailed orders regarding timetables and instructions for conducting dress rehearsals. He also recommended that the P-38s and modified B-25s be flown to the new forward base at Dobodura, near Buna on the northeast coast of New Guinea.

(Occupied in November and still undergoing expansion, Dobodura was destined to become a large and important base for the Allies. Its location provided a huge advantage over Port Moresby by eliminating the need to cross the Owen Stanley Mountains.)

Before flying back to Brisbane that afternoon, Kenney spent some time watching Major Larner's squadron practice against the SS *Pruth*. When the dress rehearsal ended, Larner boasted that his squadron wouldn't miss. Kenney admired the major's cockiness but felt compelled to warn Larner that his crews had better take their mission seriously.

OPERATION 81, as the Japanese called the new convoy, assembled in the anchorage at Rabaul on February 28. Six transports, packed to the limit with approximately six thousand soldiers and many tons of weapons and supplies, rode low in the water. They were joined by an old navy supply ship carrying six hundred SNLF troops, and by a small "sea truck" loaded with 1,650 drums of aviation fuel for the airdrome at Lae. The merchant ships would be escorted by eight veteran destroyers, all of which had fought valiantly in the waters around Guadalcanal.

Admiral Yamamoto, who in February had shifted his flag to the new super-battleship *Musashi* in Truk Lagoon, had misgivings about committing so many first-rate warships to the convoy. "The Commander of the Combined Fleet kindly spared eight of the latest type destroyers," wrote Lt. Gen. Kane Yoshihara, the Eighteenth Army chief of staff, "though the thought of dispatching them made his heart bleed."

Soon after midnight on March 1, Rear Adm. Masatomi Kimura led the convoy from Rabaul. Just as Kenney had predicted, the ships steered northwest around Crater Peninsula and entered the Bismarck Sea. Steaming parallel to the northern coast of New Britain, the convoy was limited by the speed of the slowest ship, in this case a leisurely seven knots.

The pace must have been agonizing for the men aboard the jam-packed transports as they pitched and rolled in the storm-tossed Bismarck Sea. *Kyokusei Maru,* a merchant ship originally built in Canada in 1920, was by no means large, yet an estimated 1,200 soldiers were crammed aboard. The 5,943-ton vessel, which had been used at least once to transport POWs from Sumatra to Burma, had been modified to carry humans by fitting the box-shaped cargo holds with multiple levels of wooden decks, each containing row upon row of narrow sleeping platforms.

The other transports in Operation 81 were no different. As early as 1905, the Japanese had adapted a method called the *tsubo* system for calculating the minimum amount of space an individual needed aboard a transport ship. By 1941, the original meager allowance had been cut by a third. Packed into the troopships like sardines, soldiers were expected to withstand days or even weeks of excessive heat and unsanitary conditions without complaining. They called it *chomansai*, "extreme overload," and shrugged it off as part of military life. Under the circumstances, the soldiers of Operation 81 were no doubt praying for a fast voyage.

ON THE AFTERNOON of March 1, a B-24 of the 321st Bomb Squadron/ 90th Bomb Group weaved between thunderheads while flying over the rugged mountains of New Britain. Lieutenant Walt Higgins, piloting *Miss Deed* on a methodical reconnaissance of the island, had found nothing of interest off the south coast. He encountered strong storms towering as high as forty thousand feet while crossing the island to examine the north coast, and more by accident than design he stumbled across the convoy at approximately 1500 hours. In the nose of the Liberator, the excited bombardier counted fourteen vessels. Higgins, shot down the last time he'd attempted a solo attack on a convoy, was content to orbit overhead and report the ships' position.

For the past two days, General Ennis Whitehead had scheduled only essential missions to conserve his air units, and had an impressive number of planes available for the coming battle: 75 light and medium bombers, 39 heavy bombers, and about 130 fighters. At Jackson airdrome, 7 B-17s were airborne within forty minutes of Higgins's initial sighting report, but they failed to find the convoy in the rapidly settling darkness.

Early the next morning, while short-range bombers and fighters attacked Lae to suppress enemy air support, Major Scott led eight Fortresses of the 63rd Bomb Squadron aloft from Jackson at 0630. Finding the convoy three hours later, they commenced a conventional attack at 6,500 feet. Scott and his two wingmen targeted a large transport, and for once the bombardiers achieved remarkable accuracy. Of the twelve 1,000-pounders dropped, at least four and possibly six were direct hits, and several of the remainder scored as damaging near misses. The exploding bombs tore the guts out of *Kyokusei Maru*, which carried tons of munitions in addition to 1,200 troops. It burned for two hours, then broke in two and sank with heavy loss of life. The destroyers *Yukikaze* and *Asagumo* picked up survivors and dashed ahead to Lae, delivering about 850 troops. None were in fighting form, having lost virtually all of their weapons and equipment.

Later that day an even larger attack was conducted by eighteen Fortresses of the 64th and 65th Bomb Squadrons, but the results were embarrassing. Out of sixty-nine heavy bombs dropped, only two direct hits and four near misses were claimed. Despite the dismal percentage of hits, one or two of the near misses caused hull damage to the 6,800-ton *Teiyo Maru*, killing or wounding upwards of fifty men.

The twenty-four sorties by the 43rd Bomb Group accounted for one transport sunk and another damaged on March 2, yet the day's action represented little more than preliminary jabs; a couple of telling blows that drew blood. The next day would be different. For once, the Allies had the equipment and the manpower for a major brawl.

DURING THE NIGHT of March 2–3, surveillance of the convoy was maintained by a flying boat of 11 Squadron piloted by Flt. Lt. Terry Duigan, who had made the first air-sea rescue with a Catalina eleven months earlier. Arriving over the convoy just before midnight, the radar-equipped flying boat shadowed the enemy for several hours before handing the duties off to a B-17 flown by Lt. William B. Trigg, 63rd Bomb Squadron. Trigg and his crew endured repeated attacks by fighters throughout the early morning hours but remained over the convoy by ducking in and out of rain clouds.

Well before dawn, seven Beauforts of RAAF 100 Squadron took off from Milne Bay to attack the convoy with torpedoes. The British-built attack aircraft, the same basic design from which the Beaufighter was derived, encountered heavy weather en route. Only two located the enemy ships, and one was unable to release its torpedo due to a malfunction. The other dropped its single "fish" but the crew observed no indication of a hit.

The next effort by the Allies was far more successful. More than one hundred aircraft took off from Port Moresby, Milne Bay, and Dobodura, and then assembled over Cape Ward Hunt before heading toward the coordinates provided by Lieutenant Trigg. Upon sighting the convoy, the crews followed the procedures rehearsed a few days earlier. First, at 0955 (0755 Japan Standard Time), thirteen Beaufighters of 30 Squadron swept in from the southwest at five hundred feet. When they got within range of the ships' antiaircraft guns, they descended almost to the waves and formed a line abreast while accelerating to 250 miles per hour. The destroyer captains, thinking another torpedo attack was underway, reflexively turned toward the Aussie fighters. This was normally a good defense against torpedoes, but it played right into the Beaufighters' strength, allowing them to rake the ships from bow to stern with their heavy armament. Exploding cannon shells and ribbons of machine-gun fire scythed across the decks, wiping out numerous Japanese gun crews and forcing the survivors to dive for cover.

Moments later, while the remaining Japanese gunners concentrated on the Beaufighters, thirteen B-17s of the 64th, 65th and 403rd Bomb Squadrons roared overhead at seven thousand to nine thousand feet and unleashed their bombs. Directly on their heels came thirteen B-25 Mitchells of the 38th Bomb Group, which also bombed from medium altitude. The results of the level bombing were mixed—a few hits, many misses—but the convoy was forced to break apart as individual ships maneuvered wildly to dodge the falling bombs.

With perfect timing, the modified B-25s of Ed Larner's 90th Bomb Squadron reached the scene. Larner peeled off and lined up on a destroyer, then noticed that three other B-25s were following him. "Dammit," he growled on the radio, "get the hell off my wing and get your own boat."

Racing in at full throttle, the B-25 gunships maneuvered to set up beam runs on the scattered transports and destroyers. At a distance of a thousand yards, in some cases less, the pilots squeezed the triggers rigged to their control yokes. The switch activated the electric firing mechanisms of eight Browning M2 machine guns, each with a cyclic rate of eight hundred rounds per minute. Spitting more than one hundred slugs from the combined guns every second, each of the B-25s shook to its rivets.

During the Pacific war, .50-caliber cartridges were typically belted in repeating sequences, of which two out of every five projectiles were armor-piercing. Highly effective against lightly armored warships and unarmored merchantmen, each bullet was 1.5 inches long, measured 0.5 inch in diameter, and weighed 700 grains, equivalent to about 1.6 ounces. At a casual glance, the dimensions of a single bullet might seem rather insignificant. How much damage could something the size of a pinky finger do?

What really mattered were the ballistic properties. The M2 discharged an armor-piercing round with a muzzle velocity of 2,800 feet per second—nearly three times the speed of sound—generating phenomenal kinetic energy. On impact, each bullet exerted a force of approximately fourteen thousand pounds per square inch. Naturally, because of friction and gravity, the bullet's velocity diminished as it moved through the air, but the B-25s were also traveling at around 240 miles per hour, or more than 130 yards per second. As the attacking planes drew closer to the Japanese ships, the relative kinetic energy of the bullets actually increased.

The outcome was total carnage. Most of the pilots held the trigger down for about four to seven seconds, spraying upwards of a thousand rounds at the enemy ships. Many of the heavy slugs penetrated the hulls and upper works, pulverizing equipment and tearing into crewmembers. The bullets alone often possessed the destructive power to sink a sizeable vessel, but the coup de grace was still to come. Just before hauling back on the control column to zoom over the target vessel, the pilots released one or two 500-pound bombs. Larner's squadron had not practiced skip-bombing *per se*, but instead perfected the split-second timing necessary for direct impact.

Each of the B-25s made multiple attack runs, crisscrossing the convoy to bomb and strafe ship after ship. The machine guns overheated, and several crewmen blistered their hands from clearing and recharging them. Larner almost made good on his boast that his pilots wouldn't miss. Of thirty-seven 500-pounders dropped at point-blank range, seventeen were recorded as direct hits.

The results seem to justify the claims. In a span of fifteen minutes, all seven of the remaining transports and three out of eight destroyers were left sinking or dead in the water. The first warship hit was probably *Shirayuki*, flagship of Rear Admiral Kimura. Larner's strafing run killed many of the men on the bridge and wounded most of the others, including Kimura. Of the two bombs dropped, one was a near miss; the other struck with tremendous impact near the aft main battery, rolling the big destroyer on its side. *Shirayuki* righted herself, but shortly there-after an ammunition magazine blew up, tearing off her stern. In a bold maneuver, the destroyer *Shikinami* stopped alongside and successfully transferred Kimura and some of the other wounded just before the crippled flagship sank.

Lieutenant General Adachi also had to be rescued. He was aboard the 2,490-ton destroyer *Tokitsukaze*, which lost power and was abandoned after taking four direct hits, including one that made a shambles of the engine room. In similar fashion, the destroyer *Arashio* was hit by three bombs and lost steering. The naval supply ship *Nojima* attempted to assist, but things quickly went from bad to worse as the uncontrolled *Arashio* rammed into it, causing mortal damage to *Nojima*. With seventy-two crewmen dead, including the captain, the survivors abandoned ship and were rescued by yet another destroyer, *Yukikaze*.

The nightmare for the Japanese was far from over. Six B-25s of the 405th Bomb Squadron attacked with 500-pounders at altitudes of two hundred feet or less, scoring four more hits. Next came a dozen modified A-20s, which strafed and bombed at mast height, reportedly scoring another eleven direct hits. Finally, about twenty minutes after the mayhem started, four B-17s of the 63rd Bomb Squadron approached the remnants of the convoy. The vessels that were still afloat had become scattered over an area estimated to be fifteen miles in length and five miles across.

FLYING IN FROM the north, fifteen Zeros also approached the convoy. Detached from the carrier *Zuiho*, whose fighter group had transferred to Kavieng the previous day, the Model 22s (code-named Zeke) were scheduled to reach the convoy at 0830, Japan Standard Time. The flight leader, Lt. Masao Sato, wanted to arrive on station thirty minutes early and therefore advanced the group's takeoff time accordingly.

Approaching in their dark-green fighters at eighteen thousand feet, the Zero pilots sighted the convoy shortly before the four B-17s commenced their attack. Warrant Officer Tsutomu Iwai, a veteran of the China war, watched with dread as the distant ships were suddenly enveloped by water spouts from exploding bombs. Going to full throttle, he reached the convoy within minutes, but the worst had already been done. Several ships were sinking, others burned fiercely, and columns of black smoke rose to fifteen thousand feet. The carnage on the surface, he later wrote, "was truly a scene from hell."

Spotting the four B-17s, the *Zuiho* pilots attacked vigorously. Ten or more dived in from the left on the Fortress flown by Lt. Bill Thompson, whose crew gave better than they got—or so the gunners claimed. The tail gunner, ball turret gunner, and left waist gunner all supposedly shot down Zeros, though it is possible that all three were aiming at the same plane. A pair of B-17s flown by Lt. Francis P. Denault (*Lulu Belle*) and Lt. Woodrow W. Moore (*Double Trouble*) also came under attack by an estimated ten fighters. Denault's navigator, Roger Vargas, claimed a Zero with his .50-caliber nose gun, and one of the waist gunners also claimed a fighter. Thus far the heavily armed bombers had seemed impervious, but something different transpired in *Double Trouble*.

According to American sources, a Japanese fighter came in under the wing of Moore's bomber and fired a burst upward into the fuselage, setting the B-17 on fire. Accounts differ as to whether the cockpit area or radio compartment was hit first, but the fire was evidently intense and fast-spreading, as flames were seen "spouting from the windows and tail." *Double Trouble* maintained level flight for a few moments, its bomb bay doors partially open and the fire clearly visible through a window in the radio compartment, but then gradually began descending. The bombs tumbled out, followed by seven crewmembers whose parachutes opened normally, though one man was seen to slip out of his harness and fall. Apparently three flyers remained aboard *Double Trouble*, including Moore, who perhaps intended to ditch the burning aircraft. However, it was still a few hundred feet above the water when the rear empennage suddenly crumpled and fell away. No longer under control, *Double Trouble* smashed into the sea.

In a memoir written after the war, Iwai claimed that one of his wingmen, Flight CPO Masanao Maki, deliberately rammed the B-17. "Both planes broke in two," he wrote, "and the four pieces fell, jumbled together."

His account is at odds with the recollections of the B-17 crewmen, making it difficult to believe that a Zero sneaked in and collided with Moore's plane without anyone else seeing it. Conversely, the Flying Fortresses were famous for their ability to absorb tremendous damage but keep on flying. This makes it equally hard to believe that enemy gunfire alone caused the tail of Moore's B-17 to break away. From that standpoint, the scenario of a mid-air collision gains credibility.

Wherever the truth lies, Iwai's recollection was highly sentimental: "I was struck by a deep emotion and closed my eyes in prayer as Maki fell away," he wrote. "Maki was honored with a posthumous double promotion of rank and his feat announced to all forces."

To virtually all American and Australian airmen, the notion of suicidal "body crashing" was outrageous, a fanatical act that few could comprehend. But an even more shocking event transpired immediately after the downing of *Double Trouble*. The members of Moore's crew who had bailed out were still drifting in their parachutes when three Zeros swooped down and machine-gunned them in full view of the other B-17 crews. The enemy fighters, described as clipped-wing A6M3s, were almost certainly from Air Group 204 at Rabaul or Air Group 253 at Kavieng.

As soon as the bomber crews returned to Port Moresby, word of the atrocity began to spread. On flight lines, in mess halls, in operations shacks and tent cities, the story of the men who were machine-gunned in their parachutes was told again and again. Men who had never heard of *Double Trouble* or met any of the crew were suddenly gripped by a seething hatred for the Japanese. Most were already familiar with the horror stories coming out of the jungles around Buna and Kokoda, where undeniable evidence of war crimes and even cannibalism by Japanese soldiers was being discovered.

Emotions boiled over. The airmen wanted retribution. War correspondent Quentin Reynolds, an associate editor at *Colliers* magazine, narrated the reactions of Sgt. Gordon R. Manuel, a bombardier in the 43rd Bomb Group: "We got back to the base and everybody knew what had happened to the six boys from the 63rd Squadron. We ate dinner and nobody said much. We were all burning. We couldn't wait until the next day when we might have another crack at those rats."

Some aircrews did not wait. Although the weather was deteriorating, Ed Scott and Jimmy Dieffenderfer took off at 1325 to hit the convoy again. Dieffenderfer turned back because of engine trouble, but Scott pressed on and joined five B-17s from the 65th Bomb Squadron. Soon two more B-17s slid into position on Scott's wing. Australian A-20s and American B-25s also marshaled for the attack, with P-38s providing top cover.

When the Allies located the convoy, they found five transports wallowing in the water. All were burning, little more than smoking hulks. Around them, the sea was speckled with Japanese sailors and soldiers who had gone overboard. Thousands struggled in the water, some clinging to rafts or debris, others floating in lifebelts or small boats.

A few destroyers were also in the vicinity. *Tokitsukaze*, her buckled hull surrounded by an enormous oil slick, had been abandoned. Nearby,

Asashio moved at a crawl through the debris fields to pick up survivors. Well to the north, four destroyers departed the killing zone at high speed, having pulled hundreds of men from the water. They would rendezvous the next day with two destroyers en route from Rabaul, transfer the survivors, and then return to the convoy.

Asashio, with five hundred survivors already crowding every inch of her decks, halted rescue efforts and also headed north when the Allied aircraft approached. Hundreds of Japanese, left behind in the water, watched in disbelief as the warship sped off without them. But they were the lucky ones.

Lacking most if not all of her gun crews, *Asashio* was defenseless against the swarm of attacking bombers. Ed Scott released two 1,000-pounders from seven thousand feet, and his wingmen dropped four apiece. One or two of the heavy bombs slammed into the destroyer, and several others narrowly missed, scything the hull with deadly shrapnel. Almost simultaneously, *Asashio* was attacked by several skip-bombing B-25s. Shuddering under a storm of bombs and bullets, the lone destroyer was transformed into a blackened, listing hulk. Somehow she stayed afloat, at least temporarily, but very few of her crew or the hundreds of Japanese who had already been rescued once from the sea survived the onslaught.

Despite the mayhem visited upon *Asashio*, the Allied airmen were far from satisfied. Seeking additional retribution for the machine-gunning of Lieutenant Moore's crew earlier that morning, Scott and his fellow B-17 pilots turned their heavily armed planes against the thousands of Japanese who had abandoned various sinking or sunken ships. Descending to a mere fifty feet, the seven Fortresses maneuvered slowly above the clusters of drifting survivors. Almost every crewmember who could point his weapon downward—belly gunners, tail gunners, waist gunners, even bombardiers with their nose guns—sprayed the lifeboats, rafts, and knots of Japanese clinging to debris.

For thousands of once-proud soldiers and sailors of the Rising Sun, the turn of events was incomprehensible. A few hours earlier the convoy had seemed mighty, but now several ships were underwater and most of the remainder drifted lifelessly, smoke pouring from their hulls and superstructures. Although the sea was warm, it was both alien and immense, a frightening, shark-infested atmosphere for the Japanese who found themselves struggling to stay afloat. And if the sudden reversal of fortune was not shocking enough, gigantic enemy bombers now roared just above their heads, spitting ribbons of fire in all directions. The apocalypse had come.

While the B-17s strafed men in the water, the A-20s and B-25s continued their low-level attacks. Some bombs inevitably overshot their intended targets and exploded among clusters of survivors, obliterating everyone within the blast radius. The sea literally turned red in places, attracting sharks to the blood and gore.

The number of Japanese killed in the water that afternoon is anyone's guess, but the toll undoubtedly climbed into the many hundreds as the Allied crews went on a rampage. One man in Scott's B-17 burned out two machine guns in the process of firing 1,100 rounds. Captain Jim Harcrow and his crew conducted three missions. "We'd come back and refuel, bomb up, and go back out again," he recalled. "That was the bad thing about the Bismarck Sea . . . when our guys parachuted, the Japanese shot 'em right in their chutes. So after that we did the same thing. If they were hanging onto a piece of debris, we strafed them in the water."

The slaughter continued into the next day. On the morning of March 4, a trio of B-17s came upon six enemy landing barges attempting to rescue survivors off Lae and "unmercifully" wiped them out. The following day, a B-25 crew fired 1,200 machine-gun rounds into a cluster of life rafts holding about one hundred Japanese. Time and again, whenever an Allied warplane came across a drifting lifeboat or suspicious-looking debris, the scene was repeated.

Few Allies, if any, fretted about the double standard. The Japanese were regarded as murderous and cruel for gunning down Moore's crew, whereas the Allied airmen believed their own actions were justified. Few probably stopped to consider what would have happened if Moore's crew had *not* been strafed. In basic terms, the outcome would have been the same. The parachutists had no alternative but to come down in the midst of the burning, sinking enemy convoy—and there was virtually no possibility of rescue by an Allied plane. Any survivors who fell into the hands of the Japanese would have been treated with inconceivable brutality, which means the men of Moore's crew were doomed, no matter what.

So the slaughter went on. Some airmen used revenge as a motive; others rationalized that the enemy had to be prevented, by any means, from reaching New Guinea. Among most of the aircrews, no one objected to the strafing of helpless Japanese. To the contrary, according to the 63rd Bomb Squadron's war diary, "Every man in the squadron would have given two months' pay to be in on the strafing." Pilots in RAAF 30 Squadron allegedly found it "distasteful," but they participated.

EXCEPT FOR THE TASK of mopping up small groups of survivors, the Battle of the Bismarck Sea concluded on March 4 when Japanese aircraft finished off the drifting *Tokitsukaze*. General Kenney, scheduled to leave at dawn for a trip to Washington, D.C., awakened MacArthur at 0300 and informed him of the victory. Basing his information on the early reports from Port Moresby, Kenney told MacArthur that Allied aircraft had sunk six destroyers or light cruisers and eleven to fourteen merchantmen, shot down sixty enemy planes and "probably destroyed" twenty-five more, and killed upwards of fifteen thousand Japanese. The cost: four Allied planes shot down and two crash-landed, with casualties of thirteen dead and twelve wounded.

Kenney had never seen his boss so happy. MacArthur immediately drafted a message to the participating units, which Kenney forwarded to General Whitehead along with a personal endorsement: "Congratulations on that stupendous success. Air Power has written some important history in the past three days. Tell the whole gang that I am so proud of them I am about to bust a fuse."

Three days later MacArthur issued a communiqué in which some of the claims had been reduced, others revised upward. Soon thereafter the victory was hailed in newspapers, magazines, and radio broadcasts all across America. The Japanese had allegedly lost three light cruisers, seven destroyers, twelve merchant ships, more than one hundred aircraft, and fifteen thousand troops. "Our decisive success cannot fail to have a most important effect on the enemy's tactical plans," stated MacArthur. "His campaign, at least for the time being, is completely dislocated. . . . Merciful Providence has guarded us in this great victory."

The victory against Operation 81 had been absolute—that much was true—as all eight transports and four of the eight destroyers were at the bottom of the sea. However, aerial claims had been greatly exaggerated. A total of eight Zeros had been destroyed on March 3, while thirteen Oscars were damaged. The following day, seven Oscars were shot down and three others damaged. But the most devastating effect on the Japanese was the loss of many tons of equipment and supplies—materiel that the garrison at Lae desperately needed.

Accounting for the number of Japanese killed is less precise. Estimates vary regarding the number of survivors pulled from the water on March 3 and returned to Rabaul, ranging from a low of 1,400 men to a high of 2,700. Imperial Navy submarines rescued about 275 more, and over the next few weeks several small groups of survivors fetched up on nearby islands. Many of the castaways were subsequently killed or captured. One group sailed hundreds of miles to Guadalcanal in a lifeboat, only to be cut down by an American patrol. In the final tally, probably between 3,000 and 3,500 soldiers and sailors perished during what became known as the Battle of the Bismarck Sea. More importantly, of the 6,000-plus troops embarked, only about 900—including those rescued from *Kyokusei Maru* on March 2—reached their destination.

On March 22, in the middle of his visit to the United States, George Kenney was featured on the front cover of *Life* magazine. With its accompanying story on the Bismarck Sea victory, the magazine coverage made him, at least briefly, the most famous man in America. Having reached that zenith, Kenney had no intention of modifying his boastful claims. Neither did MacArthur. Both generals not only declined to make changes, they lashed out defensively when the validity of the initial communiqué was questioned. Five months later, informed that the original communiqué had to be revised because it contradicted an extensive study completed by MacArthur's own staff, they still refused to back down.

MacArthur later softened his position, but not Kenney. In his 1949 memoir he held firmly to the same numbers he had first given MacArthur. He also embellished details about the strafing of Moore's crew, writing that "about ten Jap fighters dove down and shot all seven as they were hanging in their parachutes." Conveniently, he mentioned nothing about the reciprocal killing of Japanese soldiers and sailors in the bloodstained Huon Gulf.

No matter how much Kenney exaggerated, the annihilation of the Japanese convoy remains one of the most spectacular aerial victories of the war. Kenney illustrated what could be accomplished by aggressive aviators attacking at low level, a point that was affirmed in the official postwar history produced by the USAAF: "The fact that counts is that a major effort to reinforce Lae was turned back with mass destruction inflicted upon an enemy who never thereafter dared renew the effort."

The failure of Operation 81 to reach Lae had far-reaching ramifications for the Japanese. Not only did the loss of the convoy force them to rethink their entire strategy for the Southeast Area, it acted as the catalyst for an even more disastrous chain of events.

CHAPTER 26

Operation I-Go: Yamamoto's Last Offensive

T HE DESTRUCTION OF THE Operation 81 convoy was a severe blow to the Combined Fleet Staff, especially because it came hard on the heels of the defeats at Buna and Guadalcanal. Admiral Yamamoto, who had been reluctant to commit eight destroyers to the convoy in the first place, "was greatly incensed" by the disaster, remembered Lieutenant General Yoshihara.

The most likely recipient of Yamamoto's wrath was Vice Adm. Jinichi Kusaka. In late December 1942, all naval forces in the New Guinea and Solomon Islands areas had been combined into the Southeast Area Fleet, with Kusaka in command. He was therefore responsible for the actions of the Eighth Fleet as well as the Eleventh Air Fleet, both of which had failed to protect the convoy. Yamamoto perhaps intended to censure various members of the associated headquarters for allowing such a devastating defeat to happen, but he "was gradually mollified."

Although Yamamoto's temper was defused, the spate of defeats in the Southeastern Area had both him and his staff deeply concerned, particularly about the status of land-based aviation. In the seven months since the Guadalcanal campaign had begun, the Eleventh Air Fleet had lost the great majority of its original aircrews. "The land-based air groups at Rabaul were not effective, largely because there were only a few experienced pilots," stated Cmdr. Toshikazu Ohmae of the Southeast Area Fleet staff. Yamamoto's chief of staff was even harsher. As early as December 1942, Vice Admiral Ugaki had written: "[W]e cannot expect much of the land-based air force partly because of a passive atmosphere among them."

Ugaki did not elaborate on what he meant by "passive atmosphere," but he was probably referring to a couple of serious issues affecting the air groups. The first was poor health. The previous commander of the Eleventh Air Fleet, Vice Admiral Tsukahara, had been invalided to Japan only a few months earlier, and his case was far from isolated. In fact, the health of the entire Rabaul garrison was declining. The most widespread disease, by far, was malaria. Fully 95 percent of the soldiers, sailors, and airmen at Rabaul suffered at least one bout of malaria during their deployment, and one man out of five was incapacitated by it. Other chronic diseases included dengue fever, respiratory disorders, and kidney infections. It is worth noting that Tsukahara's replacement, Vice Admiral Kusaka, suffered from chronic diarrhea, a common problem at Rabaul.

The ailments were difficult to overcome. Petty Officer Igarashi of Air Group 705 was grounded for weeks because of malaria. "I had a mysterious fever since this morning," he lamented on March 19. "Now malaria is really showing itself. It is said that there are 50,000 parasites in a drop of blood. I cannot stand the idea of being ruined by malaria parasites. To what height can people bear fever? Fever seems to affect the brain. I don't feel clear headed. From 5 to later than 10 o'clock I tossed and turned. I can't describe how hard it is to sleep. I am about to give in to this disease. I feel helpless, as I know that this suffering will continue."

Igarashi was declared fit enough to resume flying on March 30. "I took off in high spirits," he wrote that evening, "but in the afternoon I had to go back to the hospital again because of an acute pain in my left ear." Igarashi was grounded again, this time by an ear infection. "I felt very beaten by diseases, one after another," he continued. "I am not only sorry but also embarrassed . . . I've become familiar with hospital rooms. I am not proud of this. I am ashamed of myself because I feel like I am being a pest to my section."

An even greater problem affecting the air units at Rabaul was attrition. By early 1943 most of the original veterans had been killed or wounded, and the quality of the replacements left much to be desired. "Their present skill cannot be regarded as more than one-third of that of the past," wrote Ugaki. "In a newly arrived fighter group, forty-four pilots out of sixty have had no experience with the Zero fighter. Most of them are only trained in the Type 96 fighters, so they have to be trained again after their arrival."

The example Ugaki highlighted was symptomatic of a fleet-wide trend. In trying to accelerate the flow of replacement aircrews to the front lines, the Imperial Navy shortened the training syllabus for commissioned and enlisted pilots by two months. To achieve this reduction, the amount of instructional time devoted to skill areas such as gunnery, tactics, and formation flying was reduced or in some cases eliminated.

Yamamoto himself was troubled by the decline. In November 1942 he had confided to General Imamura: "[T]hey used to say that one 'Zero' fighter could take on five to ten American aircraft, but that was at the beginning of the war. Since losing so many good pilots at Midway we've had difficulty in replacing them. Even now, they still say that one 'Zero' can take on two enemy planes, but the enemy's replacement rate is three times ours; the gap between our strengths is increasing every day, and to be honest things are looking black for us now."

Four months later, the situation was even worse. The defeats at Guadalcanal and Buna weighed heavily on Yamamoto, just as the steady attrition of veterans affected the morale of the air groups. For example, after seven months of combat only four Zero pilots from the original 2nd Air Group (renamed Air Group 582 in late 1942) were still alive.

The strain of facing death every day became a terrible burden, recalled WO Kazuo Tsunoda, one of the four survivors. In his postwar memoir, he described the mental breakdown of FPO 1st Class Hisamatsu Matsunaga, one of the other remaining pilots. Starting out in the third position of a three-plane section, Matsunaga had advanced rapidly to *shotai* leader due to attrition. As the death toll rose, he eventually became a *chutai* leader, responsible for nine aircraft. But the replacements he led were comparatively inferior to the originals, and many were lost. In early March, about the time that the Zeros of Air Group 582 advanced to Buin airfield on Bougainville, Matsunaga became withdrawn and refused to fly. He remained at Rabaul, holed up in a senior enlisted man's quarters. The group's commanding officer and vice commanding officer tried to reason with him, but Matsunaga refused to cooperate. There was talk of sending him to Japan for a court-martial, which would likely result in his execution, but Matsunaga did not care.

The problem was ultimately resolved when Tsunoda returned to Rabaul on March 9 and met with the troubled flyer. Realizing that Matsunaga was carrying far too much responsibility on his young shoulders, Tsunoda offered to take him into his own division. "I will kick in the gate of Enma, the Lord of Hell. Follow me to the bottom of Hell," Tsunoda said, borrowing a war cry used by his own former division leader. It worked. Matsunaga had been virtually paralyzed by depression but agreed to fly again, though not as a leader: he simply needed someone to remove the yoke of responsibility. "I do not like Hell," he replied, "but with you, I will go there."

Unfortunately, Tsunoda was unable to keep his promise to watch over Matsunaga. The following day, nineteen pilots of Air Group 582 were assigned to escort dive bombers on a mission against the new American base in the Russell Islands. Tsunoda led the first *chutai* and expected to have Matsunaga with him, but at the last minute Matsunaga was ordered to lead the second *chutai*, an assignment he willingly accepted despite his prior concerns. During the approach to the Russells, a gaggle of F4U Corsairs attacked Matsunaga's side of the formation. He charged at them singlehandedly, leaving the rest of the Zeros to protect the bombers. Tsunoda watched in dismay as his friend raced headlong toward the American fighters, knowing instinctively that Matsunaga would not return.*

The chronic health concerns and high death toll affected virtually all of the airmen. Petty Officer Igarashi wrote in his diary: "Generally speaking, our morale is low. This is hardly to be helped. We have had rough lives at the front for nearly a year. I understand this, but yet, where have the elite of the ocean gone? Where are the true crack units?"

The answer to Igarashi's rhetorical question was provided by Tokyo. On March 15, Imperial General Headquarters introduced a new plan called the Joint Army-Navy Central Agreement on Southeast Area

---

* A few discrepancies exist between the combat log of Air Group 582 and Tsunoda's postwar account. Matsunaga and a squadron mate were killed in action on March 10 but not by Corsairs. The credit properly belongs to P-39s of the 347th Fighter Group.

Operations, which directed the establishment of "a superior and impregnable strategic position." Pretentious language aside, the plan was clearly defensive in nature. The great Southern Offensive was dead. In its place, Tokyo implored the army and navy to "literally operate as one unit" while maintaining pressure on Allied forces in New Guinea. Simultaneously, the defenses at Rabaul and its satellite bases were to be strengthened.

The sole offensive element of the plan, buried several paragraphs deep in the document, directed the Imperial Navy to initiate an air campaign against Allied positions in the Solomon Islands—essentially a counterattack on Guadalcanal. It was to be accomplished by means of "aerial supremacy combat, interception of enemy transportation, interception of enemy aircraft, ground support, and covering lines of communications and supply." The task fell to Yamamoto, who was well aware that the Allies were developing Guadalcanal, along with bases in the New Hebrides, in order to advance up the Solomons.

In fact, the first push had already been made. On February 21, only two weeks after the Japanese pulled their troops out of Guadalcanal, American forces had advanced seventy miles to the northeast and peacefully occupied the Russell Islands. Seabees immediately began to bulldoze a pair of airstrips to support Admiral Halsey's multilateral air force for the next campaign, the invasion of New Georgia.

The Japanese would find no shortage of tempting targets on Guadalcanal, or in the surrounding anchorages. During the few short weeks since they had conceded the island, it had undergone dramatic changes. Now boasting three busy airstrips, Guadalcanal had become a supply depot with massive dumps of munitions, fuel, weapons, and other war materiel piled high. Japanese reconnaissance flights on March 25 revealed approximately three hundred Allied planes on the island, and the snoopers counted numerous transports, cargo ships, and warships riding at anchor between Lunga Point and Tulagi.

Knowing that the Eleventh Air Fleet by itself was incapable of mounting an effective strike, Yamamoto called upon Adm. Jisaburo Ozawa, commander of the Third Fleet, to contribute his carrier air groups to the effort. *Zuikaku* and *Zuiho* were already in the vicinity, and *Hiyo* and *Junyo* joined them from Japan on March 27. Ozawa initially voiced opposition to the use of his elite units, but he eventually provided the aircraft and even agreed to supervise plans for the coming operation. At about this same time, it was decided that both Yamamoto and Ozawa should shift their headquarters temporarily to Rabaul, underscoring the vital role of the fortress in Japan's latest strategy.

Yamamoto scheduled his arrival for April 3. In the meantime, Vice Admiral Kusaka sent a preliminary fighter sweep down "the Slot" on April 1, hoping to draw out and destroy a large percentage of the Allied fighters at Guadalcanal. The mission consisted of two separate waves of land-based Zeros from Air Groups 204 and 253, the first consisting of thirty-two Zekes and Haps, the second containing twenty-five fighters. Both waves were detected by coastwatchers, whose radio warnings gave Fighter Command on Guadalcanal enough time to scramble forty-two fighters. Most were marine or navy F4F Wildcats, but there were also six P-38 Lightnings and several new gull-winged F4U Corsairs, which had seen their first combat only two months earlier.

The raiders were intercepted over the Russell Islands, starting a giant melee that lasted nearly three hours. Of the ninety-nine aircraft involved, fifteen were shot down. The Americans enjoyed a distinct advantage in fighting over their own territory. Although five Wildcats and a Corsair were shot down, three of the pilots survived to fight again. Conversely, the Japanese lost the pilots of all nine Zeros brought down, in part because few, if any, wore a parachute.

The reports submitted by both sides were exaggerated, but not evenly so. The Americans claimed eighteen Zeros destroyed, exactly twice as many as the Japanese actually lost. Conversely, the Japanese bragged of shooting down forty-seven American fighters, a whopping total that exceeds the number of participating aircraft.

ADMIRAL YAMAMOTO was undoubtedly pleased with the reports from the returning Zero pilots, even if he suspected their claims were inflated. Still at Truk, he indulged in a game of *shōgi* with his liaison officer, Cmdr. Shigeru Fujii, on his last night aboard *Musashi*. (*Shōgi* is a popular Japanese variation of chess; the literal translation is "general's board game.") While discussing the impending trip, Yamamoto confided: "It seems there's a lot of talk at home lately about commanders leading their own troops into battle, but to tell the truth I'm not very keen on going to Rabaul. I'd be much happier if they were sending me back to Hashirajima."

Yamamoto's statement had nothing to do with shirking his duties; instead it was based purely on human nature. Away from Japan for almost eight months, he longed to see his mistress, Chiyoko Kawai. For the past nine years, Yamamoto had loved the former geisha "with the freshness of spirit of a far younger man." Their relationship had been kept carefully hidden, so he had to be content with writing her a letter about his forthcoming trip to Rabaul. Contrary to the comments he made while playing *shōgi*, Yamamoto expressed to Kawai his happiness "at the chance to do something."

On the morning of April 3, the day before his fifty-ninth birthday, Yamamoto and several members of his staff boarded a pair of four-engine flying boats in Truk lagoon. As a precaution, he and Vice Admiral Ugaki occupied different aircraft. In the unlikely event that one of the planes went down, the Combined Fleet Staff would not lose both of its top admirals. As it was, the big seaplanes encountered no trouble and landed in Simpson Harbor at 1340. The greeting party included Vice Admiral Kusaka, who had not seen his commander in chief for six months. Kusaka noticed that Yamamoto had bloodshot eyes and seemed on the verge of exhaustion. Years later, American writer John Prados suggested that the cause might have been beriberi, a fairly common disease in the tropics caused by acute vitamin deficiency.

Yamamoto and his staff were escorted to Southeast Fleet Headquarters, where the Combined Fleet flag was raised to signify the temporary relocation of his headquarters. After a brief visit, Yamamoto was taken to his personal quarters, a cottage at Government House on Namanula Hill, "where the nights would be cool."

The next day Yamamoto, Ozawa, and Kusaka went over the details of "Attack X," the strike against Guadalcanal, scheduled for April 5. Ozawa's carrier planes—an impressive force of 96 Zeros, 54 Vals, and a few Kate torpedo bombers—had arrived on April 2, bringing the total number of attack aircraft at Rabaul to approximately 350.

With such a large and powerful force at his disposal, Yamamoto believed he could seriously hurt the Allies in New Guinea as well as in the lower Solomons. He therefore decided to add a series of strikes against New Guinea to the overall plan, officially named A-Operation, or *I-Go Sakusen* in Japanese. The recent Central Agreement formulated by Imperial General Headquarters provided ample justification for the additional raids, because it had included the following directive: "Air operations will be intensified to destroy the enemy air strength [on New Guinea]."

Attack X was postponed for two days due to bad weather, but the early hours of April 7 found Yamamoto at Lakunai airdrome to observe the departure of the massed aerial forces. Wearing a dress white uniform, he solemnly waved his cap as scores of Zeros and dive-bombers roared aloft. Dozens more took off from Vunakanau, and several hours later most of the attack force landed either at Buin, on the south coast of Bougainville, or on the tiny island of Ballale, fifteen miles off the Bougainville coast. While the planes were being refueled, the crews received updated target and weather information. Taking off again for the attack phase of the mission, they rejoined over Shortland Island, and at midday the main force of 110 Zeros and 67 Vals turned southeast toward Guadalcanal. A separate group of 47 Zeros from the Eleventh Air Fleet took off from Buka and also headed southeast. Altogether some 224 planes, the largest Japanese strike force since the attack on Pearl Harbor, set off for Guadalcanal.

THANKS TO AN experienced and talented intelligence network, the Allies received several warnings of the impending raid. First, intercepted Japanese radio traffic was analyzed at Pacific Fleet Headquarters in Hawaii, which then issued alerts back to Guadalcanal more than three hours before the attack commenced. Later, Australian coastwatchers transmitted reports of visual sightings to Guadalcanal, enabling Fighter Command to scramble seventy-six fighters from Henderson Field and the outlying airstrips, Fighter One and Fighter Two. The outcome was a massive donnybrook that began at midafternoon southeast of the Russell Islands and spread all the way to the anchorage at Tulagi. Despite the early detection, the Japanese bought extra time by cleverly splitting the attack force into four groups, which created initial confusion among the Allied radar controllers.

The first American fighters to reach the Japanese—divisions of F4F Wildcats from three Marine Corps squadrons—had to fend off Zeros and were unable to prevent the Vals from attacking targets in Tulagi anchorage. Consequently three ships were sunk: a destroyer that had fought at Pearl Harbor, a small New Zealand corvette, and a fat tanker of 14,500 tons. In addition, a converted oiler that had been refueling the corvette was badly damaged.

Among the many individual air battles that raged overhead, one stands out. James E. Swett, a marine first lieutenant in VMF-221, was officially credited with shooting down seven Vals and probably destroying an eighth; this in an F4F-4 that, due to its limited ammunition, offered only eighteen seconds' worth of firing time. Swett's own fighter was damaged and he was wounded, all of which led to a bone-jarring forced landing in Tulagi harbor. Swett escaped from the sinking Wildcat and was later awarded a Medal of Honor for his feat, which was accepted without question at the time. In recent years, however, as historians have collated extensive details of the battle, including analysis of Japanese documentation, some have concluded that Swett could not possibly have downed all of the bombers attributed to him.

Another element of the battle worth noting is the participation of two American brothers whose lives are deeply entwined in the Rabaul story. Both were division leaders on April 7. Captain Thomas P. Lanphier Jr. of the 339th Fighter Squadron led four P-38s into the fray and personally claimed three Zeros. His younger brother, 1st Lt. Charles C. Lanphier, shot down one Zero while leading four Wildcats from VMF-214. It was a good outing for the brothers. Their father, a former commanding officer of the Army Air Corps' fabled 1st Pursuit Squadron, served as Gen. "Hap" Arnold's air intelligence officer and counted men such as Charles Lindbergh among his good friends. For his fighter-pilot sons, the future seemed bright indeed.

AFTER THE FIGHT broke up, most of the surviving Vals and Zeros headed back toward Bougainville. Some with battle damage or low fuel landed at Munda Point on New Georgia, and a few were forced to ditch. Predictably, both sides submitted exaggerated reports. Over-claiming again by a ratio of approximately two-to-one, the Americans were credited with shooting down twenty-six Zeros and thirteen Vals, whereas actual Japanese losses totaled twelve Zeros and nine Vals either shot down or missing, with another three dive-bombers ditched or crash-landed. By comparison, the Japanese over-claimed by a ratio of at least six-to-one, reporting forty-one American planes destroyed (plus thirteen damaged or uncertain), though only seven Wildcats were lost with all pilots recovered.

The biggest embellishments were made by the dive-bomber crews. The returning aviators claimed that they had sunk twelve major vessels (ten transports, a cruiser, and a destroyer), heavily damaged two additional transports, and caused minor damage to yet another. The results were forwarded to Imperial General Headquarters, and highly sensationalized accounts of the battle were soon being published throughout Japan.

Convinced that the attack had achieved everything the airmen claimed, Yamamoto and the Combined Fleet Staff proceeded with Attack Operation Y, a series of raids against bases on New Guinea. The first, conducted on April 11, did not involve the Eleventh Air Fleet's land-based bombers. Instead, one hundred planes from Ozawa's carrier groups independently attacked Oro Bay, adjacent to the rapidly expanding airdrome complex at Dobodura.

Considering the number of aircraft involved (seventy-three Zeros, twenty-seven Vals), the results were surprisingly modest. Against the loss of two Zeros and four Vals, the Japanese claimed the sinking of three transports and a destroyer. However, only one American cargo vessel was actually sunk, while a second transport sustained enough damage to warrant beaching it. An Australian minesweeper, evidently mistaken for a destroyer, was also damaged.

Early the next morning, while Vice Admiral Ugaki remained abed with symptoms of dengue fever, Yamamoto traveled to Vunakanau airdrome to personally send off another strike. An inspiring sight in his crisp white uniform, he waved to the passing crews as 17 Betty medium bombers of Air Group 751 taxied into position and then roared down the dusty strip, followed by 26 Bettys of Air Group 705. Forming the 1st and 2nd Attack Units, respectively, they were joined by a direct escort of 65 Zeros from the land-based air groups as well as the carrier *Zuiho*. A separate Fighter Striking Unit consisting of Zeros from *Zuikaku*, *Hiyo*, and *Junyo* also participated, increasing the total force to 43 bombers and some 130 fighters.

The attack units, flying in two large formations, headed initially toward Milne Bay. At 0945 they were detected by a radar station at Dona, on the New Guinea coast, resulting in the scramble of almost every operational Allied fighter on the near side of the Owen Stanley Mountains. The radar signal was lost shortly after the initial detection, but at 0955 a different warning station reported thirty bombers and sixty fighters crossing the Owen Stanley Mountains en route to Port Moresby.

The feint, aided perhaps by a glitch in radar coverage, gave the attackers an ideal opportunity to cause serious harm. Not only were most of the

Allied interceptors heading toward Milne Bay, but there were many prime targets at Port Moresby. Only two days earlier, General Kenney had arrived to spell General Whitehead for a few weeks as director of air operations. One well-placed bomb on his headquarters might have set the Allied air forces back many months.

Kenney was able to see the approaching aircraft from his headquarters. He counted twenty-seven medium bombers, undoubtedly those of Air Group 705, "flying in excellent mass formation," followed by a second group of eighteen, which could only have been the bombers from Air Group 751. Kenney also counted "between sixty and seventy fighters," again coming close to the correct number.

Although it was a formidable attack force, the Japanese failed once again to take advantage of their numerical strength. Rather than concentrating the bombers' payloads on one important target—the logical choice would have been Jackson airdrome, with its area headquarters—the two formations separately attacked outlying fields. The large formation of Bettys from Air Group 705, led by Lt. Cmdr. Tomo-o Nakamura, maneuvered to attack Schwimmer and Berry airdromes from the northwest at an altitude of approximately twenty-two thousand feet. The smaller group, led by Lt. Cmdr. Masaichi Suzuki, targeted Ward's field and the adjacent area, known as Five Mile Valley.

The attack on April 12, despite being the largest of the 106 raids on Port Moresby to date, proved relatively insignificant. At Schwimmer, three B-25s and a Beaufighter were destroyed and some fifteen aircraft damaged, though many of the latter were back in operational status within a matter of weeks. Bombs cratered the runways at three outlying fields, several buildings and tents were blasted at Berry airdrome, and a stockpile of five thousand gasoline drums went up in a spectacular blaze near Ward's field. Several men working at the fuel dump died in the massive fire, but they were evidently the only casualties on the ground.

An estimated forty-four P-38s and P-39s intercepted the attackers beginning at 1010 hours. Some pursued the Japanese eastward to the New Guinea coast, where fighters of RAAF 8 and 9 Squadrons joined in. The Allies claimed thirteen Bettys and ten Zeros destroyed, plus six bombers and one fighter as probable victories. In addition, antiaircraft batteries claimed two bombers destroyed and four probably destroyed. But the attack cost the Japanese only two Zeros among the fighter groups, while six Bettys from Air Group 751 were shot down and another was lost to a crash-landing at Lae. None of Air Group 705's Bettys were lost in combat, although eleven sustained varying degrees of damage and one was subsequently destroyed in a landing mishap at Lae.

Some of the claims submitted by the returning Japanese airmen were consistent with actual damages. Bombs dropped by Air Group 751 "started great explosions at two sections of the 5th airstrip," which correlates with the burned-out fuel dump; and the crews of Air Group 705 reported that their barrage of bombs blanketed "4 large and 10 small planes." But other claims, such as the sinking of a seven-thousand-ton ship in the harbor and the shooting down of twenty-eight Allied aircraft (plus seven more considered "uncertain" victories), were greatly exaggerated. There is no record of a vessel being attacked in the harbor, let alone hit, and Allied fighter losses totaled only two P-39s, with one pilot recovered. That afternoon, Yamamoto paid a visit to Ugaki. The chief of staff had been admitted to the hospital because of dengue fever, and was eager to hear the news of the attack on Port Moresby. Both men were highly encouraged by the deceptive reports submitted by the aircrews.

Ugaki was released the following day, his fever under control if not altogether gone. It seemed as though almost everyone at Rabaul was feeling better. Yamamoto even appeared to be healthier, exhibiting a hearty appetite. Between missions he chatted, planned strategy, and played *shōgi* with Vice Admiral Kusaka and other officers in the Southeast Area Fleet Headquarters.

The positive mood spread outward through the ranks. "The carrier-based pilots are all high-spirited," wrote Petty Officer Igarashi on April 13. "They are a good stimulus to our land-based attack units as we tend to be in low spirits."

Unfortunately for the Japanese, the boost in morale was brief, flaring like the filament in a light bulb just before it burns out.

CHAPTER 27

Death of a Warrior God

THE ASSUMPTION THAT *I-Go Sakusen* was succeeding undoubtedly helped the overall mood at Rabaul. But to an even greater degree, the mere presence of Admiral Yamamoto was a great inspiration to the Japanese soldiers, sailors, and airmen. He understood the importance of being seen by the aircrews, of mingling with them, just as General Kenney did with his "kids" in New Guinea. Yamamoto therefore continued to don his dress whites to perform highly visible, ritualistic send-offs at the start of each *I-Go* mission. On April 13, after seeing how his appearances encouraged the men at Rabaul, he announced his intention to tour the forward area "in order to raise the morale of the men stationed there."

That very afternoon, a message outlining Yamamoto's proposed visit was drafted for the purpose of notifying the outlying bases. The information was laid out precisely: the date and time of Yamamoto's departure from Rabaul (April 18, 0600), the location of the first stop and estimated time of arrival (Ballale, 0800), the type of aircraft Yamamoto and his staff would ride in (land-based medium bomber), the number of escorts (six fighters), and the exact itinerary to be followed throughout the day.

Using a new naval code that had gone into effect only two weeks earlier, the message was transmitted from Rabaul a few minutes before 1800, Japan Standard Time. Powerful, low-frequency radio waves radiated outward from the transmitter in all directions and within seconds were received by the intended addressees. Decoding the message took a bit longer, but the information was delivered as intended throughout the lower Solomons. One recipient, Rear Adm. Takatsugu Jojima, commander of the 11th Seaplane Tender Division based at Shortland Island, was immediately critical of the transmission. "What a damn fool thing to do, to send such a long and detailed message about the activities of the C-in-C so near the front," he said to his subordinates. "This kind of thing must stop."

At Rabaul, Admiral Ozawa also voiced his opposition, but Yamamoto refused to change his mind. Ozawa then appealed to Capt. Kameto Kuroshima, a senior member of Yamamoto's staff. "If he insists on going, six fighters are nothing like enough," Ozawa said. "Tell the chief of staff that he can have as many of my planes as he likes." But Ugaki was in the hospital with dengue fever, and Ozawa's pledge was not delivered.

Yamamoto's fleet commanders were right to be concerned. The radio waves that carried the encrypted message did not simply stop; instead they kept radiating outward, bending around the curvature of the Earth, bouncing from clouds, and within seconds of transmittal they were picked up by American listening posts. At Pearl Harbor, room-sized IBM card-reading machines sorted through the variables of the updated naval code and detected the message's heading: C-in-C, Combined Fleet. That alone was enough to put the human code-breakers on high alert. Veteran cryptanalysts soon filled in many of the blanks that the primitive computer missed and realized that the message represented far more than a travel itinerary. The wealth of details placed the man who had masterminded the attack on Pearl Harbor in an extremely vulnerable situation. His flight to Ballale would bring him within 325 statute miles of Guadalcanal. "This is our chance to get Yamamoto," said an officer at the Fleet Radio Unit.

That morning, April 14, a copy of the message was delivered to Admiral Nimitz. For a short while he deliberated the pros and cons of using the information to eliminate Yamamoto, but the decision was really quite simple. As author Donald Davis later put it, Yamamoto represented "the hated face of the Japanese war machine. . . . Killing him would be a horrific setback for Japan, and, for America, payback for Pearl Harbor." Nimitz gave the go-ahead, and by midmorning the message had been forwarded to South Pacific Area headquarters on New Caledonia. From there it went to Rear Adm. Marc A. Mitscher, commander of aircraft operations in the Solomons (abbreviated as COMAIRSOLS). In turn, Mitscher called a secret meeting for his staff, where it was determined that any possible interception of Yamamoto's flight would have to be conducted by P-38s, the only type of fighter at Guadalcanal with the range to fly to Bougainville and back. Because the Solomons were west of the International Date Line, it was already April 15, which gave Fighter Command less than three days to plan the most important mission of the war.

AT RABAUL, Yamamoto wore his dress whites again on April 14 to send off the next attack, a two-pronged mission labeled "Y-1" and "Y-2." Seventy-five fighters and twenty-three dive-bombers from the Third Fleet, joined by fifty-four fighters and forty-four medium bombers of the Eleventh Air Fleet, took off to attack the harbor and airfields at Milne Bay. Along the way, four bombers of Air Group 751 turned back, and two others were damaged in a midair collision, but the force remained powerful with nearly two hundred aircraft.

For all the armada's potential, however, the Japanese failed once again to deliver a knockout blow. Three Allied ships were hit at Milne Bay, but only one was seriously damaged. Forty-four Allied fighters intercepted the Japanese and claimed nineteen "confirmed" kills, plus six additional planes as probably destroyed, but the raid actually cost the Japanese only eight aircraft. Similarly, losses for the Allies amounted to just one P-40 and its pilot. Four other P-40s were "pretty badly shot up," and one P-38 crash-landed.

Back at Rabaul, the returning aircrews reported hugely inflated results again: three large transports and one medium transport sunk, six transports damaged heavily and set on fire, forty-four Allied planes shot down for certain. That night, Rear Admiral Ugaki believed he had reason to gloat in his diary:

Today's operations of Y-1 and Y-2 a great success. Congratulations! But at the same time our losses gradually increased too. This was natural. A telegram from the chief of the Naval General Staff stated that when he reported the result of Operation Y-1 and Y-2 to the emperor, His Majesty gave the following words: "Please convey my satisfaction to the commander-in-chief, Combined Fleet, and tell him to enlarge the war result more than ever."

A fighter sweep was planned for April 16, which gave the Japanese a full day to prepare the aircraft, but when reconnaissance flights failed to turn up adequate targets on New Guinea's northeast coast, the raid was called off. As Yamamoto and his staff compiled the reports from the previous missions, they were convinced that the Allies had suffered tremendous harm. Aggregate claims for ships sunk at Guadalcanal and New Guinea included one cruiser, two destroyers, six large transports, and ten medium transports. Japanese aircrews and fighter pilots also claimed to have shot down 134 Allied planes for certain and damaged another 56. But as Ugaki pointed out in his diary, Japanese losses were mounting. After a week of conducting large-scale attacks, 26 percent of the Vals had been expended along with 18 percent of the land-based Bettys. Given the apparent success of the attacks and the trend in friendly losses, Yamamoto ordered the conclusion of *I-Go Sakusen*.

The next morning, April 17, Vice Admiral Ugaki chaired a conference at 8th Base Force headquarters to review the lessons learned from the aerial offensive. Numerous high-ranking naval officers were present, including Yamamoto, who was content to observe while the aviation gurus discussed important matters. One topic that generated keen interest was the tendency of Japanese warplanes to catch fire after just a few hits with incendiary or even tracer rounds. That the experts even acknowledged the problem was unusual. The Japanese were highly reluctant to admit that hundreds of aviators had been burnt to a crisp because the aircraft engineers scorned the weight penalty of protected fuel tanks. To the contrary, the Japanese typically accounted for their losses by applying reverse psychology: whenever one of their aircraft burst into flames or was otherwise shot down during combat, it wasn't entirely because the enemy had scored fatal hits; instead, the plane had merely been damaged, and its pilot decided to blow himself up (along with his crew, if applicable) as a symbolic act of suicide.

The Japanese called this *jibaku*, which literally means to self-explode. The amazing thing is that so many aviators, for all their intelligence and technological expertise, were brainwashed by the bushido mentality. Petty Officer Igarashi was a perfect example. Upon learning that one of his friends in Air Group 705 was shot down on April 14, he evoked the concept of *jibaku* as if it were the most natural thing in the world: "In the afternoon I went to the airfield again and heard about the great progress of the battle. More than ten vessels were sunk, airfields were on fire, etc. Unfortunately, Yokozawa self-exploded with Lieutenant Matuoka."

After losing numerous dive-bombers and land-based medium bombers during the one-week operation, the conference attendees admitted that their planes needed "bullet protection," as they quaintly put it. Heretofore, the aviation community had operated under the premise that the best defense was a good offense. In applying the samurai ethic to twentieth-century war machines, fliers and engineers alike valued speed, agility, and lightness above all other qualities. If a plane and its pilot were appropriately aggressive, there was little need for heavy armor plating or protected fuel tanks. As an extension of that mindset, most fighter pilots removed the radios from their planes, and many refused to wear a parachute because they considered the weight excessive.

One positive outcome of the conference, at least from the Japanese point of view, was to affirm their belief that the Zero was still the most dominant fighter in the war. The Japanese did, however, express concern about the new American fighter they were encountering in the Solomons, the Vought F4U Corsair. In spite of themselves, they were impressed by the fighter's superior horizontal speed, rate of climb, armament, and ruggedness. "While their numbers were small, the F4Us caused no trouble," wrote Akira Yoshimura. "But as their numbers rapidly increased, it . . . became impossible to ignore this new fighter. The [attendees] had to admit that at last an American fighter able to match the Zero had appeared."

Another outcome of the conference was a situation report from Lieutenant General Adachi, who had returned from a recent inspection trip to New Guinea. Despite the string of losses there, he informed Yamamoto and the assembled leaders that if he could have another battalion, he would be able to hold his current positions. It was an illusion. Adachi was probably telling the navy what he thought they wanted to hear, but it worked. Both Yamamoto and Ugaki were pleased to receive the favorable news, which made them more eager than ever to visit the forward bases in the Solomons and inspire the men serving there.

Rear Admiral Johima, who had flown to Rabaul to attend the conference, warned Yamamoto against making his planned excursion to

Bougainville. The flight was too dangerous, Johima said, but Yamamoto would not back down. "I have to go," he replied. "I've let them know, and they'll have got things ready for me. I'll leave tomorrow morning and be back by dusk. Why don't we have dinner together?"

A STICKLER for punctuality, Isoroku Yamamoto arose early on the morning of April 18. The flight to the Solomons was scheduled to depart from Lakunai airdrome at 0600. An artistic individual, fond of writing haiku poems and creating exquisite examples of calligraphy, Yamamoto might have allowed himself a few minutes to indulge in the beauty of the tropical morning. The skies were clear, bringing the promise of a pleasant day, and a gentle sea breeze brought the scent of frangipani and bougain-villea wafting through the louvered shutters of the cottage.

For the first time since leaving Japan, Yamamoto donned a new uniform of green khaki instead of dress whites. He also wore a pair of comfortable airmen's boots, and completed his ensemble by attaching a traditional sword to his uniform belt. The weapon he selected had been a gift from his older brother, who was now deceased.

After breakfast, Yamamoto met Vice Admiral Ugaki outside his quarters. The chief of staff thought their new khakis looked "gallant," but he also had to admit that seeing Yamamoto in the dark green uniform for the first time was "a bit strange." They climbed into a car for the short ride to Lakunai and arrived precisely at 0600.

The traveling staff, arriving in several cars, pulled up alongside two Type 1 *rikko* from Air Group 705, brought over that morning from Vunakanau. Admiral Ozawa was on hand for the departure, but Yamamoto did not linger before boarding his aircraft. In accordance with standard precautionary measures, the Combined Fleet Staff was divided between the two bombers: Yamamoto and three officers climbed aboard an olive-colored Betty with the number *323* painted on its vertical stabilizer, while Ugaki and three other staff officers were seated in the second Mitsubishi, numbered *326*.

The bombers took off to the southeast, passing over Matupit Harbor and the gaping crater of Tavurvur as they climbed. Behind them, six fighters of Air Group 204 roared up from the same airdrome and formed into two *shotais*, one taking position on the right side of the bombers, the other on the left. The pilot of the trailing bomber, FPO 1st Class Hiroshi

Hayashi, tucked in close along the left side of the lead aircraft, skillfully maintaining such a tight formation that Ugaki was afraid "their wingtips might touch." But the chief of staff also appreciated being able to clearly see Yamamoto, who occupied the left front seat of the lead bomber, piloted by CPO Takashi Kotani.

THE BOMBERS' FIRST destination was Ballale, an island so tiny that its crushed-coral airstrip reached from one side of the island to the other. Officially part of the Shortland group, the arrowhead-shaped isle lay fourteen miles southeast of Moila Point on the tip of Bougainville. The airfield was built by the Imperial Navy's 18th Construction Battalion, headed by Lt. Cmdr. Noriko Ozaki, between November 1942 and January 1943. Because the Japanese had no bulldozers for such big projects, much of the labor was done by hand. In early December 1942, a shipment of 517 POWs arrived from Rabaul to work on the airfield—and therein lay another dark story of Japanese atrocities.

Known unofficially as the "Gunners 600," the prisoners sent to Ballale were among the thousands of British soldiers captured after the surrender of Singapore the previous February. Some 50,000 POWs were initially held near Changi Prison, but in mid-October about 600 Royal Artillerymen were sent to New Britain. After three weeks of misery at sea aboard a "hellship," they arrived at Kokopo on November 6. One prisoner had died en route, and many others were sick with dysentery, beriberi, and malaria. About a week later, 517 men were sent on to Ballale, leaving 82 of the sickest at Kokopo.

From the time of their arrival at Ballale, the British gunners were harshly treated. Ozaki himself was said to have beheaded a prisoner the next day, no doubt to establish his absolute authoritarianism. The POWs, housed in a compound of huts near the southwestern end of the airstrip, received no medical attention and were not allowed to dig or construct air-raid shelters. Korean laborers, Chinese prisoners, and native islanders also worked on the airfield, but they were strictly prohibited from making contact with the white prisoners.

The island's occupants were all living on borrowed time. On January 15, 1943, a single B-17 from Guadalcanal bombed the airstrip, and within a matter of weeks, aerial attacks became heavier and more frequent. Unknown to the American aircrews, dozens or possibly even hundreds of

POWs were killed by friendly bombs. The Japanese permitted the burial of the victims, whereas POWs who died due to illness or neglect were placed in rice sacks and dumped at sea. By the time Yamamoto's party approached Ballale, the tiny island had been hit at least fourteen times—and only a few dozen of the original 517 gunners were still alive.

Whether Yamamoto was aware of the British prisoners at Ballale is unknown. Either way, the gaunt, sickly survivors would probably have been kept out of sight while the commander in chief visited the garrison. There is no point in speculating further, however, because Yamamoto never reached the island.

AT 0710 ON SUNDAY, April 18, celebrated around Christendom as Palm Sunday, Maj. John W. Mitchell gunned his P-38 Lightning down the airstrip known as Fighter 2 on Guadalcanal. Behind him, seventeen hand-picked pilots—eight from the 339th Fighter Squadron commanded by Mitchell and nine from the 12th Fighter Squadron—waited their turn to roll. Over the past two days, aided by the expert staff at Fighter Command, Mitchell had carefully scripted a mission to intercept Yamamoto's flight. A circuitous route, nearly five hundred statute miles in length, would be flown well out to sea at barely fifty feet of altitude to avoid all possibility of detection by Japanese coastwatchers. Navigation would rely entirely on dead reckoning, since the airmen would be flying too low to see any landmarks. Therefore, the compass headings, air speeds, and timing of the route's five legs were laid out as precisely as possible. Yamamoto's punctuality was well known to Allied intelligence, so Mitchell designed a scheme to catch the entourage at a point along the Bougainville coast, about ten minutes before the flight neared the airdrome at Buin. Four of the pilots, led by Capt. Tom Lanphier, were assigned as the "killer" flight. The remaining sixteen Lightnings would provide cover against counterattacking Zeros.

Within minutes of Mitchell's takeoff, two Lightnings were scrubbed: one with a blown tire, the other with fuel transfer problems. Both were part of the attack flight, so two designated alternates—lieutenants Besby F. Holmes and his wingman, Raymond K. Hine—slid into the vacated spots. In all, sixteen pilots joined up and skimmed the waves as they headed outbound on the first leg of their roundabout route. At sea level the temperature was above ninety degrees, which meant the pilots sweated profusely as the sun blazed through their Perspex canopies. Mitchell's wingman, 1st Lt. Julius

Jacobson, wondered how his squadron leader was handling the extraordinary responsibilities. He could only imagine the critical questions that must have constantly cycled through Mitchell's mind:

Am I on course?

Did I turn to the compass heading on time?

Are the winds as predicted?

Will Yamamoto be there when we arrive?

Can we get him?

After completing the first four legs as carefully as he knew how, Mitchell turned to the final heading, which was pointed right into the morning sun. If everything went according to plan, the nineteen-mile-long northeasterly track would bring the P-38s to the coast of Bougainville in the vicinity of Torokina village, where they would intersect the path of Yamamoto's aircraft at right angles.

The Lightning pilots squinted hard, trying to see through the glare caused by a thin layer of haze. So far they had maintained strict radio silence, but a few minutes into the final leg, the voice of 1st Lt. Douglas S. Canning suddenly filled their earphones: "Bogeys, ten o'clock high!"

AT 0730 JAPAN STANDARD TIME, Yamamoto's flight was just beginning its descent over the jungles of Bougainville. Vice Admiral Ugaki, seated directly behind the pilot of the second bomber, was handed a note: the bombers would land at Ballale in fifteen minutes, exactly on schedule. Ugaki barely had time to digest the reassurance before the plane abruptly pitched downward. It took him a moment to realize that the pilot, Petty Officer Hayashi, was taking evasive action.

The bomber leveled off at 150 feet, and the flight crew jumped into action, opening gun blisters and the dorsal port. "It got noisy for a while with the handling of machine guns and the wind blowing in," recalled Ugaki. Only later did he learn that the escorting Zeros had spotted enemy fighters and dived to intercept them. This alerted the bomber pilots, but there was nowhere to run. Within seconds, both of the Bettys were under attack.

AFTER FLYING FOR two hours on five different compass headings using only a simple compass and dead reckoning, John Mitchell's P-38s intercepted the Yamamoto flight within a minute of the estimated time.

Jack Jacobson, like everyone else on the flight, considered Mitchell a magician. Undetected because of their olive drab paint, the Lightnings held their course and altitude until they were almost underneath the Japanese formation. Then Mitchell swung his fighters to a parallel course and hauled back on the controls in a thirty-degree climb. The other pilots followed with smooth coordination, sending their P-38s skyward like a volley of surface-to-air missiles.

"Skin 'em off," Mitchell said over the radio, and the pilots flipped the switches that released their external fuel tanks.

The four shooters tightened their formation. Flying on Lanphier's wing was 1st Lt. Rex T. Barber, followed by the two alternates, Holmes and Hine. But a problem arose when Holmes could not get his drop tanks to release. If they failed to disconnect, he would be out of the fight. He'd used up the tanks' combined three hundred gallons of gasoline getting to Bougainville, which meant they now contained raw vapor—far more explosive than the fuel in its liquid state. He finally shrugged the tanks loose, but only after putting his P-38 into a power dive and then yanking back on the wheel while simultaneously kicking full left rudder. The sudden high-g maneuver literally ripped the tanks from beneath the wings. By this time, however, Holmes and his wingman (who had faithfully stuck with his leader) were out of position to attack the Bettys.

That left only Lanphier and Barber to charge after the bombers, which crossed their path from left to right while descending through three thousand feet. As the two fighters positioned themselves for an attack run, the three Zeros on the right side of the Japanese formation raced forward to intervene. Seeing their approach, Lanphier abandoned his gunnery run and pulled up to face the Zeros head-on.

John Mitchell, leading the top-cover Lightnings in a climb to their assigned altitude, could scarcely believe his eyes. The P-38 drivers had been instructed by Rear Admiral Mitscher to get Yamamoto "at any cost," which meant ramming his bomber if need be. Tom Lanphier, the most talented young pilot in the killer group, was mere moments away from shooting down the most important target of the Pacific war—yet he deliberately turned away because of a few inconsequential Zeros. Flying on Mitchell's wing, Jack Jacobson had a similar reaction. "I cannot understand why Lanphier would give up a hero's chance of a lifetime by relinquishing his lead shot to his wingman," Jacobson later wrote. "He was a very aggressive combat fighter pilot; an 'A' type personality [with] political ambitions. Did he chicken out?"

Only one P-38 remained in position to attack the bombers, which were now down to about one thousand feet. Rex Barber rolled his big fighter to the right and simultaneously lowered the nose, not realizing that the second bomber was beneath his belly. Petty Officer Hiyashi was forced to take hard evasive action, diving to the left to avoid colliding with Barber. At the same time, the lead Betty dived out to the right, and the two *rikko* became widely separated.

Rolling wings-level, Barber found himself behind and slightly left of the lead bomber—and closing fast. He wondered briefly why the potent 20mm tail cannon didn't blast him, not learning until much later that the gunner's position was vacated to make room for the luggage brought by Yamamoto and his staff. Boring in to almost point-blank range, Barber thumbed the trigger buttons on the P-38's control wheel. Four tightly concentrated streams of .50-caliber slugs blazed from the nose of the fighter, joined by the rapid thumping of the 20mm cannon. The heavy rounds angled across the fuselage and impacted the right engine, so Barber tapped the left rudder pedal and sent the next rounds through the vertical stabilizer. Firing another burst into the right engine, he dragged his gunfire across the Betty's fuselage and into the opposite engine. Black smoke erupted from the bomber, which suddenly slowed, then rolled to the left so rapidly that the P-38 almost struck the bomber's right wingtip.

In the second bomber, Vice Admiral Ugaki had the presence of mind to check on the condition of Yamamoto's plane. He was not prepared for the shock of what he saw.

> The first plane was staggering southward, just brushing the jungle top with reduced speed, emitting black smoke and flame. It was about four thousand meters away from us. I just said to myself, "My God!" I could think of nothing else. I grabbed the shoulder of Air Staff Officer Muroi, pointed to the first aircraft, and said, "Look at the commander in chief's plane!" This became my parting with him forever. All this happened in only about twenty seconds.
>
> In the meantime, my plane turned again sharply to evade another enemy attack, and we lost sight of the commander in chief's aircraft.

I waited impatiently for the plane to get back to the level while full of anxiety, though the result seemed apparent. The next glance revealed that the plane was no more to be seen, only a pall of black smoke rising to the sky from the jungle. Oh! Everything was over now!

The sudden and erratic movements of Yamamoto's bomber, which crashed into thick jungle on Bougainville, gave Barber the impression that he may have hit the pilot. This may have been true. Admiral Yamamoto, sitting to the left of Chief Petty Officer Kotani, was almost certainly dead. In fact, he had probably died instantly when Barber's gunfire raked across the bomber from the right engine to the left. Among the bullets that penetrated the fuselage, two struck the commander in chief from behind as he sat in the left front seat. One, evidently half-spent, entered his left shoulder but did not exit; the other struck his lower left jaw and exited from his right temple, near the eye. No one could have survived such a wound from a .50 caliber slug.

The second Type 1 bomber, carrying Chief of Staff Ugaki, eluded the P-38s for only a few minutes longer. All of the available evidence suggests that Frank Holmes, after shedding his wing tanks and allegedly shooting down two of the defending Zeros, caught up with the bomber as it tried to escape seaward at wave-top altitude. The scene aboard the bomber was one of bedlam, according to Ugaki. "The enemy P-38 rapidly closed in, taking advantage of his superior speed. His gunfire caught us splendidly, and oncoming bullets were seen on both sides of our plane. I felt them hitting our aircraft from time to time. Now we were hopeless, and I thought my end was very near behind."

One of the staff officers was sprawled over a worktable, probably dead, when Petty Officer Hayashi began losing control of the bomber. Smoke trailed from at least one engine. Hayashi retarded the throttles, but the aircraft suddenly shed its right wing, rolled more than ninety degrees to the left, and slammed into the sea. By some miracle, three men were ejected from the aircraft on impact and survived. Vice Admiral Ugaki sustained serious injuries, including a broken wrist and numerous lacerations, while Petty Officer Hayashi only had a few bumps and scratches. The other survivor was the fleet paymaster, Rear Adm. Gen Kitamura, who was partially blinded and could not speak due to "a big hole in his throat."

Rex Barber had also fired upon the second bomber just before it crashed. In fact, pieces of the exploding plane damaged the belly and wing of his

P-38. Thus both of the Betty bombers were successfully shot down thanks to the split-second perfection of John Mitchell's plan. The Lightnings promptly headed back toward Guadalcanal, every man for himself, before the Zeros at Buin and Ballale could intercept them. Barber's plane was badly shot up by some of the six defending Zeros, but it got him home; Frank Holmes, low on fuel, landed at the Russells; Ray Hine never did show up. He may have been the victim of an avenging Zero, but the cause of his demise has never been positively determined.

THE "YAMAMOTO MISSION," as it came to be known, was embroiled in controversy from the moment the victorious pilots landed back at Fighter 2. Indeed the debate still rages, extending well beyond the deaths of the principal players. When the airmen returned to Guadalcanal on April 18, Tom Lanphier proclaimed, "I got Yamamoto! I got Yamamoto!" He immediately began to promote his alleged accomplishment in every way possible, from the post-mission debriefings to the writing of the official report. Donald Davis, author of *Lightning Strike: The Secret Mission to Kill Yamamoto and Avenge Pearl Harbor*, provides a convincing argument that Lanphier, who had earned a degree in journalism from Stanford and worked as a reporter for the *San Francisco News,* composed and typed the report himself.

As a result of the initial debriefings and questionable report, credit was initially awarded to Lanphier, Barber, and Holmes for one bomber each. After reviewing the case and discerning that only two bombers were present, the air force amended the victories to show one-half credit each for Barber and Lanphier against the lead bomber and one-half credit each to Barber and Holmes for the second bomber. Barber was content with the arrangement, unlike the politically ambitious Lanphier. For decades Lanphier campaigned to obtain sole credit for killing Yamamoto.

Curiously, no one actually saw Lanphier shoot at either of the bombers, and there is credible evidence, albeit circumstantial, that he never did. Possibly the most damning evidence, revealed by the 1991 publication of Admiral Ugaki's annotated diary in English, was the chronology of the attack on the lead bomber. Ugaki stated that Yamamoto's aircraft was on fire within twenty seconds of the first attack (conducted by Barber), at which point Ugaki temporarily lost sight of the lead bomber while his own underwent violent maneuvers. When he next looked, Yamamoto's plane had already crashed. As described independently by both Ugaki and

Barber, everything happened quickly.

Tom Lanphier had a different story. He asserted that after he turned toward the three attacking Zeros, he downed one and fought his way past the other two. Then, zooming up to six thousand feet, he looped over on his back and spotted a Japanese bomber far below, just above the jungle. He chopped the throttles, extended his flaps to retard the Lightning's speed, and dropped down on the bomber while firing a long burst at full deflection—the most difficult angle for shooting. Furthermore, he claimed that the rear gunner in the bomber was firing back at him.

Doug Canning, the last surviving member of the Yamamoto mission, believes that Lanphier's version is bogus: "According to the Japanese, they had a lot of luggage in the back of the bomber and there was no place for the tail gunner to fit," he said. "This indicates to me that Tom was not telling the truth. He wanted to be president of the United States. That was his goal. He thought that being famous would help him."

The biggest flaw in Lanphier's account involves time. All of the dog-fighting and maneuvering that he described would have taken at least a couple of minutes—and possibly longer. Canning is convinced that Lanphier could not possibly have accomplished all that he claimed and still manage to attack Yamamoto's bomber before it crashed into the jungle.

Over the years, Lanphier altered his story several times and wrote an autobiography to back his claims, but it was never published. Ultimately his credibility disintegrated, in part because of the inconsistencies in his ever-evolving story and partly through his acrimonious insistence that he alone deserved credit. Today, historians have come to the near-unanimous conclusion that Rex Barber, who died in 2001, deserves full credit for shooting down Yamamoto. At least one organization is pushing for a Medal of Honor in Barber's behalf.

Lesser controversies also surfaced after the Yamamoto mission. All four pilots in the "killer" flight were credited with shooting down at least one Zero during the opening moments of the interception, but the combat log of Air Group 204, together with the testimony of the only escort pilot who survived the war, proves that none of the six Zeros was destroyed. In some cases, credit for victories was later rescinded by the U.S. Air Force. Tom Lanphier lost credit for the Zero he claimed that morning and subsequently dropped from the ranks of World War II aces because he had less than five total victories.

The Japanese also contributed to the controversies surrounding Yamamoto's death. Soon after the action, most of the escorting *Rei-sen* landed at Buin, where army and navy staffs waited in full dress uniform to greet Yamamoto. They were stunned by the reports that the commander in chief's plane had been shot down. The last of the escorts to land was FPO Kenji Yanagiya. He was distraught, like the other Zero pilots, and could not bring himself to admit that he had failed his assignment.

Years later, Yanagiya's recollections of that disturbing moment were incorporated into a small paperback published by the Naval Air Group 204 Association:

> The disappointing and shocking report by the crews caused a great deal of restlessness at the base. Yanagiya, who chased the enemy to the outside of the Shortlands, came back last. He got down from the plane with tottering steps and a blank expression, just like a sleepwalker's. As if the officers could not believe the report given by the previously arrived members, they called Yanagiya and asked, "Was Admiral Yamamoto really killed?"
>
> The faces of the commanders were pale. Yanagiya could not say that the Admiral had died. He was hesitant to give further blows to the dismayed officers and push them too far. On top of that, he did not have the face to say, "Yes. He is dead," while the six escort planes had no real damage.
>
> Yanagiya answered in a roundabout way, "Because the Admiral made an emergency landing in such a fierce fire, he may not have survived. However, I cannot be assertive because I myself did not see him."

Search teams were sent out in the vain hope of finding someone alive at the crash site, which was easily visible from the air. All around the point of impact, the trees were blackened by fire. Locating the site on foot in the midst of the thick, primeval jungle was another matter. Not until the evening of April 19 did a party of soldiers stumble across the wreckage, having searched for the better part of two days. The plane was not completely destroyed—its wings and engines had broken off, yet were mostly intact—but the crumpled forward half of the fuselage was "a burned-out hulk."

The condition of the bomber is consistent with what typically happens when a large aircraft plunges in flames into a forested area. However, the accounts of what the searchers discovered *outside* the plane do not make sense. Yamamoto's body was allegedly found among some trees to the left of the fuselage, still strapped in his seat, his uniform barely singed. His appearance was peaceful, as though asleep, and his left hand gripped his sword. In virtually every account, the description of Yamamoto's condition is the same. The Japanese would have us believe that his bomber crashed in flames into dense jungle, creating secondary fires that blackened the surrounding trees, yet somehow Yamamoto was neither burned nor disfigured when his body was ejected, seat and all, from the aircraft. The depiction is patently contrived and smacks of a carefully controlled cover-up.

The army search party also found evidence of the two bullet wounds in Yamamoto's body. A navy medical officer supposedly confirmed the wounds while conducting a preliminary examination on April 20 but reported the wounds as small. This also bends logic far beyond the boundaries of common sense. If a .50-caliber bullet pierced Yamamoto's left jaw and exited near his right eye, it is highly probable that much of his skull was blown away. In that case, the Japanese went to considerable lengths to prevent any mention of this ghastly disfigurement. The other possibility is that a much smaller fragment—a piece of a bullet or shrapnel from a 20mm shell—struck Yamamoto. Either way, the doctor who examined Yamamoto's head wound declared, "This alone would have killed him outright." It is also well worth noting that a quarter of a century later, Japanese biographer Hiroyuki Agawa stated that the medical report was "tampered with, on orders from above, in order to make things look better." Ultimately, so many details regarding Yamamoto's condition were whitewashed that it is difficult to accept any of them at face value.

IN KEEPING WITH Shinto tradition, the bodies of Yamamoto and the other crash victims were placed in coffins and cremated at Buin on April 21. Some of the corpses were already burned beyond recognition, to the point of being carbonized. Yamamoto's cremation was conducted in a separate pit, after which his ashes were placed in a small wooden box.

Out of concern that the news of Yamamoto's death would cause a general panic across the empire, the story was kept secret for more than four weeks while the government and Imperial General Headquarters decided what to do. Finally, on May 21, the *Johokyoku* issued a carefully prepared statement, and the following day the press released the story of Yamamoto's "heroic end." The front pages featured a large photograph of the admiral in his dress whites, taken at Rabaul during the recent offensive. For the next several days, articles exhorting the Japanese people to "exemplify the spirit of Yamamoto" were published across the nation.

In death, Yamamoto received royal treatment. His Shinto funeral rites were spread over a period of four days. There were special ceremonies to mark the return of his ashes to Japan; others to purify the graveyard where the ashes would be interred (alongside those of Fleet Admiral Togo, the hero of the Russo-Japanese War); and, in a particularly rare honor, an imperial address "to the departed spirit" was granted on June 4 by His Majesty the Emperor.

The next day, while the funeral procession moved through the streets of Tokyo to Hibiya Park, Prime Minister Hideki Tojo gave a public address praising Yamamoto's career. An urn containing Yamamoto's ashes rode atop a gun carriage pulled by sixteen *Musashi* sailors, part of a long procession that included military bands playing traditional dirges. At the front, priests held aloft a banner that reached two stories high, its kanji characters proclaiming, "The Urn of Fleet Admiral Isoroku Yamamoto, Bearer of the Grand Order and the First Order of the Golden Kite."

At precisely 1050, virtually every person in Japan stopped whatever he or she was doing and offered a silent prayer for Yamamoto while bowing in the direction of Tokyo. And the ceremonies continued long after the burial, as tens of thousands of Japanese filed past Yamamoto's shrine to pay their last respects. Numerous public tributes followed, none more unique than the song commissioned by the Mainichi newspaper group. On the day of the funeral, the company announced that Atsuo Oki, a well-known poet, had been commissioned to write the lyrics for a "people's song" about the greatest admiral in Japanese history. The music was composed by the Imperial Navy band, resulting in a lofty tribute to the man who had led, albeit reluctantly, his people into war.

"Fleet Admiral Yamamoto"

Ah! Amidst the battle in the South Seas
Gloriously died the admiral in the sky, like a private

While commanding his force at the head.
Who says that thousands upon thousands are killed
When an admiral is accredited with victory?

No sooner had the Greater East Asia War broken out
Than Admiral Isoroku Yamamoto
Destroyed the foe beyond recognition
Taking the helm of the Grand Fleet
In obeyance to the Imperial Command.

With peerless courage and masterly strategy
Did he defeat the enemy navies instantly
At Pearl Harbor and off Malai;
Off the Solomons and in the Coral Sea.
Numberless are the brilliant naval war results!

From the southern end to the northern extremity
Rose victorious cries everywhere.
Heaven admired the admiral's valor,
Seven Seas revered his dignity
As he commanded the Imperial Navy.

Iron resolve to go to the furthest front
Never to return again
Was manifest in his poems.
Let us follow in the footsteps of the noble admiral
Who assumed the weighty responsibility without argument.

If nothing else, Oki's song gave the Japanese people a lyrical vehicle, indeed a hymn, by which they could honor the spirit of their newest deity. Many, it is certain, pondered what might have been. Yamamoto was the ideal hero. Complex, sensitive, artistic, he was descended from samurai, which made his final flight aboard a warplane all the more worthy of a warrior god.

YAMAMOTO'S DEMISE not only represented a crucial turning point for the Japanese, it coincided with a fundamental shift in American strategy. General Kenney's trip to Washington, D.C., in March had been part of the prelude to that shift, as he and several other high-ranking officers from MacArthur's and Halsey's staffs attended a high-level conference with the Joint Chiefs of Staff.

Prior to the conference, which opened on March 12, 1943, Halsey and MacArthur had hammered out an agreement regarding their responsibilities for implementing the Elkton Plan. The details were then presented to the Joint Chiefs by Brigadier General Sutherland, and for this reason alone the conference proved its worth. Heretofore the Joint Chiefs had optimistically believed that Rabaul could be captured by the end of 1943, but the representatives from the Pacific Theater revealed the flaws in such wishful thinking. MacArthur estimated that, in addition to the multinational forces already under his command, he would need five infantry divisions, 1,800 planes, and a considerable navy before he could begin the first objective of Elkton, the seizure of Lae. Naturally the Joint Chiefs wanted the theater commanders to accomplish more with less, but the latter had formed a strong alliance—and the navy delegates in Washington sided with them as well.

After several days of wrangling, the attendees got no further than to define what everyone disagreed about. The solution was left to the Joint Chiefs, who would have to decide among themselves how much war materiel could be diverted to the Pacific. At first they continued to hope that Rabaul could be taken in 1943, but eventually they conceded that the objectives for the year would have to be scaled back. Even so, MacArthur was promised a minimum of six army air groups and two infantry divisions. It was considerably less than he'd requested, but when the assets that already existed were combined with the promised allotments (including those earmarked for Halsey), the Allies could expect to accumulate some 2,500 planes in the South Pacific and Southwest Pacific theaters. It was a staggering number of aircraft, many of which would eventually be used against Rabaul.

On March 28, only a few weeks before Yamamoto's death, the Joint Chiefs released a new directive titled "Offensive Operations in the South and Southwest Pacific Areas During 1943." Consisting of three main objectives, it was based on the Elkton Plan initially proposed by MacArthur, with input from Halsey:

1. Establish airfields on Kiriwina and Woodlark Islands.
2. Seize the Lae-Salamaua-Finschhafen-Madang area and occupy western New Britain.

3. Seize and occupy Solomon Islands to include the southern portion of Bougainville.

The stated purpose of the objectives was to pave the way for "the seizure of the Bismarck Archipelago," which meant that every operation was ultimately focused on Rabaul. Within a few months, however, the plan underwent a major revision. The Joint Chiefs determined that it would not be necessary to physically invade Rabaul. Instead, Japan's greatest stronghold would be neutralized by air power. Calling the new plan Operation Cartwheel, the Joint Chiefs remained optimistic that Rabaul would be smashed by the end of 1943.

But as hundreds of Allied and Japanese airmen would learn, many at the cost of their lives, the strategists were wrong.

Epilogue

THE SOUTHERN OFFENSIVE stunned the world in December 1941. And yet, by April of 1943, just sixteen months after the fighting began, the Japanese had lost all chance of winning the Pacific war. The death of Admiral Yamamoto punctuated a series of extremely costly defeats, and the registry at the Yasukuni Shrine in Tokyo (the national Shinto temple for war dead), was filling by the tens of thousands with the names of the sailors, soldiers, and airmen who had already given their lives for the emperor.

Although the tide had turned in favor of the Allies, the mood at Imperial General Headquarters was relatively calm. The desired expansion of the Southeast Area had not progressed as planned, but there was still Rabaul. The fortress was bigger than ever—stronger too, despite more than a year of Allied bombing. Expansion continued during 1943, with two more airdromes in operation and a fifth under construction. The number of troops, warplanes, and ships would also increase throughout most of the year.

In the Home Islands, Rabaul had become a fixture in popular culture. Japanese youth enjoyed listening to a trendy new song that romanticized the South Seas fortress. "Rabaul My Love," recorded in 1942, evoked images of warm nights, tropical breezes, and even romance:

So long, Rabaul, 'til we return
Bidding farewell with teary eyes
Gazing at the island where my love resides
Forevermore the Southern Cross.

§

Rabaul was even more legendary among the Allies. The exploits of Butch O'Hare, Harl Pease, and Ken Walker were widely publicized, and the stronghold was mentioned frequently in the war news at home. Due in large measure to the cost of the Walker mission, the Fifth Air Force discontinued daylight attacks against Rabaul for months, resorting instead to small-scale night raids. However, the cumulative effect of such raids amounted to little more than harassment. The Japanese were unimpeded as they continued to make improvements and establish stronger defenses around the great caldera.

The difference-maker in the Pacific war was the output of America's factories. The pipelines were just beginning to flow in April 1943, and the volume of war materiel sent to the Pacific increased steadily thereafter until the full measure of American manufacturing capability came on line. Then it was the Allies' turn to gather overwhelming strength as they prepared to launch Operation Cartwheel. The United States and her allies had the luxury of time on their side, while the Japanese remained in a strictly defensive posture, hoarding resources and struggling to provide enough men and materiel to hold their current positions.

Although the Japanese fanatically defended each of their bases in the Solomons and New Guinea, the perimeter around Rabaul collapsed island by bloody island. With each Allied gain, the size and intensity of the air attacks on Rabaul increased. Daylight raids resumed in October 1943, when P-38 Lightnings and B-25 Mitchells flying from forward bases in New Guinea joined the heavy bombers over the target. The following month, Admiral Halsey ordered two daring carrier raids against Simpson Harbor to cover the invasion of Bougainville. Soon thereafter, generals MacArthur and Kenney declared that Rabaul was finished and mistakenly turned their attention elsewhere. Within a few weeks, carriers of the Imperial Navy delivered hundreds of planes to reinforce Rabaul's land units.

With the capture of Bougainville, the Allies established airstrips that enabled single-engine fighters to reach Rabaul for the first time. For two months beginning in mid-December 1943, huge air battles raged almost daily over the stronghold, often involving hundreds of aircraft. Attrition eventually forced the Japanese to pull their air flotillas out of Rabaul, and by early March 1944, waves of Allied bombers of every size and description had razed the township.

Although besieged by the Allied encirclement, the Japanese refused to give up. Their flow of supplies was drastically reduced, and the repeated bombing raids forced the garrison to live underground, but conditions were not terribly uncomfortable. Living and working in skillfully engineered tunnels and caves, the Japanese moved their headquarters, supply dumps, barracks, and even fully equipped hospitals under the volcanic mountains.

Prisoners of war, on the other hand, endured a wretched existence at Rabaul. Indian and Chinese POWs, shipped from captured territories to provide slave labor, died by the thousands on New Britain. Captured aviators suffered much as well. Between April 1943 and the end of the war, well over a hundred downed airmen were taken prisoner in the Southwest Pacific and brought to a separate camp run by the Kempeitai. But when the Japanese surrendered Rabaul in September 1945, only seven gaunt captives were still alive.

Their story is for another book.

Notes

Prologue

Lark Force's limitations and responsibilities: Gamble, *Darkest Hour*, pp. 46–47.

Under the circumstances . . . : Cable 152, Dec. 12, 1941.

Communiqué issued by Victoria Barracks: Johnston, *New Guinea Diary*, p. 2.

Statements by Minister Forde: *Canberra Times*, Jan. 24, 1942, p. 1.

Military experts believe . . . : Sydney *Sun*, p. 1.

Chapter 1: Volcanoes, God, and Coconuts

Why are the Japs striking . . . : Johnston, p. 1.

Geological background of the Rabaul caldera and details of the major
   eruptions: McKee, pp. 4–21; also Dr. C. Daniel Miller, interview with author,
   Mar. 26, 2002.

Development and settlement of Rabaul: Gamble, pp. 34–35.

Australian Expeditionary Force skirmish at Rabaul: Ibid., p. 35.

little tropical outpost: Johnston, p. 1.

Details of 1937 eruption: Johnson, *Volcano Town*, pp. 25–45.

Chapter 2: 24 Squadron

Weak status of Australia's military, including *a paper plan*: Hasluck, *The Government
   and the People*, p. 298.

On each of these groups . . . : Thompson, *National Geographic*, Dec. 1921, pp. 557–59.

Installment of antiaircraft guns: Gamble, pp. 46–47.

Early war status of RAAF, including *not very formidable*: Gillison, *Royal Australian
   Air Force 1939–1942*, p. 191.

Lockheed Hudson duties: McAulay, *We Who Are About to Die*, p. 39.

Arrival of Hudsons at Rabaul and first operational flight: Murphy, correspondence
   with author, June 7, 2004.

Erwin's mission to Kapingamarangi Atoll: McAulay, p. 50.

I was the first to drop a bomb . . . : Murphy, correspondence with author, June 7, 2004.

It was addressed to me . . . : Quoted in McAulay, p. 52.

Personality of Wing Commander Garing: McAulay, correspondence with author, June 17, 2008.

Lerew's *impish irreverence* and sarcastic messages: Gillison, p. 270.

owing to lack of speed: Brookes, *RAAF Operations Report from Rabaul*, p. 4.

Development of Lakunai Airdrome: McAulay, pp. 42–43, 63.

Interception of flying boats and Wirraways' poor performance: Brookes, p. 4.

Details of New Year's Day attack: Murphy, correspondence with author.

Development of Japanese pre-war strategies: Bullard, *Japanese Army Operations in the South Pacific Area*, p. 4.

Japanese plans for the Southern Offensive and Rabaul, 1941: Ibid., p. 3–5.

Great Army Order No. 992: Ibid., p. 7.

South Seas Force invasion of Guam: Rottman, *World War II Pacific Island Guide*, pp. 389–90.

Japanese plans for R Operation: Bullard, pp. 7, 23–24.

Chapter 3: Gladiators

Profile of Cornelius Page: *The Stubborn Coastwatcher*, pp. 1–2.

Explanation of Imperial Japanese Navy land attack category: Tagaya, *Mitsubishi Type 1 Rikko "Betty" Units of World War 2*, p. 6.

Mitsubishi G3M specifications: Francillon, *Japanese Aircraft of the Pacific War*, p. 357.

Approach of the first Japanese bombers: Bloomfield, *Rabaul Diary*, pp. 13–14.

Can we really fire this time?: Selby, *Hell and High Fever*, p. 15.

Antiaircraft battery's first action: Ibid., pp. 15–16; also Fisher, unpublished memoir, p. 3.

Results of the first Japanese raid, including native casualties: Stone, *Hostages to Freedom*, p. 44.

Japanese publicity: *Mainichi Daily News*, Jan. 16, 1942, p. 1.

Interception by Wirraways, including *the enemy took advantage* . . . : Brookes, p. 6; also McAulay, p. 87.

Explosion of Hudson bomber: McAulay, p. 89.

Reconnaissance of Truk Lagoon: Gillison, p. 317.

Details of Jan. 16 attacks: McAulay, pp. 99–100.

Government's refusal to evacuate civilian men: Aplin, *Rabaul 1942*, p. 26.

Composition of Rabaul invasion fleet: Bullard, p. 22.

Strength of Nagumo's carrier forces: Dull, *The Imperial Japanese Navy*, p. 102;

Wenger, correspondence with author, Nov. 7, 2004.

Profile of Commander Fuchida: Prange, *God's Samurai*, pp. 4–48.

Specifications of A6M Zero: Francillon, p. 376–77.

Initial attack by Zeros, including *desperate gallantry*: Selby, p. 27; also Gillison, p. 353.

There could be only one conclusion . . . : Selby, pp. 27–28.

Details of Zero vs. Wirraway combat: Gillison, pp. 353–56; also McAulay, pp. 109–14.

There was something sickening . . . : Selby, p, 28.

Casualties suffered by 24 Squadron: McAulay, p. 114.

Defense ministry's decision regarding medals for Wirraway crews: Stone, p. 50.

Bomb damage at Vunakanau: McAulay, p. 118.

Details of *Kaga* B5N attack, including *Our aircraft shook a lot* . . . : Werneth, pp. 111, 115.

Dive-bombing attacks on *Herstein* and *Westralia*: Gamble, p. 76.

Damaged aircraft return to Japanese fleet, including *I was scared* . . . : Werneth, p. 147.

Details of Japanese losses: Tagaya, correspondence with author, July 28, 2007.

Commander Fuchida's frustration: Prange, p. 54.

Details of messages from Lerew: Gillison, p. 356.

Norwegian and RAAF casualties, including *The battered bodies* . . . : Bowman, *Not Now Tomorrow*, p. 26.

Background of the *Morituri vos salutamus* message: May, unpublished essay, Jan. 18, 1996; also interview with author, Jan. 25, 2008. In early 1992, John Lerew supported May's version of events: "I'd done Latin up through Leaving (certificate) at Scots College," he told a reporter, "but I was a bit rusty so I got an Army padre to help me." (*Canberra Times*, Jan. 18, 1992, p. 3).

Details of last Hudson flight, including *the chief gladiator* . . . : Gillison, p. 358.

Chapter 4: Desperate Hours

Configuration of Catalina: Riddell, *Recounting the Operations of RAAF Catalinas*, p. 1.

Sighting of Japanese fleet on Jan. 21, 1942: Minty, *Black Cats*, p. 2.

Details of *Zuikaku* fighter unit: Wenger, correspondence with author, Nov. 4, 2004.

Downing of Thompson's Catalina and capture of crew: Minty, pp. 3–4.

Nagumo's objectives: Bullard, p. 24.

Reported size of enemy fleet: McAulay, p. 121; Gillison, pp. 356–57.

Colonel Scanlan's puzzling orders: Gamble, pp. 81–82.

Orders for 24 Squadron, including *all available aircraft* . . . : Brookes, p. 9.

not to reason why . . . : Tennyson, "The Charge of the Light Brigade."

Sharp's attempt to find the Japanese fleet: Gillison, p. 357.

Message from Air Commodore Bladin: Ibid., p. 358.

Last RAAF flight from Rabaul: McAulay, pp. 124–25.

Explosion of bomb dump, including *a rather botched demolition*: Stone, p. 53.

Scanlan's consent to withdraw 24 Squadron: Gamble, p. 86.

Evacuation of patients to Vunapope, including *You'll stay* . . . : May, interview with author. Jan. 5, 2008.

Send flying boats . . . : Gillison, p. 360.

Callous behavior of civilians: Brookes, p. 11.

Airlift of 24 Squadron personnel: Brookes, pp. 10–11; also McAulay, pp. 138–44.

Chapter 5: The Fall of Rabaul

Amphibious landings on January 23, 1942: Gamble, pp. 94–99.

The loss of Zero pilot Hiraishi: Shiga, quoted in Werneth, p. 249.

Collapse of Lark Force, including *every man for himself*: Bloomfield, pp. 23, 25; also Gamble, pp. 110–17.

Execution of captured officers: Gamble, pp. 132, 134, 156, 212–13.

General Horii's edict: Bloomfield, p. 25.

Outbreak of malaria: Japanese Monograph No. 143 (Army), p. 10.

Captain Robertson's warning of *certain death*: Selby, p. 57.

Assault on Tol Plantation by 3rd Battalion/8th Company: Monograph No. 143, p. 8.

Atrocities at Tol: Gamble, pp. 148–58.

Torture and execution of Captain Gray: Stone, pp. 361–62. Several references to the vivisection of Gray are found in the memoirs of Rabaul POWs and internees. As with the atrocities at Tol, the Japanese were unable to keep Gray's murder a secret. According to Peter Stone, two villagers came across Gray's shallow grave a few weeks after the incident and "examined the body, confirming that the heart was removed." Independently, a Kempeitai interpreter bragged about the vivisection in the presence of Father Josef Leo Brenninkmeyer, a priest at Vunapope.

Gray's coupe de grace: May, interview with author.

Chapter 6: Counterattack

Specifications of the PBY Catalina: Riddell, p. 1; also Swanborough & Bowers, *United States Navy Aircraft*, p. 100.

Details of first RAAF raid on Rabaul: Gillison, p. 365.

It was an amazing thing . . . : Kingsland, interview with author. Nov. 29, 2005.

snatch a nap like children in kindergarten: Minty, p. 10.

Observations of Private Hisaeda: Captured diary, Jan. 24, 1942. AWM 3DRL/4005.

RAAF damage claims: Gillison, p. 365.

Japanese friendly fire incident: AWM 54 (423/4/158).

Follow-up raid and observations of Lieutenant Duigan: Gillison, p. 365.

RAAF Shocks Japs: Sydney *Sun*, Jan. 28, 1942, p. 1.

Enemy aircraft frequently invaded . . . : AWM 54 (423/4/162).

Repairs to Lakunai: Japanese Monograph No. 120, Outline of Southeast Area Naval
   Operations, p. 5.

encourage the Army engineer troops . . . : Hata & Izawa, *Japanese Naval Aces and
   Fighter Units in World War II*, p. 103.

Arrival of first Imperial Navy fighter units: Ibid., pp. 103–4.

Capabilities and limitations of Mitsubishi A5M: Francillon, p. 347.

Air combat between Hemsworth and Nishizawa: Gillison, pp. 448–49; also
   Guttmann, "The Devil," *Aviation History*, July 1998, p. 44.

Hemsworth's return to Port Moresby: Gillison, p. 448.

Ordeal of Captain Campbell and crew: Ibid., pp. 449–50.

Capture and development of Gasmata air base: Bullard, p. 38.

Lerew's attack on Gasmata: McAulay, p. 194–95.

Interception by Japanese fighters: Tagaya, correspondence with author, Feb. 8, 2004.

Damage to Japanese transports: McAulay, p. 194–96.

Chapter 7: Stronghold

Japanese occupation of Rabaul and construction statistics: United States Strategic
   Bombing Survey, *The Allied Campaign Against Rabaul*, pp. 11–18.

Details of antiaircraft defenses and ground defenses: Ibid., pp. 11–14.

Details of infrastructure: Ibid., pp. 15–18.

Specifications of antiaircraft weapons: *Intelligence Bulletin Vol. I, No. 8*, pp. 72–76;
   also *Vol. III, No. 2*, pp. 47–48.

Radar and early warning at Rabaul: United States Strategic Bombing Survey, pp.
   15–16.

Other details regarding the development of Rabaul were found in AWM 54
   (208/2/1), containing ATIS translations of miscellaneous captured documents,
   and in AWM 55 (12/140), ATIS Information Request Report No. 103, Japanese
   statements and diary excerpts relating to prisoners of war, May 4, 1944.

Chapter 8: Task Force 11

Assessment of Yamamoto's chief of staff: Ugaki, *Fading Victory*, p. 81.

Background of Task Force 11 and the ANZAC command: Lundstrom, *The First*

Team: Pacific Naval Air Combat from Pearl Harbor to Midway, pp. 84–87.

Reconnaissance findings at Rabaul on Feb. 16: Gillison, p. 451.

Mitsubishi Type 1 specifications: Francillon, p. 386.

Critique of weight-saving measures: Tagaya, *Mitsubishi Type 1*, p. 10.

Progress of Task Force 11 from Fiji: Lundstrom, pp. 85–87.

Plentiful shipping targets . . . : Sherman, p. 80.

Plans for B-17 support: Salaker, *Fortress Against the Sun*, p. 145.

Detection of Task Force 11 by flying boats: Lundstrom, pp. 88, 91.

Launching and vectoring of Wildcats: Ibid., pp. 88–91.

Chapter 9: Medal of Honor: Edward H. "Butch" O'Hare

Profile of Lieutenant Commander Thach: Lundstrom, p. 38.

Downing of first Japanese flying boat, including Thach's observations: Thach, "The Red Rain of Battle," *Collier's*, p. 15.

Shoot-down of second flying boat: Lundstrom, pp. 93–94.

Admiral Goto's decision to send Type 1 bombers: Ibid., pp. 94–95.

Goto's message to the 4th Air Group: Quoted in Osaka *Mainichi*, Mar. 10, 1942, p 2.

Configuration of Type 1 cockpit seating: Tagaya, correspondence with author, Jan. 4, 2004.

Off we went . . . : Osaka *Mainichi*, Mar. 10, 1942, p. 2.

Ito's decision to separate the 1st and 2nd *Chutais*: Lundstrom, pp. 97–98.

Admiral Brown's decision to call off the raid: Ibid., p. 94.

Background and capabilities of USS *Lexington*: Johnson, *Queen of the Flattops*, pp. 2, 19–23.

a perfect day for bombing: Sherman, *Combat Command*, p. 81.

Details of 2nd Chutai's attack on *Lexington*: Lundstrom, pp. 97–10; also Tagaya, *Mitsubishi Type 1 Units*, pp. 36–37.

Destruction of the 2nd Chutai: Ewing & Lundstrom, *Fateful Rendezvous*, pp. 124–28. (The O'Hare biography contains revisions over Lundstrom's earlier landmark work, *The First Team*, which remains unparalleled as a moment-by-moment account.)

O'Hare's interception of the 1st Chutai: Ewing & Lundstrom, pp. 128–37.

The rest of us . . . : Thach, in *Collier's*, p. 56.

[the bombers] were coming on fast . . . : O'Hare, quoted in *Life*, p. 18.

O'Hare's first gunnery pass: Lundstrom, *The First Team, Pearl Harbor to Midway*, pp. 102–3; also Tagaya, p. 36.

As we closed in . . . : Thach, quoted in Johnston, p. 74.

By this time . . . : O'Hare, quoted in *Life*, p. 18.

Pursuit of 1st Chutai remnants: Lundstrom, pp. 104–5; Tagaya, pp. 36–37; also Osaka *Mainichi*, Mar. 10, 1942, p. 2.

Ordeal of 1st Chutai stragglers: Tagaya, p. 37; also Osaka *Mainichi*, Mar. 10, 1942, p. 2.

Observations of the raid by war correspondent Miyake: Ibid.

Obituaries in the Japanese press: Osaka *Mainichi*, May 3, 1942, p. 1.

Distribution of American medals: Johnston, pp. 78–79.

Background of E. J. O'Hare: Ewing & Lundstrom, pp. 28–38, 75–86.

I figured there wasn't much to do . . . : Quoted in *Life*, p. 18.

Chapter 10: Carmichael's Raid

making better progress . . . and *inflict strong pressure on Australia* . . . : AWM 54 (608/5/4).

Results of first Japanese raid on Darwin: Gillison, pp. 430–31.

Tomorrow we go on our first mission . . . and *mission called off* . . . : Steinbinder, personal diary, Feb. 19, 1942.

Conditions at Cloncurry: Ibid., Feb. 20, 1942.

I was there for comfort . . . : Kingsland, interview with author, Nov. 29, 2005.

Reduction of B-17s for first mission: Steinbinder diary, Feb. 22, 1942; also Salaker, p. 145.

Details of first bomb runs by Lewis and Eaton: Saleker, pp. 145–46; also Gillison, p. 152.

Eaton's forced landing: Taylan, "Swamp Ghost: B-17E 41-2446" DVD.

Carmichael's assessment of enemy fighters: USAF oral history, p. 74.

Cohen's recollection of Zero attacks: Kingsland, interview with author.

B-17 claim by Petty Officer Yoshina: Tagaya, correspondence with author, Jan. 26, 2004.

Carmichael's admission of poor bombing: USAF oral history, p. 74.

The Japanese were very alert . . . and details of the Catalina dive-bombing attack: Kingsland, interview with author.

14th Reconnaissance Squadron immobilized by dengue fever: Steinbinder diary, Mar. 11–17, 1942.

Chapter 11: Yanks Down Under

Arcadia conference: Craven & Cate, *The Army Air Forces in World War II, Vol. IV*, pp. 408–10.

Background of Brett and his troubles with MacArthur: Cox, *Air Power Leadership on the Front Line*, pp. 39–43.

MacArthur's reputation, including "Dugout Doug": Manchester, *American Caesar*, p. 236.

Brett's coziness with Australian politicians: Griffith, pp. 51–52.

Aussie work habits, including *smoke-o*: The Marauder unofficial unit history, p. 23.

Japanese attacks on Port Moresby: Tagaya, pp. 37–38; also Gillison, pp. 446, 453.

Japanese aerial superiority: Ibid., p. 453.

Fate of Petty Officer Nagatomo: Ibid.; also Hata & Izawa, p. 376.

MacArthur's reluctance to leave the Philippines: Manchester, pp. 252–54.

MacArthur's request for three B-17s: Ibid., p. 265.

Leary's reply, including *I'd like to help you . . .* : Ibid.

First attempt to rescue MacArthur: Salaker, p. 153.

Loss of Godwin's bomber: Ibid., pp. 154–55.

PT boat rescue of MacArthur and his party: Manchester, pp. 258–64.

MacArthur's message to Washington: Ibid.

Second attempt to rescue MacArthur's party: Salaker, pp. 155–57.

I came through . . . : Manchester, p. 271.

Status of U.S. Army aerial forces: Craven & Cate, *Plans & Operations*, pp. 410–11.

a P-40 with a Zero on its tail: Guttman, "Defending Port Moresby," *Aviation History*, Sep. 2002, p. 39.

God have mercy on us!: James, *The Years of MacArthur, 1941–1945*, p. 109; also Manchester, p. 270.

Invasion of Lae and Salamaua: Bullard, pp. 47–48; also Monograph No. 120, pp. 7–8.

Counterattack by Hudsons and B-17s: Gillison, p. 455; also Steinbinder diary, Mar. 8, 1942.

Planning for carrier strike on Lae, including *We had little information . . .* : Sherman, pp. 85–86.

Details of Lae/Salamaua raid and claims by carrier pilots: Office of Naval Intelligence, *Early Raids in the Pacific Ocean*, pp. 62–67; also Lundstrom, pp. 130–32.

Praise from Roosevelt and pilot awards: Gillison, p. 456; also Johnson, *Queen of the Flattops*, p. 91.

Japanese losses at Lae: Lundstrom, p. 131; also Prados, *Combined Fleet Decoded*, p. 241.

B-17 raid on Rabaul and experience of DuBose's crew: Steinbinder diary, Mar. 18, 1942.

Dispute between Carmichael and Fesmire: Mitchell, *On Wings We Conquer*, p. 102.

Chapter 12: The Last Outpost

Presumed fall of New Guinea: *Mainichi Daily News*, Mar. 14, 1942, p. 1.

Example of "victory disease": Ugaki, *Fading Victory*, pp. 118–20. On May 4, 1942, just as the Battle of the Coral Sea was starting, Ugaki wrote that he was "a bit tired after a week of continuous conferences starting with the war lessons, table maneuvers, and briefings" related to the next operation, the invasion of Midway.

Hectic pace of New Guinea aerial operations: Monograph No. 120, pp. 8–10; also Bullard, pp. 53–56.

Every afternoon and every night . . . : White, *Green Armor*, p. 55.

Stamina of Catalina crews, including *Repeatedly I saw them come in* . . . : Ibid., p. 56.

Monotonous diet at Port Moresby: Steinbinder diary, May 5, 1942.

officers would be permitted . . . : White, p. 56.

Neverhawks and *Tomorrowhawks*: Ibid.

Background of 75 Squadron personnel: Wilson, *Seek and Strike*, pp. 1–4.

Japanese reconnaissance crew over Port Moresby: Tagaya, p. 39.

Steinbinder's observations: Personal diary, Mar. 21, 1942.

75 Squadron's first combat: Wilson, pp. 13–14.

Garrison's euphoria, including *We onlookers* . . . : White, p. 75.

75 Squadron's first raid on Lae: Wilson, pp. 14–17; also Tagaya, correspondence with author, Jan. 8, 2006.

Follow-up attack on Lae by B-17s: Gillison, p. 461.

Acknowledgment of damage by the Japanese: Bullard, p. 54.

Eventual return of Wackett: Wilson, pp. 20–21.

Retaliatory attack on Port Moresby: Ibid., p. 18.

Profile of Squadron Leader Jackson and his decision to stay at Moresby: Ibid., pp. 3–4, 18.

4th Air Group's attrition and claims: Monograph No. 120, p. 10.

Chapter 13: New Guinea Interlude

Recollection of voyage aboard *Maui*: Operational History, 80th Fighter Squadron, p. 1.

22nd Bomb Group's arrival in Australia: Hickey et al., *Revenge of the Red Raiders*, pp. 42–49.

Arrival of 3rd Bomb Group: Operational History, 8th Bomb Squadron, p. 3.

First A-24 raid on Lae: Ibid., pp. 3–4; also Wilson, p. 25.

Jackson's solo raid and fighter sweep on Lae: Wilson, p. 26.

Japanese retaliatory raid on Moresby: Ibid., p. 27.

I feel that this is going to be disastrous . . . : Steinbinder diary, Apr. 5, 1942.

B-25 raid on Gasmata: *New Guinea Force War Diary*, Apr. 6, 1942; also Claringbould, *Forty of the Fifth*, p. 5.

B-17 portion of attack on Rabaul: Steinbinder diary, Apr. 6, 1942.

Developmental history of B-26: Watkins, interview with author. Dec. 18, 2003.

B-26 segment of attack: Hickey et al., p. 63; also Operational History, 22nd Bomb Group, *The Marauder*, p. 23.

Ditching of *Liberty Belle* and crew rescue: Hickey et al., pp. 63–66.

the other 69 bombs . . . : Steinbinder diary, Apr. 6, 1942.

75 Squadron's interception on Apr. 6, 1942: Wilson, pp. 28–29.

B-26 attack on Rabaul, Apr. 9, 1942: Hickey et al., pp. 67–69.

Assessment of attack by Kanazawa: Bullard, p. 56.

Two truckloads of bodies . . . : Hutchinson-Smith, "Guests of the Samurai," p. 28.

Details of B-26 attack on Rabaul, Apr. 11, 1942: Hickey et al., pp. 69–70.

Effort to sink *Kasuga Maru*: Ibid., pp. 71–72.

Chapter 14: Wild Eagles

Background of Tainan Air Group: Hata & Izawa, pp. 132–34.

Popularization of "Wild Eagles" in Japanese media: Tagaya, correspondence with author, Nov. 18, 2005.

Composition of 25th Air Flotilla: Monograph No. 120, pp. 12–13.

Description of unpleasant voyage to Rabaul: Sakai, *Samurai!*, p. 92.

Background of *Komaki Maru*: Cundall, correspondence with author, Feb. 4, 2004.

B-26 attack on *Komaki Maru*: Hickey et al., p. 74.

A few seconds later . . . : Hutchinson-Smith, p. 18.

Our antiaircraft guns . . . : Quoted in *Intelligence Bulletin Vol. I, No. 6*, p. 18.

Background of Captain Garnett and crew: Hickey et al., pp. 46–47; also Reed, interview with author, Mar. 21, 2008.

I was the engineer . . . : Reed, interview with author.

We couldn't get away . . . : Ibid.

Background of Lieutenant Junior Grade Sasai: Sakaida, *Imperial Japanese Navy Aces*, pp. 36–37.

Downing of Garnett's bomber: Reed, interview with author

Capture of Reed and Lutz: Ibid.

Diary entry of unnamed Kempeitai officer: AWM 55 (12/140).

He had a riding crop . . . : Reed, interview with author.

Casualties aboard *Komaki Maru*: Hickey et al., p. 75.

Observations by Japanese witnesses: Quoted in *Intelligence Bulletin Vol. 1, No. 6*, p. 19.

They must all be very happy . . . : Ibid.

We swooped down . . . : Sakai, p. 110.

Details of air battle over Port Moresby on Apr. 24, 1942: Wilson, p. 38.

Crash of B-17 into Mt. Obree: Salaker, p. 170.

75 Squadron's struggles, including loss of Jackson: Wilson, pp. 39–42.

Attack by B-17s on Hirohito's birthday and retaliatory strafing raid: Sakai, pp. 111–12.

Arrival of P-39s and last action of 75 Squadron: Wilson, pp. 43–46.

Chapter 15: MO: The Offensive Blunted

Japanese plans for invasion of Port Moresby: Rottman, *Japanese Army, Conquest 1941–42*, p. 21.

Background of JN-25 code and its compromise: Prados, pp. 80, 305.

Analysis of Japanese plans for MO Operation: Ibid., pp. 301–2.

Japanese order of battle: Monograph No.120, p. 12; also Bullard, pp. 65–68.

Positioning of *Lexington* and *Yorktown* task forces: Lundstrom, pp. 178–82.

Marauder attacks on Rabaul: Hickey et al., p. 87.

Loss of Herron and Gurney: Ibid., pp. 87–88.

Catalina operations and heavy losses: Riddell, p. 24. Some accounts have erroneously reported that Cpl. A. H. Lanagan died of wounds on May 4, but in fact all nine crewmembers were captured alive and taken to Rabaul. Executed six months later, they were buried in a common grave. Their remains were positively identified after the war.

Fletcher's carrier raid on the Tulagi Invasion Force: Office of Naval Intelligence, *The Battle of the Coral Sea*, pp. 5–9.

B-26 attack on Rabaul, May 4, 1942: Hickey et al., pp. 88–89.

Observations of Australian POWs: Bowman, *Not Now Tomorrow*, p. 82.

Three B-17s came in . . . : Steinbinder diary, May 7, 1942.

We couldn't hit the side of a barn . . . ": Carmichael oral history, p. 93.

Narrative of opening phases of Coral Sea battle: Office of Naval Intelligence, pp. 13–19.

Maj. Teats's recollections of B-17 attack: Teats, *Coral Sea B-17s*, 19th Bomb Group CD.

Kobayashi's search for the fleet: Tagaya, p. 41; also 25th Air Flotilla war diary, May 7, 1942.

a formation of 10 or 12 single engine monoplanes . . . : Office of Naval Intelligence, p. 53.

G4M torpedo attacks on Allied cruiser formation: Ibid., pp. 53–56; also Lundstrom, pp. 208–9.

bunched together and flying very low: Smyth, *A Coral Sea Eyewitness Account*.

4th Air Group losses: Tagaya, p. 41; also 25th Air Flotilla war diary, May 7, 1942.

Attack on the Allied cruiser force by G3Ms: 25th Air Flotilla war diary, May 7, 1942.

Erroneous damage claims by the Japanese: Ibid.

Mistaken attack on the cruiser force by B-17s: Office of Naval Intelligence, p. 55.

Failed evening attack by Japanese carrier planes on May 7: Lundstrom, pp. 209–20.

Dismay of Combined Fleet Staff: Ugaki, p. 122.

Outcome of carrier battle, May 8: Lundstrom, pp. 277–82.

Exaggerated claims by Japanese: Osaka *Mainichi*, May 9, 1942.

Subsequent actions by Japanese commanders: Ugaki, p. 124.

Ugaki's concerns, including *the past weakness*: Ibid., p. 125.

Japan take Moresby . . . : Quoted in Bowman, p. 83.

The ships that came into focus . . . : Ibid., pp. 83–84.

How differently they returned . . . : Hutchinson-Smith, p. 41.

Imperial rescript to Yamamoto: Osaka *Mainichi*, May 12, 1942, p. 1.

Propaganda speech by Captain Hiraide: Ibid.

fairly big sacrifices: Ugaki, p. 126.

For a while we'll have everything . . . Yamamoto, quoted in Agawa, p. 292.

Chapter 16: Guests of the Emperor

Arrest of the Harvey family, including *The Japanese herded them . . .* : Hutchinson-Smith, pp. 31–32.

Trial and execution of Harvey family: AWM 54 (1010/9/22), statements of Daizo Hamada (rank unknown), WO Minoru Yoshimura, and Capt. Shojiro Mizusaki.

Status of eleven-year-old Richard Harvey: roll-of-honour.org.uk/civilians/html. There are unconfirmed rumors of Australian children as young as seven being murdered by the Japanese, but the government officially recognizes Richard Harvey as the youngest.

POWs' concerns about Allied bombing: Hutchinson-Smith, p. 18.

Delivery of POW letters to Port Moresby: Johnson, Carl, *Little Hell*, p. 128.

Prisoners' reluctance to use air raid shelters: May, *Rabaul Story*, p. 8.

Japanese gunners' excessive shooting: Hutchinson-Smith, pp. 27–28.

Interrogations of American airmen: Reed, interview with author.

Phony intelligence provided by Sergeant Lutz: Bullard, pp. 62–63.

Last B-26 raid on Rabaul: Hickey et al., pp. 96–97.

Ordeal of Lieutenant Massie's B-26 crew: Ibid., pp. 96–98, 177, 179.

The jungle as *a desert*, lack of sustenance: Feldt, p. 36.

Strafing of Toboi Wharf: Hutchinson-Smith, p. 19.

Low-level attack by *Suzy-Q*: Salaker, p. 202.

Japanese shipping records: Cundall, correspondence with author. Feb. 4, 2004.

There is no food left . . . : Takamura, quoted in AWM 55 (12/140).

Departure of Lark Force soldiers from camp: Gamble, pp. 233–35.

Sinking of *Montevideo Maru*: Ibid., pp. 239–42.

Transportation of officers and women to Japan: Ibid., pp. 244–47.

Chapter 17: Fading Glory

We have lost supremacy . . . : Quoted in Bullard, pp. 100–1.

Propaganda by Information Bureau: Osaka *Mainichi*, June 10, 1942, p. 1.

Isolation of Japanese wounded: Agawa, p. 322; also Prange et al., pp. 85–87.

Deliberate cover-up by Information Bureau: Osaka *Mainichi*, July 21, 1942, p. 2.

Message from Emperor Hirohito: Agawa.

Cancellation of FS Operation and aviation assessments: Bullard, pp. 102–3.

Reduced strength of Tainan Air Group: Hata & Izawa, p. 135.

Construction and assembly methods of Zero fighter: Akira, *Zero Fighter*, pp. 137–39.

Formation of Eighth Fleet: Bullard, p. 106.

Ri Operation and Great Army Order 1180: Ibid., p. 95.

Pressure on Port Moresby, July 1942: Monograph No. 120, pp. 53–54.

Construction of airdromes at Port Moresby: PacificWrecks.org/airfields/Papua New Guinea.

As the months passed at Lae . . . : Sakai, p. 121.

Statistics for Airacobra squadrons: Stanaway & Hickey, *Attack and Conquer*, pp. 310–11; also Gillison, p. 549.

Chapter 18: MacArthur's New Airman

Distrust of MacArthur by airmen: Griffith, *MacArthur's Airman*, p. 57.

Criticisms of MacArthur and Sutherland by General Brett: Kenney Papers, "Comments of Gen. Brett re personnel, etc.," undated.

Brett's feud with Sutherland, including details of memos: Cox, pp. 53–56.

Brett's relationship with Australian political parties: Griffith, pp. 51–52.

a rather easy-going Air Force officer . . . : Cox, pp. 59–60.

either Brett or MacArthur must go: Ibid., p. 57.

I would prefer Andrews to Brett . . . : Message, MacArthur to Marshall, June 30, 1942.

I know intimately all officers named . . . : MacArthur to Marshall, July 7, 1942.

Negative response of General Andrews to job offer: Griffith, p. 56.

Background of General Kenney: Ibid., pp. 1–6.

a cocky, enthusiastic little man . . . : *Time*, Jan. 18, 1943.

Kenney's skip-bombing tests with Major Benn: *General Kenney Reports*, pp. 21–22.

Arrival of Kenney in Australia and lecture from MacArthur: Kenney diary, July 29, 1942.

Kenney's fact-finding visit to Port Moresby, including personnel assessments: Ibid., July 30, 1942.

Return to Australia and debriefing with MacArthur: Ibid., Aug. 2, 1942.

Chapter 19: Medal of Honor: Harl Pease Jr.

Early history of Guadalcanal: Rottman, pp. 98–102, 104–7.

Japanese development of Guadalcanal: Frank, *Guadalcanal*, p. 31; also Lord, *Lonely Vigil*, pp. 19–20.

Establishment of coastwatchers on Guadalcanal: Lord, pp. 25–28.

I hope they build a good one . . . : Quoted in 19th Bomb Group history, p. 53.

Joint Directive of July 2, 1942: Morton, *Strategy and Command*, pp. 619–20.

Operation Watchtower assignments and establishment of boundaries: Frank, pp. 34–35.

When I told [MacArthur] . . . : Kenney diary, Aug. 4, 1942.

Reconnaissance figures for air strength at Rabaul: Kenney diary, Aug. 5, 1942.

Kenney's expectations for group commanders: Ibid.

Japanese discovery of Milne Bay Airdrome, including *a great threat*: Bullard, p. 127.

Air strength at Rabaul on Aug. 6, 1942: Monograph No. 121, p. 2.

Arrival of 2nd Air Group at Rabaul: Hata & Izawa, p. 157.

Background of Harl Pease Jr.: Mitchell, pp. 125–27.

Operational details of Aug. 7 mission to Rabaul: Salaker, p. 226.

Crash of B-17 on takeoff: Ibid., p. 227.

Urgent radio messages from Tulagi and Guadalcanal: Frank, p. 64.

Orders from Eleventh Air Fleet Headquarters: Monograph No. 121, p. 2.

Capabilities of long- and short-range Zeros: Ibid., p. 3; also Lundstrom, *The First Team (Guadalcanal)*, p. 44.

Decision to send dive-bombers on one-way mission: Monograph No. 121, p. 3.

Arrangement of Carmichael's formation and bombardier technique: Mitchell, p. 129.

Radar and early warning capabilities: United States Strategic Bombing Survey, pp. 15–16.

Initial interception of B-17s: Lundstrom, *The First Team and the Guadalcanal Campaign*, p. 71.

Damage to *Queenie*: Salaker, p. 227.

Bomb load: Mitchell, p. 126. The B-17s were loaded with a mix of 100-, 300-, and 500-pounders.

Details of renewed fighter attacks and results: Salaker, p. 228.

Japanese fighter doctrine: Sakaida, *Siege of Rabaul*, p. 9.

Recollection of Ed Jaquet: Pacific Wrecks.com/aircraft/b-17/41-2429 (accessed Sep. 10, 2008).

Observations of Troccia and Bridges: Mitchell, pp. 125, 130.

Carmichael's opinion on auxiliary fuel tank: Air Force oral history, p. 90.

Location of aircraft wreckage: PacificWrecks.com/aircraft/b-17/41-2429.

Claims by American gunners and bombardiers: Lundstrom, p.71.

Kenney's exaggerations on damage: *General Kenney Reports*, pp. 59, 61.

Status of land attack aircraft on Aug. 7: Monograph No. 121, p. 4.

The Marines landed with no opposition . . . : *General Kenney Reports*, p. 60.

little bits of pretty ribbon . . . : Ibid., p. 43.

MacArthur's endorsement of awards: Kenney diary, Aug. 4, 1942.

had no business in the show: *General Kenney Reports*, p. 59.

We don't treat American airmen!: Quoted in Mitchell, p. 135.

Chapter 20: The Personification of Evil

Downing of Lieutenant Keel's B-25 and rescue of crewmember: *Marsh Casualty File*, encl. *52b*, statement of Cpl. Louis Murphy, Nov. 17, 1942.

only partially clad: Ibid., encl. *102a*, statement of Naohei Okabe, rank unknown, Mar. 23, 1948.

Hospitalization of Keel and unknown sergeant: Ibid., encl. *103a*, testimony of Lieutenant Yamaguchi, Sep. 9, 1949.

in a bad way: AWM 54 (1010/9/22), statement of Captain Mizusaki.

administered what comfort he could: *Marsh Casualty File*, encl. *103a*.

Execution of Lieutenant Durand: Stanaway & Hickey, p. 36.

Hunter hospitalized with *burns or light wounds . . .* : *Dept. of External Affairs*, statement of Maj. L. F. Darling, RNZAF.

Capture of Massie and King: Hickey et al., *Revenge of the Red Raiders*, p. 179.

Background of Sub-Lieutenant Page and early rescue attempts: Feldt, pp. 22–24.

Search for Page by the SNLF, including *With the use of wireless* . . . : ATIS 46, serial number 93, "Fate of Allied Coast Watchers" p. 14.

Failure to rescue coastwatchers Kyle and Benham: Feldt, p. 51–56. A synopsis of submarine *S-43*'s wartime service is found in the *Dictionary of American Naval Fighting Ships, Vol. 6*, pp. 205–6.

Executions of Page, Talmage, Kyle, and Benham at Kavieng: Roll of Honor (accessed Sep. 10, 2008).

military prisoners were held . . . : Lepping, quoted in Mitchell, p. 135.

Admiration of Captain Pease: Ibid., pp. 135–36.

Testimony of Timothy Mak: *Dept. of External Affairs*, statement of Maj. L. F. Darling.

You go tomorrow: Mitchell, p. 137.

Execution of Pease and seven other POWs: AWM 54 (1010/9/22). Warrant Officer Yoshimura stated that he did not know the identities of the prisoners, so it is impossible to ascertain which two POWs were dissected.

Chapter 21: A Shift in Momentum

Marshall's opinion on *mixing nationalities* and approval to form a new air force: *General Kenney Reports*, p. 63.

Establishment of ADVON command: Birdsall, *Flying Buccaneers*, p. 16.

Priority to *knock out the Jap air strength*: Kenney diary, Aug. 3 1942.

brains, leadership, loyalty . . . : *General Kenney Reports*, p. 12.

General Walker's professional reputation: Byrd, p. 36.

Kenney's opinion of General Wurtsmith: *General Kenney Reports*, pp. 64–65.

Claims by B-17 crews against Rabaul, Aug. 12, 1942: Salaker, p. 237.

Damage to *Matsumo Maru*: JANAC (Part VIII), p. 11.

Loss of *Chief Seattle*: Salaker, p. 238–39.

My roommate and crew . . . : Steinbinder diary, Aug. 14, 1942.

Recollection of Sergeant Phillips: Interview with author, Feb. 14, 2004.

Ghormley's request for assistance at Guadalcanal: *General Kenney Reports*, pp. 98–99.

Tempo of missions in mid-September 1942: Ibid., p. 99.

Wandering all over the place . . . : Quoted in *Seattle Daily Times*, Sep. 21, 1942.

Loss of Burcky's B-17: Pacificwrecks.com/aircraft/b-17/41-2650.html (accessed Dec. 1, 2008).

Concerns of Combined Fleet Staff regarding Guadalcanal: Ugaki, p. 177.

Additional setbacks at Guadalcanal: Ibid., p. 213.

Heavy explosions at Rabaul: Ibid., pp. 211–13; also Hutchinson-Smith, p. 18.

Major Benn assumes command of 63rd Bomb Squadron: *General Kenney Reports,*
p. 82; also Birdsall, pp. 25–26.

I happened to be the officer-of-the-day . . . : Vargas, interview with author,
Jan. 17, 2009.

He talked us into all kinds of things . . . : Dieffenderfer, interview with author,
Jan. 13, 2009.

Profile of Captain McCullar: *General Kenney Reports,* p. 105.

Naming of *Black Jack:* Bowman, *B-17 Units of the Pacific War,* p. 59.

McCullar's skip-bombing demonstration on SS *Pruth: General Kenney Reports,*
p. 105.

Application of instantaneous bomb fuses: Ibid., pp. 107–8.

Personality of General Walker: Byrd, pp. 30, 48, 55.

Walker's receipt of Silver Star: Ibid., p. 148.

Allied conference at Noumea: *General Kenney Reports,* p. 115.

rice, bullets, and soldiers; also, nicknaming of "Tokyo Express": Frank, p. 210.

B-17s move to Fourteen Mile Airdrome: Salaker, p. 251.

Rabaul attack on Oct. 2: Murphy, *Skip Bombing,* p. 42.

Lack of damage to merchant shipping: JANAC (Part VIII), p. 13.

Damage to cruiser *Tenryu:* Combinedfleet.com/tenryu_t.htm (accessed
Nov. 8, 2008).

Loss of Lieutenant Hageman and Flying Officer Davenport: Salaker, pp. 269–70.

Kenney's reaction to mission, including *I can always hire* . . . :Byrd, pp. 97–98.

Plans for major night raid on Rabaul: Salaker, p. 270.

Different weather forecasts from Walker and Kenney: Byrd, p. 98.

Catalinas' orders to *light up the town* . . . : *Bomber Command Target Report No. 9,* p. 3.

Catalina bomb loads and initial results: Ibid.

a colossal fireworks display: Salaker, p. 271.

B-17 bomb loads and results: Ibid.

Radio Tokyo announcement about Geisha girls at Rabaul: 19th Bomb Group history,
p. 59.

Experience of Father Lepping: Mitchell, p. 137.

Casualties aboard photoreconnaissance plane: Steinbinder diary, Oct. 10, 1942.

Buildup of air strength at Rabaul: Hata & Izawa, p. 150; Monograph No. 121,
pp. 29, 34; also Lundstrom, pp. 190–91.

Description and effects of wire-wrapped bombs: *General Kenney Reports,* pp. 106–7.

Damages and casualties from night attacks: Ugaki, p. 229.

fine performance over Rabaul: General Kenney Reports, p. 121.

Kenney's teasing and subsequent diplomacy with Walker: Byrd, p. 98.

Awards ceremonies in Australia: *General Kenney Reports*, p. 122.

a bastard mixture of airplanes: Carmichael oral history, p. 97.

Plans for 90th Bomb Group, including *I was not particular* . . . : Kenney, pp. 112–13.

Photoreconnaissance of Rabaul in late October: Ibid., p. 126.

First skip-bombing attack: Ibid., pp. 126–27; also *Bomber Command Target Report No. 9*, p. 6.

Andy, why don't you move over . . . : Anderson, interview with author, Jan. 16, 2009.

Initial attack maneuvers: Murphy, p. 24.

We had good moonlight . . . : Anderson, interview with author.

Results of Lieutenant Green's attacks: 63rd Bomb Squadron war diary, Oct. 23, 1942.

Damage claims by McCullar and Hustad: Ibid.

Actual damages: JANAC (Part VIII), p. 13.

the hottest outfit in the whole air force: *General Kenney Reports*, p. 121.

Chapter 22: New Identities

Establishment of identification codes: Mikesh, p. 11–12.

Background of Major McCoy and team: Ibid.

Examples of code names: Ibid., pp. 12–18.

Attack of "Vals" on invasion fleet at Guadalcanal: Lundstrom, p. 68.

Attack by "Bettys" and subsequent losses: Ibid., p. 52.

Return flight of Saburo Sakai: Frank, pp. 68–69; Cook & Cook, p. 137.

Rikko attack on Aug. 8: Lundstrom, pp. 77–78; also Tagaya, p. 46.

Type 1 lighter: Iwatani, p. 319; also Tagaya, p. 48.

Opinions of Captain Moritama: Iwatani, pp. 300–1.

Battle results reported by the Japanese: Ugaki, p. 179.

Naval battles off Savo Island: Lundstrom, pp. 82–85.

Putting the [results] together . . . : Ugaki, p. 179.

Exaggerations in Japanese newspapers: Osaka *Mainichi*, Aug. 15, 1942.

Actual damages: Frank, p. 80.

Return of Admiral Tsukahara to Japan: Ugaki, p. 220.

Arrival of Admiral Kusaka: Ibid.

Kusaka's daily activities: Excerpts from Kusaka diary. Although few entries contain significant detail, Kusaka's diary reveals numerous morning horseback rides. He was often accompanied by one or more staff officers.

Concentration of aircraft at Rabaul: Monograph No. 121, p. 17.

Details of airdrome improvements and new construction: Pacificwrecks.com/
provinces/png_rabaul.html (accessed July 19, 2009).

every time it rained heavily . . . : Ugaki, p. 227.

Battle of Santa Cruz: Lundstrom, pp. 358–407, also Frank, pp. 379–403.

Japanese claims at Santa Cruz: Ugaki, pp. 249–50.

Fulfillment of Yamamoto's goal: Lundstrom, p. 470.

Reorganization of air units on Nov. 1: Monograph No. 122, p. 4.

[It] was impossible for us to continue . . . : Iwatani, *Medium Bomber*, pp. 318–19.

Formation of Eighth Area Army and termination of Buna campaign: Ugaki,
p. 280–81.

Yamamoto's predictions: Ibid., p. 284.

Chapter 23: Heavy Bomber Blues

Shipment of P-38s to Australia: *General Kenney Reports*, p. 73.

Early defects with P-38s: Christy & Ethell, p. 67.

Controversy in 90th Bomb Squadron: Dorr, pp. 23–24.

Chronic trouble with B-24s: Woods, p. 16.

90th Bomb Group's first mission: Ibid., p. 18.

Kansas-sized dust storm: Livingstone, p. 49.

Takeoff accident at Iron Range: Ibid., p. 50.

Background of Major Morse: Woods, p. 12.

90th Bomb Group restricted to training missions: *General Kenney Reports*, p. 141.

Failed attempt to bomb Rabaul on Dec. 7: Woods, p. 27.

Operational accidents and poor morale: Ibid.

B-24 crash on Dec. 26, 1942: Woods, p. 31; also Livingstone, p. 52.

Chapter 24: Medal of Honor: Kenneth N. Walker

I shared a tent with Benn . . . : Dieffenderfer, interview with author.

Disagreements over fuse settings: *General Kenney Reports*, pp. 107–8; Byrd, p. 97.

Demonstration of instantaneous fuse on SS *Pruth*: *General Kenney Reports*,
p. 142–43.

Kenney's assessment of Walker: Ibid., p. 143.

Boyhood of General Walker; Douglas P. Walker, correspondence with author,
Dec. 3, 2008; also Byrd, p. 1.

Near total involvement with himself . . . : Byrd, pp. 30–31.

Kenney's order to stop flying combat missions: Ibid., pp. 97–98; also Claringbould,
Flightpath, p. 53.

stop flying combat missions: General Kenney Reports, p. 166.

We had plenty of evidence . . . : Ibid.

Loss of four B-17s in one week: AF History Center, 43rd Bomb Group casualty report, pp. 192–94.

B-17 attack on Rabaul, Dec. 26: 43rd Bomb Group war diary, Dec. 26, 1943.

Damage to *Italy Maru*: Joint Assessment statistics, Dec. 1942.

Death of Lieutenant Commander Hirasata: combinedfleet.com/tachik_t.htm.

B-17s obstinately attacked Rabaul . . . : Ugaki, p. 314.

large flash . . . : Quoted in 43rd Bomb Group war diary, Dec. 30, 1942.

Hits claimed by Lieutenant Murphy: *Skip Bombing*, pp. 79–80. Murphy wrote that the two ships he attacked were located "between Protto Point and Micaca Island just out of the Rabaul Harbor [sic]." The points almost certainly equate to Praed Point and Makada Island, respectively, which define a sizeable area east of Crater Peninsula. But the only Japanese ship that sank that night at Rabaul went down near Vulcan Island, on the western shore of Simpson Harbor.

Loss of *Tomiura Maru*: JANAC (Part VIII), p. 15.

Opinion of wire-wrapped bombs: Murphy, p. 81.

Ugaki's reflections about the year 1942: Ugaki, p. 319.

Japanese casualties on Guadalcanal: Rottman, p. 116.

Reinforcements at Buna; soldiers *only keeping themselves alive . . .* : Ugaki, p. 314.

Death of General Horii: Ballard, pp. 202–3.

Construction of new army and navy airdromes: Rottman, pp. 160–61; also Ugaki, p. 308.

Simpson Harbor shipping on Dec. 30, 1942: Craven & Cate, *Guadalcanal to Saipan*, p. 136.

When the Jap accumulates that much tonnage . . . : Kenney papers, Jan. 1, 1943.

break up the movement at the source . . . : General Kenney Reports, p. 175.

Walker's request to change takeoff time: Ibid.

Noon attack vs. dawn attack rationale: Byrd, p. 108.

Kenney repeats orders for a dawn attack: *General Kenney Reports*, p. 176.

full-scale bomber attack: Ibid., p. 175.

You're going to lose two airplanes . . . : Quoted by Dieffenderfer, author interview.

Fine, we just won't take your squadron: Ibid.

Walker conducts mission briefing: Ibid.

When this was announced . . . : Wesche, oral history. His statement contradicts biographer Martha Byrd, who wrote that Walker may have been motivated to delay the attack until noon because "most of the crews preferred a total daylight mission."

Early mission on Jan. 5, 1943 to suppress fighters: pacificwrecks.com/aircraft/b-17/41-24538.html.

First interception by Ki-43 Oscars: Ichimura, *Ki-43 Aces*, p. 74.

Japanese "infuriated" by the shoot-down of a Ki-43: Quoted in Dunn, "Timing Factor," p. 3.

Attack on Captain Jack's B-17: pacificwrecks.com/aircraft/b-17/41-24538.html.

Start of main mission, crew of *San Antonio Rose*: MACR 15359.

Participation of B-24s on Jan. 5, 1943: Woods, p. 32.

at least three ships hit . . . : Ibid.; also Alcorn, *The Jolly Rogers*, pp. 18–19.

Minor damage to B-24s: Alcorn, p. 18.

Downing of Ki-43 pilot Takagaki: Ichimura, p. 74.

We went over the target . . . : Wesche, oral history.

Last observation of *San Antonio Rose*: MACR 15359.

Japanese losses: Combinedfleet.com/tachik_t.htm; also Ichimura, p. 74.

Walker off late . . . : Kenney papers, Jan. 5, 1943.

Kenney's intension to reprimand Walker: *General Kenney Reports*, p. 176.

If he doesn't come back . . . : Quoted in Griffith, p. 102; also Kenney papers, Jan. 5 1943.

quite disappointed . . . : quoted by Dieffenderfer, correspondence with author. The remark was made by Colonel Jack when Dieffenderfer worked with him at Wright-Patterson AFB in the 1950s.

Downing of Rose's B-24 on Jan. 6, 1943: Pacificwrecks.com/aircraft/b-24/walker search.html.

Loss of Higgins's B-24 and subsequent rescue of crew: Woods, p. 33.

MacArthur's communiqué: Byrd, photo gallery (*Glendale News Press* image).

Kenney's belief that Walker was dead: *General Kenney Reports*, p. 177.

The attacking planes . . . : Scharmach, *This Crowd Beats Us All*, p. 120.

Information regarding Walker learned by Lieutenant Holguin: Pacificwrecks.com/aircraft/b-17/41-24458/pow.html.

We do not know . . . : Scharmach, p. 120.

It is the considered opinion of Headquarters . . . : Quoted in Byrd, p. 121.

Chapter 25: Blood in the Water

Eleventh Air Fleet's attempted raid on Port Moresby: Asai, *History of Air Group 705*, p. 178.

Raid aborted due to weather: Ibid.

Attacks on the Lae convoy and successful landings: *USAF Study 113*, p. 73.

Skepticism of Japanese: Diary of Igarashi quoted in Asai, p. 178.

Symbol conference and allocation of resources: Morison, *Breaking the Bismarcks Barrier*, pp. 4–5.

withdrawing from commitments . . . : Ibid., p. 5.

MacArthur's appreciation of air power: *USAF Study 113*, p. 25.

Joint Directive: Kenney papers, July 2, 1942.

Kenney's expectations for Ramey: *General Kenney Reports*, p. 182.

Loss of Major Benn: Pacificwrecks.com/aircraft/b-25/41-12485.html.

Status of Fifth Air Force units: *USAF Study 113*, p. 7.

an elevator shot out . . . : 63rd Bomb Squadron war diary, Jan. 26, 1943.

Night patrols by Zeros of Air Group 204: Mikesh, *Moonlight Interceptors*, p. 37.

the weather was generally bad . . . : *USAF Study 113*, pp. 74–75.

Descriptions and assessments of combat stress: King, "Some First Hand Observations," pp. 2–5.

They just went out and that was the end of it . . . : DeLoach, appearing in "Black Jack" documentary.

We lost a lot of airplanes . . . :Harcrow, interview with author.

I had to have seven airplanes available . . . : Dieffenderfer, interview with author.

really take Rabaul apart and *burn down the town*: Kenney, p. 191.

Rabaul mission on Feb. 14, 1943: *USAF Study 113*, p. 82; also 63rd Bomb Squadron war diary. Japanese assessment of damages: *SWPA Intelligence Summary 146*.

loud sound of antiaircraft guns . . . : Asai, p. 191.

Praise from Colonel Ramey: 63rd Bomb Group war diary, Feb. 15, 1943.

I had a terrible headache . . . : Asai, p. 191.

less than satisfactory record against shipping: *USAF Study 113*, p. 84.

Background of Paul Gunn: Henebry, *The Grim Reapers*, pp. 52–55.

Kenney's recommendations for B-25 mods: *General Kenney Reports*, p. 144.

help Pappy with testing . . . : Ibid., p. 169.

Larner assigned to 90th Bomb Squadron: Ibid., p. 173.

Successful Japanese convoys: Frank, p. 595; also Morison, pp. 54–55.

Intel on Lae convoy: *General Kenney Reports*, p. 197.

Kenney and Whitehead plot the convoy route: Ibid.

tsubo system and *chomansai*: Cundall, correspondence with author, Feb. 4, 2004.

Higgins finds the convoy: Wood, p. 43.

Allied aircraft availability: *USAF Study 113*, p. 86.

Initial attack by B-17s on Mar. 2: JANAC (Part VIII), p. 18; also McAulay, *Battle of the Bismarck Sea*, p. 47.

Nighttime surveillance of the convoy: Riddell, p. 41; also 63rd Bomb Squadron war diary, Mar. 2, 1943.

Dawn attack by 100 Squadron: *USAF Study 113*, pp. 90–91.

Subsequent attack by B-17s: Ibid., p. 92.

Dammit, get the hell off my wing . . . : Quoted in Birdsall, p. 57.

Low-level attacks on Mar. 3: MacAulay, pp. 63–97.

Scattering of convoy over fifteen miles: 63rd Bomb Squadron war diary, Mar. 2, 1943.

Details of B-17 attack: *USAF Study 113*, p. 93; 63rd Bomb Squadron war diary, Mar. 3, 1943.

Account of Warrent Officer Iwai: Tagaya, correspondence to Edward Rogers, June 20, 2007.

Reaction of Sergeant Manuel to strafing: Reynolds, *70,000 to One*, p. 60.

Positioning of destroyers, afternoon of Mar. 3: McAulay, pp. 102–3.

Details of B-17 attacks and strafing: McAulay, pp. 114–16; 63rd Bomb Squadron war diary, Mar. 3, 1943.

We'd come back and refuel . . . : Harcrow, interview with author.

Details of Mar. 4 attacks: 63rd Bomb Squadron war diary; McAulay, p. 149.

Every man in the squadron . . . : 63rd Bomb Squadron war diary, Mar. 3, 1943.

RAAF pilots' opinion on strafing: Griffith, p. 107.

Claims reported to MacArthur: *General Kenney Reports*, pp. 205–6.

Congratulations on that stupendous success . . . : Kenney, quoted in 63rd Bomb Squadron war diary, Mar. 5, 1943.

Our decisive success . . . : MacArthur, quoted in *Time*, Mar. 15, 1943.

Estimates of casualties: McAulay, p. 164.

Kenney's refusal to modify claims: Griffith, pp. 110–11.

about ten Jap fighters . . . : *General Kenney Reports*, p. 204.

The fact that counts . . . : Craven & Cate, *Vol. IV*, p. 146–47.

Chapter 26: Operation I-Go: Yamamoto's Last Offensive

Yamamoto *greatly incensed*: Yoshihara, "Attitudes to the War" (accessed Feb. 6, 2004).

gradually mollified: Ibid.

The land-based air groups . . . : quoted in Prados, p. 449.

We cannot expect much . . . : Ugaki, p. 316.

Health of Admiral Kusaka: United States Strategic Bombing Survey, pp. 33–34.

I had a mysterious fever . . . : Quoted in Asai, p. 205.

Their present skill . . . : Ugaki, p. 316.

Shortening of Imperial Japanese Navy training syllabus: Prados, p. 540.

They used to say . . . : Agawa, p. 342.

Narrative of Petty Officer Matsunaga: Tsunoda, pp. 159–62.

Health concerns of Igarashi: Asai, pp. 178–79.

Joint Army-Navy Central Agreement (Japanese): Morton, p. 637.

American build-up on Guadalcanal: Craven & Cate, p. 212; also Dunn, "X Attack," pp. 4–5.

Admiral Ozawa's reluctance to contribute carrier planes: Prados, p. 452.

Transfer of Combined Fleet Headquarters to Rabaul: Agawa, p. 339.

Outcome of Apr. 1 fighter sweep: Hata & Izawa, p. 428; also Dunn, p. 11.

Exaggerated claims: Morison, p. 118; Monograph No. 122, p. 47.

Yamamoto confides in liaison officer: Agawa, p. 340.

Yamamoto's relationship with Chiyoko Kawai: Ibid., pp. 59, 341.

Possibility that Yamamoto had beriberi: Prados, p. 458.

Preliminary plans for *I-Go*: Ugaki, p. 321.

Yamamoto adds strikes to the original plan: Morton, p. 636.

Statistics of Japanese participation, Apr. 7: Dunn, p. 20; also Morison, p. 120.

Warnings and alerts to Guadalcanal: Dunn, p. 21.

Feat of Lieutenant Swett: Tillman, *Above and Beyond*, pp. 165–66.

Analysis of Swett's victories: Dunn, pp. 26–27, 32, 43.

Actual Japanese losses: Monograph No. 122, p. 47.

Claims by Imperial Japanese Navy dive-bomber units: Dunn, p. 42.

Exaggerated coverage in Japanese media: *Mainichi Daily News*, May 1, 1943.

Operation Y attacks, Apr. 11, 1943: Ugaki, p. 329; Morison, p. 125.

Medium bomber attacks, Apr. 12, 1943: Tagaya, p. 70.

Details of attacks on New Guinea: *General Kenney Reports*, p. 227; also AWM52 (1/5/51-0335), *Air Operations Daily Review*, Apr. 11, 1943, p. 2.

flying in excellent mass formation: *General Kenney Reports*, p. 227.

Results of Japanese attacks on Apr. 12, 1943: Gillison, p. 701; also 43rd Bomb Group war diary.

Interception by American fighters and comparison of claims: Monograph No. 122, p. 47; also Tagaya, p. 70.

Improved mood at Rabaul: Agawa, p. 344.

The carrier-based pilots . . . : Igarashi, p. 209.

Chapter 27: Death of a Warrior God

Yamamoto's decision to tour forward areas: Agawa, p. 346.

Outline of Yamamoto's itinerary: Davis, *Lightning Strike*, p. 222; also Agawa, p. 346.

What a damn fool thing to do . . . : Agawa, p. 347.

If he insists on going . . . : Ibid., p. 346.

This is our chance to get Yamamoto . . . : Davis, p. 227.

Nimitz gives approval for the mission: Ibid., pp. 228–33.

Attack Y-1, Apr. 14, 1943: Monograph No. 122, pp. 43, 48; also Tagaya, p. 70.

Results of attack Y-1: *General Kenney Reports,* p. 230; Monograph No. 122, p. 43.

Today's operations . . . *a great success* . . . : Ugaki, p. 328.

Overall Japanese claims compiled on Apr. 16: Ugaki, pp. 329–30.

more than ten vessels were sunk . . . : Asai, p. 209.

Belief in dominance of the Zero: Yoshimura, p. 160.

While their numbers were small . . . : Ibid., p. 161.

Situation report from General Adachi: Ugaki, p. 351.

Admiral Johima's protest: Akawa, p. 347.

Yamamoto's wardrobe: Ugaki diary, p. 353. A year after the event, Ugaki wrote a highly detailed account of the journey, covering such topics as the weather and his appearance in uniform; also Agawa, p. 360 (details of Yamamoto's sword).

Yamamoto and his staff board their bombers: Tagaya, p. 71.

Positioning of formation: Ugaki, p. 353. Riding in the second plane, the chief of staff trailed the lead bomber in standard echelon formation on the left. Ugaki wrote that he "could clearly see the commander in chief in the skipper's seat," a reference to the aircraft commander's position on the left side of the cockpit. On this day, Chief Petty Officer Kotani served as both commander *and* chief pilot. He therefore occupied the right-hand seat, which made the left seat available to Admiral Yamamoto as a special privilege.

POWs at Ballale: Wall, *Kill the Prisoners*, p. 115.

First raid on Ballale: Hammell, *Air War Pacific*, p. 124.

Lieutenant Jacobson's concerns: Jacobson, "Julius, His Story," p. 33.

Mitchell's pinpoint navigation: Davis, p. 254.

Bogeys, ten o'clock high!: Canning, "The Yamamoto Mission," dougcanning.com/ yamamoto1943.html.

It got noisy for a while . . . : Ugaki, pp. 353–54.

Mitchell considered *a magician*: Jacobson, p. 33.

Mitchell's radio call to *skin 'em off* . . . : Canning.

Instructions to get Yamamoto *at any cost*: Sherrod, *History of Marine Corps Aviation,* p. 139.

I cannot understand why . . . : Jacobson, p. 34.

Maneuvering by Lanphier and Barber: Davis, pp. 259–62; also Canning.

Barber's first gunnery pass: Davis, pp. 261–62.

The first plane was staggering . . . : Ugaki, p. 354.

The enemy P-38 rapidly closed in . . . : Ibid.

Crack-up of second bomber: Davis, p. 269.

a big hole in his throat: Ugaki, p. 357.

Fate of Lieutenant Hine: Davis, p. 269.

I got Yamamoto!: Lanphier, quoted in Davis, p. 276.

This indicates to me . . . : Canning, interview with author, Apr. 10, 2009.

The disappointing and shocking report . . . : *Naval Air Group 204*, pp. 185–86.

Evidence of fire at crash site: Agawa, p. 355.

a burned-out hulk: Ibid., p. 358.

This alone would have killed him . . . : Ibid., p. 362.

News releases in Japan: *Mainichi Daily News*, May 21 and May 23, 1943.

Funeral procession and imperial address: Ibid., June 6, 1943.

Processional banner slogan: Ibid.

"Fleet Admiral Yamamoto" lyrics: Ibid.

Details of new Joint Cheifs of Staff directives: Morton, p. 641.

Epilogue

"Rabaul My Love" lyrics: Translated by Herbert S. Kadowaki from a cassette recording of *Songs of War-Time Japan 1937–1945*. (A teenager during World War II, Setsuzo Kadowaki lived with his grandmother in Kyoto, Japan.)

Selected Bibliography

Agawa, Hiroyuki (translation by John Bester). *The Reluctant Admiral: Yamamoto and the Imperial Navy*. Tokyo: Kodansha International, 1979.

Alcorn, John. *The Jolly Rogers: History of the 90th Bomb Group During World War II*. Temple City: Historical Aviation, 1981.

Asai, Tatuzou. *The History of Air Group 705*. Tokyo: Naval Air Group 705 Association, 1975.

Birdsall, Steve. *Flying Buccaneers: The Illustrated Story of Kenney's Fifth Air Force*. Garden City: Doubleday, 1977.

Bloomfield, David. *Rabaul Diary: Escaping Captivity in 1942*. Loftus, NSW: Australian Military History Publications, 2001.

Bowman, Alice. *Not Now Tomorrow*. Bangalow, NSW: Daisy Press, 1996.

Bowman, Martin. *B-17 Flying Fortress Units of the Pacific War*. Botley, Oxford: Osprey, 2003.

Brosius, J. W. *The Marauder: A Book of the 22nd Bomb Group*. Sydney: Halstead Press, 1944.

Byrd, Martha. *Kenneth N. Walker: Airpower's Untempered Crusader*. Maxwell AFB: Air University Press, 1997.

Bullard, Steven (translator). *Japanese Army Operations in the South Pacific Area: New Britain and Papua Campaigns, 1942–43*. Canberra: Australian War Memorial, 2007.

Chihaya, Masataka (translator). *Fading Victory: The Diary of Admiral Matome Ugaki, 1941–1945*. Pittsburgh: University of Pittsburgh Press, 1991.

Christy, Joe, and Jeffery Ethell. *P-38 Lightning at War*. London: Ian Allen, 1978.

Clairingbould, Michael. *Forty of the Fifth: The Life, Times, and Demise of Forty U.S. Fifth Air Force Aircraft*. Kingston: Aerothentic, 1999.

———. *The Forgotten Fifth: A Photographic Chronology of the U.S. Fifth Air Force in World War Two*. Hyde Park: Balus, 2007.

Clayton, James. *The Years of MacArthur: 1941–1945*. Boston: Houghton Mifflin, 1975.

Cook, Haruko, and Theodore Cook. *Japan at War: An Oral History.* New York: The New Press, 1992.

Cox, Douglas. *Airpower Leadership on the Front Line: Lt. Gen. George H. Brett and Combat Command.* Maxwell AFB: Air University Press, 2006.

Craven, Wesley, and John Cate. *The Army Air Forces in World War II: The Pacific: Guadalcanal to Saipan, August 1942 to July 1944.* Chicago: University of Chicago Press, 1950.

———. *The Army Air Forces in World War II: Plans & Early Operations, January 1939 to August 1942.* Chicago: University of Chicago Press, 1948.

Davis, Donald. *Lighting Strike: The Secret Mission to Kill Admiral Yamamoto and Avenge Pearl Harbor.* New York: St. Martins (Griffin edition), 2005.

Department of the Navy. *Early Raids in the Pacific Ocean: February 1 to March 10, 1942.* Washington: Office of Naval Intelligence, United States Navy, 1943.

Department of the Navy, Naval History Division. *Dictionary of American Naval Fighting Ships, Volume VI.* Washington: U.S. Government Printing Office, 1976.

Dorr, Robert. *B-24 Liberator Units of the Pacific War.* Botley, Oxford: Osprey, 1999.

Ewing, Steve, and John Lundstrom. *Fateful Rendezvous: The Life of Butch O'Hare.* Annapolis: Naval Institute Press, 1997.

Feldt, Eric. *The Coastwatchers.* New York: Bantam, 1979.

Francillon, Rene. *Japanese Aircraft of the Pacific War.* Annapolis: Naval Institute Press, 1979.

Frank, Richard. *Guadalcanal: The Definitive Account of the Landmark Battle.* New York: Penguin, 1990.

Gamble, Bruce. *Darkest Hour: The True Story of Lark Force at Rabaul—Australia's Worst Military Disaster of World War II.* St. Paul: Zenith Press, 2006.

Gillison, Douglas. *Royal Australian Air Force, 1939–1942 (Series 3, Vol. I, Australia in the War of 1939–1945).* Canberra: Australian War Memorial, 1962.

Gorham, J. R., and C. J. L. Hewett. *The Torch Bearers: War Service of Shore Old Boys, 1939–1999.* North Sydney, NSW: Sydney Church of England Grammar School, 1999.

Griffith, Thomas. *MacArthur's Airman: General George C. Kenney and the War in the Southwest Pacific.* Lawrence: University Press of Kansas, 1998.

Hammel, Eric. *Air War Pacific Chronology.* Pacifica, CA: Pacifica Press, 1998.

Hasluck, Paul. *The Government and the People (Series 4, Vol. 1, Australia in the War of 1939–1945).* Canberra: Australian War Memorial, 1952.

Hata, Ikuhiko, and Yasuho Izawa. *Japanese Naval Aces and Fighter Units in World War II.* Annapolis: Naval Institute Press, 1989.

Henebry, John. *The Grim Reapers at Work in the Pacific Theater: The Third Attack Group of the U.S. Fifth Air Force.* Missoula, MT: Pictorial Histories, 2002.

Hickey, Lawrence et al. *Revenge of the Red Raiders: An Illustrated History of the 22nd*

Bombardment Group During World War II. Boulder, MT: International Research and Publishing, 2006.

Ichimura, Hiroshi. *Ki-43 "Oscar" Aces of World War 2.* Botley, Oxford: Osprey, 2009.

Iwatani, Fumio. *Medium Size Bomber.* Tokyo: Hara Shobou, 1976.

Johnson, Carl. *Little Hell: The Story of the 2/22nd Battalion and Lark Force.* Blackburn, VIC: History House, 2004.

Johnson, R. W., and N. A. Threlfall. *Volcano Town: The 1937–43 Rabaul Eruptions.* Bathurst, NSW: Robert Brown & Associates, 1985.

Johnson, Stanley. *Queen of the Flattops.* New York: Dutton, 1942.

Johnston, George. *New Guinea Diary.* Sydney: Angus and Robertson, 1945.

Joint Army-Navy Assessment Committee (JANAC). *Japanese Naval and Merchant Shipping Losses During World War II by all Causes.* Washington: Government Printing Office, 1947.

Kenney, George. *General Kenney Reports: A Personal History of the Pacific War.* New York: Duell, Sloan and Pearce, 1949 (Air Force History and Museums reprint, 1997).

Livingstone, Bob. *Under the Southern Cross: The B-24 Liberator in the South Pacific.* Paducah: Turner Publishing, 1998.

Lord, Walter. *Lonely Vigil: Coastwatchers of the Solomons.* New York: Viking Press, 1977.

Lundstrom, John. *The First Team: Pacific Naval Air Combat from Pearl Harbor to Midway.* Annapolis: Naval Institute, 1984.

———. *The First Team and the Guadalcanal Campaign: Naval Fighter Combat from August to November 1942.* Annapolis: Naval Institute Press, 1994.

Manchester, William. *American Caesar: Douglas MacArthur 1880–1964.* Boston: Little, Brown, 1978.

Martin, Charles et al. *The Reaper's Harvest: The Story of the Third Attack Group.* Sydney: Halstead Press, 1945.

McAulay, Lex. *Battle of the Bismarck Sea.* New York: St. Martin's, 1991.

———. *We Who Are About to Die: The Story of John Lerew—A Hero of Rabaul, 1942.* Maryborough, QLD: Banner Books, 2007.

McKee, Chris. *Field Trip C1: Rabaul Caldera.* Canberra: Australian Geological Survey Organization, 1993.

Mikesh, Robert. *Japanese Aircraft Code Names and Designations.* Atglen: Schiffer, 1995.

———. *Moonlight Interceptor: Japan's "Irving" Night Fighter.* Washington: Smithsonian Institution Press, 1995.

Minty, A. E. *Black Cats.* Point Cook, VIC: RAAF Museum, 2001.

Mitchell, John. *On Wings We Conquer.* Springfield: G.E.M., 1990.

Morison, Samuel. *History of United States Naval Operations in World War II, Vol. 6: Breaking the Bismarcks Barrier, 22 July 1941–1 May 1944.* Boston: Little,

Brown, 1959.

Morton, Louis. *The U.S. Army in World War II: The War in the Pacific: Strategy and Command: The First Two Years*. Washington: Office of the Chief of Military History, Department of the Army, 1962.

Murphy, James, with A. B. Feuer. *Skip Bombing: The True Story of Stealth Bombing Techniques used in 1942*. Westport: Praeger, 1993.

Naval Air Group 204 Association. *The Record of Rabaul Air Battles*. Tokyo: Asahi Sonorama, 1987.

Okumiya, Masatake. *Rabaul Naval Air Group*. Tokyo: Asahi Sonorama, 1976.

Prados, John. *Combined Fleet Decoded*. New York: Random House, 1995.

Prange, Gordon, with Donald Goldstein and Katherine Dillon. *God's Samurai: Lead Pilot at Pearl Harbor*. Washington: Brassey's, 1991.

Riddell, Jack. *Catalina Squadrons: First and Furthest—Recounting the Operations of RAAF Catalinas, May 1941 to March 1943*. Murwillumbah, NSW: Print Spot, 1992.

Rottman, Gordon. *Japanese Army in World War II: Conquest of the Pacific, 1941–42*. Botley, Oxford: Osprey, 2005.

———. *Japanese Army in World War II: The South Pacific and New Guinea, 1942–43*. Botley, Oxford: Osprey, 2005.

———. *World War II Pacific Island Guide: A Geo-Military Study*. Westport: Greenwood, 2002.

Sakai, Saburo. *Samurai!* Garden City: Doubleday, 1957.

Sakaida, Henry. *Imperial Japanese Navy Aces 1937–45*. Botley, Oxford: Osprey, 1998.

———. *The Siege of Rabaul*. St. Paul: Phalanx, 1996.

Salaker, Gene. *Fortress Against the Sun: The B-17 Flying Fortress in the Pacific*. Conshohocken: Combined Publishing, 2001.

Selby, David. *Hell and High Fever*. Sydney: Currawong, 1956.

Sherman, Frederick. *Combat Command: The American Aircraft Carriers in the Pacific War*. New York: Dutton, 1950.

Stanaway, John, and Lawrence Hickey. *Attack and Conquer: The 8th Fighter Group in World War II*. Atglen: Schiffer, 1995.

Stone, Peter. *Hostages to Freedom: The Fall of Rabaul*. Maryborough, VIC: Australian Print Group, 1995.

Swanborough, Gordon, and Peter Bowers. *United States Navy Aircraft Since 1911*. London: Putnam, 1990.

Tagaya, Osamu. *Mitsubishi Type 1 "Betty" Units of World War 2*. Botley, Oxford: Osprey, 2001.

Tibbs, O. E. *Production Flight Test Procedure for the Martin B-26*. Baltimore: Glenn L. Martin Company, 1941.

Tillman, Barrett. *Above and Beyond: The Aviation Medals of Honor*. Washington:

Smithsonian Institution Press, 2002.

———. *Wildcat: The F4F in WWII*. Annapolis: Naval Institute Press, 1990.

Tsunoda, Kazuo. *The Wing of Shura*. Tokyo: Konnichi no Wadai-sha, 1989.

United States Strategic Bombing Survey. *The Allied Campaign Against Rabaul*. Washington: Government Printing Office, 1946.

Wall, Don. *Kill the Prisoners!* Smithfield, NSW: Alken Press, 1996.

Werneth, Ron. *Beyond Pearl Harbor: The Untold Stories of Japan's Naval Airmen*. Atglen: Schiffer, 2008.

Wigmore, Lionel. *The Japanese Thrust (Series 1, Vol. IV, Australia in the War of 1939–1945)*. Canberra: Australian War Memorial, 1957.

Wilson, David. *Seek and Strike: 75 Squadron RAAF 1942–2002*. Maryborough, QLD: Banner Books, 2002.

Woods, Wiley. *Legacy of the 90th Bombardment Group: "The Jolly Rogers."* Paducah: Turner Publishing, 1994.

Yoshimura, Akira. *Zero Fighter*. Westport: Praeger, 1996.

Articles

Claringbould, Michael. "Rabaul's Ultimate Mystery: The Loss of Brigadier-General Kenneth N. Walker." *Flightpath*, Volume 14, Number 1.

Field, John. "How O'Hare Downed 5 Jap Planes in One Day." *Life*, April 13, 1942.

Gann, Timothy. "Fifth Air Force Light and Medium Bomber Operations During 1942 and 1943." School of Advanced Airpower Studies, 1992.

Guttman, John. "Defending Port Moresby." *Aviation History*, September 2001.

Thach, John. "The Red Rain of Battle." *Collier's*, December 5, 1942.

Thomas, Gordon. "In Rabaul, Under the Japs." *Pacific Islands Yearbook*, 1950.

Thomson, J. P. "The Islands of the Pacific." *National Geographic*, December 1921.

Military Documents—Australian

AWM A705 (166/1/319 Part 3): Presumption of Death—Casualties in Royal Australian Air Force Units—Minutes (Casualty file regarding Sgt. Thomas Marsh).

AWM 52 (1/5/51): New Guinea Force Headquarters and General (Air) War Diary, March–April 1942 (Australian Military Forces, Army headquarters, formation and unit diaries, 1939–1945).

AWM 54 (629/1/11): "The Stubborn Coastwatcher" unattributed document giving an account of Sub-Lt. Cornelius L. Page, RANVR.

AWM 54 (81/4/194): RAAF Operations From Rabaul, compiled by Sqn. Ldr. W. D. Brookes, February 24, 1942.

AWM 55 Item 12/32 Part 2: (ATIS Report 46 serial number 93).

AWM 113 (MH 1/121, Part 1): Official inquiry into the Japanese landings at Rabaul, with attached summary by R. W. Robson, editor of *Pacific Islands Monthly*.

MP729/6 (16/401/493): Cable 152, Chief of Naval Staff, Prime Minister's Department to Australian Minister (Naval Attache), Washington, D.C., December 12, 1941.

War Cabinet minutes, Melbourne, October 15, 1941.

Department of External Affairs, Memorandum 13973, July 20, 1950, Extract of letter from Maj. L. F. Darling concerning the execution of Lt. David S. Hunter, USAAF.

Military Documents (Translated)—Japanese

AWM 3DRL/4005: Diary of Akiyoshi Hisaeda, March 10, 1941, to November 16, 1942.

AWM 54 (208/2/4): ATIS translations of miscellaneous captured documents.

AWM 54 (423/4/158): ATIS Enemy Publications, Detailed Battle Report No. 2 (Rabaul Occupation Operations), June 2, 1943.

AWM 54 (423/4/1162): "Military Intelligence Section, Full Translation of a Report on the Japanese Invasion of Rabaul," May 9, 1946.

AWM 54 (608/5/4): "Japanese South East Area Operations Record (South Seas Detachment Operations) Monograph No. 143 (Army)," circa 1946.

AWM 55 (12/140): ATIS Information Request Report No. 103, Japanese statements and diary excerpts relating to prisoners of war, May 4, 1944.

Monograph No. 120 (Navy): Outline of Southeast Area Naval Air Operations, Part I. Second Demobilization Bureau, 1949.

Monograph No. 121 (Navy): Outline of Southeast Area Naval Air Operations, Part II, August 1942–October 1942. Second Demobilization Bureau, 1949.

Monograph No. 122 (Navy): Outline of Southeast Area Naval Air Operations, Part III, November 1942–June 1943. Second Demobilization Bureau, 1949.

Military Documents—United States

"Extracts From Diaries," War Department, Military Intelligence Division, Intelligence Bulletin Vol. I, No. 6, Section II, February 1943.

"A General Review of Japanese Weapons," War Department, Military Intelligence Division, Intelligence Bulletin Vol. III, No. 2, Section II, October 1944.

Headquarters, 19th Bombardment Group (H), 19th Bombardment Group History, Question-Answer Document, Pyote, TX, 1943.

"The Imperial Rescript," War Department, Military Intelligence Division, Intelligence Bulletin Vol. III, No. 5, January 1945.

"Japanese A/A Guns," War Department, Military Intelligence Division, Intelligence Bulletin Vol. I, No. 8, Section II, April 1943.

"Japanese Explanation of 'Duty' and 'Spirit'," War Department, Military Intelligence Division, Intelligence Bulletin Vol. II, No. 9, Section IX, May 1944.

U.S. Air Force Historical Study No. 113, "The Fifth Air Force in the Huon Peninsula Campaign, January to October 1943," AAF Historical Officer. Headquarters, Army Air Forces, 1946.

Unpublished Material

Dunn, Richard L. "Japanese Observations of the Timing and Other Evens in the 5 Jan 43 Attack: A Compendium," electronically forwarded to the author on June 24, 2009.

———. "X Attack of I-Operation: The Anti-shipping Mission to the Guadalcanal-Tulagi Area on April 7, 1943," 2007.

Fisher, Peter W. "New Britain, December 1941 to April 1942," via Warwick Fisher.

Hutchinson-Smith, David, "Guests of the Emperor," AWM Private Collections No. MSS 1534, Australian War Memorial.

Jacobson, Julius. "Julius, His Story," typewritten memoir, 2003.

King, James. "Some First Hand Observations on Combat Flying Stress in a Heavy Bombardment Group," New Guinea, 1943.

May, John L.. "Kokopo 1942," Undated, Kingston, Tasmania.

———, "Morituri Vos Salutamus," Undated, Kingston, Tasmania.

———, "Rabaul Story," Undated, Kingston, Tasmania.

Teats, Edward. "Coral Sea B-17s" (as told to John McCullough), December 1942.

Websites

Bowen, James. "Battle of the Coral Sea: The Events of 7 May 1942." http://www.users.bigpond.com/pacificwar/CoralSea/May.7th.html

Canning, Douglas. "The Yamamoto Mission." http://www.dougcanning.com/yamamoto1943.html

Nevitt, Allyn. "Arashio." http://www.combinedfleet.com/arasho_t.htm

———. "Asashio" http://www.combinedfleet.com/asashi_t.htm

———. "Japanese Destroyers: Tabular Movement Records (TROMs)." http://www.combinedfleet.com/lancers.htm/

———. "Tokitsukasze." http://www.combinedfleet.com/tokits_t.htm

———. "Yukikazi." http://www.combinedfleet.com/yukika_t.htm

Smyth, Dacre. "A Coral Sea Eyewitness Account." http://www.users.bigpond.com/pacificwar/coralsea/theyserved/DacreSmyth.html

Taylan, Justin. "B-17D 'The Swoose, Old Betsy' Serial Number 40-3097." http://www.pacificwrecks.com/aircraft/b-17/40-3097.html

———. "B-17E Flying Fortress Serial Number 41-2650." http://www.pacificwrecks.

com/aircraft/b-17/41-2650.html

——. "B-17F Flying Fortress Serial Number 41-24538." http://www.pacificwrecks. com/aircraft/b-17/41-24538.html

——. "B-24D Serial Number ?" http://www.pacificwrecks.com/aircraft/b-24/ walker_search.html

——. "B-25C Algernon IV Serial Number 41-12485." http://www.pacificwrecks. com/aircraft/b-25/41-12485.html

——. "Kenneth N. Walker-A Brief History." http://www.pacificwrecks.com/ people/veterans/walker/biography.html

——. "Papua New Guinea Airfields and Seaplane Anchorages." http://www. pacificwrecks.com/airfields/png/index.html

——. "Prisoners from B-17F San Antonio Rose 41-24458." http://www. pacificwrecks.com/aircraft/b-17/41-24458/pow.html

Unattributed. "Roll of Honour, Britain at War: To Honour Those United Kingdom Civilians Who Died in the Far East." http://www.roll-of-honour.org.uk/ civilians/index.html

Unattributed. "Terence 'Terry' Lawless Duigan." http://www.ctie.monash.edu/ hargrave/duigan_terry_aircraft.html

Yoshihara, Kane. "Attitudes to the War: Southern Cross, Chapter 10, 81 Operation." http://ajrp.awm.gov.au/ajrp/AJRP2.nsf/pages/NT0000A696?openDocument

Correspondence Received by Author

Cundall, Peter. February 4, 2004.

Dieffenderfer, James. February 15, 2009.

Kingsland, Sir Richard. November 17, 2005.

May, John. (Undated).

McAulay, Lex. July 14, 2007; July 15, 2007; July 17, 2007; June 17, 2008.

Murphy, John. June 7, 2004.

Tagaya, Osamu. December 20, 2003; January 13, 2004; January 15, 2005; January 8, 2006.

Wenger, Michael. November 7, 2004.

Interviews

Anderson, Lloyd. January 16, 2009.

Canning, Douglas. April 10, 2009.

Carmichael, Richard (U.S. Air Force oral history interview). September 8–10, November 10–11, 1980.

Dieffenderfer, James. January 13, 2009.

Fields, John (with Kenneth Fields). October 9, 1982.

Harcrow, James. December 16, 2008.

Kingsland, Sir Richard. November 29, 2005.

Loisel, John. November 20, 2008.

May, John. January 25, 2008.

Phillips, Carthon. February 14, 2004.

Reed, Sanger, March 21, 2008.

Vargas, Roger. January 17, 2009.

Watkins, John. December 18, 2003.

Wesche, Frederick III (with Shaun Illingworth and Kathryn Tracy, Rutgers University). May 10, 2001.

Index